Fearing Others

CW00957665

Social phobia and disruptive social anxiety are features of the lives of many thousands of people. But exactly what is social phobia? What causes it? What is its nature and what kinds of treatments can improve it? Using key concepts and methods and a substantive body of research, this book aims to answer these questions and clarify social phobia by means of critical discussions and examination of evidence. It takes a skeptical stance towards the received view of social phobia as a species of disease caused by a deficient inner mechanism and considers and alternative construal of social phobia as a purposeful interpersonal pattern of self-overprotection from social threats. The possibility that social phobia might not actually exist in nature is also considered. *Fearing Others* will appeal to researchers, clinicians, and students in clinical and health psychology and psychiatry.

ARIEL STRAVYNSKI is Professor of Clinical Psychology in the Department of Psychology at the University of Montreal.

Fearing Others

The Nature and Treatment of Social Phobia

Ariel Stravynski

University of Montreal

CAMBRIDGE
UNIVERSITY PRESS

CAMBRIDGE UNIVERSITY PRESS
Cambridge, New York, Melbourne, Madrid, Cape Town, Singapore, São Paulo

CAMBRIDGE UNIVERSITY PRESS
The Edinburgh Building, Cambridge CB2 8RU, UK

Published in the United States of America by Cambridge University Press,
New York

www.cambridge.org
Information on this title: www.cambridge.org/9780521671088

First published 2007

Printed in the United Kingdom at the University Press, Cambridge

A catalogue record for this book is available from the British Library

Library of Congress Cataloging in Publication data

Stravynski, Ariel, 1949–
Fearing others: the nature and treatment of social phobia / Ariel Stravynski.
      p. ; cm.
   Includes bibliographical references and index.
   ISBN-13: 978-0-521-85487-0 (hardback: alk. paper)
   ISBN-10: 0-521-85487-3 (hardback: alk. paper)
   ISBN-13: 978-0-521-67108-8 (pbk.: alk. paper)
   ISBN-10: 0-521-67108-6 (pbk.: alk. paper)
   1. Social phobia. 2. Social phobia–Treatment. I. Title.
   [DNLM: 1. Phobia Disorders. 2. Interpersonal Relations. 3. Social
Isolation–psychology. WM 178 S912f 2006]
   RC552.S62S77 2006
   616.85′225—dc22

                                                                2006038543
ISBN-13 978-0-521-85487-0 hardback
ISBN-13 978-0-521-67108-8 paperback

To my wife
and to
the memory of my mother — who taught me to read.

Epigraph

"Brave, carefree, mocking, forceful − this is how wisdom wants us to be."
Friedrich Nietzsche

Contents

Tables

Acknowledgments

I got underway during sabbatical leave and completed the book while on sabbatical leave — 7 years later. I thank the University of Montreal for this enlightened policy.

Much of the writing took place at the Fernand-Seguin Research Centre of the L. H. Lafontaine Hospital. I am much obliged to the directors of both Centre and Hospital, for creating conditions propitious to such a sustained intellectual effort.

Marc-Yvan Custeau, Jacqueline Rochefort and their colleagues at the library of the L. H. Lafontaine Hospital were most helpful in tracing and obtaining numerous articles from not always easily accessible journals.

Suzanne Lepage coordinated the making of the book while uncomplainingly typing and retyping references, valiantly struggling to match them with the ever-changing text. Her helpfulness and constancy are much appreciated.

I have learned much about fear and self-protection from Devi. On a more abstract plane, I have been enriched by the work of Isaac Marks, Howard Rachlin and Theodore Kemper; I wish to acknowledge these intellectual debts.

In my attempt to assimilate a vast range of publications, I have been assisted most ably and with unwavering dedication by Suzie Bond and Danielle Amado. Starting off as students, they became discerning critics and collaborators. This book would not be the same without them.

I am grateful to Nira Arbel for reading the whole manuscript and helping to straighten crooked sentences and clarifying obscurities.

I wish to thank Kieron O'Connor and Mark Freeston (chapter 7), Frank Vitaro (chapter 9) and David Greenberg (chapters 4 and 5) for their incisive comments on parts of the manuscript.

Nonetheless, errors either obstinately committed or ones of oversight are mine alone.

Chapter 8 is an updated and substantially modified version of chapter 6 in S. G. Hofmann & P. M. DiBartolo (Eds.), *From social anxiety to social phobia: multiple perspectives*. Boston: Allyn & Bacon, 2001. It is reprinted with the permission of the publishers.

Preface

Although the term social phobia was coined early in the twentieth century, it first found little resonance. A seminal paper authored by Marks & Gelder (1966) sparked off the modern interest in social phobia. It culminated in the creation of a clinical entity bearing that label in the DSM-III. Soon followed by the ICD-9, this formal recognition by influential institutions – respectively, the American Psychiatric Association (APA) and the World Health Organization – proved to be a watershed. Starting with a trickle – to stay with the water imagery – the stream of publications has turned to flood and continues unabated, threatening by its very abundance. For what does all this information amount to? Unfortunately, we cannot hope for knowledge to result from the accumulation of information ordering itself in a meaningful, intelligible way. The organization of the bits (of information) in different patterns while articulating the logic inherent in them and considering them critically is a task separate from the production of information. Has the wealth of research broadened and enriched our knowledge? Has it deepened our understanding? To answer these questions, we must pause, to take stock and consider. This is the main purpose of this book.

Is there really such a disease entity as the "diagnosis" purports to identify? Is social phobia a valid entity (as opposed to a fanciful albeit popular construction driven by various interests)? The vast majority of studies approach the reality of social phobia unquestioningly. Such a bold assumption, however, requires justification. After all, the history of medical psychology and psychiatry is littered with discarded entities once fashionable and carrying great conviction, and new ones (e.g. fibromyalgia) proclaimed – or is it discovered – regularly.

Can we pin down with greater accuracy what is social phobia? In what sense is it an "anxiety disorder"? Is it a clinical problem in its own right or perhaps a feature of some other entity or even entities? Causal accounts of social phobia abound; are they equally valid? These are some of the queries that need to be answered.

To attempt this, the book is structured mostly as a series of critical discussions centering on four questions: What is social phobia? What is its nature? What causes it? And what kinds of treatments are likely to help?

The best approximation to an accurate answer is likely to be achieved by viewing it from various angles. Accordingly, I have considered multiple theoretical approaches towards answering each question. Specifically, I have selected only approaches that lend themselves to critical assessment, by providing key concepts, methods for their measurement and a substantive body of research. In each case, the specific chapter includes an analysis of the key theoretical concept underpinning the approach, followed by a discussion of its assessment (the two are inextricably linked) and finally an examination of the available evidence.

Although useful for analytic purposes, such separation of perspectives is artificial and, if taken beyond a certain point, barren. What is to be gained in terms of understanding by ignoring, for example, awkward results arising from a rival perspective? Ultimately, the various perspectives are at their most illuminating when cross-referenced and considered as a meaningful whole. Thus, integration is the second purpose of this book. Although it will be attempted piecemeal throughout, the concluding chapter will be devoted to such a synthesis.

Perhaps the reader might be curious at this point to know something about where I stand. In a nutshell, I would describe my approach as naturalistic; I incline towards observing life as it is lived – rooted in its natural and social habitat. This requires a certain discipline: observation must take precedence over speculation.

As to substance, I take it as incontrovertible fact that only whole living beings – as opposed to minds or brains for instance – are afraid. Similarly, self-protection from harm is something only whole living creatures are capable of. Fearing and protecting oneself are ways of representing an integrated corporeal activity. Such response is elicited by and directed toward danger – either tangible or one foreseen. In the latter case the fearful reaction is acted out imaginatively. Fearsome circumstances and fearfulness form a unity. Attempting to understand fear without reference to the object of fear (i.e. the dangerous context) is inadequate and unsatisfactory; if elevated to principle, misguided. To paraphrase Schoppenhauer, an inquiry into fear "in between the pages of which one does not hear the tears, the weeping, the gnashing of teeth and the din of mutual universal murder" is hardly worthy of that name. Has not fear evolved and proven its worth in the context of precisely such a monstrous, murderous reality extended over millennia?

After this exposition of first principles, I shall turn to the content itself. Although much research strains to explain social phobia, astonishingly there are hardly any definitions or even descriptions of it. Paradoxically, methods of assessment have been developed but what do these measure? What then is social phobia? Clearly, there is some uncertainty about it. Part I attempts to fill the gap. Chapter 1 systematizes the description of social phobia as an integrated and extended fearful interpersonal pattern aimed at self-protection. It argues that social phobia gains from being considered holistically and contextually while emphasizing the purposeful nature of social phobic conduct as a way (albeit inadequate) of managing the terrors arising from concrete social situations. The chapter sharpens the description of social phobia in contrasting available cases from different cultures highlighting similarities and unique responses to culturally defined social demands. Chapter 2 traces the historic evolution of the notion of social phobia and its equivalents (mostly from the end of nineteenth century France) in the context of a rising interest in anxiety-related phenomena and the desire to give them a medical footing. It traces the links between that historic movement in medicine and the modern formulation of social phobia.

In part II several ideas about the nature of social phobia (i.e. what category does it belong to) are examined. Chapter 3 considers social phobia as a disorder of social anxiety – the most common construal of social phobia today. It analyzes the concept of social anxiety that underpins this perspective, with a related inquiry into issues concerning its assessment. Then, key questions concerning the existence of a specific social phobic kind of anxiety and whether it is distinguishable from normal anxieties (and other kinds of pathological anxieties) are raised.

Many treat social phobia as a disease; chapter 4 examines the grounds for considering it as such. As a preliminary, the chapter analyzes the notion of disease and its assessment (e.g. diagnosis, validating tests). Subsequently, various definitions of disease are considered and relevant research examined so as to determine whether social phobia might be considered one.

Social phobia is taken (in practice) by many as a valid natural entity recently discovered. Its validity however is not self-evident; nor does the fact that it is listed in diagnostic manuals provide proof of it. Chapter 5 examines whether there are grounds for considering social phobia a valid entity at this time. It starts from the premise that the validity of social phobia must be considered hypothetical and, therefore, put to a test, rather than assumed. It then proceeds first to outline a procedure for the process of validation of a hypothetical construct and, second, to examine critically all relevant research.

Part III is concerned with various attempts to elucidate what might cause social phobia. Chapter 6 outlines the biomedical view, highlighting the two related features central to its account of social phobia: neurobiological abnormalities (specifically brain abnormalities) and the possibility of their genetic transmission. Relevant evidence is critically reviewed. Chapter 7 outlines the cognitive account of social phobia as an instance of distorted thinking. The assessment of cognitive processes deemed central to social phobia as well as difficulties inherent in the measurement of thought in general are discussed and relevant evidence is considered critically. Chapter 8 outlines the account of social phobia as an instance of inadequate social skills. The chapter emphasizes the measurement of social skills while critically summarizing all relevant research. Chapter 9 examines historical accounts of social phobia. Two theoretical approaches are considered within a broad developmental perspective: the cornerstone of the first is the notion of temperament, and of the second, attachment. The assessment of each is set forth in detail and all relevant research is critically examined.

Part IV deals with treatment. Chapter 10 briefly describes available pharmacological and psychological approaches. These have been selected for having an extensive empirical basis of controlled studies documenting their effects. These are critically discussed.

Part V (Chapter 11) synthesizes themes previously considered in isolation. It ends with an integrated account that accords with current knowledge about what social phobia is, how it comes about, and the available treatment strategies most suited to it.

Part I

What is Social Phobia?

"Of all the many wonders, none is more wonderful than man ... who has learnt the arts of speech, of wind-swift thought, and the living in neighborliness." Sophocles

1 Social Phobia: a Self-Protective Interpersonal Pattern

What is social phobia? How can it be described? Before attempting that, it is perhaps well to remember that the "criteria" found in diagnostic manuals are not depictions of social phobia. Rather, these list its indicators; features considered as particularly prominent, allowing spotting social phobia – typically from someone's self-representation. As is the case with DSM and ICD, in principle there could be several sets of indicators, potentially all useful (not necessarily to the same degree) in identifying social phobia.

What conditions ought a description of social phobia satisfy? First, as an abnormal condition, social phobia has to be a significant behavioral or psychological pattern associated with considerable distress and impaired functioning, compromising the ability of such individuals to pursue desired goals and to participate fully in the life of their community.

Second, as a phobic pattern it concerns a state of anxious distress in the face of a looming threat. The state of fright may be widened to include attempts of the individual to come to grips with it; this straddles both the somatic and the interpersonal elements.

Third, it ought to give prominence to the social or interpersonal environment within which the social phobic pattern is embedded. This is indispensable because the fearful distress is evoked quite precisely by specific activities as actually performed or only when imagined in the presence of others or by interpersonal transactions in which the goals pursued, namely getting one's way and gaining approval from others, are experienced as dangerously unattainable or likely to fail. Finally, to describe the social phobic pattern is to depict the activity of the whole human organism, not the workings of a putative system (e.g. state of mind) or organ (e.g. brain) within it.

A concrete way of representing how persons embody social anxiety and enact the social phobic pattern is to depict three social phobic individuals.

Case Descriptions

"A" was a 47-year-old married woman with two grown-up children from a previous marriage and unemployed. She described her fears of others as originating with the death of her father when she was 5 years old. She felt then very much alone and defenseless. She found her mother domineering, harsh and unresponsive, neglecting her while favoring an older son. A's first marriage strengthened these fears as her husband repeatedly criticized her appearance and her clumsiness.

When seen, she reported being unable to interview for jobs or go into a store for fear of blushing and becoming incoherent when addressed by sales people. She avoided speaking in groups or on the telephone because of the "foolish" impression she might give, as well as avoiding public toilets where other women might hear her.

Socially, she was at ease only with her supportive second husband and grown-up children from the first marriage. She experienced small gatherings in which confident-looking and sounding people were present, as especially intimidating. When speaking about herself she was disparaging and apologized often for various shortcomings. She seldom expressed opinions, backed away from confrontation, and tended to be passive. She defied however, her French husband's insistence to move to France, on the grounds that her poor vocabulary and French-Canadian accent would make her a target of ridicule.

A lived (with her husband) in an apartment above that of her mother, reluctantly looking after the elderly woman who still dominated her. She approached her mother with trepidation, mostly choosing to do as told over being criticized sarcastically. The occasional non-compliance was justified by elaborate excuses repeated many times.

"B" was a 32-year-old woman, married and mother to two young children. While she considered herself as having always been shy, her difficulties began at the age of 14 when, in the middle of a presentation of a classroom assignment, she began experiencing a paroxysm of anxiety and could not go on. Since that day, she avoided all public speaking (e.g. classes at university in which this was a requirement).

At work in a bank, she gravitated towards assignments requiring no meetings or face-to-face contact with clients. She was able to function within these constraints until becoming pregnant, when she developed an intense discomfort ("hot in the face") in response to the attention that her pregnancy drew. She then began to dread the possibility of blushing while being the focus of interest. Gradually the discomfort generalized to other situations and she began fearing anyone approaching her – especially unexpectedly. At first, she attempted dissimulation (moving a lot, sitting in dark places) and then avoidance of work (she did not go back to it after maternity leave) She began progressively to shun friends and family and apprehended going to the grocery store where she dreaded the supermarket owner's greetings and offers of help.

Her husband's business activities included a certain amount of socializing with partners, prospective clients and their spouses in which she was expected to take part. Her unacknowledged desire to avoid these was a source of constant friction; nevertheless she successfully hid her difficulties from her husband in whom she confided only 3 months before being admitted into treatment. During these outings she feared silences, being contradicted or queried.

Her relationship with her husband was beset by conflict as she dissembled by being evasive and "irresponsible" and he often found fault with her. In retaliation, she rarely expressed affection or appreciation of things he did or features of his personality. Their sex life was unsatisfactory. She was similarly stern with her children although much concerned about them. By contrast, she found it difficult to issue instructions and otherwise oversee the maid (e.g. criticize her work) who cleaned her apartment, for fear of blushing.

She set great store by propriety and attempted to achieve perfection in everything (e.g. appearance, manners). Imperfections of any kind (blushing, being in therapy) were carefully concealed. Circumstances in which she fell short of such standards were experienced with disquiet, especially if other people personified them with seeming ease.

"C" was a 35-year-old single man who worked as a machine operator at a printing plant. He felt always uneasy about meeting new people, as he would tend to stammer and slur his words initially. This was especially true in regards to meeting and dating women. At work he was uneasy in exchanges with the foreman and other people in authority. He was leading a rather inactive social life but had a small group of (mostly male) friends with whom he met regularly and whom he accompanied on outings to bars. He found it difficult to share intimacies even with them, and hardly ever spoke of himself (e.g. none was aware of his fears) or expressed an opinion. He confided only once – in a former girlfriend.

His most acute fear however, concerned writing, typically signing in front of others. The onset of this problem could not be established, but the triggering event took place in a bank. In order to draw money from his account, C would prepare a check at home and present it to the teller. On one occasion a teller demanded that he countersign the check. He argued meekly and inarticulately with the teller with anxiety mounting. Finally, he complied reluctantly and attempted to sign while in the grip of panic. The teller refused to accept the check and C fled the bank premises with all eyes fixed on him. Since then he has drawn money from cash-dispensing machines and made purchases with cash and readymade checks only. Although wishing to take holidays abroad he avoided those for fear of trembling while signing, for example, credit-card slips under scrutiny.

While not as acutely distressing as the inability to write in public, his loneliness stemming from his fear of approaching available women and initiating courtship must be considered the most important problem in the long run.

The Social Phobic Response

Social anxiety or fear — evoked by engaging with others and thereby submitting to their reactions and scrutiny — is at the heart of the social phobic pattern of conduct. It involves a looming sense of danger accompanied by a heightened activation of the bodily mechanisms supporting defensive action. Figuratively speaking, social phobic individuals ready themselves for a desperate flight from or, with every evasive tactic failing, for a losing struggle with menacing others during various social interactions. Social anxiety has simultaneously a somatic and an interpersonal locus.

Somatic: In the face of an emergency, the body is readied for self-protective action. At such moments, it bustles with intense activity:

1. Palpitations — the heart pumps faster for the more blood circulates, the greater the energy. The blood is shifted from the skin to where it is needed most: muscles and brain. This results in cool extremities and pallor.
2. Fast breathing — supplies more oxygen.
3. Tensing up of muscles as readying for action occurs; at peak it results in trembling and incoordination of the hands and a mask-like rigidity of the face.
4. Sweating — through evaporation it cools off straining muscles.
5. An urge to urinate (in some an inability to do it). Intestinal cramps and alternating diarrhea and constipation and sometimes vomiting occur — needless processes in an emergency are aborted and waste evacuated.
6. Speech difficulties might arise due to labored breathing and incoordination of the muscles involved in articulation (being "tongue-tied").

7. Otherwise diminished responsiveness and blunted perceptiveness as vigilance is focused on identifying danger before it arises and reacting to it as soon as it does.
8. Pupils dilate to increase visual acuity.
9. Hair stands on end. Disappointingly, it is of little use. Unlike cats' enemies, those of humans are usually not impressed by such displays.

As a consequence, social phobic individuals frequently report neck and shoulder stiffness and headaches. Ahead of feared situations they experience palpitations, rapid breathing, tightening of the chest, heat and sweating, a queasy sensation in the stomach and gut and a pressing need to have a bowel movement or urinate. Some paradoxically are unable to relieve themselves in public.

Generally, these individuals describe experiencing an almost unrelieved dread, uncertainty and helplessness with much rumination directed towards guessing various conjunctures that may arise in the future and what various important people might be thinking of them. All the while they would also be brooding over their own awkwardness, unattractiveness, incompetence, and cowardliness. These are beheld with a sense of impending doom. Periods of discouragement and hopelessness, especially following setbacks, punctuate a fluctuating but uninterrupted sense of menace.

Some social phobic individuals dread blushing. Although this reddening of the face, ears, neck, and upper chest is a psychosomatic manifestation, it is not one of anxiety. Blanching rather than blushing prevails in fear. The facial expressions accompanying blushing (e.g. smiling, averting one's gaze and lowering one's head) are unlike the strained vigilance typical of fear. Finally, blushing occurs in a state of passivity and immobility, in contrast to the restlessness and agitation common to anxious states. Consequently, I shall consider blushing as a facet of a wider interpersonal pattern to be discussed below.

All anxious disorders might be said to involve an exacerbation of the above normal "stress-response," chronically extended. Social phobia is marked off from other such anxious states by the insistent attempts of such individuals to hide the physical manifestations of fear from the critical gaze of others. Some adopt a disguise: dark glasses, wide-brimmed hats, make-up, and turtlenecks to conceal blushing for example. The surest means to safety however, is keeping a distance from danger (i.e. avoiding evocative social occasions altogether or, if it cannot be helped, escaping) and hiding (i.e. remaining out of sight) or not drawing attention (e.g. saying little). As the cumulative social cost of such actions might be very high indeed (e.g. none are compatible with working) most attempt dissembling. This is a "hair-raising" strategy: feigning poise while dreading exposure as an impostor; the "nervousness" (detailed above) or blushing threatening to let slip how uncomfortable one really is. Use of alcohol or medication is common. Acting as inhibitors of a fearfully overexcited nervous system, these substances chemically induce a decrease in palpitations, hand tremors, etc. and therefore offer some relief from the fear of attracting unwanted attention.

While simultaneously seeking to master the bodily aspects of fear, dissembling is essentially an interpersonal act aimed at creating a positive impression or at the very least to conceal what is presumed to elicit an unfavorable one. It hints at the paramount importance of being in the good graces of others and the necessity to conform to their alleged expectations – typical of the social phobic individual.

Interpersonal

Although wishing not having to deal with many frightening aspects of social life and at times actually avoiding threatening social situations, few social phobic individuals forgo it and literally choose seclusion. Although weary, they recognize the opportunities that social life provides (e.g. for a mate, companionship) as well as the harsh necessity (e.g. making a living) dictating taking part. While specific challenges (e.g. public speaking or eating, joining a group) might be desperately avoided, social phobic individuals do participate in social life, but exceedingly prudently. In addition to outright avoiding certain situations and concealing the physical manifestations of fear and blushing mentioned earlier, four interpersonal patterns woven into an overall strategy minimizing risk-taking stand out.

First, social phobic individuals seek security in being liked. To this end, they make themselves agreeable, smiling and nodding with interest and approval with those they know. When not preoccupied with themselves, they can be well attuned to the needs of others and readily lend an attentive ear or a helping hand. To put it negatively, they are not unresponsive, demanding, critical, capricious or petulant. They are conciliatory and tend to give in or take the blame for mishaps so as to minimize frictions. Resentment and disappointment are carefully dissimulated for fear of retaliation. Being treated correctly but impersonally (i.e. not obviously appreciated) is experienced as disquieting. Relationships of any kind, therefore, tend to be personalized with much effort invested in being likable and gaining approval.

Second, to minimize strife and the possibility of loss of face in a skirmish they are bound to lose, social phobic individuals prefer to propitiate and appease. They are soft spoken, docile, and mild; not challenging or provocative. They keep out of power struggles, they are neither masterful nor eager to take charge. Rather, they readily fall in with the initiatives of others and tend to give in to pressure or intimidation, or at least give that impression. When not complying, they resort to elaborate justifications so as not to give offence; when in opposition they resist surreptitiously. When embarrassed (e.g. blundering, receiving praise, being teased) they turn their heads away, bow them, avert their eyes, grin or giggle, and some blush. This disarming pattern might be considered an appeasement or a submission display (Stein & Bouwer, 1997), thereby mitigating threats from potentially hostile others. Blushing considered narrowly as the reddening of the skin is baffling; it acquires meaning only when understood relationally and contextually.

Third, to stay out of trouble, social phobic individuals strive to lead a blameless life. For this, they adopt stringent standards of propriety and scruple; attempting, but not necessarily succeeding, to be beyond reproach. Despite being keen to please, they refrain from making promises lightly or manipulatively, as these might come to haunt them. In a similar vein various activities (e.g. work, grooming) are carried out in a spirit of seeking "perfection" designed to eliminate the possibility of mistakes or being in the wrong.

Fourth, social phobic individuals tend to lead a shadowy and furtive existence. They prefer escaping notice and staying out of the limelight at all costs, fearing, as all attention is on them, embarrassment will disable them from performing the required social activity (e.g. dancing, speaking in public, responding graciously to praise, engaging in sexual activities) to the standards they find respectable; plodding mediocrity is not. Social phobic individuals are rather self-effacing and pliant. Being singled out for criticism or even praise in front of a group is experienced as an ordeal, with so many witnessing their potential discomfiture (e.g. blushing) and ensuing disgrace.

Finally, social phobic individuals are rather passive participants in social life, given more to observation of others and ruminations about their own shortcomings. Others find them uninvolved, reserved, and inscrutable. They shun novelty (e.g. attractive strangers) as too dangerous for being unpredictable. Imposed changes (e.g. new neighbors) are experienced as menacing unless experience proves otherwise. Faults of commission (e.g. blundering) are guarded against as far more dangerous than faults of omission (i.e. missing out on opportunities).

Evocative Social Situations

Social phobic behavior or patterns of behavior listed by themselves are puzzling. They gain in meaningfulness by being considered contextually. Four categories of evocative situations highlight most social phobic responses.

First, judging by the intensity of the somatic manifestations of fear and associated subjective distress, fulfilling a social role and dealing with individuals enacting sanctioned authoritative and powerful roles embedded in hierarchical structures present the most threatening challenges to the social phobic individual. For most, these difficulties occur in formal/institutional situations (e.g. meetings, presentations at work) and concern acting authoritatively and dealings with people occupying positions of power. When facing authorities, social phobic individuals assume an obedient and overall submissive posture designed to placate and pacify, fearing otherwise to be found in the wrong, cut down to size – their pretentiousness soon punctured. Objectionable demands are resisted passively and stealthily. When exercising authority (e.g. instructing or leading) they are hesitant to assert themselves and to impose their views for fear of being challenged or sullenly resented, trying instead to satisfy everyone.

Yearning for approval while dreading criticism and dissatisfaction, social phobic individuals feel unable to argue their case, defend their point of view against critics, expose weaknesses in contending arguments, convince and carry the day. Rather, they feel powerless – at the mercy of others, having only themselves to blame for their shortcomings. Given their heightened anxious state while participating in meetings or presenting, such individuals typically fear blushing, shaking (e.g. hand tremor) or incapacitating surges of anxiety (i.e. panic) that would make it all but impossible to speak in public. Their embarrassing lack of poise, combined with what they consider a lackluster performance, adds insult to injury. During meetings they prefer to remain silent. If addressed directly and made to speak, they cannot refuse – but do not quite comply either. When attempting to communicate they are liable to meander inarticulately and inexpressively, talk rapidly in a strained and barely audible voice, usually failing to make an impact.

When faced with complex tasks to be performed in the presence of others (e.g. while instructed) social phobic individuals are liable to be distracted, failing to understand or even remember information or operations they have been shown recently.

Second, group membership and participation in its activities is a difficult area of social life for the social phobic individual. Collaborative activities as a group (e.g. a dinner party) are entered upon defensively, in which self-protection (e.g. silence) is far more prominent than participation (e.g. describing an amusing incident, expressing an opinion). Such passive involvement marginalizes social phobic individuals.

Relationships among members of a group are not equal. All groups (e.g. family, peers, community) naturally involve ranking. Some members personifying the highest values of their community are more admired than others, some exercise leading roles. Unless otherwise organized, group life involves, in addition to collaboration, a fair amount of rivalry among others, for standing within it. Social phobic individuals find competitive activities, either symbolic (e.g. games) or in earnest (e.g. for a position or a desirable mate) threatening and forgo them. Consequently, they also shun self-promotion (as well as denigrating others, often its flip side), alliances with like-minded people in the furtherance of their interests, and the company of authoritative, glamorous, seemingly self-assured people.

Unsure of their ability to impress and be chosen, they fear that attempts to gain recognition might attract contempt and ridicule instead, further diminishing their rather uncertain standing within the group. Concerned both about losing and winning – thereby stoking the resentment of other competitors – they find it safer keeping out of the running.

Performing symbolic rituals (e.g. leading a prayer, toasting the bride and groom, performing a ritual dance at a wedding) and affirming group membership (e.g. sharing a meal or a drink with colleagues at work while participating in the conversation) are experienced as ordeals to be performed to the satisfaction of others and on which one's uncertain standing hinges. Failure to satisfy or, worse, ridicule if one is not up to standard, bring closer the possibility of becoming an outcast or being banished from the group in disgrace.

Third, strangers as unfathomable sources of threat are watched warily and studiously avoided. An attempt of establishing contact with an individual or joining a group after all might be greeted with indifference or end in rebuff, confirming the social phobic individual's insignificance. Accepting strangers' attentions might be exciting but it opens the door to potentially disastrous entanglements, as their interest is likely to turn to disappointment and rejection. Strangers among a group of familiar people (at a party, at work), although less threatening, are nevertheless assessed for their potential of being dismissive and overbearing, especially if sounding and looking confident or particularly attractive.

Such diffidence with relative strangers typical of social phobia is a major handicap for personal life in the countries of the industrialized world where meeting potential partners and subsequent courtship depends entirely on individual initiative and ability to win someone over, sometimes against keen competition. Many social phobic individuals are chosen rather than actively pursuing somebody they have singled out. Men are at a greater disadvantage under such arrangements, as they are culturally expected to take the initiative. Furthermore, the choices open even to the more adventurous social phobic individuals are restricted, for the more attractive potential mates are viewed as in great demand and therefore more likely to be dismissive or soon to lose interest and pursue brighter prospects elsewhere.

Fourth, intimate relations set in relief both strengths and weaknesses in the social phobic pattern. The eagerness to please and gain the appreciation of others, while dreading disapproval, is one of the threads running through the description of social phobia so far. If striving for the liking and high regard of someone while wishing to satisfy them is at the core of relations of intimacy and love, it might be said that social phobic individuals are driven to try to form a manner of intimate relations as a rule, even where they are unlikely to be found, as in group and institutional life, normally characterized by rivalry (as well as cooperation) and impersonal power relationships. Such misdirected efforts undermine adequate functioning in the public sphere.

However, the longing to be liked and treated with consideration and kindness common to social phobia brings a great strength to love relationships or intimate friendships – once they are formed. Social phobic individuals are in their element in relationships where affection, respect and dependency are reciprocated. In such a secure context they may learn to drop their guard, take initiative or even take charge, become less calculating, more spontaneous and adventurous (e.g. more reckless) and powerful, and therefore less than perfect. Domineering partners, however, exacerbate the anxieties and frustrations of submissive social phobic individuals, stoking their insecurities. Emotional expressivity (e.g. of affection but especially anger) is circumscribed. Passive/aggressive gestures of omission or commission – enacted unseen – abound instead.

It is important to note that fearful and self-protective responses are not monolithic; social phobic individuals are most discerning. Their responses therefore are highly differentiated from situation to situation, the danger inherent in it dependent on the category and other parameters. The most dangerous are those concerning competitive performances as a social actor on public occasions. The formality of the occasion, what is at stake, the kind of participants (e.g. authorities) and their numbers, act as exacerbating factors. The least dangerous would be engaging in an intimate relationship that is obviously requited, under conditions where privacy is guaranteed.

In summary, fears of blushing, shaking, panicking or of eating, writing, speaking (in public) or their avoidance – on occasion invoked as descriptions of social phobia – only point to some of its facets. Abstracted from the specific responses to the myriad of social dangers, social phobia is simultaneously an inordinate fear of humiliation resulting from public degradations that one is powerless to prevent, ending in subsequent loss of standing or membership in the social worlds to which one belongs, as well as a comprehensive defensive interpersonal pattern (constituted of various sub-patterns) protective against the threat of being hurtfully treated by others. The integrated pattern seriously compromises the ability of the individual to carry out desired personal goals and to participate fully in the life of the groups and communities to which she or he belongs.

If this narrowly pure definition of social phobia were to be widened, it might also include other fears, intermittent or chronic depressed mood and dependency on substances used towards self-medication. Which is the true social phobia? The question might be somewhat evasively but truthfully answered that it is a matter of perspective, for where the boundaries are drawn is to some extent artificial.

Cultural Differences

Are social phobic individuals the same the world over? It is difficult to answer this question with any certainty for relevant descriptions are scarce.

If separating again the integrated social phobic pattern into a somatic and an interpersonal dimension, one could assume that the bodily activation supporting self-protective action has to be similar (could it be otherwise?), as it is orchestrated by various systems in the brain involved in emotional regulation. Its expression, however, being culturally molded, might be altogether different. The self-protective interpersonal patterns issued from culturally constituted social roles embedded in social structures organized into a way of life, might in principle vary a lot, although not necessarily in all particulars. Everywhere, the social phobic pattern makes itself evident by disrupting to a considerable degree the ability to enact social roles and participate in the life of the community.

An informal comparison between the earlier-described French-Canadian social phobic individuals and social phobic ultra-orthodox Jewish men residing in the state of Israel (Greenberg, Stravynski, & Bilu, 2004) is illustrative.

First, it is meaningful that only men are included in the Jewish orthodox sample; there are women in the Canadian sample. As marriages are arranged, women are confined only to the private sphere in Jewish orthodox life, raising children and in contact mostly with other women in a private capacity; social phobia in such a cultural context is hardly imaginable. Neither is agoraphobia in housebound pious Muslim women (El-Islam, 1994).

Second, as marriages are arranged it is almost impossible to fail to secure a spouse among orthodox men, no matter how bashful and lacking in social graces they might be. In other cultures where marriages are also arranged, the requirements might be somewhat more onerous. These however would not be of a personal nature. Among most Indians, matching language, caste, status and horoscope are indispensable. By contrast, the Canadian male social phobic was at a considerable disadvantage within a culture placing the onus of courtship on men, reliant mostly on their ability to charm and sustain a relationship, often in the face of competition. Although pining for a life-companion he remained alone. Things were easier in this respect for the Canadian social phobic women who were both spotted as desirable partners and courted by their future husbands. They had only to provide some encouragement.

Third, both Canadian and orthodox social phobic individuals were principally handicapped in the performance of public social roles, for fear of failure and disgrace. For the Canadians it was acting as a bank official, as a saleswoman, and as a customer in the market place. The orthodox men, by contrast, could not lead a prayer or preside over a religious ritual, either in the presence of other worshippers in the synagogue or at home; this interfered with the performance of religious duties. Most hurtful however was the inability to act authoritatively as teachers and interpreters expounding on matters of observance and religion. Not daring to act as befitting a religious authority, fearful of being unable to defend their claim to the prestige reserved to the religious scholar, they forwent an exalted status in their community, keeping out of the limelight and out of danger.

In summary, social phobic individuals living very different ways of life share defensive self-protecting interpersonal patterns. Whether these are activated depends on the social demands placed on the individual by the way of life of their community. These determine the situational contexts evocative of the social phobic responses.

Individual Differences

Even within the same culture, social phobic individuals are not all identical. Individual cases of social phobia are variations on the theme of fear of, and self-protection against, possible interpersonal injury. Some differences among such individuals are quantitative, for instance in the degree of somatic activation supporting self-protective action in the face of threat. Similarly, the number of triggering social situations might provide a crude index of severity. Another difference in degree is in the severity of the fearful distress and the manner it is reported.

Some differences are qualitative. First, there are the somatic aspects of discomfort come to the fore (e.g. shaking, panicking, blushing). Second, there is the prominence of certain interpersonal sub-patterns described earlier and their proportion in making up the social phobic pattern as a whole.

As the social phobic response and the situations evoking it are inseparable, some individual differences are embedded in circumstances, both present and past. Gender, changes in position or occupation or personal status (e.g. marriage) modulate the social phobic response considerably.

Altogether, it is likely that personal history is the most important source of individual differences (see chapter 9). If social anxiety is at the heart of social phobia, underlying it is in all likelihood a broad genetic propensity, perhaps best described as emotionality (see chapter 3). Fearfulness is not a readymade and enduring characteristic evident at the onset of life (see chapter 9). For instance, fear is not present in the repertoire of newborns and appears to emerge as the result of maturation. It is on the individual propensity – the raw material as it were – that the social environment acts; it will mold the propensity from birth (or even before) and subsequently, in the course of development.

In summary, the differences in the potential endowment as well as life histories (the process of molding the individual propensity including learning as well as unlearning) translate into individual differences in the integrated social phobic pattern of fearfulness and interpersonal self-protection. While various social fears might precede it in childhood, the social phobic pattern is forged by adult demands made on the individual by the way of life of the community to which he or she belongs. These crystallize in late adolescence or early adulthood; so does the onset of social phobia (see chapter 5).

2   The Genealogy of Social Phobia

If something can be said to exist formally and definitively only when it acquires an official name, social phobia came into the world fully formed with the publication of the DSM-III in 1980. The notion designated by the name, however, is much older; the fearful self-protective pattern itself is likely as old as humanity.

The dual purposes of this chapter are to trace the intellectual history of the term, and to establish whether and how it has evolved. In carrying out this overview I shall rely mostly on the invaluable historical survey of Pelissolo & Lépine (1995) concerning social phobia as such as well as the broader overviews of the conceptual history of anxiety disorders by Berrios (1999) and Glas (1996).

Before embarking on the historical survey, it is well to consider what perspective regarding the nature of social phobia would serve our purpose best. In principle, on a continuum of the nature of psychopathology, two seemingly contradictory positions face off. On the one hand, social phobia might be envisaged as a distinct entity occurring in nature and obtaining universally that went unrecognized until discovered. On the other hand, social phobia could be taken for a linguistic construction denoting several ambiguous phenomena (lending themselves to numerous readings) lumped together. This construction is a cultural product of various social forces embedded in a particular way of life. On that view, as the factors sustaining its use fluctuate, social phobia might fall into disuse, could be replaced (e.g. "social anxiety disorder") so as to better serve the purposes of those who advocate the change, or find its meaning transformed with reversals in circumstances.

These two – admittedly extreme – perspectives would likely give rise to quite different histories. I shall take an intermediate position, one that attempts to reconcile the apparent contradictions. From the "naturalistic" perspective one could argue that the core of social phobia is fear (or anxiety, I use the terms interchangeably – see chapter 3) evoked by interpersonal transactions and their social/cultural contexts. Fear, like emotion in general, is a loosely linked cluster of responses incorporating feelings, thoughts, behaviors and physiological activation, in this case geared towards self-protection. Thus, fear is *incorporated* and *visceral*, associated with a fairly well-defined physiological and endocrinological pattern of responses coordinated by various systems in the brain involved in emotional regulation (Misslin, 2003; Marks, 1987, pp. 177–227).

Furthermore, social phobia relates to one of four classes of common (i.e. normal) fears reproduced in numerous surveys (Ohman, 2000, p. 575). These are of: (1) interpersonal strife, criticism, rejection; (2) death, disease, injuries, pain; (3) animals; (4) being alone and/or trapped or amidst strangers far from a secure and familiar base. Social phobia is obviously linked to the interpersonal cluster of fears, as the fear-evoking situations triggering it are predominantly social.

From the "constructivist" perspective it could be said that the social experiences, interpersonal behaviors and patterns of behavior generated under the state of fear as well as the manner they are construed are largely malleable, and as such indeterminate. Although tending to cluster, they nonetheless vary among individuals, across cultures and social practices.

Bearing these considerations in mind I shall proceed with the historical review.

Background

The term phobia derives from the Greek word *phobos* (attendant and son of Ares – the god of war) denoting fear, terror, panic. Its source is the worship of Phobos, who had the power to instill terror in enemies of ancient Greeks. The deity was often depicted on weapons, especially shields.

The term phobia only reappears in the literature in the mid-nineteenth century, after an absence of 1,300 years. In the intervening period, irrational fears combined with glum mood and much else went under the heading of *melancholia* (black bile). For according to Hippocrates "temporary fears and terrors are due to overheating of the brain and are associated with an expansion and preponderance of bile in that structure" (Errera, 1962, p. 327).

In European culture before the eighteenth century, anxiety was mostly linked to spiritual anguish, of interest to theologians and philosophers. A common Christian belief for example was that such fear resulted from sin. In this view timidity reflected an insufficient faith (in god) and shyness expressed insufficient love (charity) for one's neighbor.

With the secularization of life, the eighteenth century witnessed the beginning of the medicalization of the abnormal experiences of fear.

Thus, medical treatises dedicated to the gut and the heart, for example, described what today would be regarded as anxious complaints (e.g. abdominal cramps, dry mouth, oppressive feeling in the chest: Berrios, 1999, p. 84). Palpitations, for instance, were described as symptoms of heart disease and hyperventilation a disease of the lungs (1999, p. 84). While the process of medicalization reached its peak in the first half of the nineteenth century, a process of psychologization (e.g. Freud) got under way in the second half. What in the former era were regarded as symptoms of independent disease, in the latter period become facets of putative entities (e.g. neurasthenia, anxiety-neurosis).

Launched in the USA and later adopted in Europe, neurasthenia was conceived as a new disease category induced by "modern life." As defined, it involved fatigue and a vast range of depressive and anxious manifestations. Anxiety-neurosis as proposed by Freud narrowed the field to encompass an anxious state of distress combined with a "nervous over-excitement" involving flushes, sweat, tremors, diarrhea, etc. Both neurasthenia and anxiety-neurosis were considered by their proponents diseases of the nervous system, the putative sexual etiology of the latter notwithstanding. The continued failure however to find any neurological or other cause accounting for "nervous disorders" during the nineteenth century, cleared the way for psychological theories.

The Notion of Social Phobia

The term "social phobia" originated with Janet (1903). While the label is roughly 100 years old, the pattern of behavior it denotes has been noticed and described since antiquity. Burton (1621, quoted in Marks, 1987, p. 362) for example set forth a state of fear that "amazeth many men that are to speak, or show themselves in public assemblies, or before some great personages, as Tully confessed of himself, that he trembled still at the beginning of his speech; and Demosthenes that great orator of Greece, before Phillipus." Burton gave further the example of Hippocrates who "through bashfulness, suspicion, and timorousness, will not be seen abroad; loves darkness as life, and cannot endure the light, or to sit in lightsome places; his hat still in his eyes, he will neither see nor be seen by his good will. He dare not come in company, for fear he should be misused, disgraced, overshoot himself in gestures or speeches or be sick; he thinks every man observes him" (1987, p. 362).

Systematic and mostly medical interest in the phenomena clustered around the construct of social phobia crystallized late in nineteenth-century France. There were several strands to this trend.

First, it was construed as a phobia. Within the context of a classificatory scheme Janet (1903) conceived of four types of phobias: situational, bodily, of objects, and of ideas. Situational phobias were further subdivided into those related to places (open — agoraphobia; enclosed — claustrophobia) and those related to social occasions. Janet emphasized repeatedly the social nature of the phobic fear. This arises only in response to having to act in public or interact with someone, for such individuals do not fear shaking or blushing when alone, for instance. Janet proposed the term social phobia or phobia of society to stress this point. He conceived social phobia broadly as ranging over fear of blushing, of intimacy (and sex), public speaking and acting from a position of authority, among others.

Second, several detailed descriptions of cases of *ereutophobia* (blushing phobia) and discussions of related conceptual issues were published. Notable is a Swiss psychologist, Claparede's (1902), contribution. Although narrowly conceived as concerning only blushing, the social and the phobic aspects were emphasized. Neither was necessarily recognized as such by all authorities; some construed the morbid dread of blushing as an obsession; others of a more traditional medical bent, a cardiovascular problem.

Attempts at treatment are mentioned: alcohol, and opium among others, but also hypnosis and psychotherapy. In a refractory case, leeches were applied, followed by a sham operation designed to simulate a ligature of the carotid arteries. Improvement was short-lived.

Thirdly, Dugas (1898), and especially Hartenberg (first published in 1901; I have used the available 4th edition of 1921) approached the crippling fears of the social phobic pattern of behavior as an exacerbation of a common dimension of personality — namely shyness ("social anxiety" in modern parlance) — rather than as a putative abnormal entity, as did Janet and Claparede. Philosophically, Hartenberg considered himself a positivist psychologist "more interested in behavior than in the soul" and believed in "the predominance of the affective life and in the James–Lange theory of emotions" (Berios, 1999, p. 90). Both Dugas and Hartenberg trained under Ribot and with him "believed that both in psychiatry and in education the emotions were more important than the intellect" (1999, p. 91).

Hartenberg (1921) emphasized the situational nature of social anxiety. Furthermore, he conceived of social anxiety as an admixture of two basic emotions: fear and shame. He related primarily the somatic experiences (e.g. palpitations, tremor, sweating), but also the experience of dread — to fear. Self-consciousness, a heightened sense of propriety and blushing were expressions of shame. Social anxiety is evoked socially by engaging with others and thereby submitting to their scrutiny. It is generated through the dread of falling short of expectations or of appearing inferior or ridiculous.

Hartenberg (1921, pp. 21–40) gave a most comprehensive and detailed description of a paroxysm of social anxiety (*acces de timidite*). This involves, among others: (1) cardiovascular reactions (e.g. palpitations and due to peripheral vaso-constriction, cool extremities, and pallor); (2) respiratory difficulties; (3) gastro-intestinal and bladder muscle malfunctioning giving rise to vomiting, cramps, and alternating diarrhea and constipation and the urge to urinate; (4) muscle tension in the face, trembling and incoordination of the hands; (5) speech difficulties due to troubled breathing and incoordination of muscles involved in articulation; and (6) mentally: blunted perceptiveness, diminished responsiveness (e.g. ability to concentrate), and confusion. An indirect testimony to the social nature of such anxiety is the almost universal tendency to dissimulate its manifestations (1921, p. 83).

Hartenberg's (1921, pp. 157–182) dimensional conception of social anxiety is in evidence in his singling out several occupations whose practitioners are at risk of what might be termed stage fright or performance anxiety ("*le trac*"). Namely, these are stage actors, musicians, lecturers, preachers and trial lawyers. Were they not bound to perform in front of an attentive (and possibly critical) audience, there would be no fear. To Hartenberg (1921, pp. 183–184), common social anxiety becomes morbid when it is exaggerated, becomes over-generalized and chronic. Anxiety however is embedded in a personality constellation characterizing the shy. Interpersonally, these tend to sensitivity, propriety, dissembling, passivity, isolation, pessimism, and suppressed resentment among others (1921, pp. 47–100).

As a man of his time, Hartenberg (1921, p. 217) was unequivocal about the main cause of morbid social anxiety: *predisposing* inherited constitutional defects. His analysis of causality however also included *determinant* causes (e.g. physical, psychological) or social defects (real or imagined) as well as *occasional* (i.e. situational) causes. As to the latter, he commends English education for its emphasis on physical exercise and the encouragement of freedom and initiative as the key to its success in producing the least shy individuals.

His approach to treatment was reassurance and a behavioral therapy. In today's terminology this would include exposure in vivo, role-rehearsal for public speaking and modification of posture and other non-verbal elements of social behavior. For fear of reading in public, for example, he recommended graduated exercises of reading in the classroom. First it was to be done in unison with the whole class, followed by reading with a diminishing number of other participants ending with reading by the socially phobic individual alone. Treatment also included self-administered tasks to be performed in between sessions (1921, pp. 222–250).

Over the next 50 years interest in social phobia – the hypothetical construct – waned while the name fell into disuse. Myerson's (1945) description of social anxiety neurosis is striking in its resemblance to social phobia with an emphasis on chronic physiological over-activation and an intense concern with related bodily sensations. Myerson pointed to some similarities between social anxiety neurosis and certain forms of schizophrenia. First, there is the common tendency towards withdrawal. Second, certain features of social phobia taken in isolation might appear delusional (ideas of reference) such as a sense of being closely watched or taken advantage of.

A similar dual focus on the physical aspect of fear and its interpersonal consequences is also manifest in a Japanese version of an entity reminiscent of social phobia. Characterized by vivid social fears and labeled *tai-jin kyofu* by Morita in 1930 (Takahashi, 1989), it consists of a dread of the negative reactions of others to the bodily manifestation of fear (shaking, sweating, blushing, being inappropriate). Such conspicuous displays are considered disgraceful.

The years after World War II see the rise of psychology and the application of its psychometric methods to the study of social phobia. The first scale for the measurement of social anxiety – the psychological construct at the heart of social phobia – is devised and put to the test by Dixon, De Monchaux & Sandler (1957).

A factor analysis extracts a large factor of social anxiety with small factors denoting fears of losing control of bodily functions, fears of drawing attention to oneself and appearing inferior.

Marks & Gelder (1966) resurrected the term social phobia by providing, for the first time, some supporting evidence of its validity. Social phobia is distinguishable from agoraphobia and specific phobias on the basis of age of onset. Subsequent work (Marks, 1987, pp. 362–371) refined the identifying features of the construct by singling out anxious distress evoked by social activities, a tendency to avoid them and as a result, impaired functioning. In essence these indicators were adopted by the DSM-III in 1980 and the ICD-10 in 1990. While the ICD used specific descriptors, the DSM opted for abstract definitions (see chapter 5). Consequently, social phobia in the ICD is more narrowly defined. This was the culmination of descriptive work carried out over a century, enshrining social phobia as a putative entity or a psychopathological pattern of behavior.

An attempt to reduce the heterogeneity of the vast expanse of psychological content encompassed by social phobia led to the creation of two subtypes in DSM-III-R, hypothetically distinguished by the number of situations evocative of social anxiety. This proved an impetus to research, that overall disconfirmed the contention that generalized and "specific" social phobia are distinct sub-entities. Rather, (as can be seen in chapter 5) most available evidence is consistent with the view that the putative subtypes, together with avoidant personality disorder, are degrees of severity of social phobia.

Recently, social phobia found itself in a process of "rebranding" as social anxiety disorder. This label was first proposed as an alternative by the DSM-IV taskforce on anxiety disorders, aligning it semantically with the other "anxiety disorders." Subsequently, the desirability of a change in name was justified by the image it projects; social anxiety disorder, it is argued, "connotes a more severe and impairing disorder than implied by the label social phobia" (Liebowitz, Heimberg, Fresco, Travers, & Stein, 2000).

The appropriateness of labeling social phobia a phobia may be queried on more substantive grounds, for a phobia ought by definition to be a highly specific response to a concrete stimulus. The wide-ranging and at times diffuse social anxiety experienced by most social phobic individuals fits with strain the narrow definition of a phobia. However that may be, the proposed new name — social anxiety disorder — while perhaps striking a more ominous note, does not call into question the construct of social phobia as such. That has remained consistent since its inception.

Discussion

Anxiety-related experiences and behaviors were well known before the nineteenth century. Palpitations, dizziness, intestinal cramps, and other somatic manifestations, however, were taken to be expressions of separate diseases. There was a major conceptual shift when these phenomena began to be considered as neuroses (i.e. resulting from disorders of the autonomic nervous system). Against this background, gradually social phobia, agoraphobia, depersonalization, and paroxysmal surges of anxiety were described. Perhaps the emergence of these constructs may be related to the process of psychologization that set in with the failure to find any support for considering them neurological diseases.

The construct of social phobia began to emerge with the realization that this pattern stands out among other anxiety-linked problems for having a dual locus. As in all such disorders, the anxious response is all-pervasive and largely *incorporated* (i.e. somatic). In social phobia uniquely, it is integrated into interpersonal behavior (e.g. dissembling) in response to social circumstances. It is Hartenberg's, Dugas', and Janet's valuable contribution to have emphasized this in their formulations.

Both Hartenberg and Claparede saw poor heredity ("congenital taint") as the main cause of social phobia, relegating environmental circumstances to a triggering role. Such views prefigure a certain bio-medical outlook prevalent today. Then as now there was a tendency to see in agglomerations of social phobia in some families, support for genetic transmission. Claparede reported "family antecedents" in 83% of his sample. Few of these, however, might be described as social phobic individuals as many were labeled alcoholic, hysteric, neurasthenic and nervous. However that may be, preponderance of social phobia or even social anxiety (a more vast category) in the family cannot be taken by itself as proof of genetic inheritance; social anxiety might be transmitted and maintained in the family through psychological processes. Environments are inherited as much as genes.

"Congenital taint" notwithstanding, social phobia was from the outset considered as amenable to treatment. Early psychopharmacotherapy included alcohol and opium – both sound "anxiolytics" with some undesirable "side effects." Although no longer prescribed, these are still widely consumed in social phobic circles today. A sophisticated use was made of medical placebos: leeches were applied and mock operations performed. Attesting to the power of such procedures, the results, although short-lived, were not negligible.

Psychological approaches specifically devised for social phobia were pioneered applying many of the principles that were subsequently refined and in use today; namely exposure, role practice, and cognitive restructuring. The outcomes of the various treatments, however, were not systematically assessed and reported.

Two outlooks, the categorical and the dimensional, were put forward in the initial attempts to formulate social phobia. The categorical (e.g. Janet, 1903) treated social phobia in Kraeplinian fashion (Roelcke, 1997) as an entity sharply distinguished from both normality and other hypothetical entities of psychopathology. Underlying it is the assumption that social phobia is a morbid manifestation due to a break-down in normal processes. In that sense it is similar to social phobia as conceived in DSM-III and onwards. The dimensional (e.g. Hartenberg, 1921) envisaged social phobia in continuity with normal social anxiety. From that perspective, the anxious response differs from the normal not in kind but in degree. In comparison to the normal, the social phobic response is exaggerated, over-generalized, and chronic. The issues raised by these incompatible points of view attending the inception of the notion of social phobia are as relevant now as they were then; they are as controversial and not anywhere near being settled.

Part II

What is The Nature of Social Phobia?

3 Social Phobia as a Disorder of Social Anxiety

Individuals consulting for social phobia convey vividly the pall of fear hanging over their lives. It is all the more surprising therefore to find no trace of obvious danger in these accounts that mostly focus on seemingly mundane social events. The main source of threat looming is the possibly indifferent or demeaning reactions of others. Although these are not without practical consequences (in terms of social standing), at worst, the immediate prospective harm would be loss of face, not of limb or life. Irrespective of how likely such embarrassing incidents are to occur, the foreseen response to them seems exaggerated by any standard. Indeed, these individuals describe experiencing an almost unrelieved dread, uncertainty, and helplessness with much rumination directed towards guessing various conjunctures that may arise in the future while also brooding over their own awkwardness and incompetence. These are contemplated with a sense of pending doom. Periods of discouragement and loss of hope, especially in the face of setbacks, punctuate the uninterrupted sense of threat.

If these individuals cannot help being in fear-evoking situations, they typically fear shaking (e.g. hand tremor) or blushing or, if all attention is on them, experiencing incapacitating surges of fear (e.g. panic) that would make it all but impossible, say, to speak in public. These might give away their inner turmoil leading to embarrassment and disgrace, adding insult to injury.

When attempting to communicate, they are liable to be tongue-tied and inexpressive, talk in a strained and barely audible voice and ultimately either fail to express themselves in a coherent fashion or, paradoxically, become over-animated and talkative. When faced with demanding tasks (e.g. at work) to be performed in the presence of others, they are liable to be distracted and find it difficult to concentrate.

Their overall manner of participation in social life is characterized by caution or outright avoidance of many social situations (if they can) while fleeing social encounters during which they might become the focus of attention. When this outlet is not available, they dread that

their performance might not be up to standard, and that their inade-
quacies and discomfiture will become plain for all to see. In the
social situations in which they do participate they tend to be proper,
self-effacing, conciliatory, deferential, and eager to please. Undesirable
demands are resisted passively and surreptitiously. Discomfort and displeasure are carefully dissimulated.

Physically, such individuals report muscular (neck, shoulders) stiffness, headaches, and cramps. Furthermore, ahead of a feared situation
or while being in it, they experience palpitations, heat and sweating,
tightening of the chest, rapid breathing, and a pressing need to urinate
or to have a bowel movement. Some, however, are unable to relieve
themselves in public toilets.

What might account for this (social phobic) partly self-reported,
partly observed pattern of behavior? A widely held opinion is that it is
the outcome of clinical (abnormal) anxiety (Noyes & Hoehn-Saric,
1998, p. ix) and specifically its bodily aspects (Scholing &
Emmelkamp, 1993a; Mersch, Hildebrand, Mavy, Wessel, & van Hout,
1992a). In this view, the manifestations of social phobia are driven by
(or in medical terminology are symptoms of) anxiety. According to the
DSM-IV, "Individuals with social phobia almost always experience
symptoms of anxiety (e.g. palpitations, tremors, sweating, blushing) in
the feared social situations" (APA, 1994, p. 412). From this perspective,
avoidance of fear-evoking situations might be conceived of as an anxiety-
reducing maneuver (see Goodwin, 1986) performed in order to lessen
the "immediate psychological instability" that "permeates all anxiety
disorders" (Putman, 1997, p. 4). Similarly, the rather disorganized execution of verbal, manual or other tasks might be seen as illustrating the
dramatic drop in performance typically associated with high degrees of
anxiety (see Lader & Marks, 1971, p. 7); and so is the self-reported high
level of psycho-physiological activation. It is for this reason that social
phobia is to be found among the anxiety disorders in contemporary
classification manuals (e.g. DSM-IV, ICD-10). All the above illustrations notwithstanding, the conundrum of whether it is abnormal anxiety
that generates social phobia or, alternatively, the complex pattern
of social phobic behavior that might generate anxiety admits of no
simple solution. What is more, in considering it we are cast in a
theoretical vacuum.

It seems a safe assumption that the entities found among the anxiety
disorders relate, in one way or another, to four classes of *common*
(i.e. normal) fears that have been highlighted in numerous surveys
(Ohman, 2000, p. 575). These are of interpersonal strife, criticism,
rejection; death, disease, injuries, pain; animals; being alone

and/or trapped or amidst strangers far from a secure and familiar base (Arrindell, Pickersgill, Merckelbach, Ardon, & Cornet, 1991a). The various hypothetical entities found in the cluster of anxiety disorders are considered as sharing a predominantly abnormal anxious response albeit to differing evoking situations. Other abnormal patterns (e.g. irritable bowel syndrome, dysmorphophobia, sexual aversion, bulimia-anorexia nervosa) however, that might plausibly be considered as anxiety-driven, have not found their way into the category of anxiety disorders.

Social phobia is obviously related to the interpersonal cluster of fears, highlighted in Arrindell et al. (1991a) as the fear-eliciting situations triggering it are predominantly social. As other phobias, it might be also seen as "a fear of a situation that is out of proportion to its danger, can neither be explained nor reasoned away, is largely beyond voluntary control, and leads to avoidance of the feared situation" (Marks, 1987, p. 5). The view that social phobia is a disorder of anxiety has had a profound impact on treatment development in that most attempts at psychological treatment and pharmacotherapy have sought to provide help to patients by means of various methods aiming directly or indirectly at anxiety reduction.

Aim and Method

My main goal in this chapter is to examine critically the relevant evidence pertaining to the "disorder of anxiety" account of social phobia. This cannot be done however before clarifying the concept of anxiety in general, and inquiring into its application to the social domain (social anxiety) and social phobia in particular.

Consequently, as concepts cannot meaningfully be used divorced from the way they are measured (and vice versa), I shall examine the validity of the measures devised to ascertain and quantify social anxiety, as this is most relevant to social phobia.

Examination of the validity both of the construct and of the methods assessing it is indispensable for interpreting the results arising from different experiments testing the hypotheses relevant to our concern. Once the issues of their validity are settled, we will be free to grapple with specific questions such as whether sub-groups of social phobia differ from one another in this respect and whether social phobic individuals differ in their anxiety from normal and other contrast populations. The demonstration of such differences is a necessary precondition for the ultimate query: what (if any) causal role does anxiety play in social phobia?

Anxiety: Emotion or Construct?

What then is anxiety and what is the meaning of abnormal anxiety? A striking fact about much psychological and psychiatric research into anxiety is that the term itself is seldom defined (e.g. MacLoed, 1991). Nevertheless, "anxiety" is measured by a variety of inventories constructed for the purpose. What then is being assessed?

Anxiety is a word: what does it signify? Dictionaries define anxiety as "A painful or apprehensive uneasiness of mind usually over an impending or anticipated ill" (Webster, 1962) or "A condition of agitation and depression with a sensation of tightness and distress in the praecordial region" (The shorter Oxford English dictionary, 1972).

There are two scholarly views of anxiety: either as an emotion or as a psychological (i.e. hypothetical) construct. In a very general sense (see Levenson, 1999 for a comprehensive discussion), an emotion may be said to be an evaluative appraisal of the world – especially the social world – from the perspective of the individual's well-being. Emotions are ineluctable and strongly embodied, thus closely geared to action. Emotions register forcibly, both as communications to oneself as well as to others (Oatley, 1992, p. 59). In that sense emotions mark off certain activities (Rachlin, 1995, p. 114). In recognition of their vital role in social life, emotions also may be artfully simulated or painstakingly dissembled.

According to Lader & Marks (1971): "Anxiety is an emotion which is usually unpleasant. Subjectively it has the quality of fear or of closely related emotions. Implicit in anxiety is the feeling of impending danger, but there is no recognizable threat or the threat is, by reasonable standards, disproportionate to the emotion it seemingly evokes" (p. 1). Almost identically, Goodwin (1986, p. 3) defines anxiety as "an emotion that signifies the presence of danger that cannot be identified, or, if identified is not sufficiently threatening to justify the intensity of emotion." Fear by contrast, "signifies a known danger . . . the strength of which is proportionate to the degree of danger" (1986, p. 3). Fear in this view represents a response to actual danger, whereas anxiety represents a response to a potential danger whose degree of likelihood is slim. Nevertheless, the anxious response may arise in anticipation to potential pain and suffering vividly imagined however improbable their occurrence might seem.

In a variation on this outlook, May (1979, p. 205) argued:

It is agreed by students of anxiety – Freud, Goldstein, Horney, to mention only three – that anxiety is a diffuse apprehension, and that the central difference between fear and anxiety is that fear is a reaction to a specific danger while anxiety is unspecific, vague, objectless.

The glossary of the *Diagnostic and statistical manual of mental disorders* (APA, 1994) defines anxiety as "apprehensive anticipation of future danger or misfortune accompanied by a feeling of dysphoria or somatic symptoms of tension" (p. 764). Fear, by contrast, has an identifiable eliciting stimulus.

Exceptionally among theoreticians, Izard & Youngstrom (1996, p. 35) maintain that anxiety is an admixture of fear (a permanent component) and other shifting emotions (e.g. sadness, guilt). "Although fear may represent a common element in anxiety's permutations, it is inappropriate to equate anxiety with fear" (1996, p. 35).

Thus the mainstream distinction between fear and anxiety seems to rest on the salience of the trigger context evoking the reaction, the specificity of the reaction and its proportionality. McNeil, Turk, & Ries (1994) by contrast see anxiety as "associated with more cognitive symptoms and less visceral activation and cues for its manifestation are more diffuse and changeable, relative to fear" (p. 151). Chorpita & Barlow (1998, p. 3) consider anxiety as concerned with detection and preparation for danger while fear concerns the "actual confrontation with danger." Bowlby (1981b, pp. 151–152), by contrast, regards emotion – fear – as constituting the appraisal phase, itself a prelude to action. Rosen & Schulkin (1998, p. 325) similarly divide the extended pattern into a schematic "fear or anxious apprehension" phase – the terms are used interchangeably – when the first whiff of danger is identified, perhaps to be followed by a "defensive" phase, displayed in the face of actual danger. Ohman (2000, p. 574) recasts the difference as one between a "prestimulus" (anxiety) and "poststimulus" (fear) reaction. Epstein (1972), however, doubts that the nature of the external stimuli determines the difference between fear and anxiety. Rather, fear is tightly bound to action (i.e. flight). When acting on the fear (e.g. escaping) is not possible, the resulting emotion is one of anxiety (i.e. an unresolved or undirected fear). In the final analysis, how the above-enumerated distinctions can be made practically, and whether they hold up under rigorous and sustained scrutiny, is not altogether clear.

The social context – most relevant to our concerns – illustrates well the ambiguities involved. Social settings, the participants and what they do (e.g. talking, listening, dancing) are very concrete indeed; we can hear, see, touch, and smell them. The interactive processes however are not easy to characterize. With the exception of being literally brutally pounded into submission, it is usually difficult to point to specific moments when the social threat (eroding capacity to stand one's own ground, diminished standing) actually becomes manifest. Social transactions are an unfolding pattern that can be clearly spotted only when complete. Is the queasy feeling then one of fear or anxiety? Does one worry about pregnancy in a state of fear or anxiety? What about nightmares? Do we wake up bathed in sweat with heart racing anxiously or fearfully?

Another and this time a non-social example: In 2001 the USA experienced a terrorist onslaught by means of anthrax spores sent by post in envelopes. Fear stalked the country, or was it an epidemic of anxiety that was spreading? The danger was very real — five people who had the misfortune of inhaling anthrax died of the infection, and more were found to be suffering from the cutaneous form. The bacteria — unfortunately for humans — are invisible and therefore could be anywhere. The danger was manifest to the senses only in the alarming information disseminated by various media. While anthrax is not contagious, fear (or anxiety) as well as courage clearly are. Vast numbers of people became uneasy, their worries amplified by warnings from various sources. The citizenry was primed to be zealously vigilant. The upshot was that the authorities were constantly alerted to suspicious-looking envelopes and some individuals went to the extraordinary step of self-medicating as a preventative measure.

How shall we classify the various reactions? The source of danger was concrete enough and so were the fatal consequences (see Alexander & Klein, 2003), yet the virulent microorganisms were not easily identifiable. In this incident they were delivered by the mail in envelopes. By association, many became vigilant about the mail, but envelopes (conveyed by the postal service) were not the only possible means of dissemination. The reactions to the danger varied from the stoic to the heroically self-protective. As usual the extreme reactions were a minority pursuit whereas most people reacted in a moderately cautious sort of way. Who manifests fear and who manifests anxiety?

The impossibility of resolving ambiguities such as these without resorting to dogmatic pronouncements has led Levitt (1980, p. 9) to conclude that: "it seems prudent to eliminate, for most part, any distinction between anxiety and fear and regard them as interchangeable terms with perhaps minor shades of meaning." In keeping with Levitt's (1980, p. 9) recommendation, I shall use the terms anxiety and fear as rough equivalents from now on.

Moreover, even if the above definitions of the two terms and the distinctions drawn between them were of interest and perhaps of some clinical value, they would hardly be meaningful so far as research and theory are concerned (Levitt, 1980, p. 9).

From that perspective, anxiety has to be considered a construct conceptually linking and, if found valid, potentially explaining various sets of observable phenomena. In the case of anxiety these manifestations are held to be a bodily activation and its (e.g. motor) consequences and related self-protective behavior. As such activation is non-specific and occurs in many "exciting" situations (e.g. parachuting for sport, dancing, gambling, attempting an elaborate deception, narrowly avoiding being hit by a car, an angry row, getting intimate with an alluring and sexually receptive partner), the state of anxiety fails to explain it. Are self-protective actions such as keeping a vigilant watch, literally jumping to conclusions (e.g. fleeing while taking evasive action, or "freezing" into immobility in an attempt to make oneself unnoticeable, and if everything else fails, appeasing or fighting when cornered) made any clearer by postulating an anxious state of mind? Rather, considering these activities in context renders them transparently meaningful; the (mental) state of anxiety adds little to understanding and may be dispensed with.

It is most likely that the use of a mental state as an explanatory device is a conceptual habit inherited from a dualistic view (identified with Descartes, see Sprigge, 1984, pp. 13–14) of the substances a person is composed of. According to Descartes a human may be divided into body and mind (thereby providing the metaphysics for the immortal soul dwelling within a perishable body of Christian theology). In this view, actions (such as described earlier) are the doings of the machine-like body. In contrast, conscious experiences (e.g. thoughts, images) that cannot easily be formulated in occurrence terms (Sarbin, 1964, p. 631), are postulated to be made of a mental (i.e. a non-physical) substance, revealed to introspection alone. Translated into today's psychological parlance, these are mental states formulated as psychological constructs. Although existing nowhere, the mental is often spoken of as a kind of space where "cognitions" (i.e. judgments, beliefs, memories, intentions, etc.) are (metaphorically) stored, retrieved and allegedly exert their influence (Lourenco, 2001).

Whatever the history of its use, a construct denotes a hypothetical process (or an unseen system) postulated to relate two or more observable events (Craighead, Kazdin, & Mahoney, 1981, p. 42). It must be remembered that constructs are hypothetical abstractions, attempts at understanding by delineating and linking phenomena. Eventually it may be shown that what was hypothesized as a hypothetical construct is no more than an intellectual tool (i.e. an intervening variable) and therefore may not refer to anything definite in nature at all. Nevertheless anxiety and other constructs are spoken of as if they were "things" actually existing within a person. Indeed the very existence of a label is in itself suggestive to many of a corresponding "object" in the world. However, an autopsy will not locate anxiety or for that matter intelligence or introversion within the brain or any other organ of a person. Furthermore, attempts to identify specific biological correlates ("markers" − Hoes, 1986) or processes of anxiety (e.g. salivary cortisol, carbon dioxide inhalation, lactate infusion, levels of monoamine oxidase, among others) have failed to yield such an "essential or non-reducible component" (Friman, Hayes, & Wilson, 1998, p. 139).

To have scientific merit, a construct must be defined in terms of acts, not words alone (Levitt, 1980, p. 5). Word definitions of anxiety are typically made up of constructs in need of definition themselves (e.g. danger, threat, arousal). Thus, such verbal refinements do not add much clarity to the meaning of the construct; only objectively quantifiable definitions are of value in this respect. As with other psychological constructs so with anxiety, objectively measurable features are highly desirable but hard to come by. It is therefore a commonplace that there is no unequivocal operational definition of anxiety (Sarbin, 1964, p. 630).

It is in part the absence of such referents as well as the fact that most measurements of anxiety in practice rely solely on subjective estimates (even of objectively measurable features such as bodily reactivity), that leads some authors to question the standing of anxiety as a scientific construct.

In his thorough analysis of the construct of anxiety, Hallam (1985, pp. 2−3) lays stress on the fact that it does not have a unique and stable set of referents. On this view it is rather a *lay* construct redefined afresh by every user in pursuit of an idiosyncratic purpose in expressing complaints or providing information about his or her state of anxiety. Thus according to the author, anxiety has no objective standing, but, for example, the (social) practice of complaining of it might have purposes such as deflecting social obligations (1985, p. 175). From that perspective, an interesting question is: what are the functions of the various uses of the term "anxiety" (see also Friman et al., 1998)?

In an earlier critique of the term anxiety, Sarbin (1964) called for its discontinuation for scientific purposes. His key argument was that anxiety must not be regarded a scientific construct but, rather, a literal rendering of a metaphor. Etymologically (Lewis, 1967) the term anxiety stems from the ancient Greek root *angh* meaning to press tight, to strangle (p. 105). It was transmitted into medieval English as *anguish* (suffering of a spiritual kind) via the French *anguisse* (preceded by the Latin *angustus*) that denoted an oppressing or choking sensation. The modern word anxiety is a translation of Freud's German term *angst* (that kept the original Latin spelling) denoting a hypothetical state of mind (Sarbin, 1964, p. 634) of unconscious origins and arising from inner conflict (Michels, Frances, & Shear, 1985, p. 598). Thus, it is very much unlike fear that is presumably set off only by objectively dangerous events. Firstly, the word that originally denoted an oppressive physical sensation came by analogy to be used for a spiritual (religious) distress. Finally, the inner state of disquiet shorn of its religious connotation came to be seen as causing the sensation. It is for this reason that Sarbin (1964) considers anxiety (i.e. the state of mind) of no definite referents but possessing agency, a reified metaphor.

On this reading, far from describing the workings of nature (i.e. a mental structure underpinned by brain structures and neuropsychological processes, e.g. Gray, 1979), anxiety is better considered as the product of a historic and social process of the (mis)use of words (Sarbin, 1964). In consequence, the term anxiety, although always the same word, will carry many meanings, determined by the particular definitions attached to it. As such, it is liable to be highly misleading. This applies with special force to attempts to measure "anxiety" and the interpretation of the ensuing results. These difficulties notwithstanding, the call for the abolition of anxiety, needless to say, has not so far been heeded.

Social Fear

Social fear might be defined abstractly as an apprehensive response to individuals or to social situations involving a number of people. That dealings with others induce powerful emotions, delight as well as fear, is self-evident. Most relevant to social anxiety (used interchangeably with fear) are the dimensions of *power* and *status* (Kemper, 2000, p. 46) inherent in social interactions (see Kemper & Collins, 1990 for the evidence in support of these dimensions). These are relational notions, describing the dynamic connection between two individuals, or a pattern of relationships between an individual and others that form a group. Power is a construct tightly associated with the ability to deliver punishment (e.g. to constrain, to harm, to inflict pain and ultimately death). To accord status, in contrast, is for example to hold someone in awe as possessing superior qualities (e.g. assurance, knowledge, courage, purity of purpose) or single out someone – as in courtship – by means of high regard, rewards, and attention. Correspondingly, to suffer diminished regard or lose it altogether is experienced painfully as loss.

An authority inspires both fear and awe; it wields power and has high status. Dominance (a synonymous construct to power) and submission are played out in sequences of symbolic "scripted" reciprocal behaviors (see Keltner & Buswell, 1997, p. 263). A direct fixed stare is met with lowered eyes and averted gaze, a fierce expression with a smile, criticisms (or orders) delivered in a loud and imperious voice are acknowledged (or obeyed) with bowed head, a submissive posture and in soft-spoken and apologetic tones. Dominance is recognized by deference; the dominant party is not challenged, contradicted or ignored. In many cultures (e.g. Cambodia) such exchanges are ritualized as marks of rank and are part of proper etiquette.

Although dominance might be difficult to determine objectively at every specific point, in time, as the pattern unfolds, it becomes plain who influences (e.g. compels) whom and, correspondingly, who yields (if they do). Briefly stated, insufficient power or an erosion or loss of it (and correspondingly the interlocutor's gain in influence) at the present, or previously established disparities of power, are typically associated with feelings of fear or anxiety (Kemper, 2000, pp. 46–47). The degradation of status as manifested in the manner one is treated is associated with shame (e.g. one does not count for much) and humiliation (e.g. disdain from others). The worst cases of humiliation are those in which the humiliator seeks, by degrading the victim, to exclude him or her from the group (Statman, 2000, p. 531).

In addition to yielding specific and immediate power and status estimates, circumscribed social interactions also convey wider as well as longer-term implications (e.g. reflecting a deteriorating social environment, for instance at the workplace). The recognition of one's weakness for not having been able to prevent or soften the blow in a specific encounter insinuates the possibility of similar defeats in future confrontations. It counsels caution (e.g. submission).

In sum, if the realization of cherished plans depend on someone who pays little heed to one's well-being or, if one is made to do things one does not wish to do while being ignored or worse (say treated with contempt or one's discomfiture mocked), one feels threatened, ashamed, and humiliated. Unsurprisingly, this is the sort of social encounter most dreaded by social phobic individuals. It could equally involve a fierce bully and his acolytes, a child who might insolently disobey a command or a sexually alluring ("overpowering") relative stranger.

Is it legitimate however to separate social anxiety from what might be an overall propensity towards timidity (i.e. responding anxiously to a host of dangers)? Several arguments might be invoked justifying such a step. First, the largest and the most common factor extracted from responses to multidimensional personality inventories has been identified as "social shyness" (Howarth, 1980). Similarly, factor-analytic studies of various inventories of fears consistently yield a factor or two concerning social anxieties (i.e. in relation with conflict, criticism, rejection: Arrindell et al., 1991a). These are typically elicited by meeting new people, being interviewed for a position, addressing a group, taking charge or speaking in public (e.g. Gursky & Reiss, 1987). Adult concerns are prefigured in studies of children's fears – adjusted for age – such as being called to the blackboard, reading in front of the class, being ridiculed or bullied, or making people angry (e.g. Rose & Ditto, 1983; Spence, Rapee, McDonald, & Ingram, 2001; see also Schlenker & Leary, 1982 for a review). Thus, phobic patients of all stripes report similar fears to varying degrees; these are not exclusive to social phobia (Stravynski, Basoglu, Marks, Sengun, & Marks, 1995b).

Second, social anxieties in the guise of fear of separation from caregivers (or familiar figures) and fear of strangers appear at an early stage in development (the second half of the first year) and persist – albeit in different form – in most adults. Third, fear arising from interactions with conspecifics (members of the same species) is a fundamental fear in non-humans (Boissy, 1995) and humans alike (e.g. in competitive interactions with peers or dealings with powerful members of a group).

The Dangers Inherent in Social Life

Does social anxiety then fit for example Goodwin's (1986) definition of anxiety as an "emotion that signifies the presence of danger that cannot be identified, or, if identified is not sufficiently threatening to justify the intensity of emotion" (p. 3)? At the heart of the definition is our understanding of "sufficiently threatening danger." "In nature," for instance "the most important threats of injury that an individual encounters during its lifetime come from predators or competing or attacking conspecifics" (Boissy, 1995, p. 166). Thus, in animal societies, (unlike in the laboratory where it is artificially induced by means of noise or electric shock – see LeDoux, 1996) fearful behavior is typically observed as a response to threat arising from their conspecific group members (Boissy, 1995, p. 182). In light of this, the main question to be answered is: are there any grounds to suspect that humans might injure or cause harm to fellow humans?

If personal or second-hand experience does not serve, a brief perusal of newspapers from the most high-minded to the lowest offers an unequivocal answer. Harmful acts ranging from the viciously criminal (e.g. murder, assault, rape, theft, fraud), via the immoral (e.g. deceit, slander, breach of faith) to the unscrupulous ill-use of others (e.g. manipulative exploitation, shifting the blame) are daily occurrences affecting numerous people directly or at once removed. Although statistically aberrations, such experiences are nevertheless commonplace enough.

Some of the worst acts, either criminal (e.g. arson, massacres) or not (e.g. ritual humiliations, turning on members who question profoundly held beliefs, hostility to strangers), are carried out by bands. These are composed of members acting together (Canetti, 1981, p. 385) often organized and led by individuals who assume a position of leadership – formal or not. Men acting under orders are capable of the most appalling deeds (e.g. Kelman & Hamilton, 1989).

Human societies and their various institutions (e.g. places of work, government) are almost universally organized hierarchically (Mousnier, 1969; Hawley, 1999). At different levels of social stratification (Barber, 1957) much power resides in the hands of small ruling groups (Sidanius & Pratto, 1999, pp. 31–33); these may change or perpetually cling to power. Within that system – where this is permitted or even encouraged – intense competitions for power and resources ensue. The structures expressing and enforcing such systems of power may either encourage and reward collaboration or, alternatively, through intimidation or even brutality, discourage and punish challenges to it (e.g. Corner, 2002). Although not necessarily visible, these structures of power are manifest and exert tight control (e.g. as contingencies determining consequences or matrices of cost–benefit) over behavior (Gerth & Mills, 1953, pp. 185–374). A vast majority of adults (let alone children) often find themselves in a subordinate position to whom commands are issued, depending on the goodwill of those holding power over them. Furthermore, millions daily find themselves in situations in which a hastily spoken word or a misplaced gesture might have dire consequences (e.g. Conquest, 1990). The displeasure of the mighty may be expressed as anger (suggestive of darkening prospects), scorn (put-downs, questioning one's standing) and other methods of intimidation and manipulation (Kemper, 2000, p. 46), for "anyone who wants to rule men, first tries to humiliate them" (Canetti, 1981, p. 245; see Sofsky, 1997, pp. 82–85). Concrete sanctions in addition to symbolic threats might follow. Obviously, the consequences of crossing high-ranking individuals (e.g. employer, manager) who hire and fire, control access to resources and privileges, as well as punitive sanctions by those belonging to a lower stratum (i.e. status group, e.g. employee), may prove to be costly (e.g. Donkin, 2000). The actual consequences depend on the range of arrangements prevailing in particular countries or sections of society at a given time. In fascist Italy favorite forms of intimidation through humiliation were shaving off half a moustache, or forcibly administering large quantities of castor oil to those who over-stepped the limits (Paxton, 2004, pp. 61–64). Grimmer fates awaited the recalcitrant: beatings, loss of employment, torture, prison camps, and death (Corner, 2002).

Military society, for instance, "makes dissatisfaction with a superior, once expressed, a criminal offence; even 'dumb insolence' attracts confinement, while fomenting dissent is mutiny, in times of war an act punishable by death" (Keegan, 1988, p. 335). Needless to say, not being duly appreciative of or openly disagreeing with tyrants, let alone conspiring against them, puts one in quite a delicate position (e.g. Sebag Montefiore, 2003).

Unlike earlier examples (e.g. crime) that might be considered as touching on the exceptional, functioning in groups as well as their social stratification (with power flowing from the top) and all its ramifications in terms of the hazards involved, are woven into the very fabric of social life.

In the interest of comprehensiveness, to the previous account must be added the occurrence of various organized (or impersonal) social systems of discrimination favoring the interests of some to the detriment of others. Thus, the dominance hierarchy represents the crystallization of an unequal distribution of benefits. Furthermore, no less organized brutalities and violence directed against members of its own society designated as enemies or foreigners in the form of atrocities, mass executions, torture, war, dispossession, deportation, slavery, as well as political, ethnic and religious persecutions and campaigns of exterminations that are sanctioned by the state (or competing political organizations as in civil war) and enacted by its officials, are rife (see Pedersen, 2002; Mazower, 2002). Within such political contexts, spying on and denunciations of individuals considered members of "enemy" groups by those (e.g. neighbors, colleagues) making a show of their loyalty are commonplace (Paxton, 2004, p. 230). Such occurrences, although not part of life in the rich industrialized West at the present and viewed as an aberration, were pervasive in it in previous (and not too distant) times (see Naimark, 2002) and could conceivably return. However that may be, this is very much part of the plight of humanity elsewhere at the present (e.g. Green, 1994), let alone in the past. If such is the potential inherent in possible dealings with others either as individuals or in an official capacity (enacting social roles embedded in a social structure), little wonder that most humans approach them warily.

Russell (1958, p. 122) put it thus: "We are accustomed to being the Lords of Creation; we no longer have the occasion, like cave men, to fear lions and tigers, mammoth and wild boars. Except against each other, we feel safe." The fact that among humans, "the weakest has strength enough to kill the strongest, either by secret machination, or by confederacy with others," Hobbes wrote, is sufficient to make everyone afraid of everyone else.

Social Life as a Necessity

Human life is universally organized in societies (subdivided in communities and other groupings) and within these frameworks it is intensely social. People seek safety in groups, as do many other species (see Marks, 1987, pp. 83–89). Fitting in and being part of groups is a necessity dictated by survival, but also brings ample rewards. It provides pleasure; it is protective, enriching (culture, higher standards of living), and the source of most human companionship (mates, allies), comfort, and joy. Group membership is a fundamental social category, second only to gender, and the demarcation between the social group(s) to which one belongs and members of other groups is vital. Conformity with the group in dress, manners, and opinions is an important social force (Bond & Smith, 1996). Standing out, (e.g. by challenging customs or cherished social beliefs) evokes resentment and hostility. This is especially true when the group feels threatened (Rothgerber, 1997). Being cast out from community restricts access to resources and diminishes prospects of reproduction (Buss, 1990) and survival. Excommunication and forced exile, nowadays in disuse, were once among the harshest of punishments. Membership in groups, however, extracts a high cost. Groups impose demands and diminish freedom. Invariably, group life involves conflict. As Buss (1990) put it, others "will injure you, steal your cattle, covet your mate and slander your reputation" (p. 199).

Nevertheless, sociability comes naturally to humans. Seeking to establish durable affectional bonds "is as intrinsic a system of behavior as feeding and sex" (Lader & Marks, 1971, p. 13). Quintessential human characteristics such as language and self-consciousness are likely to have evolved in the process of social living (Humphrey, 1976) and now sustain it. Fearful behavior, for example, or at least some acts related to it, might be considered communicatively, say as means of raising the alarm and thus instigating the coordination of an appropriate communal response.

The survival of newborns depends on careful long-term nurturing by others. Conversely, the restriction of social contact during infancy and childhood (as well as other forms of inadequate care) exerts powerful effects on psychopathology across the lifespan. "Disruptions of personal ties, through ridicule, discrimination, separation, divorce, bereavement, are among the most stressful events people must endure" (Cacioppo, Bernston, Sheridan, & McClintock, 2000, p. 831).

Thus the selfish striving of every individual in the ceaseless struggle to promote its well-being and existence, often in competition with others or at their expense, is mitigated by the thoroughgoing sociability and propensity to cooperate of humans (Glassman, 2000).

Social Danger as an Erosion in Environmental Conditions

Social dangers are concrete in terms of the very real harmful consequences they entail. On the one hand it may mean to be forced to do what one does not wish to do. On the other hand it may mean making enemies, becoming the target of violence, being vilified, suffering diminished standing, being driven out, as well as being denied access to resources with an attendant loss of opportunity. The consequences of these might not necessarily be felt strongly at once but rather be extended in time. These would unfold gradually while gaining strength in the manner of countrywide economic decline for instance (falling of hours worked, rising unemployment, rising numbers of unemployment benefit claims, jumps in welfare spending, collapse of tax revenues). In that sense these might be signs of *deteriorating environmental conditions* in train. In the face of these, existence becomes increasingly precarious. Historic experiences, for example the mass Stalinist repressions of 1937–1938 in the Soviet Union (the "Great Terror," see Conquest 1990), provide a wealth of illustrations. In the face of worsening prospects, many strove to find some safety in detecting predictable patterns. In the words of a survivor:

We never asked, on hearing about the latest arrest, what was he arrested for? But we were exceptional. Most people crazed by fear, asked this question just to give themselves a little hope: if others were arrested for some reason, then they wouldn't be arrested because they hadn't done anything wrong (Mandelstam, 1970, p. 10).

Mineka & Kihlstrom (1978) note that in non-humans anxiety increases markedly when environmental events of vital importance to them become unpredictable and uncontrollable (p. 257). This observation suggests that although danger may not be specific or salient (e.g. a human, a predator), environmental patterns conveying dynamic information of an unfolding threat through distal clues (e.g. smell, moving noise, staring eyes) are detectable nevertheless (Bowlby, 1981b, pp. 109–111). This information would be inherent in the patterning of various elements foreshadowing deteriorating environmental conditions or responsiveness. In the long haul, the assessment of one's environment (and by extension one's prospects in it) as poor may lead to a general decrease in activity including socialization and reproduction in a variety of animals (Lima & Dill, 1989) and doubtless in humans (Williams, 1998). Thus, the dangers inherent in social life are varied and might not be on every count like losing one's footing on a high cliff. Nor are social dangers like being under well-aimed artillery fire, when sensing the earth shake with deafening explosions, being showered with falling debris, mouth parched, stomach in knots, bladder emptying, bowels loosened and legs gelatinous, one experiences a mind-shattering terror suffused with fear of pain, injury, and death. Social fears, however seemingly different, nevertheless bespeak of the implications of diminished prospects and capacities of survival and, as any fears, ultimately concern suffering and death. On the battlefield, however, where armies function in small fighting units of strongly bonded men (Holmes, 1985, pp. 290–315), the social consequences of letting one's comrades down often outweigh fear of mutilation, pain, and death (1985, pp. 138–142).

Bridging the two sets of fears (the social and of pain and death) is Darwin's (1872, quoted in Marks, 1987, p. 3) imaginative reconstruction of the origins of social fears.

Men during numberless generations, have endeavored to escape from their enemies or danger by headlong flight, or by violent struggling with them; and such great exertions will have caused the heart to beat rapidly, the breathing to be hurried, the chest to heave and the nostrils to be dilated. As the exertions have been prolonged to the last extremity, the final result would have been utter prostration, pallor, perspiration, trembling of all muscles... Now, whenever the emotion of fear is strongly felt, though it may not lead to any exertion, the same results tend to reappear, through the force of inheritance or association.

This example leaves us in no doubt that social dangers were once and still are very real and concrete indeed. Thus, fearing others to a degree that does not interfere overall with other activities is normal and the attendant anxieties might be expected to be highly pervasive in the overall population. As we shall see shortly, much evidence supports the view that social anxiety is not the exclusive province of social phobia (albeit such individuals report it subjectively to a higher degree). Normal individuals (e.g. Purdon, Antony, Monteiro, & Swinson, 2001) and patients meeting criteria for a variety of psychiatric disorders (and not only those that primarily concern anxiety) also report social anxiety. So do individuals suffering from highly visible medical conditions such as essential tremor (spasmodic torticollis: Gündel, Wolf, Xidara, Busch, & Ceballos-Baumann, 2001), loss of hair (alopecia: Hunt, & McHale, 2005) or disfigurement (Newell & Marks, 2000). This conveys the possibility that there is continuity and therefore differences in degree (rather than in kind) of social anxiety between various groups and individuals. The upshot would be that the dividing line between justified (i.e. proportional to the danger) degree of social anxiety and an excessive one would be to an extent arbitrary, depending on what is taken to be the norm.

Furthermore, this would suggest that social anxiety tends to arise in reference to and from concrete transactions with the social environment. On this reasoning, the view that social anxiety is for example solely or primarily a state of mind (e.g. "a subjective cognitive-affective experience": Leary, 1983, p. 67) is unsatisfactory. Social fear abstracted from its relationship to the social world is unintelligible; fear cannot be usefully divorced from what evokes it (Gerth & Mills, 1953, p. 184). The concrete social situations feared, as well as the range of the appropriate responses to them, would be embedded in a pattern of life or culture, typical of a time and place. I shall return to this point later.

Individual Differences

Given the importance of social life to humans and the dangers inherent in it, it is hardly surprising that social anxiety is a permanent fixture of human life. However, individuals do not exhibit such fears to the same degree. Undeniably, the subjectively reported (but not necessarily the objectively measured, see Edelmann & Baker, 2002) anxious reactions of social phobic individuals stand out in their severity. How are we to understand such differences?

Underlying social anxiety and fearfulness in general is in all likelihood a broad genetic propensity, perhaps best described as emotionality; (Marks, 1987, p. 153). Fearfulness is not a readymade and enduring characteristic evident at the onset of life. Fear is not present in the repertoire of newborns, and appears to emerge as the result of maturation (Izard & Youngstrom, 1996, p. 41). Furthermore, "in all mammals, friendly, affiliative, or positive approach behaviors emerge developmentally before fearful (and thus also aggressive) behaviors. Human infants, for example, typically first evidence clearly positive, affiliative behavior at around 6 to 8 weeks when the social smile appears; they first show clear signs of social fear at around 8 months when fear of strangers ordinarily appears" (Chisholm, 1999, pp. 31–32). Thus, "emotions are socialized as they emerge in development; therefore, the possible configurations of any pattern are limited both by what society (and particularly the family) dictates and by which basic emotions are developmentally available" (Izard & Youngstrom, 1996, p. 41). Fear (or anxiety) therefore is not a unitary characteristic but an amalgam of various features without any fixed relationship to the other. It is on the individual propensity – the raw material as it were – that the environment acts on and which would mold the propensity from birth (or even before) and subsequently, in the course of development. The differences in the potential endowment as well as life histories (the process of molding the individual propensity including learning as well as unlearning) translate into individual differences in social fears.

Social Anxiety Viewed Developmentally

The distress occasioned by separation from a caregiver is in all likelihood the earliest form of social anxiety experienced by a child (age range between 8 to 24 months, peaking at 9 to 12 months; Marks, 1987, p. 139). It is the first instance of a variety of experiences in a child's life as a supplicant, depending entirely on the goodwill of his or her carers. Closely allied to this is a fear of strangers – mostly of adults but also of children – occurring about the same time (1987, p. 134). "Despite widely varying patterns of child-rearing, fears of strangers and of separation are seen in children all over the world" (Marks, 1987, p. 109). While both fears (of strangers and of separation from the caregiver) appear almost simultaneously, they are nonetheless different. At the appropriate age a child reacts with alarm to strangers even in the arms of the caregiver. Anxiety at separation from the carer is manifest even in the absence of strangers. The two fears are compounded when the child is separated from the carer in the presence of a stranger (Marks, 1987, p. 142). These two complementary fears are the raw material that, further transformed through life's vicissitudes within a particular society (and its culture) at a given time, will make up social anxiety. This developmental process, characterized in terms of attachment, is traced in detail in chapter 9.

Abnormal Social Anxiety

Although it is a commonplace that social phobia is characterized by abnormal anxiety and patients seeking treatment describe themselves as prey to it, it is surprisingly difficult to verify that assertion. Firstly, we face the uncertainty of whether clinical (to be used interchangeably with abnormal) anxiety is different in kind or only in degree from normal social anxiety or shyness. The first possibility is more or less unimaginable for we would not know how to define, let alone measure, clinical anxiety in isolation. The second option is easier for definitions and some means to assess social anxiety conceived as a continuum are available. However, another difficulty is where and how to set the demarcation point between normal and abnormal social anxiety.

Two examples illustrate the dilemma. Within various groups of subjects (socially phobic, normal community residents) there is a wide variation in self-reported social anxiety scores. Although, statistically, social phobic subjects as a group on average score significantly higher than normal subjects, there is an overlap between the two score distributions. The upshot of this is that some social phobic subjects report only moderate levels of social anxiety, whereas some fairly socially anxious normal individuals do not satisfy defining criteria for social phobia. The reason for this is that the criteria that matter most in order to satisfy the definition of social phobia are those of social functioning in various spheres of life. That is where the distinction between the highly anxious normal subjects and moderately anxious social phobic subjects lies; the former function adequately in the absolute sense and far better than the latter, relatively speaking.

Furthermore, in a study of single cases of social phobic patients undergoing treatment (Stravynski, Arbel, Lachance, & Todorov, 2000b), striking individual differences in scores of social anxiety emerged. For instance, the initial anxiety levels of some of the patients were lower than those reported by other patients at follow-up who, at that stage, were in remission. Both examples suggest that the relationship between social anxiety, social functioning and social phobia is not a simple one.

What do the above imply as to the definition of abnormal anxiety? An immediate conclusion seems to be that whatever definition and its corresponding demarcation point we adopt, it is bound to be arbitrary to some extent. This is not without consequences, for even minute methodological variations in "cut-off" levels tend to have considerable repercussions (e.g. on prevalence estimates in epidemiological studies, Furmark, Tillfors, Everz, Marteinsdottir, Gefvert, & Fredrikson, 1999).

The functional standard (i.e. one taking into account the wider patterns of social behavior) is far more significant than the severity of anxiety experienced at any point. Practically, the severity of anxiety notwithstanding, a "significant restriction on the ability to engage in deliberate action . . . and to participate in the social practices of the community" (Bergner, 1997, p. 241) appears the more meaningful definition of psychopathology, social phobic or other (see also Adams, 1964).

The Measurement of Social Anxiety

As we have seen earlier, a variety of meanings are attached to the term anxiety (and fear). This implies that there could be substantive variations in one construct of anxiety or even a variety of quite different scientific constructs of anxiety. Inevitably, these would be reflected in the different rating scales devised to assess the construct. Nevertheless, "there is often a general assumption that all of them assess the same construct of anxiety and that selection of a scale is purely a matter of personal preference or convenience" (Keedwell & Snaith, 1996, p. 177).

A clinician, for example, might be interested in whether a patient's social anxiety is diffused and all-encompassing or arises in reference to specific social situations. Or, whether it is pervasive or occurs in sudden surges (panic); whether it is long-standing or of recent onset; whether it is proportional – normatively speaking – to the difficulty inherent in the evoking situation(s) or not. Typically, an inventory cannot provide answers to all these queries; it will usually privilege some limited aspects at most.

Furthermore, the phenomena that might fit the term "social anxiety" range widely. These could include

a specific mood equivalent to fear, feelings of insecurity and apprehensive antic- ipation, content of thought dominated by disaster or personal incompetence, increased arousal or vigilance, a sense of constriction leading to hyperventilation and its consequences, muscular tension causing pain, tremor and restlessness, and a variety of somatic discomforts based upon overactivity of the nervous system (Keedwell & Snaith, 1996, p. 177).

To this list, a variety of associated fearful (e.g. self-protective) behav- ioral patterns might be added if assessment of fear might be conceived as involving "three systems" (Eifert & Wilson, 1991). These might be meas- ured at a given point or monitored at length to capture patterns extended in time. An assessment of the three systems might include verbal reports of subjective distress, behavior (e.g. startle, immobility and escape), and physiologic activation (e.g. increased heart rate; sweat- ing, i.e. electrodermal activity expressed as skin-conductance).

Ideally, if the construct of social anxiety or fear were a good one (i.e. fairly valid) the sampling of its different facets would converge. As it is, most "three systems" measurements of anxiety show rather disconcert- ing "desynchrony" among the different aspects of what a priori is thought of as a unitary fear response (Eifert & Wilson, 1991).

Is it any different in the case of social anxiety? Only one study attempted to trace the links among the three factors. In Douglas, Lindsay, & Brooks (1988) 28 subjects complaining of anxiety in a wide range of social situations, but without satisfying formal diagnostic criteria, subjectively reported assessments of autonomic, behavioral and cognitive systems. Objective measurements were obtained from observations of a social task performed in the laboratory. Subjects participated in a short (5 min.) conversation with a stranger that was video recorded and then rated. Pulse rate was also taken while the subjective distress was self-reported. Heart rate correlated significantly at 0.41 with self-report of autonomic arousal. However, it correlated neither with self-reported subjective distress nor with behavioral difficulties of any kind (verbal as well as non-verbal). The cognitive score correlated significantly with difficulties in verbal self-expression at 0.73 but correlated neither with non-verbal behavior or heart rate. Interestingly, there was a good correlation (0.73) between both objective and subjective measures of the bodily but not of the other two systems.

In sum, the poor synchrony between the three factors observed in various anxious subjects has been also found to occur in the context of social anxiety. Especially striking is the lack of association between behavior and bodily activation. Perhaps what these results reflect is an artifact of the specific methodology employed (laboratory simulation). Thus, the relevant unit of observation might be that of behavioral patterns extended in time rather than discrete observations of reactions at one specific point. Finally, studies with social phobic subjects are still to be carried out. All the same, the results of available studies comparing social phobic and normal subjects are in agreement and consistently suggest desynchrony. For example, specific social phobic subjects (concerned only with public speaking) have a higher heart rate than generalized social phobic or normal subjects. However, generalized social phobic subjects overall behave far more anxiously than their specific or normal counterparts (e.g. Heimberg, Hope, Dodge, & Becker, 1990b; Levin, Saoud, Strauman, Gorman, Fyer, Crawford, & Liebowitz, 1993).

Whether the measurement model of an ultimately sound construct, or alternatively, the very conception of anxiety itself is at stake, is for the time being unknown but this remains an important conceptual as well as practical question.

Some authors (e.g. Leary, 1983, p. 66) have explicitly argued for the exclusion of behavior from the measurement of (social) anxiety not specifically as a potential remedy to the problem of "desynchrony," but rather on the theoretical grounds that social anxiety is by definition "a *subjective* cognitive-affective experience" (1983, p. 67).

In view of the differences of outlook as to what constitutes social anxiety (e.g. does it include or exclude fearful or self-protective behavior?)

meaningful differences in the choice of kinds of observable events (the *referents* (McFall & Townsend, 1998, p. 317) are bound to arise, that will provide the concrete grounding for the abstract construct. Whether in the different cases and despite the similar label — social anxiety — the assessment procedure, or more likely the self-report inventory, would provide a measurement of the same construct is rather doubtful. Furthermore, as in most inventories, behavior and bodily activation, while observable in principle, are estimated subjectively by the participants (as is distress), it is not clear what relationship these ratings would bear to the same phenomena were they to be objectively assessed.

With these reservations in mind I shall turn to commonly used inventories of social anxiety, often (but not exclusively) for the purpose of assessing the outcome of both psychological and pharmacological treatments.

The Inventories

Two main instruments are in use for the measurement of social anxiety usually in the context outcome studies of social phobia. The Social Avoidance and Distress (SAD: Watson and Friend, 1969) is mostly used in studies of psychological treatment, whereas The Social Anxiety Scale (SAS, Liebowitz, 1987) is widely used in studies of pharmacological treatment. Anxiety and fear are used as conceptual synonyms in the SAS (1987, p. 152), but not in the SAD. Neither publication describing the inventories includes the definitions of the constructs of social anxiety, nor is the reader referred elsewhere for such definitions.

What the construct of social anxiety might involve may be guessed from what the authors of these inventories include or exclude from their measurements. The SAD, for example (and the SAS), excludes bodily activation or impaired performance since Watson and Friend (1969) conceive of social anxiety as involving only subjective distress and avoidance. The excluded elements are thought of as correlates, to be tested as elements of predictive validity (1969, p. 449).

Similarly, the SAS considers anxiety as involving subjective discomfort and a tendency to avoid the potential evoking social situations. Unlike the SAD, the SAS lists social contexts that are divided into those requiring performance in front of and those involving interaction with others (both rated for subjective distress and avoidance).

Avoidance is taken to be *the* behavioral sign of social anxiety, in both inventories. Doubtlessly, this is an important index of fear and a case can be made that this is the crucial one. In measurement terms, however, it may lead to the unwarranted conclusion that a low frequency of avoidance indicates a low degree of fear. If avoidance is considered the only behavioral pattern worthy of notice in assessing social anxiety, most behaviors (as described in chapter 1) displayed in the face of a social threat might remain undetected. "Freezing" into immobility or looking away in an attempt to make oneself inconspicuous, behaving ingratiatingly and submissively in attempts to appease, being evasive, and if everything else fails threatening or fighting, are some of the self-protective fearful social behaviors that might occur. Thus although avoidance is a referent of social fear it cannot justifiably be considered *the* criterion to the exclusion of all others.

With these reservations in mind, I shall briefly overview the validity of each instrument.

Social Avoidance and Distress (SAD: Watson & Friend, 1969)

The SAD is a self-report scale of 28 items rated as true or false concerning the degree of either avoidance or distress in various social situations. The final score is a summation of the "true" responses. The test was developed with a student population and norms were established.

Reliability This refers to the accuracy of measurement, conceived of as agreement between occasions of testing or between different items and the overall score.

1. *test–retest* – In Watson & Friend (1969), 154 students took the test twice over a period of 1 month. The correlation between the two moments was r = 0.68.
2. *internal consistency* – This was estimated at 0.94 with a sample of students (n = 205) in Watson & Friend, (1969). The two subscales (avoidance and distress) correlated at r = 0.75. Oei, Kenna, & Evans 1991), reported that the scores of 265 patients with a diagnosis of one of the anxiety disorders (35 were social phobic) had an internal consistency of 0.94.

Predictive Validity This aspect of validity relies on the ability of the measure to predict aspects of behavior.

In Watson & Friend, (1969), high SAD scores predicted a reluctance to participate in a group discussion at a future time as well as a greater concern about such a possibility. Finally, subjects who scored highly on the test spoke less during various social experiments.

Convergent Validity   This type of validity concerns the degree of correspondence between measurement of the kind of process under investigation and other measures of similar factors.

The SAD (Watson & Friend, 1969) correlated as follows with other measures: Taylor Manifest Anxiety −0.54 (n = 171), Audience sensitivity Index −0.76 (n = 42), Jackson Personality Research Form (affiliation) −0.76 (n = 42) and Marlowe-Crowne Social Desirability Scale −0.25 (n = 205).

Discriminant Validity   This type of validity concerns the degree to which the measure under investigation may be distinguished from other measures assumed to be different or whether it is able to differentiate two groups assumed to be different.

In Oei et al. (1991) SAD scores of social phobic subjects were significantly higher than those reported by simple phobic individuals and panic disorder patients.

In Turner, McCanna, & Beidel (1987) however, severity of SAD scores did not distinguish social phobic individuals from those with most other anxiety disorders (agoraphobia, panic, OCD, GAD) save for specific phobia (206 outpatients in all).

To sum up, it is usually ignored that the distribution of scores in this inventory is skewed (i.e. relatively few subjects even among social phobic individuals score extremely high on this scale). Furthermore the average score for women is significantly lower than that for men. Altogether, this inventory shows moderately satisfactory psychometric characteristics, while aspects of predictive validity add especially to its overall validity.

Social Anxiety Scale (SAS: Liebowitz, 1987)

The original SAS is a 24-item clinician-administered scale rather resembling a semi-structured interview; a self-rated version by the subject is now available. Situations are presented to the subjects who rate the degree of fear or anxiety they experience; these however remain undefined.

This scale divides difficulties associated with social anxiety into two categories: "performance" (in front of an audience − seemingly without interaction) and "social" (requiring extended interactions with others). Each item is rated on a 4-point continuum (0−none to 3−severe) as to the degree of fear or anxiety it evokes and the frequency of its avoidance

(0—never to 3—usually). The scale results in 4 scores: performance (rated for anxiety and for avoidance) and social (rated for anxiety and for avoidance).

Reliability Internal consistency was found to be 0.96 (Heimberg, Horner, Juster, Safren, Brown, Schneier, & Liebowitz, 1999) but test—retest reliability is unavailable.

Concurrent Validity In Heimberg, Mueller, Holt, Hope, & Liebowitz (1992), 66 social phobic (DSM—III) subjects were administered the SAS, the Social Phobia Scale (SPS: Mattick & Clark, 1989) and the Social Interaction Anxiety Scale (SIAS; Mattick & Clarke, 1998).

The two subscales of the SAS correlated with SPS as follows: social − 0.29 (not significant), performance −0.6. As to its correlation with the SIAS, it was: social −0.69, performance −0.45.

Convergent Validity In Heimberg et al. (1999), the responses of 382 social phobic subjects from different studies correlated with their scores on the SAD at 0.63. Avoidance and anxiety correlated with the SAD at 0.64 and 0.59 respectively.

Divergent Validity SAS scores correlated less (0.48) with general anxiety scales such as the Hamilton Anxiety and 0.39 for the Hamilton Depression Scale. The LSAS scores however correlated at 0.52 with the BDI.

Construct Validity In Safren, Heimberg, Horner, Juster, Schneier, & Liebowitz (1999) the responses of 382 social phobic subjects (pooled from different studies) to the SAS were factor-analyzed so as to test the proposition that the original factors distinguishing between performance in front of others and interaction with others would be recreated. The preliminary analysis did not reconfirm the original factors. Ultimately, four factors were established (social interaction, public speaking, observation by others, and eating in public). As before, these did not uphold the original structure of the test.

In summary, the psychometric characteristics of this widely used scale, especially in pharmacological outcome trials, did not consistently confirm its validity. The fact that it correlates modestly (0.63) with the SAD might be seen as strength; the fact that one of its subscales correlates poorly with another measure of social phobia gives pause.

As a general conclusion, the two inventories possess acceptable psychometric characteristics while relating to a fairly close (albeit not identical) conception of the scientific construct of social anxiety.

The Relationship between Social Anxiety and Social Phobia

As will be seen below, the studies that have attempted to shed light on the relationship between social anxiety and social phobia make little use of instruments (such as those reviewed earlier) with known psychometric properties designed to assess a *scientific construct* of anxiety. Rather, and for the most part, subjects who took part in those studies were instructed to rate in terms of anxiety (as well as fear, nervousness, etc.) situations that they had to define idiosyncratically – guided by their own lights. Thus either by design or inadvertently the *lay construct* of anxiety was adopted. How the ratings based on it might be related to any scientific construct of social anxiety is unknown and remains to be clarified.

Social Fears Among Normal Populations

Children and adolescents   Bell-Dolan, Last, & Strauss (1990) interviewed a selected sample of 62 children without any psychiatric history (mean age 11; range 5 to 18) from the area of Pittsburgh. With regard to social fears, 22% reported a fear of public speaking, 11% a fear of blushing; 15% feared dressing in front of others, and 15% were apprehensive about social contacts. At 1-year follow-up, none of the subjects met diagnostic criteria for anxiety disorders.

In Ollendick, Matson, & Helsel (1985), 126 subjects (from the USA) filled out the Fear Survey Schedule and were divided in 4 age groups: 7−9, 10−12, 13−15 and 16−18. Social fears (as well as other fears) remained stable across age groups. Among the 10 most feared situations, only one (# 8 – looking foolish), was social. However, this stability in the degree of fears may mask the fact that the content of fears changes.

In a later study (Ollendick, Neville, & Frary, 1989), involving a mixed sample from Australia (n = 591) and the USA (n = 594), subjects ranging from 7 to 16 years of age filled out the Fear Survey Schedule. With the exception of fearing poor grades that might be construed as a fear concerning low social rank, other most feared events concerned mostly physical harm.

The paucity of social fears (with prominence of fears of being harmed) among the 10 most feared situations reported by children and adolescents was also observed by Gullone & King (1993) from Australia and Muris, Merckelbach, Meesters, & van Lier (1997) from the Netherlands.

By contrast, Westenberg, Drewes, Goedhart, Siebelink, & Treffers (2004a) in a study of 882 children (aged 8 to 18) from Holland, found that an overall decrease in fearfulness masked two contradictory processes. On the one hand, fears of harm and punishment decreased with age, while on the other hand, social fears of evaluation and falling behind in achievement were on the rise especially in adolescence.

In Poulton, Trainor, Stanton, McGee, Davies, & Silva, (1997) (conducted in New Zealand) only 2% of the children reported the same categories of fears after 2 years (from 13 to 15). The top 4 fears in this sample did include 3 social fears: speaking in front of the class, speaking to strangers and meeting new people. These findings as well as those of Westenberg, Stein, Yang, Li, & Barbato, (2004b) contradict Ollendick et al. (1985). The transient nature of the fears is likely due to the particular maturational experiences of adolescents and the greater insistence of social demands being made on them; this may account for the preponderance of social fears in this group. This aspect is also prominent in surveys of college students described below.

In Brown & Crawford (1988) 1119 university students (mean age 19) responded to a Fear Survey Schedule. 59% of the men and 78% of the women reported one or more extreme fears. Of these, 18% reported an extreme fear of speaking in public and between 12% to 15% reported fearing being rejected, disapproved of, or looking foolish. More women consistently reported extreme fears, both social and not.

Strikingly similar results have been also reported by Bryant & Trower (1974) from the UK, as well as Essau, Conradt, & Petermann (1999) and Wittchen, Stein, & Kessler (1999b) from Germany. A factor analysis of the latter results yielded several factors, the most important of which (accounting for 70% of the variance) was interpersonal fears (e.g. being teased, criticized, disapproved of).

The dynamic as well as transitional aspect of fears are well highlighted in Gullone & King (1997) who carried out a longitudinal study on 273 subjects aged 7 to 18 from Australia. This is a subset of the 918 subjects described in Gullone & King (1993). The participants in the study who had been followed for 3 years, reported a lesser degree of fear overall but an increased discomfort about talking in front of the class. The same trend was also apparent in a cross-sectional study of various age groups (Gullone & King, 1993) in which 7 to 10 year olds reported a much lower degree of distress about talking in front of the class than did 15 to 18 year olds.

In summary, the evidence regarding social fears in childhood is inconsistent. In some studies social anxieties are hardly reported while in other studies, especially involving adolescents and young adults, these become prominent, thus prefiguring adult sensitivities regarding loss of face in front of one's peers and superiors.

Adults   In Costello (1982) a random sample of 449 women (age range 18−65) drawn from the community (Calgary) underwent the Present State Examination interview. Fears were rated for intensity and avoidance. A continuity of severity combined with a tendency to avoid was established. 26% reported mild social fears without avoidance, 8% reported mild social fears with avoidance, 4% reported intense fears without avoidance and 2% reported intense social fears and avoidance. The highest prevalence of social fears (all intensities confounded) was reported between the ages of 18 and 25.

In Stein, Walker, & Forde (1994b), a random sample of 3,000 telephone subscribers in Winnipeg were contacted for a telephone interview of 32 minutes; the 519 who accepted were representative of the population of the city. During the interview the subjects were presented with 6 situations: speaking in public (either to a large or a small group), meeting new people, writing or eating in front of others, attending social gatherings, and dealing with people in authority. They were asked to rate the degree of distress these might evoke as well as to identify the worst situation and what impact the problem had on their lives.

Approximately 61% of the respondents were of the opinion that their distress ("nervousness") was average or more in at least one situation; the most frequently mentioned situation was public speaking in front of larger groups (55%), followed by speaking in front of a small group of familiar people (25%). Consistently with these results, 85% of the subjects reported public speaking to be the worst situation in terms of "nervousness." 47% of the subjects however reported difficulties in other situations in addition to public speaking. For example, approximately 15% found that they are apprehensive ("somewhat" or "much more than other people") attending social gatherings. But fully 46% reported nervousness about dealing with people in positions of authority. However, only a quarter (26%) of those feeling nervous reported a moderate (19%) or marked (7%) distress that interfered with their daily life. It is the latter that the authors considered as equivalent of those who satisfy criteria for social phobia.

In a reanalysis of the previous study, Stein, Walker, & Forde (1996) found that speaking in front of a large audience as opposed to a small group of people evoked a different anxious self-reported response. Thus 34% of the subjects reported being "much more nervous than other people" with regard to public speaking. Less than 12% of these subjects, however, rated themselves as "much more nervous than other people" in small groups.

Pollard & Henderson (1988) surveyed by telephone a sample of 500 subjects (half men, half women) in the St Louis area. 23% of the sample was identified as meeting criteria for social phobia (DSM-III), with fears of public speaking predominating (21%). When the criterion of significant distress and interference with daily life was applied, however, the prevalence rate fell to 2%. This finding implies that the bulk of subjects experiencing lesser degrees of distress and interference represent on a continuum, various degrees of normality. As do the Stein et al. (1994b, 1996) studies, it does also suggest that the norm is a varying degree of social anxiety rather than none at all.

In a study investigating the boundary of social phobia, Furmark et al. (1999) had postal questionnaires sent to a sample of 2,000 (divided equally between men and women) drawn from Stockholm and Gotland (rural Sweden); 1,202 subjects responded. The questionnaire included both situations similar to those encountered in Stein et al. (1994) as well as new ones such as: expressing opinions in front of others. Ratings of distress and impairment were included as well.

The prevalence rate of social phobia varied widely with the varying cut-off points assigned as definition. This suggests a wide gray area of varying degrees of normal social anxiety even at the boundary between normality and social phobia. The authors conclude: "It is virtually impossible to determine non-arbitrarily where normal social anxiety ends and pathology begins" (Stein et al., 1994b, p. 422).

In Pelissolo, André, Moutard-Martin, Wittchen, & Lépine (2000) 12,873 subjects (15 years and older, representative of the population of France) responded to a mailed questionnaire concerning social phobia. Two sets of definitions were used (broad and narrow) distinguished by the persistence of avoidance and impairment of daily life. Fully 67% of the sample reported at least one strong fear in social situations, while either 3% or 8% (according to the definition) reported that such fears interfered with daily life. Unsurprisingly, the more demanding the criteria, the smaller the proportion of subjects meeting these criteria.

In summary, social anxieties are widespread in the normal population; with single-situation fears (e.g. speaking in public) reported by roughly between two thirds to three quarters of the individuals questioned.

Public speaking and handling individuals in position of authority are normally situations evocative of anxiety. Thus, social fearlessness is exceptional and statistically abnormal. The greater the severity of anxiety and number of situations evoking such a response (and in parallel the functional handicap), the rarer the phenomenon. Nevertheless, it lies on continuity with normality. However defined, it is marked off in a somewhat arbitrary manner.

Social Anxiety in the Socially Phobic Compared to Normal Subjects

In Beidel, Turner, & Morris (1999) 55 social phobic children (mean age 10) were compared to 22 normal control children (mean age 12) on a social phobia and anxiety inventory for children (SPAI-C) and on a behavioral assessment task. This included an interaction with a peer as well as reading aloud in front of an audience. On the SPAI-C, social phobic children scored 6 times as high as the control group (26 vs. 4), the surprising result being how few social fears were reported by the normal children.

Similarly, "blind" judges observing the behavioral assessment tasks rated the social phobic children as highly anxious while normal subjects were considered a little anxious. Interestingly, the phobic children rated themselves as less anxious than did the judges, but the difference in ratings of the social phobic and the normal children was still significant.

By means of advertisements in newspapers, Hofmann & Roth (1996) recruited 24 (public speaking) social phobic and 22 control subjects who were then compared. Both groups were subdivided in those who reported experiencing distress in either one or several situations. While participants categorized as generalized social phobia reported more anxiety than did patients identified as single-situation phobia (and similar controls), there was no difference in the degree of reported anxiety between the non-generalized social phobic and the normal subjects who reported distress in several situations.

In summary, there were differences in the degree of anxiety reported by social phobic subjects compared to normal control subjects. Qualitative differences were observed in children, but not in adults.

Social Anxiety in Subtypes of Social Phobia

With the advent of DSM-III-R, subtypes of social phobia have been proposed. The specific was circumscribed in terms of fear-evoking situations, typically public speaking. The generalized was defined as including most social situations. To these must be added a related construct – that of avoidant personality disorder, that closely resembles the generalized subtype. These rather loose definitions proved difficult to define operationally, therefore complicating any attempt to compare results issued from different studies.

In these, typically the participants were asked to give an impromptu speech or to engage in a brief conversation with a stranger. Behavior as well as physiological activity was observed while subjects rated subjective anxiety on various scales.

The generalized social phobia subjects rated their subjective anxiety higher than did the specifics (Heimberg et al., 1990b), while both rated higher than the normal subjects (Gerlach, Wilhelm, Gruber, & Roth, 2001). Participants meeting criteria for both generalized social phobia and avoidant personality disorder, rated higher than generalized subjects (Boone, McNeil, Masia, Turk, Carter, Ries, & Lewin, 1999). However, when the specific and generalized subtypes were separated, in some studies the specifics rated no higher than the normal subjects (Hofmann, Newman, Ehlers, & Roth, 1995b).

As to heart rate – used frequently as an index of physiological acti-vation, the generalized subjects tended to be alike normal subjects while the specific subjects were characterized by significantly higher heart rates (Levin et al., 1993; Hofmann et al., 1995b). Interestingly, social phobic subjects who blushed had a significantly higher heart rate than those who did not, while the latter were alike normal subjects (Gerlach et al., 2001). Thus subjective distress and somatic activation were not found to be highly correlated in these rather contrived experiments.

As to fearful behavior during the simulation in the laboratory, overall the generalized participants displayed it (e.g. avoidance or escape) more than did the specific subjects (Boone et al., 1999). In another study (Levin et al., 1993), generalized subjects behaved more anxiously than did the specific and normal subjects. The normal participants, however, spoke more than both groups of social phobic subjects (1993).

In summary, as seen in an earlier section, no coherent pattern of responding across the three domains was found to characterize subtypes of social phobia. Generalized subjects reported more subjective anxiety and displayed more anxious behavior. Specific social phobic subjects were observed to react more in terms of heart rate. Most importantly, each group rated no higher than the normal subjects in some respects.

The Shy Compared to the Non-Shy

Shyness is a cognate (lay) construct to social anxiety; their relationship, however, cannot be established with any precision. Perhaps for our purposes shyness may be conceived of as an apprehensive pattern of *normal* behavior involving rather high levels of social anxiety. In that manner, comparisons of the shy with the non-shy shed light on social anxiety.

Children   Lazarus (1982) studied the prevalence of shyness among children. A representative sample (n = 396) of the population of Florida (grade 5) was interviewed. To the question "do you consider yourself shy?", 38% of the children replied yes (49% girls and 26% boys). Of those 73% said they would prefer being less shy. 28% considered themselves shy 50% of the time, 5% most of the time and 2% all the time.

Fatis (1983) studied 152 male subjects (aged 15 to 18) who were divided in 3 groups (shy n = 30, occasionally shy n = 26, not shy n = 96) on the basis of self-definition. The 3 groups were then compared in terms of their responses to the Stanford Shyness Survey (Zimbardo, Pilkonis, & Norwood, 1975). The shy as well as the occasionally shy reported a greater frequency of unpleasant thoughts than the non-shy. A similar pattern of adverse bodily reactions (e.g. heart pounding, tremors, dry-mouth) was obtained.

In so far as "shy behaviors" (e.g. avoidance, reluctance to talk) were concerned, the shy exhibited many more of those than the non-shy, but the occasionally shy were not different from either group, implying that shyness is a dimensional rather than a categorical construct.

Stevenson-Hinde & Glover (1996) studied 126 mothers and their 4-year-old children who were divided into highly shy (n = 33), moderate (n = 59), and low in shyness (n = 20). These were determined by results of "temperament assessment battery for children" taken by the parents and observations of the interaction of the child with a stranger in the laboratory. The highest and the lowest ratings of both defined high-and low-shy children, whereas the medium required "lab rating as the norm." Shyness and negative mood were highly correlated. The highly shy children were also withdrawn in the playground. Most of the children were shy in one context (lab) but were not in another (home) suggesting that shyness is best considered contextually as well as a dimensional rather than an all-or-nothing state. Mothers interacted better with their moderately shy daughters than with the highly shy ones, suggesting that the highly shy pattern evoked less pleasant and more unpleasant interactions. This however did not hold true for the boys. The very shy had as many pleasant interactions with their mothers as did the moderately shy. No observations were carried out with the fathers.

50 of the original child-participants were reexamined 5 years later; the consistency of observed shyness (a composite score of observations by the mother, teacher and home observation) was 0.66. This result suggests that shyness is a rather stable characteristic in children.

Adolescents and Young Adults Ishiyama (1984) studied the repercussions of shyness (self-defined) and attempted to characterize them on various dimensions in 96 high-school students in British Columbia. The shy had greater academic difficulties, had greater difficulties in establishing relations with peers and reported greater loneliness.

Significantly, both shy and non-shy reported similar frequencies of avoidance of eye contact, talking in an inaudible voice and fidgety movements among others. The only distinguishing characteristic was stammering.

The social situations that evoked shyness in both the shy and the non-shy were similar: unfamiliar places and unfamiliar people (shy 69%, non-shy 72%), talking about personal matters, being judged and being rejected, making mistakes in front of others, being unsure as to how to behave. Furthermore, the shy and the non-shy shared many bodily reactions: blushing (shy 71%; non-shy 61%), "butterflies in the stomach" and a racing pulse. Some reactions however, such as bodily shaking (5% vs. 9%), nervous sweating (38 vs. 26%) were significantly more prevalent among the shy.

Goering & Breidenstein-Cutspec (1989) studied the friendship networks of 23 individuals divided into highly shy, moderately shy and non-shy (based on the Shyness scale; Cheek & Buss, 1981). The highly shy individuals had fewer friends who appeared to be connected to each other and tended to befriend only people in their immediate environment (e.g. belonging to the same sports team). Their friendships tended to last longer but contacts were less frequent. Interestingly, the highly shy individuals reported deriving the same degree of satisfaction from their friendships as did the little-shy individuals.

Is shyness perhaps another word for lack of sociability rather than an expression of social fears? In other words, do similar behaviors (e.g. keeping a distance) serve the same function or two different ones: safety and lack of interest? In Asendorf & Meier (1993) 140 (grade 2) children from Munich were divided into 4 groups the result of the combination of extremes (on the basis of cut-off scores) of shyness and sociability. The 41 subjects were observed both at school and outside it when they had a measure of influence on the degree of exposure to social situations.

An analysis of variance revealed one main effect: sociable children had more contacts (regardless of whether they were shy) while non-sociable children spent more time with their siblings at home (again regardless of whether they were shy or not). Shy children spoke less in all school situations (e.g. in class), but particularly so in social situations (e.g. break). Similarly, they spoke less in unfamiliar situations outside school. In familiar situations (i.e. at home) shy and non-shy children spoke to a similar extent. No differences in heart rate between the groups were found. The fact then that the two dimensions did not interact supports the authors' contention that sociability (the seeking out of social opportunities) and shyness (the manner of responding to them) are unrelated.

Bruch, Gorsky, Collins, & Berger (1989) asked similar questions but in answering them studied young adults (undergraduates). 4 groups were created on the basis of sociability and shyness scores (the median was the dividing point for both), and those were subdivided on sex. Shyness was found to be the main determinant of behavior, negative and positive thoughts and heart-rate change. Sociability did not mediate any of the responses as in Asendorf & Meier (1993). The results, however, emphasize the independence of the manner of responding from the tendency of seeking out social interactions.

Schmidt & Fox (1995) investigated 40 23-year-old women selected out of 282 subjects for representing extremes of shyness and sociability. In this study, highly shy and little sociable subjects spoke less than the subjects in the other groups suggesting, contrary to Asendorf & Meier (1993) and Bruch et al. (1989), that the two dimensions are interrelated. The highly shy individuals rated themselves as being less talkative than the non-shy, but were not rated as different by their partners in a simulation. Similarly, they rated themselves as more anxious than the non-shy but ratings of the partners in the simulations did not distinguish between the two.

In summary, shyness lies on a continuum and is manifest in different degrees in the shy and the non-shy. The shy are less socially active but inwardly tend to be more reactive than the non-shy. All this is entirely consistent with the literature on social anxiety. Shyness (or social anxiety) is not to be confounded with lack of sociability; it is a manner of managing the dangers of social life, not a lack of interest in social contacts.

However shyness is defined, the link between childhood shyness and adult social phobia remains indeterminate. For instance, in a study of a sample representative of the population of the USA, approximately 50% of individuals meeting criteria for social phobia (lifetime) did not consider themselves shy when growing up (Cox, MacPherson, & Enns, 2005). Conversely, only 28% of shy women and 21% of shy men reported social phobia over the lifetime (2005, p. 1024).

Discussion

The investigation of social phobia through the perspective of social anxiety, while helpful descriptively, has not brought our understanding of social phobia into a sharper focus. It is a commonplace that social phobic individuals are prone to a fearful gearing up for a desperate (and losing) figurative struggle, either during various actual social interactions or while imagining them from the remove of relative safety. Specifically, this way of being is usually associated with a looming sense of threat accompanied by a heightened self-reported activation of the bodily mechanisms (see Sapolsky, 1992) supporting self-protective action (e.g. fleeing or feigning) without actually engaging in either most of the time. Social phobic individuals as compared to normal or other phobic subjects do not experience unique physiological reactions during threatening social situations, at least as measured (objectively and subjectively) in the laboratory (see section on "psycho-physiological responding" in chapter 5; Edelmann & Baker, 2002 is illustrative). Although marked by exacerbations, these are within the range of normal reactions to threat.

With the exception of perhaps avoidance of social interactions, neither specific social phobic behaviors nor complex patterns have been brought into sharper relief by the construct of anxiety. Even avoidance or lack of it must be interpreted with caution. For little avoidance or none does not (as is implicit in many assessment inventories) mean little or no fear; nor does it imply well-adjusted social behavior. Fear, like any emotion, is a loosely linked network of responses spanning feelings, thoughts, behaviors, and physiological events (Marks & Dar, 2002, p. 508).

The dearth of aggressive and dominant behavior in the repertoire of social phobic individuals is another case in point. How would one conceive of this observation in terms of anxiety? Maintaining that anxiety inhibits social assertion would be tautological and redundant. The same reservations might be raised regarding anger (the emotion) and its display. How does anxiety seemingly inhibit anger at being dominated and consequently mistreated in some social phobic individuals, but not in others who are as anxious (Kachin, Newman, & Pincus, 2001)? Setting the behavior or its absence in an interpersonal context is more helpful. Angry behavior (to be distinguished from the stifled emotion) is a display of power in conveying a threat (as a mobilization for fighting) to others. Insufficiency of (social) power is at the root of social fear (Kemper, 1978, p. 56).

In sum, the notion of anxiety contributes little to illuminate either the minutiae of concrete social phobic behaviors or its manner of organization in patterns as well as the variety of their manifestations in different social contexts. Why for instance is the same person struggling laboriously while speaking monotonously and barely audibly (mouth parched, heart pounding, and bathed in sweat) during a presentation before colleagues, while being expressively opinionated or bitingly funny in the company of appreciative friends? To say that she behaves the way she does because she is anxious in one but not in the other situation is tautological. The two *descriptions* are equivalent, formulated in a different idiom, reflecting a different perspective; one does not cause (or provide an explanation for) the other. Social fears have both a physiological and an interpersonal locus.

A social interactive perspective, taking into account the transactional process in terms of power and status might offer a more observable explanatory framework; this however would transfigure the term anxiety altogether. From the received view of anxiety as an *intra*-personal concept it would become an *inter*-personal or a relational one. As such, it would inevitably be embedded in the social life of a society at a given time in place. Several examples would serve to illustrate the importance of this wider societal/cultural context.

First, in the western nuclear family in which usually only the mother is available as a carer, a lot rides on the attachment relationship. It might be different in a social life based on an extended family (or a collective life of sharing with neighbors) where many adults might be available physically as well as emotionally to the child. Thus the unavailable and fearful mother who shares the burden of raising the children with some other adults belonging to several generations would exert far less influence with likely a different outcome in terms of attachment and subsequently social anxiety for the growing child.

Second, the way of life prevalent in the industrialized West today (organized mostly as a marketplace) is relatively lightly structured thus affording relatively great freedom to the individual to participate in numerous competitions. This begins at a relatively young age (being accepted at school, making the grade) and never stops. The process also includes personal relationships (finding and keeping a mate) as well as a way of being (making a living), getting and keeping positions, making a success of them. This might account for the fact that, although quite secure, life in the western countries is nevertheless attended by many anxieties, as reported by surveys. Might social anxiety be greater in individualistic and highly competitive societies in which no social positions are guaranteed, no alliances permanent, as opposed to societies more rigidly stratified, in which one's way through life and one's social standing are to a large extent determined by kinship (i.e. on being the member of a family in a larger social structure)?

Third, in segments (e.g. samurai) of certain societies (Japan) in a given period (twelfth–nineteenth centuries), one could arguably maintain that social anxieties (and perhaps fear altogether) did not exist. Among members of such a warrior caste (King, 1993, pp. 37–60), the very experience of fear would be disgraceful; giving expression to it unthinkable. Through years of drilling and training in swordsmanship and other martial skills since an early age, and the provision of example and encouragement of lording it over the lower orders (who could be killed with impunity for being less than obsequiously deferential), the treatment of one's equals with utmost consideration, and unquestioning obedience to one's superiors, fear might be said to have been eliminated from this way of life. It would neither be shown objectively nor acknowledged subjectively.

In sum, while fear might be considered a "basic" human emotion it is modulated in important ways by the social form of life and culture of the individual.

Anxiety conceived intra-personally involves certain assumptions that need to be highlighted. Anxiety as a state of mind or construct is abstracted from the living human organism taking part in unceasing dynamic transactions with the social environment. The human agent and the environment are separated, with the environment serving as stage on which unfolds a plot dictated from within. Whether these assumptions are warranted is uncertain.

Conceptually as well as practically, understanding the actual social phobic behavior is vital; the impaired social functioning (a necessary condition for the definition of social phobia) of the social phobic individual is its direct consequence. An obvious type of understanding is the historical; it was sketched in an earlier developmental perspective on social anxiety and described in detail in chapter 9. While the end – safety – is fixed, the behavioral means towards realizing it vary. These come about through a continuous process of social learning, binding the individual to the social environment that selects as it were the proper behavior through its consequences.

While some behaviors (taking alcohol and/or medication) might be conceived of also as attempts to self-regulate, most other behaviors (and certainly broader patterns such as submission) are direct attempts to cope with threats in the environment. These would be actions directed towards other people, either as individuals or as social actors performing social roles nested in social structures and in reference to interpersonal (e.g. power or status) processes embedded in them. In chapter 1 a case was made for describing social phobia in terms of interpersonal behavior, conceiving it as the enactment of various circumscribed patterns embedded in wider patterns ranging over various spheres of life (e.g. work, intimacy). The various acts are embedded in an overall pattern of self-protection and expressing an inadequacy of social power. The social meaningfulness of phobic behavior (either as a single act or as an extended and evolving pattern) is illuminated by the context within which it is displayed, as well as by its function (determined by the effects). In sum, rather than being the cause of social phobia, fear in such a conception is its emotional facet. It emanates from and supports the social phobic pattern of behavior rather than generating it.

Why is the construct of social anxiety so widely used despite its evident flaws and rather uncertain empirical support? Perhaps the outlook that assigns a central place to anxiety (social phobia as an anxiety disorder) is not formed in response to evidence alone. It draws its strength from being consistent with "an intuitive concept of disorder that underlies medical judgment and is widely shared by health professionals – that the symptoms of disorder are due to an internal process that is not functioning as expected (i.e. an internal dysfunction)" (Wakefield, Pottick, & Kirk, 2002, p. 380). On this view (social) anxiety is the expression of the dysfunction of certain (as yet unknown) regulatory mechanisms *within* the individual; social phobia would be its ultimate consequence. It is consistent with a Cartesian model of the human body as a machine (Shepherd, 1993, p. 569), inhabited by a ghostly mind.

Conceptually, the project of establishing abnormal (social) anxiety as a proximate cause of social phobia stumbles on the fact that anxiety itself is such a problematic concept. The ambiguity of its status is well illustrated by the availability of multiple competing definitions on the one hand and numerous measurement inventories devised without reference to a specific construct (of anxiety) on the other hand. Furthermore, most studies surveyed earlier had actually relied on a *lay* construct of anxiety since the participants in those studies have defined it subjectively and idiosyncratically.

Perhaps the most questionable assumption embedded in the studies we have surveyed is that social anxiety – construed intrapersonally – might be regarded as a *fixed* characteristic embodied in the individual that may be accurately and repeatedly measured. Since being socially anxious is an actively emergent process, it should have been properly expressed as a verb. Instead it is regarded as a *thing* and accordingly identified by a noun. Fittingly, it is often spoken of as something one has.

This is a highly inadequate characterization. Going about social transactions fearfully is the product of a process; one emerging from specific circumstances and firmly embedded in the dynamic shifts (in say power and status aspects) of the relationships in that situation and the context in which the interaction takes place. It is therefore highly sensitive to situational variations and the dangers inherent in them. Nonetheless, social anxiety is typically considered a fixed quality within the individual regulated by a (figurative) mechanism that, when functioning properly, can be turned on and off as well as modulated. In morbid conditions this putative mechanism is seen as dysfunctional. In sum, various instances of a fluid process of social interactions taking place on different occasions are abstracted, reified, and located inside the individual.

The single most important practical consequence of the construction of social phobia as a disorder of anxiety is that the remedies that have been devised for it on the whole seek to reduce anxiety. Consequently, outcomes are assessed and claims to efficacy are formulated mainly in anxiety terms. This flows from the rationale that difficulties in social functioning are consequences of the morbid anxious process underlying social phobia, while this in turn is considered as consequences of pathological processes on a more fundamental level (e.g. cognitive, neurobiological) to be elucidated. This way of construing social phobia is in analogy to a medical view separating the disease (within) and the resulting social impairment (measured as a diminished quality of life) displayed in the environment. Whether a reified social phobia may be separated from the manifest problematic social functioning of such individuals is most doubtful.

Although the view that social phobia is a *disorder* of anxiety might appear plausible on the face of it, the evidence in support of it is slim at best, even when taking the subjective estimates (of uncertain validity) at face value. In absolute terms no specific sort of social phobic (or abnormal social) anxiety has been identified. Palpitations, trembling, sweating, and blushing, for example, are self-reported not only by social phobic subjects but also by various other categories of individuals (e.g. normal, shy, other anxiety disorders). In quantitative terms, no specific demarcation point cuts abnormal social anxiety off from the normal sort. Thus, although social phobic individuals typically rate themselves subjectively as more anxious than do normal individuals, the difference between the two is one of degree rather than of kind.

This also applies to the various subtypes of social phobia. Additionally, if intermediate degrees of severity (sub-clinical fears) are taken into account (Chavira, Stein, & Malcarne, 2002), the results become consistent with a continuum of social fears, with social phobic individuals, as a group, at its high end. Furthermore, when physiological indices of anxiety (admittedly evoked by somewhat artificial social tasks) are objectively measured in the laboratory, the differences — significant on the continuum of subjective anxiety — blur (e.g. Gerlach et al., 2001) and in some studies vanish altogether (e.g. Edelmann et al., 2002).

In a survey seen earlier (Stein et al., 1994b), 85% of the 519 subjects (a sample representative of the population of Winnipeg) identified public speaking — a typical social phobic concern — as the worst situation in terms of "nervousness." While the degree of distress varied, it is obvious that "nervousness" in such social situations is the norm. Similarly, musicians and singers, for instance, commonly report "stage fright" (performance anxiety) and so do other artists; for a minority the problem is handicapping (see Lederman, 1989).

Thus, social anxiety, unlike social phobia, is commonplace. It is prefigured to some extent in childhood and adolescence, and fully manifest in adulthood, evoked by dealings with authority and a variety of socially competitive activities (e.g. for status or power). Given its ubiquity, social anxiety has to be considered an adaptive mechanism conferring a protective advantage from an evolutionary point of view (see Gilbert, 2001). Social anxiety or sensitivity (Stravynski et al., 1995b) about evoking displeasure in others is protective of the individual and doubtlessly plays a role in reducing strife and hence increases cohesion within the group. Viewed from that vantage point, the maladaptive interpersonal pattern of social phobia might be seen as the extended misuse of highly adaptive short-term defensive tactics.

In sum, social phobic individuals do not strike one as obviously abnormal in any specific comparison either in their anxious responses or in the social situations evoking these. The differences that have been identified (in self-reported subjective distress) are exacerbations (at times extreme) of apparently normal tendencies. Social phobic individuals differ markedly from normal ones not so much in terms of the anxiety reactions as such or fear in concrete interactions (e.g. when evaluated) but cumulatively, in various self-protective patterns of conduct displayed at different times in various spheres of social life. As described in chapter 1, these many continuous acts combine in the extended pattern of maladjustment and fearful distress we identify as social phobia.

4   Social Phobia as a Disease

We have seen in chapter 3 that social phobia can neither be characterized as an instance of a "disordered" anxiety nor be considered a disorder of a singular kind of anxiety. The nature of social phobia then, remains an open question.

A potential answer might be found in the fact that social phobia is considered by some physicians a disease. An introduction to a series of articles published in *International Clinical Pharmacology* (James, 1997), for instance, had as title: "Social phobia – a debilitating disease with a new treatment option."

That much is also implied by the vocabulary in use. Typically, individuals seeking help are "diagnosed" as "suffering from" social phobia – "a debilitating condition with an etiology that has yet to be established." Fearfulness of and an inclination toward avoidance of social occasions are said to be its "symptoms."

Moreover, social phobia is at least implicitly recognized as a disease by international official authorities and by some national professional bodies. Its "diagnosis" may be found listed in both the International Classification of Diseases (ICD-10; Classification of Mental and Behavioral Disorders) compiled by the World Health Organization (1992) as well as in the Diagnostic and Statistical Manual (DSM-IV) published by the American Psychiatric Association (APA, 1994).

Is social phobia a disease then? Ostensibly, the answer is simple but as we shall see later, it is bedeviled by complex conceptual issues and the fact that there is rather little evidence to rely on.

The arguments for considering social phobia a disease are mostly rhetorical and abstract, rooted in the nature of psychiatric problems in general. For this reason, I shall take a roundabout route, and before coming to a conclusion I shall examine the notion of disease and whether it is applicable to social phobia.

Disease or Disorder?

The distinction between disease, illness and sickness is a commonplace in theoretical medicine. Disease is by definition an organic phenomenon independent of subjective experience or social conventions. It is measured objectively; such measurements are the *signs* of disease. Illness refers to the subjective complaints communicated by the individual; these are typically known as *symptoms*. Sickness is the social phenomenon; it refers to the individual's performance of various social roles and the manner of his/her participation in the life of their community (see Hofmann, 2002, pp. 652–653).

In the ICD-10 and DSM-IV diagnostic manuals social phobia is found under the heading of anxiety disorders. What is a disorder? Is it a synonym of disease?

In its introductory note on terminology, the ICD-10 (World Health Organization, 1992) explains:

The term "disorder" is used throughout the classification, so as to avoid even greater problems inherent in the use of terms such as "disease" and "illness." "Disorder is not an exact term, but it is used here to imply the existence of a clinically recognizable set of symptoms or behaviors associated in most cases with distress and with interference with personal functions." (p. 5).

A similar line is taken in the DSM-III and subsequent revisions. In the DSM-IV we find a caveat stating,

although this manual provides a classification of mental disorders, it must be admitted that no definition adequately specifies precise boundaries for the concept of mental disorder... In DSM-IV, each of the mental disorders is conceptualized as a clinically significant behavioral or psychological syndrome or pattern exhibited by an individual and that is associated with present distress (e.g. a painful symptom) or disability (i.e. impairment in one or more important areas of functioning) or with a significantly increased risk of suffering death, pain, disability, or an important loss of freedom (p. xxi).

Significantly, however, it is argued elsewhere (by some of the individuals who have been in the forefront of the creation of the DSM-III): "a mental disorder is a medical disorder whose manifestations are primarily signs and symptoms of a psychological (behavioral) nature" (Spitzer & Endicott, 1978, p. 18).

While the ICD is reticent in coming to grips with the issue and shies away from providing a definition of disease or disorder, the DSM appears to have it both ways; it provides no real definition of disease but insinuates it is dealing with them nevertheless. It explains,

all medical conditions are defined on various levels of abstraction – for example, structural pathology (e.g. ulcerative colitis), symptom presentation (e.g. migraine), deviance from a physiological norm (e.g. hypertension), and etiology (e.g. pneumococcal pneumonia). Mental disorders have also been defined by a variety of concepts (e.g. distress, dyscontrol, disadvantage, disability, inflexibility, irrationality, syndromal pattern, etiology, and statistical deviation). Each is a useful indicator for a mental disorder, but none is equivalent to the concept, and different situations call for different definitions (p. xxi).

A somewhat less bookish way to shed light on the concepts of disease and disorder is to look to the use of these terms in medicine. Wiggins & Schwartz (1994, p. 98) maintain that "medical doctors rarely speak of disorders; they refer instead to diseases … Physicians do employ the term disorder to express the idea that the patient has a functional rather than a structural problem." What kind of functioning, however, do these authors refer to? Is it psychological and behavioral or physiological? The distinction is of utmost importance as the functional problem in social phobia is maladjustment to life-demands rather than a bodily one.

As the final step I shall turn to pathology – the authority on disease – for its applied understanding of the terms disease and disorder. According to the Robbins Pathologic Basis of Disease, pathology is "devoted to the study of the structural and the functional changes in cells, tissues, and organs that underlie diseases" (Cotran, Kumar, & Robbins, 1994, p. 1). Disease, then, spans the anatomy (structure) and the physiology (function) of the human organism. In other words it is "the structural alterations induced in the cells and organs of the body (morphologic changes), and the functional consequences of the morphologic changes" (1994, p. 1). By "functional" Cotran et al. (1994) mean that "The nature of the morphological changes and their distribution in different organs or tissues influence normal function and determine the clinical features (symptoms and signs), course and prognosis of the disease" (p. 1). In other words, in disease functional abnormalities flow from structural changes; they are not independent of them.

As functional abnormalities are the consequence of structural ones, the structural/functional perspectives on disease must not be seen either as a dichotomy or as mutually exclusive. In some circumscribed instances, however, one would be able to separate the two perspectives as during the period when the structure – say of an organ – is abnormal while it is still functioning adequately.

In summary, disease is viewed materialistically in terms of (observable) lesions to cells, tissues or organs, identifiable biochemical imbalances, etc. These manifest themselves through signs (e.g. fever), symptoms (e.g. expressions of suffering) or a combination of the two. These indicators are used to arrive at a tentative diagnosis. In practice, some diagnoses may never be validated independently. As a matter of principle, however, there is a concrete disease independent of its manifest indicators. In the absence of disease the use of the related term of diagnosis hardly makes sense.

Mental Disorder – a Metaphoric Disease?

For the reasons evoked above, Szasz (1987, pp. 135–169) considers the use of the term "mental illness" or its modern equivalent – disorder – misleading and a fallacy. In his view the use of the term "disease" ought to be limited to material disease only. The definition of disease by distress and maladjustment is, according to him, a metaphoric one, arrived at by analogy.

The reasoning is as follows: since individuals with a bodily (i.e. material) disease suffer and may have trouble leading well-adjusted lives, those who resemble them may be deemed to be diseased as well. As one might look at disease functionally (in terms of physiology e.g. when no lesions are observed) poor psychological functioning by an inversed logic could also be conceived along the lines of a disease (disorder). According to Szasz (1987) if such patients may be said to be sick at all, it is figuratively (in terms of metaphor), as when saying "sick with love" to describe someone driven to distraction or "it makes me sick" to express disgust and disapproval.

In a similar vein, Lenin, whose chief preoccupation after seizing power in October 1917 was to hold on to it, diagnosed (some) of his more upright comrades' scruples about abandoning principle for expediency, as symptoms of left-wing communism – an infantile disease.

Social Phobia – a Neurological Disease?

Recent decades have been characterized by an intensification of a biologizing trend in the search for explanations of abnormality, especially in US psychiatry. Consequently, some authors have come to denounce and reject the distinction made between the two kinds of disease – mental and otherwise (described above) – striving to show that mental disorder (defined psychologically) is medical (i.e. material disease) after all. This quest – despite its modern ring – has actually a long pedigree as suggested by Griesinger's (1845) maxim: "*Geisteskrankheitn sind Gehirnkrankheitn*" (mental diseases are diseases of the brain, quoted in Mooij, 1995).

As a working hypothesis, such a possibility is eminently plausible – either for social phobia or for any other problem. Andreasen (1984, p. 29), for example asserts, "The major psychiatric illnesses are diseases. They should be considered medical illnesses just as diabetes, heart disease and cancer are." On what grounds? Because

The various forms of mental illness are due to many different types of brain abnormalities, including the loss of nerve cells and excesses and deficits in chemical transmissions between neurons; sometimes the fault may be in the pattern of the wiring or circuitry, sometimes in the command centers and sometimes in the way messages move along the wires 1984, (p. 221).

To sum it up, "Mental illnesses are diseases that affect the brain, which is an organ of the body just as the heart or the stomach is. People who suffer from mental illness suffer from a sick or broken brain."

What evidence is there to bolster such claims? Concerning anxiety disorders as a group (social phobia is not discussed on its own), the author first expresses the hope that "anxiolytic" medication might shed light on the neurochemistry of anxiety. As to actual evidence, we are told that there is a possibility of a genetic component to anxiousness, that panic may be induced in certain patients with the infusion of lactate and that there is a link between panic and mitral-valve prolapse (see Andreasen, 1984, pp. 239–243). These hardly give support to the rather sweeping assertions of "brain abnormalities."

Sheehan (1986) advocates a broadly similar approach. Although in his book *The anxiety disease* social phobia is broached tangentially – as a stage in the development of what he terms the anxiety disease – his views have a bearing on our topic.

"The proposed model suggests that at the center of this disease, feeding it like a spring, is a biological and probably a biochemical disorder" (p. 90). Secondary (exacerbatory) roles are accorded however to psychological (i.e. conditioning) processes and environmental stresses.

In support of his construal, the author asserts that there is evidence that vulnerability to the disease may be genetically inherited, and that it is

possible that such a genetic weakness could give rise to biochemical abnormalities ... What are the precise biochemical abnormalities in this disease? No one yet knows with certainty ... The best guesses so far involve certain nerve endings and receptors in the central nervous system which receive and produce chemical messengers and excite the brain. These nerve endings manufacture naturally occurring stimulants called cathecolamines. It is believed that in the anxiety disease, the nerve endings are overfiring. They are working too hard, overproducing these stimulants and perhaps others ... At the same time there are nerve endings that have the opposite effect: they produce naturally occurring tranquilizers, called inhibitory neurotransmitters that inhibit, calm down, and dampen the nerve firing of the brain. It appears that the neurotransmitters or the receptors may be deficient, either in quality or quantity ... [In summary] A chain of events apparently runs from the inherited gene or genes through the cell nucleus to the cell membrane to the nerve ending and the chemicals it uses, involving some or all of the above mechanisms (Sheehan, 1986, pp. 91–92).

Even without carefully examining each argument introduced by both authors conceptually and methodologically at this point (this is done in Chapter 6 critically reviewing available studies), it is clear that the insubstantial and tangential proof provided hardly makes the case that social phobia is an instance of neurological disease. Furthermore, in a comprehensive review of all studies having a bearing on the neurobiology of social phobia, Nickell & Uhde (1995, p.128) conclude that: "what available data have been collected across different laboratories suggest that tests of biological function in patients with social phobia are more typically similar to, rather than different from, those of normal control subjects." A more recent review (Dewar & Stravynski, 2001) concurred. Despite continuing attempts – all based on the general notion that a difference between social phobic and matched control subjects on some neurobiological parameter would reveal an abnormality – the hypothetical biological substrate of social phobia, fails to materialize.

The implications of this are far reaching. Either the paradigm and methodologies used in this research program are inadequate and need to be radically rethought, or there is no neurobiological deficit or excess underlying social phobia to be found. In the words of Nickell & Uhde, (1995): "While this continuum view of social anxiety to social phobia might appear self-evident in some scientific circles, it is, in truth, a different theoretical construct from the disease model"(p. 128).

The Social Context of the Disease Model

The use of the term disease in reference to social phobia occurs mostly in publications describing and (wittingly or not) promoting the use of psychotropic medication as a treatment. It is disconnected from its scientific basis and used rhetorically, implying that in the face of disease only medication will do.

Clinicians,

tell patients that they suffer from a chemical imbalance in the brain. The explanatory power of this statement is about of the same order as if you said to the patient "you are alive". It confuses the distinction between etiology and correlation, and cause and mechanism, a common confusion in our field. It gives the patient a misleading impression that his or her imbalance is the cause of his or her illness, that it needs to be fixed by purely chemical means, that psychotherapy is useless and that personal efforts and responsibility have no part to play in getting better (Lipowski, 1989, p. 252).

Thus the notion of disease complements the designation of certain compounds (which have many other applications) as indicated for social phobia. These are typically elements in marketing campaigns orchestrated by pharmaceutical companies. Pharmaceutical Marketing, a trade publication, "singled out social phobia as a positive example of drug marketers' shaping medical and public opinion about a disease" (Moynihan, Heath, & Henry, 2002, p. 888).

Is Social Phobia a Disease?

Ultimately, it is a matter of definition. The possibilities are as follows:

most physicians, when they give the matter any thought at all, believe that disease is a scientific term whose sphere of application should be determined by doctors on technical or scientific grounds, but that in practice, they apply the term inconsistently, often in response to what are quite clearly social or political considerations of various kinds. What should the architects of a classification of diseases or a classification of psychiatric disorders do in this unsatisfactory and confusing situation? A total of four alternative strategies are available. The first, adopted by the World Health Organization, is to ignore the problem, perhaps in the hope that others will do the same, and to make no attempt to define the term disease or any of its analogues. The second, adopted by the task force responsible for DSM-III, is to provide a definition, which is vaguely worded to allow any term with medical connotations to be either included or excluded in conformity with contemporary medical opinion. (A subsidiary strategy, adopted by both WHO and the APA, is to refer throughout to mental disorders rather than diseases, on the assumption that the undefined term disorder will be both less contentious and broader in scope than the similarly undefined term disease.) The third strategy, which so far as I am aware has never yet been adopted, at least for a psychiatric classification, is to provide an operational definition of disease (or disorder), which provides unambiguous rules of application, and then abide by the unsatisfactory constraints imposed by that definition. The fourth is to concede openly that psychiatric classifications are not classifications of diseases or disorders, but simply of the problems psychiatrists are currently consulted about, and that the justification for including such categories as oppositional disorder or pyromania (DSM-III) or specific reading retardation

(ICD-9) is merely that in practice psychiatrists are consulted by, or about, people with such problems.

My own view is that this is probably the best course, at least until we have resolved some of the problems discussed above. It avoids the ambiguity and intellectual dishonesty of the first two options and the serious constraints of the third. It does, of course, leave unresolved the question of which of the conditions listed in the glossary is a disease and which merely a problem resulting in a psychiatric consultation, but the use of the term "mental disorder" does that anyway (Kendell, 1986, pp. 41–42).

In the final analysis, if disease is an organic problem, scientifically demonstrated, social phobia is not a disease. If disease is any problem attended to by a physician, social phobia may be considered one.

5   Social Phobia as a Hypothetical Construct

Both the International Classification of Disease (10th edition) and the Diagnostic and Statistical Manual (4th edition) list social phobia as one of the "mental disorders." As such, it ought to be a "significant behavioral or psychological pattern" associated with distress and impaired functioning. Both glossaries are primarily "field-manuals" providing checklists of identifying features to guide the spotting of individuals whose self-description matches the appropriate, (in our case the social phobic) pattern of conduct. Although the manuals might be thought of as dictionaries, this is mistaken for they do not clarify what social phobia is.

Two definitions of social phobia (DSM-IV and ICD-10) are currently available for the purpose of assessment, using somewhat different indicators (defining criteria). These may be seen in Table 5.1 below. While ICD-10 specifies various facets of fear, DCM-IV stresses impaired social functioning. (Tyrer, 1996 provides a detailed comparison.)

Most research has adopted the DSM definitions that, besides emphasising impairment since DSM-III-R, have remained, with slight changes, essentially the same.

The definitions, however, leave unanswered the question of what proof there is that what is defined actually exists? And if it does, whether it constitutes a distinct entity?

The necessity of asking such questions arises from the somewhat philosophical uncertainties as to the nature of what is defined in the classification manuals.

Frances and some of his fellow creators of the DSM-IV (Frances, Mack, First, Widiger, et al., 1994) put the dilemmas thus:

Do psychiatric disorders exist as entities in nature, or do they arise as mental constructs created in the mind of the classifiers?

At one extreme are those who take a reductionistically realistic view of the world and its phenomena and believe that there actually is a thing or entity out there

Table 5.1. *Main defining criteria of social phobia in the International Classification of Diseases (ICD-10) and the Diagnostic and Statistical Manual of Mental Disorders (DSM-IV)*

ICD-10	DSM-IV
Pronounced and persistent fear of being the focus of attention or of acting in an embarrassing or humiliating manner and/or tending to avoid social situations involving eating/speaking in public, meeting strangers or dealing with people in positions of authority.	Pronounced and persistent dread of one or more social situations in which one is exposed to scrutiny by others or unfamiliar people.
Complaining of 2 or more of the following: palpitations, sweating, trembling, dry mouth, breathing difficulties, sensation of choking, hot flushes, nausea, dizziness, numbness or tingling, experiencing loss of control or depersonalization; and complaining of fearing at least one of the following: blushing, shaking, wetting or soiling oneself.	
The above complaints are evoked mostly by feared situations or when envisaging involvement in those.	Involvement in social situations or envisaging it evokes heightened anxiety.
Anxious experiences and the inclination to avoid situations that evoke them generate considerable distress; such responses are recognized as excessive and unreasonable.	Dreaded social situations tend to be avoided or else, endured with intense anxiety and distress. Such responses are recognized as excessive and unreasonable.
	The tendency to avoid social situations and/or anxious participation in them, significantly impair social functioning.

that we call schizophrenia and that it can be captured in the bottle of psychiatric diagnosis. In contrast, there are the solipsistic nominalists who might contend that nothing, especially psychiatric disorders, inherently exists except as it is constructed in the minds of people.

DSM-IV represents an attempt to forge some middle ground between a naive realism and a heuristically barren solipsism. Most, if not all, mental disorders are better conceived as no more than (but also no less than) valuable heuristic constructs. Psychiatric constructs as we know them are not well-defined entities that describe nature on the hoof. (Frances et al., 1994, p. 210).

Social phobia then, as one of the hypothetical entities found in the diagnostic manuals, is best seen as a tentative "heuristic construct." Although the fact that it has been listed in diagnostic manuals since the advent of DSM-III lends it a certain dignity, it does not confer on it a seal of validity. It is a hypothesis considered by a group of experts to be worthwhile and, on current evidence, promising enough to be put to further tests.

The precariousness of the construct of social phobia, at least conceptually, is well illustrated by theoretical positions that dissent from those mooted in the diagnostic manuals. Tyrer (1985) for example argues for an undifferentiated view of anxiety disorders. That would make social phobia a variant of "anxiety neurosis." Similarly, Andrews (1996) presents noteworthy evidence in favor of a "general neurotic syndrome"; social phobia would be one of its facets.

Historic experience also counsels prudence. That abnormalities are not etched in stone is well illustrated by the fact that the history of psychopathology is littered with entities that came into being and then fell into disuse (e.g. dissociative fugue, Hacking, 1996). During the more recent past similar upheavals were in evidence: former abnormalities with a venerable history as sin (e.g. homosexuality) have been recast as normal variations, and old vices (e.g. gambling) have been relabeled as (tentative) psychopathologies. New potential disorders are clamoring for consideration (e.g. chronic fatigue syndrome: Jason, Richman, Friedberg, Wagner, Raylor, & Jordan (1997) or "acedia" (Bartlett, 1990) arguably themselves reincarnations of neurasthenia of old. Finally, it must be borne in mind that alongside scientific considerations, the rise of new constructs is also driven by social concerns in specific countries (e.g. the emergence of "post-traumatic stress disorder" in the USA: Young, 1995).

The Validation of a Construct

How could we tell if a hypothetical construct represents a real entity, or in other words is valid? Various strategies have been proposed for the validation of hypothetical constructs (e.g. Gorenstein, 1992; Nelson-Gray, 1991; Blashfield & Livesley, 1991). All draw on the indispensable work of Cronbach & Meehl (1955) who have outlined the rationale as well as the methods to be used for the purpose of validation of instruments (tests) measuring psychological characteristics (constructs). Such an approach may be usefully applied to psychopathological entities (Morey, 1991) for in both cases the end is the same: developing, measuring, and validating a concept denoting a pattern of psychological functioning.

A somewhat different approach to validation identified as "clinical" (Kendell, 1989) or "diagnostic" (Robins & Guze, 1970) has been outlined from a medical perspective. It does share some features with the approach to construct validation I shall outline later, but differs from it in its relative unconcern with the issue of measurement while emphasizing "etiology" as the ultimate step in validation. This is hardly a practical strategy in light of past experience; as we shall see in later chapters what causes social phobia is both elusive and contentious. Furthermore, an entity of ambiguous validity can hardly be expected to yield clear-cut causes. It seems practical and prudent, therefore, to separate the question of whether social phobia is indeed an entity, from that of what may cause it.

What follows is the outline of a framework of validation that draws mostly on Gorenstein (1992, pp. 65−90).

As with any scientific notion, the formulation of a construct springs from observation. Typically certain behaviors seem to co-occur (e.g. self-protective withdrawal, anxious distress) as well as manifest themselves in particular contexts (e.g. in rather formal social gatherings, with people in authority or who act authoritatively).

The clinician (or any observer) might be struck at some stage with the coherence of it all; behavior (the immediately observable as well as involved patterns of conduct unfolding over extended periods of time), expressions of feeling, and reasoning seem all intricately arranged to fit a certain mold. Inspiration might provide a name for the pattern (interpersonal phobia!!), but this is not the construct yet. Smug complacency at this critical moment − although most tempting − must not be yielded to, for risk of committing the fallacy "to believe that whatever received a name must be an entity or a being, having an independent existence of its own" (J. S. Mill). At this stage, the name may only be used as shorthand for a set of tentative observations.

When logically unrelated behaviors are observed to co-vary with some regularity it seems not too unreasonable to conclude that another overarching factor accounts for this. What might this factor be?

A not implausible working hypothesis could state that the unifying factor is the peculiar organization of functioning of the organism − overall or under certain circumstances. In other words it is the very "significant psychological or behavioral pattern," or construct or entity (I shall use these terms interchangeably).

Construct validation then is a simultaneous process of measurement and testing of the hypothetical entity. Initially, since the processes involved in the construct are unknown to us, the measurement of it (i.e. the indicators or criteria) can only be an approximation through tapping certain features deemed to be central to it. There cannot be – even hypothetically – the unquestionably proper criteria, since we could not possibly know what these might be. This is the direct consequence of the direst feature of our predicament – namely that no independent proof of the presence or absence of the entity is available.

In practice, however, things might not be necessarily so grim. As when groping in the dark, any accessible features that could be readily (if only dimly) outlined, might turn out to be worthwhile and therefore must not be overlooked. All told, the defining characteristics can only have a probabilistic relationship to the construct they flag; the best would obviously be those that bear the most likely (i.e. closest and steadiest) relationship to the construct.

The measurement of a construct must clearly satisfy certain standards of accuracy. For one, the measurement of the construct ought to give similar results (i.e. the same classification decision, when applied by different assessors). If repeated, the measurement ought to yield approximately similar consequences – unless there is good reason to believe that social phobia is volatile; this is unlikely to be the case. This aspect of measurement is technically known as reliability and is typically expressed as a coefficient of agreement between classifiers who apply the same set of criteria. Finally, the indicators ought to show adequate consistency in defining the construct.

Once a reliable enough measurement has been developed through assembling the proper indicators, we are ready to test the construct further. Basically, this means putting forward hypotheses regarding aspects of the behavior (most broadly defined) of individuals we identify as exhibiting or, as usually is the case, reporting the social phobic pattern of conduct in various circumstances. Obviously, for these to be of more than passing interest, the predictions have to go beyond the defining characteristics of the construct (e.g. anxious distress, avoidance).

Hypothetically speaking, social phobic individuals might be expected to be more liable to sexual dysfunctions (Beck & Barlow, 1984) or to tend toward submissiveness to authority (Allan & Gilbert, 1997).

Furthermore, the hypotheses might be better put to a test by using contrasting circumstances and populations as controls (e.g. normally shy subjects, individuals consulting for other problems). These procedures, applied in various permutations and from a variety of theoretical perspectives, have the potential to highlight stable links between the construct and certain features of conduct – on condition, of course, that this pattern of links consistently obtains in nature.

This then – in the briefest outline – is the process by which a putative entity (not much more than a label initially) may become, in the fullness of time, a distinctive pattern of psychological functioning. It bears reminding that we are trying to validate the measure (consisting of the criteria/indicators) and the construct (social phobia) at the same time. When our experiments go well, both measure and the hypothetical entity gain in strength and vitality. When results disappoint (e.g. a wildly variable "epidemiology" of social phobia) we face a dilemma. Is our measure imprecise (i.e. do we mistakenly include some wrong individuals and miss some of the right ones?) or is the construct not quite what we speculated it to be? Worse still, the construct may not be what we had imagined altogether.

In practice, the process of validation is bound to be equivocal and the results it would yield, as we shall see later, often surrounded with ambiguities. Furthermore, the fact that validation is a process implies that it is cumulative and may never be fully completed. Nevertheless, even a partially validated construct may be worthwhile (if only in a limited sense) on certain pragmatic grounds. Conversely, a limited amount of a certain kind of information (e.g. a consistently unacceptable level of reliability) may be sufficient to seriously undermine a construct.

The process of validation of the hypothetical construct of social phobia is then an ongoing undertaking being carried out collectively over a number of years by numerous uncoordinated researchers, although some of those would have collaborative ties.

In this chapter, I shall consider most publicly available evidence while sorting it in different types of validity. An outline of the structure of the analysis is found in Table 5.2; it is divided in three types of validity.

Content validity concerns the extent to which the specific indicators capture the main relevant facets of the construct (i.e. the hallmark clinical features, in our case).

Another way of estimating content validity is to attend to the reliability or precision with which the construct may be measured. It is typically conceived as the degree of agreement between various raters and the stability of agreement-in-time regarding the construct. Content validity and especially reliability might be considered a necessary but not a sufficient condition for overall validity. It is the stepping-stone for higher things if it holds; everything else founders if it does not.

Criterion validity refers to the ability of the construct to estimate a way of behaving or other features (the criteria), not inherent in the definition of the construct itself or its indicators (e.g. anxious disquiet, avoidance of threatening situations). Two types of criteria are typically sought to aid the process of validation: such that occur at the same time,

Table 5.2. *A conceptual outline of validity elements and ways of testing them*

Validity

| | Criterion (empirical) | | Construct (conceptual) | | | |
| | | | internal | | external | |
Content (descriptive)	concurrent	predictive	convergent	discriminant	generalizability	ecological
Clinical features agreement about salient features	**Co-occurrence** *Clinical studies* e.g. rates of prevalence of SP *Community studies* e.g. rates of prevalence of SP	**Familial history** e.g. rates of prevalence of SP in first-rank relatives compared to normal controls	**Factor and principal component analysis** statistical analysis that identifies the main fears shared by members of a hypothetical group.	**Distinctiveness** tests for factors that distinguish SP from normal individuals and those with other disorders	**Epidemiological studies** *Prevalence* e.g. comparisons of rates of prevalence found in a variety of populations drawn from different countries and cultures *Co-occurrence* as above	**Social phobic behavior** 1. observation of SP behavior naturalistically 2. observation of SP behavior in the laboratory (role-plays)
Reliability *Inter-rater agreement* agreement between two observers	*Associated characteristics* e.g. links with sociological, psychological and neurobiological variables	**Response to treatment** e.g. pre-treatment features that predict response to treatments	**Associations with other constructs** e.g. rates of co-occurrence			

Table 5.2. (cont.)

Content (descriptive)	Criterion (empirical)		Construct (conceptual)			
	concurrent	predictive	internal		external	
			convergent	discriminant	generalizability	ecological
Test–retest agreement between two assessments at two points in time		**Longitudinal studies** e.g. follow children over years				
Internal consistency relationship between individual ratings and a global score						

Note: SP = Social phobia.

therefore concurrent and those that might obtain in the future, therefore predictive. Predictive validity, for example response to treatment, is the most useful in the practical sense. Theoretically, however, the most meaningful series of studies are usually those contributing to construct validity; this is central if an abstract concept is to pulsate with life.

Construct validity concerns the relationship of the construct under study — social phobia — to other psychological constructs (e.g. introversion, sexual functioning). This offers the best indirect possibility to gauge its nature. For it to be particularly meaningful, the relationship must first be specified on theoretical grounds and only then tested empirically. The process of construct validation is at its best when theory-driven. A well-articulated theoretical model would greatly aid the validation process. So far, most research has been conducted without the benefit of such a model. However, research would have stalled without even a tacitly understood and barely articulated theory (e.g. social phobia as a putative disease entity) in which the construct is embedded and which charts its possible relationship with other constructs.

Put simply, the relationships could be of two kinds: sharing features with constructs with which it is deemed to have a kinship (convergent validity) and being distinguishable from constructs purportedly different (discriminant validity). What is shared and that which distinguishes do not have to be completely unrelated; these might be seen as two sides of the same coin.

Last but not least, construct validity may be gauged from the degree to which the results observed in a specific study (or a series) carried out with a limited number of subjects and under particular conditions, may be said to apply in general (external validity). It is all too easy to get carried away when internal validity (i.e. convergent and discriminant) is sufficiently established and rashly assume that the construct may be extrapolated as obtaining universally and forever in human nature. Generalizability needs to be tested and shown.

This, then, concludes the outline of the process of validation of a hypothetical construct; I shall now turn to the available evidence.

Content Validity

Reliability: Agreeing About the Entity

Reliability provides a potent preliminary test of validity, as interviewers using the defining indicators ought in principle to be able to identify the pattern with relative ease.

Calculations of Agreement   As most of the studies that follow will be concerned with quantifying degrees of agreement, an important consideration is the choice of the best method to this end.

The plainest way to calculate agreement would take the following form: number of cases of social phobia for which there is agreement, plus the number of cases which are not of social phobia for which there is agreement, divided by the total number of cases. That would give a figure known as the "overall percentage of agreement."

Its great merit is that it is obvious and easily understood. Its deficiency in the eyes of its critics is that some (likely) or all (unlikely) of the agreements could be due to chance. To guard against this, Cohen (1960) devised a method that attempts to exclude chance. As such, the kappa statistic represents the probability that the agreement between two raters is not due to chance.

Mathematically it varies between -1 and $+1$, the range from 0 to -1 representing chance. Its significance is more symbolic than practical; a negative probability is nonsense. Practically speaking the closer the probability value is to zero, the greater the likelihood of chance agreements. Technically, the kappa statistic is much under the influence of the prevalence of individuals fulfilling criteria for social phobia in a given sample (i.e. the "base-rate"). Consequently, the greater the prevalence of social phobic individuals in a given group, the likelier the agreement on a case between interviewers. As base-rates vary considerably among studies, this has the unfortunate consequence of making kappas not quite comparable. Although proposals were made (see Spitznagel & Helzer, 1985) to replace the kappa with another statistic (Yule's Y for example) not as dependent on the "base-rate," for the time being at least, the kappa remains much in vogue.

Another problem with the kappa arises from how it is interpreted. Typically (see Mannuzza, Fyer, Martin, Gallops, Endicott, Gorman, Liebowitz, & Klein, 1989, p. 1094 for example) a kappa, (κ) of 1.00 to 0.75 is considered excellent, that between 0.74 to 0.60 as indicating good agreement, whereas values between 0.59 to 0.40 are considered moderate and those below 0.4 as indicating poor agreement. Such use treats the probability value (which allows the assignment of rank but not more) as a coefficient (which presupposes ratios) and could be read to imply that a kappa of 0.75 is 50% better than that of 0.50. That would be wrong. Nor is a kappa of 1.00 suggestive of perfect reliability; it is rather indicative of an absence of agreement due to chance.

Equipped with these rather technical considerations, we are ready to tackle the relevant literature.

To my knowledge, none of the versions of the DSM reported rates of reliability arising from its field trials involving clinicians relying only on the diagnostic manual. Instead, most available reliability results are based on structured interviews. These (e.g. DIS, SCID, ADIS) were devised soon after the publication of the DSM-III and its successors – primarily for epidemiological purposes – to be administered either by clinicians or lay-interviewers. Typically, the reported results are based on retrospective interviews yielding "diagnoses" over the "lifetime" rather than during the interview. It is not always clear whether requisite criteria were satisfied simultaneously at some time in the past or participants were reporting experiences occurring disparately on different occasions. The latter possibility is disquieting.

Table 5.3 summarizes reliability studies of both DSM and ICD criteria. The results suggest that social phobia, as a "clinically significant pattern of behavior," is reasonably well recognizable from its defining indicators – be they those of the DSM or the ICD. These results obtain especially when two assessors interview or observe the patients at the same time without the benefit of structured interviews to guide them.

Results obtained with ICD-10 or DSM-III, III-R or IV appear roughly equivalent. Differences however are far from negligible. Andrews, Slade, & Peters (1999), on the basis of 1,500 interviews addressing both sets of criteria, found that only 66% of potentially social phobic individuals corresponded to both sets of criteria.

A special perspective on reliability is raised by the agreements between two types of assessors: psychiatrists and lay-interviewers using standard structured interviews (DIS). The study (Neufeld, Swartz, Bienvenu, Eaton, & Cai, 1999) was carried out 13 years after the original Epidemiologic Catchment Area study in Baltimore aiming to estimate the incidence of social phobia using DSM-IV criteria. Respondents reporting any new problems to the lay-interviewers were subsequently invited to an interview with a psychiatrist who ignored the DIS diagnosis established by the lay-interviewer. Among the 43 social phobic individuals according to the lay-interviewers, psychiatrists identified only 16. Conversely, 10 subjects subsequently considered socially phobic by the psychiatrists, were not initially identified as such by the lay-interviewers. If psychiatrists may be assumed to provide the best available operational definition of social phobia (can it be otherwise?) the poor reliability in evidence in Neufeld et al. (1999) questions the results obtained by lay-interviewers using structured interviews.

Table 5.3. *Reliability: agreeing about the entity of social phobia*

Study	Participants	Criteria	Instrument	Reliability	Comments
Brown et al. (2001b)	1,127 outpatients (186 SP)	DSM-IV	1. ADIS 2. Clinical interview	$k = 0.77$	In 67% of the cases, the disagreement was about the threshold of clinical significance of the problems reported.
Sartorius et al. (1995)	3,493 outpatients (28 SP)	ICD-10	1. Clinical interview 2. Watched interviews from 1	$k = 0.33$	WHO/ADAMHA field trials.
DiNardo et al. (1993)	267 outpatients (45 SP)	DSM-III-R	1. ADIS 2. Attended interviews from 1	$k = 0.79$	The students were trained until reaching a rate of 3 out of 5 agreements with experienced interviewers.
Sartorius et al. (1993)	2,460 outpatients (22 SP)	ICD-10	1. Clinical interview 2. Watched interviews from 1	$k = 0.41$	WHO/ADAMHA field-trials.
DiNardo et al. (1993)	60 outpatients (8 SP)	DSM-III	1. ADIS 2. Structured interview	$k = 0.77$	Highly selected sample: clinic specializing in anxiety disorders.

Study	Sample	Criteria	Method	Results	Comments
Skre et al. (1991)	34 twin siblings 18 non-twins 2 parents of the twins (12 SP)	DSM-III-R	1. SCID 2. Listened to taped interviews from 1	$k = 0.72$ (SP alone) $k = 0.58$ (SP + DP) $k = 0.75$ (SP + AA) $k = 0.71$ (SP + DP + AA)	High rates of agreement may be an artifact arising from the use of audiotaped interviews. These narrow the clinical material according to the line of investigation pursued by the original interviewer.
Wittchen et al. (1991)	575 outpatients (45 SP)	DSM-III-R or ICD-10 criteria	1. CIDI 2. Watched interviews from 1	Agreement: 99% $k = 0.97$	WHO/ADAMHA field-trials, including 18 centers around the world.
Burnam et al. (1983)	220 outpatients (11 SP)	DSM-III	1. DIS 2. Clinical interview	Agreement: 85–88% $k = 0.32 – 0.38$	

Note: AA = alcohol abuse; ADAMHA = Alcohol, Drug Abuse and Mental Health Administration; ADIS = Anxiety Disorders Interview Schedule; CIDI = Composite International Diagnostic Interview; DIS = Diagnostic Interview Schedule; DSM = Diagnostic and Statistical Manual of mental disorders; ICD = International Classification of Diseases; DP = depression; SCID = Structured Clinical Interview for DSM; SP = social phobia; WHO = World Health Organization; + = combined with; k = Kappa statistic.

Reliability: Agreeing about Features of the Entity

Whereas the previous studies dealt with social phobia as an entity, this section examines agreement about some of its salient features.

Turner, Beidel, & Townsley (1992) focused on two features of social phobia: circumscribed performance anxiety (n = 27) and fear of common social gatherings (n = 61) in 88 social phobic subjects. Experienced clinicians using the ADIS-R obtained k = 0.97 in agreeing on which feature characterized each patient.

In Mannuzza, Schneier, Chapman, Liebowitz, Klein, & Fyer (1995b), the medical charts of 51 social phobic subjects (identified by the SADS-LA) seen in an anxiety clinic, were classified as generalized or specific social phobia by two clinicians in a discussion until consensus was reached; agreement was at k = 0.69.

In Brown, Di Nardo, Lehman, & Campbell (2001b), in which 152 individuals met criteria for social phobia either as the main or secondary problem, the agreement on the features of avoidance and fear were both r = 0.86.

In summary, both specific responses and typical constellations of these were identified reliably, ranging from modest to very good. All-pervasive fears were identified more reliably; discrete features less so. On the whole results are positive as manner of responding may be expected to vary much more than the overall pattern of social phobia, in reaction to situational and other factors.

Criterion (empirical) Validity

Concurrent Validity

This perspective on validity seeks to establish whether the construct of social phobia is systematically associated with certain factors (e.g. socio-demographic, psychological or biological) or behaviors.

Association with Age of Onset and Sex Distribution   Epidemiological rather than clinical studies are probably a better source for this information on account of the representativeness of these samples of their community. Such a procedure allows us to identify the critical age-range rather then provide a specific figure. As the subjects in these studies were children, their parents were typically also interviewed. Social phobia, however, was identified on the basis of the interview with the child.

The rate of prevalence of social phobia among children between the ages of 7 to 11 was at about 1% in Pittsburgh, USA (Benjamin, Costello, & Warren, 1990); it was still 1.1% in a sample of 15 year olds in Dunedin, New Zealand (McGee, Feehan, Williams, Partridge, Silva, & Kelly, 1990). The rate rose to 3.7% among 13 to 18 year olds in Rotterdam, Holland and was fully 11.6% among 18 year olds from the northeastern USA (Reinherz, Giaconia, Lefkowitz, Pakiz, & Frost, 1993). From that age on, no apparent increases in prevalence were reported. The critical period for onset of social phobia is therefore likely to be between the ages of 15 to 18. This is compatible with reports of patients seeking treatment (e.g. average age of onset was 14.4 in Goisman, Goldenberg, Vasile, & Keller, 1995). It is well to remember, however, that a meaningful percentage of subjects report that they "were always that way" (e.g. 14% in Lépine & Lellouch, 1995).

An approximately equal distribution of sexes is a feature of social phobia throughout (e.g. Turk, Heimberg, Orsillo, Holt, Gitow, Street, Schneier, & Liebowitz, 1998); this is already apparent in surveys of children.

Some similarities are also found in demographic and clinical features. Men and women (n = 212) in Turk et al. (1998) were similar in terms of age, marital status and educational attainment. Duration of social phobia as well as other associated problems was also similar as were self-reported anxiety ratings to numerous social situations. Some differences were noted: men reported higher anxiety levels for urinating in public and returning goods to a store. Women, by contrast, rated significantly higher situations such as working while being observed, talking to persons in positions of authority and being the center of attention.

In summary, social phobia is associated with a distinctive age-range of onset and equal sex distribution.

Association with Demographic Factors   Some studies allow us to trace the correspondence between the construct of social phobia and certain demographic factors and features of development.

Davidson, Hughes, George, & Blazer (1993a) studied a subset of the ECA sample (N = 1,488) divided in 3 groups: social phobic individuals (n = 123), those who met criteria for social phobia but were not distressed (n = 248), and control subjects. No differences in terms of demographic characteristics were found between the two social phobic groups. When lumped together, they tended to be less frequently married and employed and had fewer years of education than the control group. Fewer also reported having a close friend. Unfortunately, the social processes leading to this remain uncharted. This must become a priority research area in the future.

In terms of their development, social phobic individuals reported more early parental separations and a tendency to repeat grades at school.

Association with Psychological Factors: Cognition   An extensive review of this field of study is available in chapter 7. The conclusion most relevant to our purposes is that no "cognitive" process inherently and exclusively typifies social phobia. Consequently, there is no systematic evidence to support the claim that there is a "cognitive bias" that is inherently social phobic.

Association with Psychological Factors: Social Skills Deficits   A general overview of this area of research is available in chapter 8. This shows no evidence linking social phobia consistently with deficits of "social skills."

Association with Psychological Factors: Sexual Functioning   A study from Israel (Bodinger, Hermesh, Aizenberg, Valevski, Marom, Shiloh, Gothelf, Zemishlany, & Weitzman (2002) compared 40 social phobic and 40 normal individuals in terms of sexual functioning, experiences, and problems. Male social phobic subjects rated the ease of their sexual arousal, frequency of orgasm during sex, and satisfaction with their sexual performance lower than did normal subjects. Although statistically significant, these differences were not psychologically meaningful. For example, both groups rated their arousal within the "very easy" range (p. 876). More social phobic individuals reported some sexual problems (e.g. retarded ejaculation: 33% vs. 5%). Similarly, social phobic women rated the frequency of their desire for sex, ease of sexual arousal, frequency of coitus and satisfaction with their sexual performance as less than did normal women. They also reported more sexual problems, such as painful coitus (42% vs. 6%) and loss of desire during intercourse (46% vs. 6%) than did normal women.

As to sexual history, social phobic women reported having fewer sexual partners than did normal women. This was not the case with socially phobic men. They were, however, older (20 vs. 17) than normal men at the time of their first sexual experience. More social phobic men paid for sex (42% vs. 8%) and 21% of them compared to none of the normal men had only experienced paid sex.

In summary, social phobic individuals were neither characterized by a specific pattern of sexual functioning nor by a frankly dysfunctional one. At most, certain sexual problems were more prevalent among social phobic than among normal subjects, who were not entirely free of them either.

Association with Typical Psycho-physiological Patterns of Responding In numerous studies a variety of cardiovascular, respiratory and skin-conductance (as well as resistance) functions were measured so as to establish whether any were characteristic of social phobia. The most important comparison would undoubtedly be with normal subjects.

In Turner, Beidel, & Larkin (1986) 17 social phobic individuals were compared to 26 socially anxious and 26 non-socially-anxious normal participants. All subjects simulated interactions with a member of the opposite and the same sex and gave an impromptu speech. Overall, there was a difference between both socially anxious groups (phobic and not) and the non-anxious group in terms of greater systolic and diastolic blood pressure, and heart rate. There were, however, significant variations in physiological responses from task to task.

With the view to characterize the autonomic responses of 15 social phobic and 15 normal subjects, Stein, Asmundson, & Chartier (1994a) had them undergo: postural challenge (shift from sitting to standing); isometric exercises (gripping a dynamometer); cold-pressor test (immersing the dominant hand into cold water); and the Valsalva maneuver (blowing into a plastic mouthpiece connected to a pressure gauge).

At baseline the two groups did not differ on any measure of cardiovascular and respiratory functions. Surprisingly, given the number of measures taken, few differences between the responses of the social phobic and the normal control subjects were found. The phobic individuals had greater vagal withdrawal during the isometric exercise task, higher mean arterial pressure and a greater range of heart-rate responses during the Valsalva task. On this backdrop, it is difficult to justify the conclusion that "social phobics exhibited selective, subtle evidence of autonomic dysregulation" (p. 218).

Levin et al. (1993) compared the responses of 28 generalized, 8 single-situational social phobic individuals, and 14 normal subjects while simulating a speech. During baseline, no differences were found between the groups. "Discrete" social phobic participants had higher heart rates than did the generalized phobic subjects, with normal subjects in-between. When baseline heart rates were taken into account, however, differences vanished (see 1993, Fig. 2, p. 215).

In summary, no overall systematic differences between social phobic and normal participants emerged during experimental tasks. Moreover, these highlighted basically a similar pattern of responding. Some differences were observed on certain tasks, varying with the measures employed. In short, individual differences as well as factors related to particular situations tended to overshadow group differences.

A number of studies concerning primarily panic disorder/agoraphobia, have included social phobic (and normal) subjects as controls. Although not on center-stage, social phobia is still illuminated albeit from perspectives relevant to panic disorder.

In the first of such studies, Holt & Andrews (1989) compared the responses of participants identified as panic disorder (25), panic disorder/agoraphobia (25), social phobia (19), and generalized anxiety disorder (10) to those of 16 normal controls on a variety of respiratory parameters. Every subject was tested while at rest, hyperventilating, breathing normally (a control phase for the next condition), breathing CO_2, and pedaling an exercise bike.

At baseline some differences were found among the groups, depending on the measure used. For example, at rest all panic subjects had a higher respiratory rate than the social phobic and generalized anxiety disorder (GAD) groups. In contrast, some differences were found on the same measure between normal subjects and those with panic. All experimental conditions were amalgamated and compared to the two control conditions. Of all measures used, social phobic/GAD participants exhibited somewhat higher changes in respiratory volume from control to provocation than those of the panic group; otherwise responses were closer to those of normal subjects.

In Gorman, Papp, Martinez, Goetz, Hollander, Liebowitz, & Jordan (1990) 22 social phobic subjects were compared to 25 panic disorder and 14 normal subjects. Participants had to inhale a mixture of 35% CO_2 and 60% oxygen while a variety of measures were being taken. At baseline, panic subjects had higher tidal volume as well as higher pulse rates than social phobic and the control subjects who were both equivalent. During experimentation, no differential responses were observed; all subjects reacted similarly on all measures.

In Stein, Tancer, & Uhde (1992), the responses of 14 social phobic, 14 panic, and 14 normal control subjects to an abrupt change in posture, were compared. Social phobic participants were found to have a significantly higher diastolic heart pressure; no differences were found between panic and normal participants in this respect. Panic subjects had a significantly higher heart rate than the normal controls with social phobic subjects in-between without reaching statistical significance. In terms of cardiovascular reactivity, hyperventilation, and response to the inhalation of CO_2, the social phobic subjects were on the whole alike normal participants.

In Tancer, Stein, & Uhde (1990a) social phobia, panic disorder, and normal subjects (10 of each) were injected with 500mg of thyrotropin-releasing hormone that simulates an incipient episode of panic. At baseline all groups were equivalent on all cardiovascular measures, but one minute after the injection, social phobic subjects were found on average to have higher systolic and mean arterial pressure than subjects of the other two groups. It is rather doubtful that this is indicative of the "autonomic hyperactivity" (Tancer et al., 1990a, p. 782) of social phobia, as overall in similar experimental situations, social phobic participants tended to respond more like normal individuals while both were differentiated from the panic group.

In Asmundson & Stein (1994) 15 social phobic, 15 panic, and 15 normal control participants underwent three breathing tasks: hypoventilation (6 breaths/min), normal ventilation (12 breaths/min) and hyperventilation (20 breaths/min). No differences were observed between groups either during baseline or experimental conditions.

In summary, no consistent differences between social phobia and other anxiety disorders (mostly panic) emerged. Task-related factors and individual variability were more potent determinants of responses than group membership. Overall, none of the physiological functions (mostly respiratory and to some extent cardiovascular) under investigation was found to be a characteristic and distinctive feature of social phobia.

Association with Neurobiological Factors A comprehensive review of this body of research is available in chapter 6. The main conclusion relevant to our concerns is that the literature relative to a putative neurobiological substrate of social phobia is inconclusive at best. With the possible exception of some studies, most reports of significant differences have not withstood replication. By default, I am led to the conclusion that the neurobiological activity detected in social phobic individuals by current methods appears to be very much alike that of normal control subjects.

Predictive Validity

As can be seen in chapter 10, neither psychological nor pharmacological treatments are specific to social phobia. Similar therapies and compounds are applied with comparable effects to other types of problems (e.g. anxiety and depression). Are there nonetheless aspects of social phobia that make for a differential response?

Response to Treatment: Psychological   Clinical features of social phobia as potential predictors for response to therapy have been investigated in several studies; these are summarized in Table 5.4. While social phobic patients generally respond well to behavioral and cognitive-behavioral types of therapies, regardless of severity (see in chapter 10), few predictors, based on either entity notions (subtypes, APD or other personality disorders) or discrete features, have held up consistently. Even when statistically significant, effects were small in size. Promising features (e.g. also meeting criteria for APD) were likely to be no more than gradations of severity of social phobia or artifacts of policies of admission into treatment programs resulting in commensurate outcome.

Response to Treatment: Pharmacological   Similar conclusions apply also to pharmacological treatment (Table 5.4), although response to medication appears almost a mirror image of response to psychological treatments. Moclobemide was at its most potent with the circumscribed type of social phobia and in cases with high levels of anxious and depressed mood. The latter was not true of clonazepam – an anxiolytic.

By contrast, response to psychological treatments was not affected by additional problems and widespread difficulties in social functioning were not an obstacle to improvement (although they predicted the ultimate level of functioning of the patient after treatment). Finally, unlike psychological treatments, improvement with medication was contingent on taking it; improvement was not sustained in the majority of cases after medication was stopped.

Social Phobia in the Family   Studies examining the extent to which social phobia predicts a first-degree relative with a similar problem are summarized in Table 5.5 (a detailed review is found in chapter 6). Prevalence rates in relevant studies are always over the "lifetime" – not concurrent – with all the limitations inherent in such statistics.

All told, although the evidence for moderate family aggregation of social phobia in most studies is statistically significant, its meaningfulness is not evident, especially in light of a wider array of disorders in such families (see next paragraph). Given the wide confidence intervals (95%) and the mostly low RRs (e.g. 2.4), the predictability of "lifetime" social phobia in relatives of social phobic patients was generally modest. If present social phobia were adopted as the standard, it is likely that the significant association would vanish.

Furthermore, when other disorders (e.g. depression, generalized anxiety disorder) were also included in the investigation, their prevalence

Table 5.4. *Predictors of response to treatment*

Study	Participants	Therapy	Predictors	Response to treatment	Comments
Rosser et al. (2004)	133 SP Anxiety disorders clinic Sydney (Australia)	CBT	Taking antidepressants before therapy (continued while being treated)	antidepressant = no antidepressant	Specific medication unknown.
van Ameringen et al. (2004b)	204 SP Anxiety disorders clinic Ontario (Canada)	Sertraline	Age of onset Co-occurrence (other disorders) Sex Duration of social phobia Psychosocial variables (e.g. marital status)	later-onset (19 yrs and older) > earlier-onset	This advantage for later-onset can be accounted for neither by severity nor by duration of social phobia.
Clark et al. (2003)	40 SP Clinical referrals Oxford (England)	Fluoxetine CT	Age Gender Marital status Initial level of difficulties Duration of social phobia Co-occurrence (APD)	could not be predicted	
Stein et al. (2002a)	390 SP Study sites in Europe and South Africa	Moclobemide	Co-occurrence (other ANX)	SP < SP + ANX	All other tested variables (not mentioned) did not discriminate between responders and non-responders.
Stein et al. (2002b)	829 SP Multicenter trials North America, Europe and South Africa	Paroxetine	Age Gender Baseline heart rate/pressure Initial level of difficulties Duration of social phobia Paroxetine dose Treatment duration	overall could not be predicted, except by treatment duration (longer = better response)	

Table 5.4. (cont.)

Study	Participants	Therapy	Predictors	Response to treatment	Comments
Mennin et al. (2000)	75 SP Center for Stress and Anxiety Disorders New York (USA)	CBT	Co-occurrence (GAD)	SP = SP + GAD	Clinician severity rating scores differed significantly between the groups at pretreatment, but converged at post-treatment
Otto et al. (2000)	45 SP Clinical referrals Local advertisement Massachusetts (USA)	Clonazepam BT	Baseline severity Baseline scores on anxiety and avoidance measures	could not be predicted	Improvement in avoidance following clonazepam was not similar across levels of severity as it was following behavioral therapy.
Chambless et al. (1997)	62 SP American University Agoraphobia and Anxiety Program (USA)	CBT	Depressed mood Treatment expectancies PD traits Severity of social impairment Frequency of negative thoughts during social interaction	could not be predicted	Severity of depressed mood and higher tendency to avoid were both related to poorer outcome in certain areas.
Safren et al. (1997)	113 SP Center for Stress and Anxiety Disorders New York (USA)	CBT	Initial expectancies for positive outcome	this variable was a significant but weak predictor (7%) in a statistical regression	Pretreatment scores were used as covariate.

Study	Sample/Setting	Treatment	Variable	Predictor/Relationship	Result
van Velzen et al. (1997)	30 SP Clinical referrals Co-occurrence (other ANX) Local advertisement The Netherlands	BT	Co-occurrence (APD) Co-occurrence (MOOD) Co-occurrence (PD)	could not be predicted	All groups benefited equally from treatment.
Versiani et al. (1997)	93 SP Federal University of Rio de Janeiro (Brazil)	Moclobemide	Subtype of SP (generalized) Co-occurrence (APD) Co-occurrence (other ANX) Co-occurrence (DYS or AA)	all predictors of poor response	
Feske et al. (1996)	48 SP Clinical referrals Pennsylvania (USA)	CBT	Co-occurrence (APD)	SP > SP + APD	27% of the patients (equally distributed) were on psychotropic medication.
Sutherland et al. (1996)	56 SP Duke University Medical Center Durham (USA)	Clonazepam	Anxious mood	inversely related to therapeutic response	
Leung and Heimberg (1996)	91 SP Center for Stress and Anxiety Disorders New York (USA)	CBT	Homework compliance	significant predictor of reduced post-treatment interactional anxiety	Homework compliance accounted for 6.3% of the variance in post-treatment social anxiety.
Turner et al. (1996b)	84 SP Western Psychiatric Institute and Clinic Pittsburg (USA)	Atenolol, BT	Subtype of SP Co-occurrence (other disorders)	could not be predicted	A higher number of specific patients than generalized ones achieved a moderate or high level of improvement.

Table 5.4. (*cont.*)

Study	Participants	Therapy	Predictors	Response to treatment	Comments
Brown et al. (1995)	63 SP Center for Stress and Anxiety Disorders New York (USA)	CBT	Subtype of SP Co-occurrence (APD)	could not be predicted	More severely phobic patients in all groups remained more impaired.
Hofmann et al. (1995b)	16 SP Local advertisement Palo Alto (USA)	BT	Subtype of SP Co-occurrence (APD)	could not be predicted	
Hope et al. (1995b)	23 SP Local advertisement Nebraska (USA)	CBT	Subtype of SP Co-occurrence (APD)	could not be predicted	More severely phobic patients in all groups remained more impaired.
Mersch et al. (1995)	34 SP Local advertisement Limburg (The Netherlands)	BT CBT + SST	Co-occurrence (PD)	SP = SP + PD	SP + PD group reported greater distress and avoid-ance at pretreatment. No effect of treatment condition.
Turner et al. (1992)	20 SP Western Psychiatric Institute and Clinic Pittsburg (USA)	BT	Subtype of SP	could not be predicted	

Note: AA = alcohol abuse; ANX = anxiety disorder; APD = avoidant personality disorder; BT = behavior therapy; CBT = cognitive-behavioral therapy; CT = cognitive therapy; DYS = dysthymia; GAD = generalized anxiety disorder; MOOD = affective disorder; PD = personality disorders; SP = social phobia; SST = social skills training; + = combined with.

Table 5.5. *Social phobia in the family*

Study	Probands	Relatives (proband)	Prevalence of social phobia among relatives	Comments
Bandelow et al. (2004)	50 SP 120 NC Gottingen (Germany)	First-degree relatives ? (SP) ? (NC)	SP (8%) > NC (0%)	Prevalence of other disorders among relatives of social phobic individuals was far greater than that of social phobia, e.g. depression 56%, any anxiety disorder 62%.
Stein et al. (1998a)	23 GSP 24 NC Manitoba (Canada)	Relatives 106 (GSP) 74 (NC)	GSP (26%) > NC (3%) RR = 9.7	Similar results obtained in regards to APD (20% vs 0%), highlight the close kinship of the two constructs. No difference between the groups for the prevalence of discrete and non-generalized SP.
Beidel & Turner (1997)	16 ANX (4 SP) ? DP 14 ANX + DP ? NC Pittsburgh (USA) Charleston (USA)	Children (Age: 7–12) 28 (ANX) 24 (DP) 29 (ANX + DP) 48 (NC)	ANX (0%) DP (13%) ANX + DP (7%) NC (2%)	This study, albeit lacking a group of social phobic parents, questions the notion that children of social phobic parents are at greater risk for social phobia.
Mancini et al. (1996)	26 SP Ontario (Canada)	Children (Age: 12–18) 47 (SP)	SP (23%)	Uncontrolled study. The rate exceeded the prevalence reported in the general population of similar age.
Fyer et al. (1995)	39 SP 15 SiP 49 PAN + AG 77 NC New York (USA)	First-degree relatives 105 (SP) 49 (SiP) 131 (PAN + AG) 231 (NC)	SP (15%) = SiP (10%) = PAN + AG (8%) = NC (6%) SP (15%) > NC (6%) RR = 2.4	

Table 5.5. (cont.)

Study	Probands	Relatives (proband)	Prevalence of social phobia among relatives	Comments
Fyer et al. (1993) Mannuzza et al. (1995a)	30 SP 77 NC New York (USA)	First-degree relatives 83 (SP) 231 (NC)	SP (16%) > NC (5%) RR = 3.1	Greater family aggregation among GSP (16%) than among relatives of the specific (6%) and normal (6%) probands.
Perugi et al. (1990)	25 SP 26 AG/PAN + SP 82 AG/ PAN Pisa (Italy)	First-degree relatives 25 (SP) 26 (AG/PAN + SP) 82 (AG/ PAN)	SP (4%) = AG/PAN + SP (0%) = AG/PAN (2%)	
Reich & Yates (1988)	17 SP 88 PAN 10 NC Boston and Iowa City (USA)	Relatives 76 (SP) 471 (PAN) 46 (NC)	SP (7%) > PAN (0.4%) SP (7%) = NC (2%)	The most prevalent disorder among relatives of SP was MD (13%).

Note: AG = agoraphobia; ANX = anxiety disorder; APD = avoidant personality disorder; DP = depression; GSP = generalized social phobia; MD = major depression; C = normal control; PAN = panic disorder; SiP = specific phobia; SP = social phobia; RR = relative risk; + = combined with.

rates among relatives of social phobic individuals were far greater than that of social phobia.

Social Phobia in Children of Social Phobic Parents   Relevant studies are summarized in Table 5.5. Some evidence suggests that a social phobia agglomerates in some families; this being especially true of the generalized/avoidant personality end of the spectrum (Stein, Chartier, Hazen, Kozak, Tancer, Lander, Furer, Chubaty, & Walker, 1998a). The meaning of this finding, however, is rendered ambiguous by the fact that it is unclear who are the relatives at risk. Most importantly, the greater risk in first-degree relatives obtains only over the "life-span."

Moreover, the finding of a greater risk is contradicted both by studies of first-degree relatives in general (Reich & Yates, 1988; Perugi, Simonini, Savino, Mengali, Cassano, & Akiskal, 1990) and children of parents with anxiety disorders (Beidel & Turner, 1997).

What Predicts Social Phobia: Prospective Studies

Longitudinal studies have a great potential for predicting specific steps in an unfolding process, but these are rare. In view of the importance of a longitudinal perspective on the one hand and the paucity of such studies (only one meets the definition with some strain) I shall include also investigations describing dimensions of behavior closely related to social phobia even if the requisite defining criteria of social phobia are lacking. These will be considered later.

In Hayward, Killen, Kraemer, & Taylor (1998) 2,242 pupils from 4 high schools in California were recruited and interviewed. Diagnostic interviews were administered on a yearly basis at grades 9 to 12; the average age at the onset of the study was 15. Ultimately, 4 experimental groups were created: social phobia (n = 122), major depression (n = 240), social phobia and depression (n = 34), and neither (n = 1,846). Conceptually, the study is framed by the notion of behavioral inhibition – BI – (reviewed extensively in chapter 9). The participants' history of BI was obtained retrospectively by means of a self-report questionnaire (Reznick, Hegeman, Kaufman, Woods, & Jacobs, 1992) and the results were factor-analyzed. Three factors emerged, labeled social avoidance, fearfulness and illness behavior.

Social avoidance reported retrospectively at the beginning of the study (i.e. at adolescence) predicted social phobia but not depression. This obtained equally in girls and in boys. Fearfulness, by contrast, in addition to predicting social phobia also predicted depression, while illness behavior predicted depression in girls only.

When subjects who met criteria for social phobia at the beginning were excluded, results remained almost the same, with the exception that social avoidance no longer predicted social phobia in girls. Combining social avoidance and fearfulness in childhood increased the predictive power for social phobia fivefold for boys and sevenfold for girls. Thus, a female adolescent reporting being socially avoidant and fearful in childhood was 21% likely to fulfill criteria for social phobia (males: 23%). By contrast, female adolescents who were neither fearful nor avoidant in childhood were only 3% likely to meet criteria for social phobia at adolescence (males: 4%).

This study, in addition to following adolescents over 4 years, has also the merit of studying a very large sample. Its main weakness is that the behavioral inhibition was obtained by self-report and retrospectively rather than by observation and prospectively. The test−retest reliability over 3 days (social avoidance −0.59, fearfulness −0.64; illness behavior −0.68) gives pause.

Goodwin, Fergusson, & Horwood (2004) report a longitudinal study of an unselected cohort of 1,265 children born in Christchurch, New Zealand. At the age of 8, an index of "anxious withdrawal" (e.g. fearfulness of new situations and people, shyness with other children, worries about illness and death) was created by means of parent and teacher ratings. A diagnostic interview was carried out between the ages of 18 and 21. Although a statistically significant association was found between severity of anxious withdrawal and social phobia at young adulthood, only 12% of the 146 most anxiously withdrawn children at the age of 8 met criteria for social phobia. Moreover, anxious withdrawal during childhood was associated to a similar degree with other phobias, but with 26% of adult major depression.

In Mason, Kosterman, Hawkings, Herrenkohl, Lengua, & McCauley (2004) 765 fifth-grade pupils (mean age−10) from 18 elementary schools in Seattle were interviewed. Parents, teachers and the participants rated a checklist of child behavior. A diagnostic interview was carried out at the age of 21. Self- and parent-reported "shyness" (undefined) at the age of 10 rather weakly (OR = 1.6) but significantly by statistical standards, predicted social phobia.

An additional longitudinal study focusing on behaviors relevant to social phobia is that of Schwartz, Snidman, & Kagan (1999) carried out in Boston. In it 112 2 year olds were divided into "inhibited" (52) or "uninhibited" (57) based on the observation of the child's reaction to several events in the laboratory (e.g. a stranger entering the room in the presence of his/her mother). Responses indicative of behavioral inhibition were: "apprehensions, withdrawal, long latencies to approach the unfamiliar person or object, clinging to mother, crying . . . and cessation of play" (Schwartz et al., 1999, p. 1010). The children fulfilled no condition for psychiatric disorder.

79 subjects were reassessed at the age of 13 by means of the DISC – a children's version of a structured interview used in epidemiological studies. This instrument identifies among others the following difficulties: generalized social anxiety, performance anxiety, separation anxiety, and specific fears (e.g. of darkness). 61% of the adolescents who had been inhibited as young children reported current social anxiety (compared with 27% of the subjects previously uninhibited). Furthermore, inhibition at a young age predicted neither performance nor separation anxiety nor specific fears.

When the threshold for generalized social anxiety was raised to include in addition to anxious distress also impaired functioning thereby bringing it closer to the definition of social phobia, the rate of the previously inhibited toddlers presenting generalized social anxiety as adolescents fell to 34%. By contrast, only 9% of the uninhibited toddlers were considered as (generalized) socially anxious adolescents.

Furthermore, these results sharply differentiated boys from girls. Whereas, 22% of the previously "inhibited" boys were considered (generalized) socially anxious, 44% of the girls were. Similar (but inverse) proportions obtained with the previously uninhibited: 5% of the girls, compared with 13% of the boys, qualified as (generalized) socially anxious in adolescence.

These results suggest a link between behavioral inhibition at a very young age and "generalized social anxiety" in adolescence. Its predictive strength was greater for girls especially when aspects of functioning are affected. Whether "generalized social anxiety" is equivalent to social phobia remains to be established.

In summary and somewhat trivially, social phobia or its features at the threshold of adolescence predicted social phobia later on. Other constructs (e.g. behavioral inhibition) did not predict social phobia overall more revealingly, for the association held only for a minority of the subjects. Thus, 66% of the "behaviorally inhibited" toddlers were not characterized by "generalized social anxiety" in adolescence.

Retrospective Studies: What Predicts Social Phobia?

Manicavasagar, Silove, & Hadzi-Pavlovic (1998) measured "early separation anxiety" in two samples: (1) 74 patients with an anxiety disorder (none of social phobia), (2) 136 women residents in a public housing estates who were administered the DIS (21 – 15% – met criteria for

social phobia). The authors concluded that high levels of "early separation anxiety" (SA) were predictive (in terms of "odds ratios" of
social phobia in adulthood (see 1998, p. 186, Table 3). This
seems questionable, as the calculation, by comparing only "high SA"
social phobic (n = 11) and normal subjects, ignored fully 48% (n = 10)
of the sample of social phobic individuals reporting a low level of early
separation anxiety and to whom the conclusion would not apply.

What Does Social Phobia Predict?

The hypothesis that social phobia might predict depression was tested
(Regier, Rae, Narrow, Kaelber, & Schatzberg, 1998) by reanalyzing the
results of the ECA (n = 202,911). In 72% of the cases social phobia did
precede depression by at least two years. Only in 5% of the cases the
reverse sequence was found. Social phobia stood out as the anxiety
disorder most likely to be followed by a depressive episode.

A similar test was carried out using a study (Stein, Fuetsch, Müller,
Hoffler, Lieb, & Wittchen, 2001a) of 3,021 subjects from Munich. As in
Regier et al. (1998), the likelihood for a depressive disorder was far
higher among social phobic than normal participants. Social phobia
was not unique in this respect; all other anxiety disorders were likely
to be followed by depressive episodes.

Schatzberg, Samson, Rothschild, Bond, & Regier (1998) reconfirmed
the by now typical sequence in their study of 85 depressed participants;
77% reported the onset of social phobia preceding that of major depression by an average of 2 years.

Two independent studies carried out in Canada and the USA showed
that social phobia also preceded the onset of alcoholism in a great
majority, namely 80%, of cases (Sareen, Chartier, Kjernisted, & Stein,
2001; Schuckit, Tipp, Bucholz, Nurnberger, Hesselbrock, Crowe,
et al., 1997).

Overall, Brown, Campbell, Lehman, Grisham, & Mancill (2001a)
who had studied 1,127 subjects, found that "social phobia was associated with the earliest age of onset (mean = 15.7) and was the disorder
that most often preceded other conditions" (p. 592).

In summary, neither prospective nor retrospective available studies
have highlighted specific predictors of social phobia (the entity); nor
has social phobia been shown to predict distinct outcomes. Results of
studies stretching from childhood to mature adulthood − a formidable
undertaking − are still awaited.

Construct Validity

Internal – Convergent Validity

In the absence of a theory of social phobia to postulate conceptual links with other constructs, most such research has been carried out opportunistically by casting the net wide as it were and observing what comes up. Such prosaic procedures limit considerably the conclusions that can be drawn from any results, since these can neither be in support of nor against theory.

Factor-analytic Studies   Factor-analytic studies shed some light on social phobia by allowing a glimpse into features it might share with other constructs. Stravynski et al. (1995b) factor-analyzed responses of 80 agoraphobic, 25 social phobic, and 35 specific phobic individuals to Wolpe's (1983) Fear Survey Schedule. A factor of social sensitivity (e.g. being criticized, feeling disapproved of) was identified that accounted for 24% out of 50% of the variance (other factors extracted were agoraphobia – 7% and blood/injury – 5%, etc). On social sensitivity, social phobic and agoraphobic participants overlapped, sharing many similar concerns. More social phobic individuals, however, had the highest positive scores.

In summary, social phobia shares a range of social fears especially with agoraphobia.

Association of Social Phobia with Other Disorders   Relevant studies are summarized in Table 5.6. In summary, the most apparent associations with social phobia are those with other anxiety disorders – chiefly agoraphobia, generalized anxiety disorder and specific phobia and the avoidant, obsessive-compulsive, paranoid, and dependent personality disorders. The link between social phobia and depression (the entity – not the mood) is variable and perhaps overstated; in some studies it is not more pronounced than that between panic and alcoholism.

In certain clinical problems such as eating disorders, the co-occurrence of social phobia is very high ranging from 20% to 59%. The most common association however was with obsessive-compulsive disorder.

Internal – Discriminant Validity

An important aspect of the validity of social phobia as a "significant psychological pattern" is how distinguishable it is from comparable

Table 5.6. *Association of social phobia with other disorders*

Study	Site	Sample (N)	Co-occurrence	Comments
Any additional Axis I disorder				
Lampe et al. (2003)	Australian National Survey of Mental Health and Well-Being (Australia)	10,641 (2.3% SP)	78% (current)	
Brown et al. (2001a)	Center for Stress and Anxiety Disorders Boston and New York (USA)	968 (186 SP)	46% (current) 72% (lifetime)	Although high, the co-occurrence of SP with other disorders was among the smallest (e.g. PTSD: 92%; DP: 71%).
Anxiety disorders				
Lampe et al. (2003)	Australian National Survey of Mental Health and Well- Being (Australia)	10,641 (2.3% SP)	Any anxiety disorder 53% (current)	
Brown et al. (2001a)	Center for Stress and Anxiety Disorders Boston and New York (USA)	968 (186 SP)	Any anxiety disorder 28% (current) 37% (lifetime)	SP were the least likely to meet criteria for an additional current anxiety disorder. By contrast, 62% of the individuals with PTSD met criteria for additional anxiety disorders.
Lecrubier & Weiller (1997)	Primary care Paris (France)	405 (38 SP)	AG OR: 10.4 (15%, current) GAD OR: 1.4 (16%, current)	
Goisman et al. (1995)	Harvard Brown Anxiety Disorders Research Program Multicenter Study of Anxiety Disorders New England (USA)	711 (199 SP)	PAN + AG 36%, 42% (current, lifetime) GAD 34% 35% (current, lifetime)	See also Goldenberg et al. (1996)

Study	Setting	Sample (SP)	Findings	Notes
Lépine et al. (1993)	18 clinical settings around the world	543 (112 SP)	Significantly associated with: AG (current, lifetime) SiP (current, lifetime) PAN (current) DP (current)	Representative sample.
Schneier et al. (1992)	Epidemiologic Catchment Area study Baltimore, St Louis, Durham, Los Angeles (USA)	13,537 (361 SP)	OCD OR: 4.4 (11%, lifetime) PAN OR: 3.2 (5%, lifetime) AG OR: 11.8 (45%, lifetime) SiP OR: 9.2 (59%, lifetime)	Probability sample.

Affective disorders

Study	Setting	Sample (SP)	Findings	Notes
Lampe et al. (2003)	Australian National Survey of Mental Health and Well-Being (Australia)	10,641 (2.3% SP)	MD 41% (current)	
Brown et al. (2001a)	Center for Stress and Anxiety Disorders Boston and New York (USA)	968 (186 SP)	Any mood disorder 29% (current) 57% (lifetime)	
Brown et al. (2001a)	Center for Stress and Anxiety Disorders Boston and New York (USA)	968 (186 SP)	MD 14%, 44% (current, lifetime) DYS 13%, 17% (current, lifetime)	
Perugi et al. (2001)	Treatment program for anxiety disorders Pisa (Italy)	153 SP	BP-II 9% (lifetime) MD 46% (lifetime)	In this study, SP was the only disorder with an increased risk of lifetime dysthymia.

Table 5.6. (*cont.*)

Study	Site	Sample (N)	Co-occurrence	Comments
Kessler et al. (1999)	National Comorbidity Survey 48 states (USA)	8,098 (1,077 SP)	MD OR: 2.9 (34%, lifetime) DYS OR 2.7 BP OR: 5.9	68.5% reported occurrence of social phobia before the mood disorder.
Schatzberg et al. (1998)	Hospital Depression Research Facility Standford (USA)	85 (DP as main problem)	SP 13% (current)	
Lecrubier & Weiller (1997)	Primary care Paris (France)	405 (38 SP)	DP OR: 7.0 (49%, current)	
Alpert et al. (1997)	Depression research program Boston (USA)	87 typical DP 87 atypical DP	SP 8% (current) 13% (current) SP + APD 10% (current) 26% (current)	The co-occurrence of SP with APD among depressed patients was associated with an earlier age of onset of DP, a greater number of additional disorders, and greater impairment of social adjustment and assertiveness.
Pini et al. (1997)	Community mental health center University Hospital Pisa (Italy)	24 BP 38 DP (unipolar) 25 DYS	SP 0% (current) 11% (current) 4% (current)	The bipolar group was studied in the depressed phase.
Dilsaver et al. (1992)	Clinical Research Unit Houston (USA)	42 (DP as main problem) 35 seasonal depression	SP 45% (current) 46% (current)	This lends some support to the association between atypical depression and SP noted by Alpert et al. (1997).

Study	Setting	Sample	Prevalence	Comorbidity/OR	Comments
Schneier et al. (1992)	Epidemiologic Catchment Area study Baltimore, St Louis, Durham, Los Angeles (USA)	13,537 (361 SP)		MD OR: 4.4 (17%, lifetime) BP OR: 4.1 (5%, lifetime) DYS OR: 4.3 (13%, lifetime)	Probability sample.
Eating disorders					
Kaye et al. (2004)	Price Foundation Collaborative Genetics Study. Academic sites in North America and Europe	97 AN 282 BU 293 AN + BU	SP 20% (lifetime)		The most common ANX was OCD (40%) followed by SP.
Godart et al. (2000)	Clinical centers Paris (France)	29 AN 24 BU 59% (lifetime)	SP 55% (lifetime)		As a control, fears of eating in public were discounted as inclusion criteria for SP. 90% of bulimic and 65% of AN subjects reported that SP preceded at least by a year the onset of eating disorders.
Schwalberg et al. (1992)	Eating Disorder Clinics Center for Stress and Anxiety Disorder New York (USA)	20 BU 22 OBE	SP 45% (lifetime) 36% (lifetime)		The onset of SP in the great majority of cases preceded that of the eating problems.
Body dysmorphic disorder					
Wilhelm et al. (1997)	Outpatients seeking treatment Massachusetts (USA)	25 SP 80 PAN 40 OCD 20 GAD	BDD 12% (current) 4% (current) 8% (current) 10% (current)		SP preceded the onset of BDD. It is not clear whether there is a special connection between the two.

Table 5.6. (cont.)

Study	Site	Sample (N)	Co-occurrence	Comments
Sexual dysfunction				
Figueira et al. (2001)	Anxiety and Depression Program Rio de Janeiro (Brazil)	58 ANX (30 SP)	Premature ejaculation 47% (lifetime) Male orgasmic disorder 5% (lifetime) Other sexual dysfunction (male) 0% (lifetime) Female orgasmic disorder 18% (lifetime)	These rates are higher than those obtained in community studies (e.g. 21% premature ejaculation).
Alcoholism				
Thomas et al. (1999)	Treatment-seeking alcoholics Participants in Project MATCH Multi-site (USA)	1,726 AA	SP 23% (lifetime)	
Lecrubier & Weiller (1997)	Primary care Paris (France)	405 (38 SP)	AA or dependence 25% (current)	
Schuckit et al. (1997)	Six rehabilitation centers St Louis, New York, Farmington, Indianapolis, Iowa City, San Diego (USA)	954 AA 919 NC	SP 4.3% (lifetime) 1.4% (lifetime)	The results may have been influenced by considerable emphasis on dependence on alcohol rather than on its use as an anxiolytic agent.
Schneier et al. (1992)	Epidemiologic Catchment Area study Baltimore, St Louis, Durham, Los Angeles (USA)	13,537 (361 SP)	AA OR: 2.9 (13%, lifetime)	Probability sample.

Personality disorders

Grant et al. (2005)	National Epidemiologic Survey on Alcohol and Related Conditions USA (including Alaska and Hawaii)	43,093 (1207 SP)	One or more PD 61% (current) Most prevalent: 33% OCPD (current) 30% APD (current) 29% PAR (current) 21% SCZ (current)	
Dyck et al. (2001)	Hospital patients Harvard Brown Anxiety Disorders Research Program	622 (103 SP)	One or more PD 39% (current) Most prevalent: 11 sites (USA) 8% OCD (current) 7% PAG (current) 6% DPD (current)	SP was the only ANX predicting APD. 28% APD (current)
Sanderson et al. (1994)	Treatment-seeking outpatients Center for Cognitive Therapy Pennsylvania (USA)	347 ANX (51 SP)	One PD 61% (current) Two PD16% (current) Most prevalent: 37% APD (current) 18% DPD (current)	

Note: AA = alcohol abuse; AG = agoraphobia; AN = anorexic; ANX = anxiety disorder; APD = avoidant personality disorder; BDD = body dysmorphic disorder; BP = bipolar mood disorder; BU = bulimic; DP = depression; DPD = dependent personality disorder; DYS = dysthymia; GAD = generalized anxiety disorder; MD = major depression; NC = normal control; OBE = obese binge-eater; OCD = obsessive-compulsive disorder; OCPD = obsessive-compulsive personality disorder; OR = odd-ratio; PAN = panic disorder; PAG = passive-agressive personality disorder; PAR = paranoid personality disorder; PD = personality disorder; PTSD = post-traumatic stress disorder; SCZ = schizoid personality disorder; SiP = specific phobia; SP = social phobia; + = combined with.

normal patterns (e.g. shyness) on the one hand, and related putative clinical entities (e.g. other phobias) on the other hand.

Few studies have attempted such contrasts. The most frequently performed comparisons were of certain shared features, typically anxiety. These are less satisfactory for if differences are found, it remains uncertain whether they are of degree or of kind.

Social Phobia as Distinct from Normality   The distinctiveness of social phobia from normality is one of the most important questions for discriminant validity. This aspect may be found in many studies as most include normal control subjects. The following studies have been selected to illustrate the general trend; chapter 3 provides a comprehensive review.

Davidson et al. (1993a) have reanalyzed epidemiological data obtained from the Duke site of the ECA to create three groups: social phobia (DSM-III) (n = 123), those who met anxiety-related but not impairment criteria ("subthreshold"; n = 248) and normal controls (n = 1,117). Social phobia was undistinguishable from its so-called "subthreshold" counterpart on any clinical features. Unfortunately, no clinically relevant features (e.g. anxiety) of the normal subjects were measured, precluding any comparison.

Hofmann & Roth (1996) recruited 24 social phobic participants (DSM-III-R; public speaking) and 22 normal controls each identified as specific or generalized (discomfort in more than 4 social situations) through a newspaper ad. On most measures of social anxiety generalized social phobic participants rated significantly higher than the other groups who ranked in diminishing intensity of anxiety: specific social phobia, generalized controls and specific controls. Although their anxious discomfort is less than that reported by patients seeking treatment, it seems nevertheless part of the normal make-up.

All the above studies (as well as those in chapter 3) demonstrate the fact that normal subjects subjectively report a certain degree of social anxiety.

Another way of testing the difference between social phobic and normal individuals would be to study social behavior. In Baker & Edelmann (2002) 18 social phobic and 18 control participants were asked to simulate a social encounter with a confederate. Untrained undergraduate observers did not find differences in specific features (e.g. time spent talking, being silent, smiling, eye contact while listening). However, the overall social phobic social behavior (e.g. fluency and clarity of speech) was considered significantly less adequate, perhaps because it involved more "manipulating gestures" (e.g. self-touching).

In summary, although social phobia is usually distinguishable from normality in terms of intensity of subjective reports of anxiety experienced in a variety of social situations, it is not clear whether and how these differences in degree become differences in kind. As many fears reported by social phobic individuals are also observed in normal persons (e.g. public speaking) more studies contrasting the two groups on a variety of responses to multiple situations are needed. How some make the necessary adjustments to life-demands despite apprehensions, whereas others become gradually crippled by self-protective withdrawal from them, is likely to be more than a matter of degree of anxiety.

Life-Consequences of Social Phobia

Its Chronic Nature

In a study (Pine, Cohen, Gurley, Brook, & Ma, 1998) carried out in the state of New York, a representative sample of 776 children (age 9–18) were interviewed by means of the DIS (administered by trained lay-interviewers) in 1983, 1985 and 1992. In terms of age, the average at each point was 14, 16 and 22 respectively. Social phobia was identified only when the parents corroborated the interview with the subjects.

There was a greater propensity among girls to remaining socially phobic; boys tended to grow out of it. 10% (n = 39) of the girls fulfilled criteria at first assessment, 13% at the second, and 10% at the third. By contrast, 7% (n = 26) of the boys did at first and second assessment, but only 2% met defining criteria at third assessment. Overall, however, and if sex differences were ignored, social phobia at initial assessment predicted social phobia at final assessment. Relatively few subjects were socially phobic at the final assessment in the absence of previous social phobia. By contrast with social phobia in adolescence that precisely predicted social phobia in adulthood, other related patterns such as overanxious disorder of childhood had little specificity. It was found to be a predictor of major depression, generalized anxiety disorder, and social phobia, among others. The results ought to be read with caution however, as the test–retest reliability between the first and second assessment was poor (k = 0.26).

Yonkers, Dyck, & Keller (2001) assessed all patients treated at 12 sites (involved in the Harvard-Brown project) in Massachusetts; 163 met criteria for social phobia and were followed up for 8 years. Remission rates after 1year were 13% and 14% for women and men respectively. After 8 years these were 38 and 32% for women and men.

On average 64% of the social phobic sample were still socially phobic after 8 years.

The chronic nature of social phobia is put in sharp relief by comparing it with the duration of other disorders (Keller, 2003). Patients meeting criteria for panic disorder, for example, had a 26% probability of recovery within 6 months while rising to 72% after 8 years (2003 p. 87). For major depression, the recovery rate after 8 years was approximately 90% (2003 p. 89, Fig. 3).

A facet of the chronic nature of social phobia is that relatively few sufferers seek help. Zimmerman & Mattia (2000) found that only 54% of a sample of 114 patients meeting criteria for social phobia sought treatment; this compared to 99% among the depressed and 89% among patients complaining of panic. The relatively low rate of consultation is probably partly motivated by the fact that many social phobic individuals perceive their problems as a character trait; a destiny no more treatable than sex.

Furthermore, social phobic complaints tend to remain undetected at the level of the general practitioner – the person most likely to be consulted first – especially if accompanied by low mood as is often the case (Weiller, Bisserbe, Boyer, Lépine, & Lecrubier, 1996).

Economic, Educational and Social Consequences

In a study from New York, social phobic as compared to normal individuals (Schneier, Heckelman, Garfinkel, Campeas, Fallon, Gitow, Street, Del Bene, & Liebowitz, 1994) reported at least a moderate impairment in education, employment, family relationships, friendships, and romantic relationships at some times in their lives. A similar study from Munich (Wittchen, Fuetsch, Sonntag, Müller, & Liebowitz, 1999a), compared 116 social phobic participants to 65 control subjects with a herpes infection in terms of their subjective estimation of disability. Social phobic participants rated their disability as higher than did the controls in almost all areas of functioning (work, studies, romantic and family relations).

Patel, Knapp, Henderson, & Baldwin (2002) compared 63 social phobic subjects drawn from the community with 8,501 normal controls from London. Social phobic subjects did not differ in terms of qualification attainment. But, significantly more social phobic subjects (19% vs. 8%) were unemployed and significantly more social phobic individuals were inactive economically (40% vs. 22%). Furthermore, fewer were working full-time (30% vs. 54%). Significantly more social phobic individuals left their job in the last year than did controls (24% vs. 5%) on account of "mental health problems." Altogether, a greater proportion of social phobic subjects had a low income. Conversely, there were fewer social phobic individuals practicing in the professions than the controls (1.6% vs. 7.1%). There were no differences in all other categories of employment.

A countrywide (n = 10,641) study from Australia (Lampe, Slade, Issakidis, & Andrews, 2003) corroborated the above findings that social phobic individuals tend to be unemployed or not in the labor force. Furthermore, they were more likely to be separated, divorced or never have married. According to Hart, Turk, Heimberg, & Liebowitz (1999) single social phobic individuals were more severely social phobic as well as tended to meet criteria for mood disorders.

Stein & Kean (2000) analyzed relevant data from the Ontario Mental Health Survey (n = 9,953) and found that social phobic individuals reported a higher degree of dysfunction in daily activities compared to non-social phobic controls. Surprisingly in light of these difficulties and the results of Patel et al. (2002), no differences in personal income were found.

Stein, Torgrud, & Walker (2000) compared 138 social phobic individuals identified in a community survey in Winnipeg and various cities and settlements in rural Alberta to subjects reporting normal social fears (n = 281). The social phobic group had a higher proportion of subjects reporting a "lot" of interference with their education (22% vs. 9%), dropping classes (49% vs. 25%), being hindered a lot in getting a job (20% vs. 6%), being turned down for a job or a promotion (17% vs. 10%), and an interference with personal life (21% vs. 3%).

In a study from Zurich (Merikangas, Avenevoli, Acharyya, Zhang, & Angst, 2002), of 62 social phobic participants drawn from a cohort of 4,547, 57% reported "impairment" at work, but astonishingly only 44% of social phobic individuals reported impairment in social life. Furthermore, 29% of the social phobic group reported no impairment of any kind. The last two findings seriously question the validity of the social phobic group in that study.

In Bruch, Fallon, & Heimberg (2003), 113 social phobic patients from two centers in the USA were found to be overeducated for their work in contrast to the 53 normal individuals whose qualifications matched their position.

In summary, social phobia is distinguished by its chronicity and lower economic attainments. Social and personal life are considerably perturbed.

Table 5.7. *Social phobia as distinct from other disorders*

Study	Participants	Features	Results	Comments
Anxiety disorders				
Bienvenu et al. (2001)	42 SP 25 AG Community sample Baltimore (USA)	Five-factor model of personality (e.g. neuroticism, extraversion)	SP = AG	Epidemiologic Catchment Area program (ECA) follow-up study.
Hoyer et al. (2001)	22 SP 36 GAD Veterans Administration Hospital	Duration of daily worrying Number of worrying topics Category of worrying	SP < GAD SP < GAD SP (people/relationship), GAD (work/school, health, daily hassles)	
	Palo Alto (USA)	Experiencing worry as unwanted Experiencing worry as excessive Bodily sensations accompanying worrying	SP < GAD SP < GAD SP < GAD	
Figueira et al. (2001)	30 SP 28 PAN Anxiety and Depression Program Rio de Janeiro (Brazil)	Age of first sexual intercourse (male) Lack a current sexual partner (male) Use a prostitute as a first sexual partner (male) Masturbation (male) Masturbation (female)	SP > PAN SP > PAN SP > PAN SP > PAN SP > PAN	
Nardi et al. (2001)	22 SP 26 PAN Laboratory of panic 25 NC Volunteers Rio de Janeiro (Brazil)	Reported panic subsequently to a task of hyperventilation	SP: 23% PAN: 62% NC: 4%	

Study	Sample	Variable	Result
Tükel et al. (2000)	51 SP 32 PAN University of Istanbul, oupatient clinic Istanbul (Turkey)	SR fear SR avoidance Work disability Social life and leisure disability	SP > PAN SP > PAN SP > PAN SP > PAN
Perugi et al. (1999)	71 SP 119 PAN Treatment Program Institute of Psychiatry Pisa (Italy)	Co-occurrence of APD	SP > PAN
Antony et al. (1998b)	49 SP 35 PAN 51 OCD Anxiety disorders clinic Hamilton (Canada)	Interference with life Interference in social relations Ability of self-expression	SP = PAN, OCD SP > PAN, OCD SP > PAN, OCD
Antony et al. (1998a)	70 SP 15 SiP 44 OCD 44 PAN 49 NC Anxiety disorders clinic Local advertising Hamilton (Canada)	Dimensions of perfectionism: Concerns about making mistakes Doubts about performance Parental criticism Standards for self-evaluation Emphasis on order and organization	 SP > SiP, PAN, OCD, NC SP > SiP, PAN, NC; SP< OCD SP > OCD, NC SP = OCD, PAN, NC SP = OCD, PAN, NC
Noyes et al. (1995)	46 SP 72 PAN (some with AG) Local advertising (USA)	Duration Age of onset Avoidant personality traits Schizotypal personality traits	SP > PAN SP < PAN SP > PAN SP > PAN

Saboonchi, Lundh & Ost (1999) comparing SP, AG and PAN in Sweden reported similar results.

Table 5.7. (*cont.*)

Study	Participants	Features	Results	Comments
Stravynski et al. (1995a)	25 SP 80 AG 35 SiP Referred hospital outpatients London (England)	SR measures of common fears (socially relevant or not)	Two discriminant function analyses allowed a reclassification fully 97% accurate on average.	
Jansen et al. (1994)	32 SP 85 PAN Regional Institute Mental Health Services The Netherlands	Co-occurrence of personality disorders or their features	Strongest discriminator. "schizo-typal feature" score. Avoidant feature score did not enhance the discriminative power of the function analysis. Fear of embarrassment (criterion of APD) discriminated the most between the two disorders.	It is odd that only a few schizo-typal patients were included in the study and that avoidant features (but not APD) were found significantly more often among SP than PAN patients.
Page (1994)	69 SP 69 PAN Clinical referrals Sydney (Australia)	Reported being troubled by being anxious and felt upset	SP = PAN	A discriminant function analysis allowed the correct classification of 87% of the cases.
Gelernter et al. (1992)	66 SP 60 PAN Anxiety clinic Pennsylvania (USA)	SR social anxiety and avoidance SR agoraphobic fear and avoidance SR depressive mood SR avoidance of many common situations	SP > PAN SP < PAN SP < PAN SP = PAN	A discriminant function distin-guished significantly the two groups and reclassified correctly 91% cases of social phobia.

Study	Sample / Setting	Measure	Results	Findings
Lelliott et al. (1991)	118 SP 260 AG 52 SiP Hospital referrals (data gathered from medical charts of patients) London (England)	SR anxiety of: being criticized speaking or acting to an audience all other social situations examined	SP = AG SP = SiP SP > AG, SiP	A discriminant function analysis allowed the correct reclassification of 88% of the social and agoraphobic patients.
Rapee et al. (1988)	35 SP 35 AG 35 PAN 36 GAD 19 SiP Clinical referrals and community New York (USA)	SR fears of being observed SR preoccupation with embarrassment SR avoidance in such situations	SP = AG, PAN, GAD, SiP SP > AG, PAN, GAD, SiP SP > AG, PAN, GAD, SiP	A considerable rate (21–42%) of subjects in the non-social phobic groups also met criteria for SP.
Amies et al. (1983)	87 SP 57 AG Clinical referrals Oxford (England)	Most severe SR fears on a measure of common fears	SP = being introduced, meeting people in authority AG = being alone, unfamiliar places	
Amies et al. (1983)	87 SP 57 AG Clinical referrals Oxford (England)	Number of participants reporting: blushing weakness in limbs difficulty breathing faintness ringing in ears other somatic complaints	SP > AG SP < AG SP < AG SP < AG SP < AG SP = AG	

Table 5.7. (*cont.*)

Study	Participants	Features	Results	Comments
Affective disorders				
Ham et al. (2002)	54 SP 23 DYS 27 NC Advertising Nebraska (USA)	Alcohol consumption expectancies: greater assertiveness tension reduction global positive change Number of drinks per month	SP > DYS, NC SP = DYS > NC SP = DYS > NC SP = DYS = NC	
Cox et al. (2000)	26 DP 32 SP Clinical referrals Toronto (Canada)	SR self-criticism	SP < DP	Self-criticism scores failed to predict group membership; the differentiation between social phobia and depression in that regard is rather tenuous.
Nelson et al. (2000)	$N = 1,344$ (219 life time SP) Missouri Adolescent Female Twin Study Missouri (USA)	Prevalence of DP Tendency to suicidal ideation	SP: 30% Other disorders: 12% SP: slight (statistically significant) SP + DP: dramatic increase	When DP is combined with SP, preparations of suicide plans, attempted suicide and admissions to a hospital following an attempt increase.
Alpert et al. (1997)	23 MD + SP 27 MD + APD 42 MD + SP + APD Depression Research Program Boston (USA)	Impairment in social functioning	MD = MD + SP MD < MD + APD MD < MD + SP + APD	

	Sample	Measure	Results	Comments
Eating disorders				
Bulik et al. (1991)	23 AN inpatients 54 BU inpatients 43 SP Western Psychiatric Institute and Clinic 50 ST Pennsylvania (USA)	SR fear of negative evaluation of their weight and appearance	AN = BU = SP > NC	A discriminant function analysis allowed the correct classification of 83% of SP.
Schwalberg et al. (1992)	20 BU 22 OBE Eating disorder clinics 20 SP 20 PAN Center for Stress and Anxiety Disorders New York (USA)	Co-occurrence (other ANX) Co-occurrence (MOOD)	BU > PAN > OBE > SP BU > OBE > PAN = SP	GAD and SP were the most common anxiety disorders among both eating disorders.
Alcoholism				
Thomas et al. (1999)	1,726 AL (397 SP; 397 no SP) Treatment seeking individuals Project MATCH Multi-sites (USA)	Alcohol consumption expectancies: improve sociability improve general functioning pattern of drinking (e.g. solitary)	SP + AL > AL without SP SP + AL > AL without SP SP + AL = AL without SP	
Avoidant personality disorder				
van Velzen et al. (2000)	28 GSP 24 GSP + APD Clinical referrals Local advertising The Netherlands	SR social anxious thoughts Co-occurrence (other disorder) SR depressed mood General psychopathology Neuroticism and introversion Impairment in social and occupational functioning	GSP < GSP + APD GSP = GSP + APD GSP < GSP + APD GSP = GSP + APD GSP < GSP + APD GSP < GSP + APD	

Table 5.7. (cont.)

Study	Participants	Features	Results	Comments
Brown et al. (1995)	38 NGSP 36 GSP 28 GSP + APD Center for Stress and Anxiety Disorders New York (USA)	SR social anxiety SR depressed mood Social phobia scales Co-occurrence (MOOD) Co-occurrence (other ANX)	NGSP < GSP = GSP + APD NGSP < GSP = GSP + APD NGSP < GSP = GSP + APD NGSP = GSP < GSP + ADP NGSP, GSP + APD < GSP	There was little evidence that the generalized type of SP is distinguishable from APD.
Hofmann et al. (1995a)	8 SP 34 APD Local advertisements California (USA)	All measures of anxiety	SP = SP + APD	
Tran & Chambless (1995)	16 NGSP 13 GSP 16 GSP + APD Agoraphobia and Anxiety Program Washington DC (USA)	SR social anxiety SR depressed mood SR & observer ratings of social skills	NGSP < GSP = GSP + APD NGSP = GSP < GSP + APD (NGSP > GSP + APD) = GSP	As use of medication was not controlled, these results must be viewed with caution.
Herbert et al. (1992)	9 GSP 14 GSP + APD Advertising Pennsylvania (USA) 27 NGSP	SR measures (including social anxiety) Impairment in functioning Co-occurrence (other disorder) Observer ratings of social skills SR anxiety (during performance) SR social anxiety and general distress	GSP < GSP + APD GSP < GSP + APD GSP < GSP + APD GSP = GSP + APD GSP < GSP + APD NGSP < GSP, GSP + APD	

Study	Sample / Location	Measures	Results	Comments
Turner et al. (1992)	61 GSP (some with APD) Anxiety Disorders Clinic Pittsburg (USA)	Impairment in social functioning SR distress during a speech Speech length Heart rate during a speech	NGSP < GSP, GSP + APD NGSP = GSP = GSP + APD NGSP = GSP = GSP + APD NGSP = GSP = GSP + APD	The difference between subgroups is one of degree not one of kind.
Holt et al. (1992)	10 NGSP 10 GSP 10 GSP + APD Center for Stress and Anxiety Disorders New York (USA)	Age at onset Clinician's severity rating SR social anxiety and avoidance SR depressed mood	NGSP > GSP = GSP + APD NGSP < GSP < GSP + APD NGSP < GSP = GSP + APD NGSP < GSP = GSP + APD	
Stravynski et al. (1986)	8 SP 34 APD Alcoholism rehabilitation center Montreal (Canada)	Measures of phobic anxiety Measures of alcoholism Measures of depression	SP = APD SP = APD SP = APD	APD patients were less likely than those with SP to identify "being observed in groups" as the most anxiety-evoking difficulty (36% vs. 80%).

Note: AG = agoraphobia; AL = alcoholic; AN = anorexic; ANX = anxiety disorder; APD = avoidant personality disorder; BU = bulimic; DP = depression; DYS = dysthymia; GAD = generalized anxiety disorder; GSP = generalized social phobia; MD = major depression; MOOD = affective disorder; NC = normal control; NGSP = non-generalized social phobia; OBE = obese binge-eater; OCD = obsessive-compulsive disorder; PAN = panic disorder; SiP = specific phobia; SP = social phobia; SR = self-reported; ST = undergraduate psychology students; + = combined with.

Social Phobia as Distinct from Other Disorders

Social phobia has been compared in various ways with other disorders. These studies are summarized in Table 5.7.

Anxiety Disorders

Social phobia is well distinguishable from other anxiety disorders on a host of features including personality traits, social and sexual functioning. Additionally, some demographic and clinical features distinguish social phobia in comparisons with other anxiety disorders. Social phobic patients tended to be male (Perugi, Nassini, Socci, Lenzi, Toni, Simonini, & Akistal, 1999) and single (Noyes, Woodman, Holt, Reich, & Zimmerman, 1995; Perugi et al., 1999; Tükel, Kiziltan, Demir, & Demir, 2000) in some studies. Social phobia had an earlier age of onset (Tükel et al., 2000) and tended to be of much longer duration (Noyes et al., 1995).

Affective Disorders

Although not many studies were carried out, nevertheless social phobia is distinguished from depression by a lesser degree of self-criticism and expectancy toward greater assertiveness when consuming alcohol.

Eating Disorders

It is a commonplace of clinical lore that bulimic or anorexic individuals fear negative evaluation about their weight and appearance. Eating disorders, however, are not a peculiar version of social phobia (Bulik, Beidel, Duchmann, Weltzin, & Kaye, 1991).

Personality Disorders

Most available comparisons concerned avoidant personality disorder (APD). The main conclusion to be drawn is that, there is little evidence that generalized social phobia can be distinguished from APD; moreover, APD alone is scarcely imaginable. All evidence points to there being one social phobic pattern of differing degrees of severity, revealed, among others, by higher ratings of subjective anxiety and depression and poorer social functioning. Comparisons with other personality disorders than APD are yet to be performed.

Conclusion

The social phobic pattern is well distinguished from normal reactions to a range of social situations. Most importantly, it also separates well from other phobic disorders, this despite having much in common with them. This finding has the most weight as far as discriminant validity is concerned.

The separateness of social phobia from avoidant personality disorder is tenuous; it is likely that these represent the same pattern but at different degrees of severity.

Overall though, social phobia is well distinguished from other phobic disorders on various clinical parameters, despite sharing much in common with them. This aspect of validity strongly supports the social phobic pattern.

Other features such as age of onset (lower), sex distribution (equal) and chronicity distinguish social phobia mainly from agoraphobia/panic. Comparisons with other anxiety disorders (e.g. generalized anxiety) are to be performed.

Construct Validity

External – Generalizability

External validity denotes the extent to which the construct may be said to apply generally (i.e. over and above the original circumstances) to either the subjects or the social environment in which it is embedded. Specifically it attempts to answer the questions of who are the individuals and groups to whom the construct might be said to apply generally (as opposed to those who were studied) and, most importantly, is the construct of wide (universal?) application or true only in the original circumstances in which it was developed (e.g. the rich industrialized countries of the late twentieth century)?

Epidemiological studies, although not carried out for that purpose, lend themselves well to a reading concerning generalizability. First, they study whole populations; this allows the drawing of general conclusions. Second, by varying grossly or subtly either the samples under inquiry, the definitions of social phobia or the instruments measuring it, the studies may be construed as replications of the same basic experiment and, as such, shed a valuable light on the generalizability of the construct.

Most studies under review concern representative samples of whole regions (e.g. Porto Rico) or cities (e.g. Paris, Florence, Pittsburgh).

Table 5.8. *Prevalence of social phobia among adults (community)*

Study	Location	Sample (N)	Instrument (criteria)	Prevalence period and rate (%)	Comments
North and Central America					
Canada					
Stein et al. (2000)	Winnipeg and Alberta	1,956	CIDI (DSM-IV)	1 year: 7.2	Six social situations were added to the original CIDI version.
Stein et al. (1996)	Winnipeg	499	Telephone survey (DSM-IV)	Point: 9.8	
Offord et al. (1996)	Ontario	9,953	CIDI (DSM-III-R)	1 year: 6.7	
Stein et al. (1994)	Winnipeg	526	Telephone survey (DSM-III-R)	Point: 7.1	
Dick et al. (1994)	Edmonton	3,258	DIS (DSM-III)	6 months: 1.2 Lifetime: 1.7	
Bland et al. (1988)					
Costello (1982)	Calgary	449	Structured interview (DSM-III)	Point: 2.9	Only women in the sample.
United States					
Grant et al. (2005)	Continental USA District of Columbia Alaska Hawaii	43,093	Structured interview similar to CIDI (DSM-IV)	12 month: 2.8	Face to face interviews with a representative sample (National Epidemiologic Survey on Alcohol and Related Conditions).
Vega et al. (1998)	Fresno county	3,012	CIDI (DSM-III-R)	Lifetime: 7.8 (urban) Lifetime: 6.6 (small town) Lifetime: 6.8 (rural)	Mexican Americans in California.

Study	Location	N	Instrument (criteria)	Prevalence	Notes
Magee et al. (1996)	48 states	8,098	CIDI (DSM-III-R)	1 month: 4.5 Lifetime: 13.3	National Comorbidity Survey (NCS).
Kessler et al. (1994)	48 states	8,098	CIDI (DSM-III-R)	1 year: 7.9	National Comorbidity Survey (NCS).
Davidson et al. (1993a)	North Carolina	3,801	DIS (DSM-III)	6 months: 2.7 Lifetime: 3.8	Epidemiologic Catchment Area program (ECA).
Schneier et al. (1992)	Baltimore Durham Los Angeles St Louis	13,537	DIS (DSM-III)	Lifetime: 2.4	Epidemiologic Catchment Area program (ECA).
Puerto Rico Canino et al. (1987)	Nationwide	1,513	DIS (DSM-III)	6 months: 1.1 Lifetime: 1.6	Slightly higher prevalence for urban area.
Mexico Caraveo-Anduaga & Colmenares (2000)	Mexico City	1,932	CIDI (ICD-10)	1 year: 0.1 Lifetime: 2.6	
South America *Brazil* Vorcaro et al. (2004)	Bambui	1,037	CIDI (DSM-III-R)	1 month: 7.9 1 year: 9.1 Lifetime: 11.8	Probability sample in a poor community of 15,000 inhabitants.
Europe *Iceland* Arnarson et al. (1998)		775	Postal survey (DSM-IV)	6 months: 4.0	Random sample from the census registry.
Lindal & Stefanson (1993)		862	DIS (DSM-III)	Lifetime: 3.5	50% of the people born in 1931.

Table 5.8. (*cont.*)

Study	Location	Sample (*N*)	Instrument (criteria)	Prevalence period and rate (%)	Comments
Norway					
Kringlen et al. (2001)	Oslo	2,066	CIDI (DSM-III-R)	1 year: 7.9 Lifetime: 13.7	
Sweden					
Furmark et al. (1999)	Stockholm Gotland	1,202	Postal survey (DSM-IV)	Point: 15.6	Significant regional differences in prevalence were not observed.
Russia					
Pakriev et al. (2000)	Udmurtia	855	CIDI (ICD-10)	1 month: 44.2 1 year: 44.2 Lifetime: 45.6	The prevalence rates were even higher when using DSM-III-R criteria (49% 1 year; 53% lifetime).
The Netherlands					
Bijl et al. (1998)		7,076	CIDI (DSM-III-R)	1 month: 3.7 1 year: 4.8 Lifetime: 7.8	
Germany					
Wittchen et al. (1992)	Munich	483	DIS (DSM-III)	6 months: 4.1 Lifetime: 8.0	Specific and social phobia.
France					
Pélissolo et al. (2000)	France	12,873	Postal survey (DSM-IV)	1 month: 2.3 Lifetime: 7.3	Using a more narrow definition, the 1 month and lifetime prevalence decreased to 0.9% and 1.9% respectively.

Study	Location	N	Instrument	Prevalence (%)
Lépine & Lellouch (1995)	Paris	1,787	Modified version of DIS/CIDI (DSM-III-R)	1 year: 1.2 (male), 2.9 (female) Lifetime: 4.1
Switzerland				
Degonda & Angst (1993)	Zurich	591	Structured interview (DSM-III)	1979–1988: 3.8
Wacker et al. (1992)	Basel	470	CIDI (DSM-III-R, ICD-10)	Lifetime: 16.0, 9.6
Italy				
Faravelli et al. (2000)	Florence	2,355	Structured interview (DSM-III-R)	Lifetime: 4.0
Faravelli et al. (1989)	Florence	1,110	Structured interview (DSM-III)	Point: 0.5 Lifetime: 1.0
Spain				
Roca et al. (1999)	Formentera island	242	Structured interview (ICD-10)	Point: 0.9
Asia				
United Arab Emirates				
Abou-Saleh et al. (2001)	Al-Ain	1,394	CIDI (ICD-10)	Lifetime: 0.4
Korea				
Lee et al. (1990a)	Seoul	5,100	DIS (DSM-III)	Lifetime: 0.5 (urban)
Lee et al. (1990b)			DIS (DSM-III)	Lifetime: 0.7 (rural)
Hwu et al. (1989)	Taiwan	11,004	DIS (DSM-III)	Lifetime: 0.6 (urban) Lifetime: 0.5 (small town) Lifetime: 0.4 (rural)

Table 5.8. (cont.)

Study	Location	Sample (N)	Instrument (criteria)	Prevalence period and rate (%)	Comments
Oceania					
Australia					
Lampe et al. (2003)		10,641	Modified version of the CIDI (DSM-IV)	1 month: 1.4 1 year: 2.3	Australian National Survey of Mental Health and Well-Being.
New Zealand					
Feehan et al. (1994)	Dunedin	930	DIS (DSM-III-R)	1 year: 11.1	18 year olds only.
Wells et al. (1989)	Christchurch	1,498	DIS (DSM-III)	Lifetime: 3.9	

Note: CIDI = Composite International Diagnostic Interview; DIS = Diagnostic Interview Schedule; DSM = Diagnostic and Statistical Manual of mental disorders; ICD = International Classification of Diseases.

Table 5.9. *Prevalence of social phobia among adults (clinical)*

Study	Location	Sample (*N*)	Instrument (criteria)	Prevalence period and rate (%)	Comments
Faravelli et al. (2004)	Sesto Fiorentino (Italy)	2,363	SCID (DSM-IV)	Lifetime: 3.7	Randomly selected from the lists of 15 general practitioners.
Brown et al. (2001b)	Boston, Albany (USA)	968	ADIS (DSM-IV)	Current: 19.2	
Weiller et al. (1996)	Paris (France)	405	CIDI (DSM-III-R)	1-month: 4.9 Lifetime: 14.4	
Lépine et al. (1993)	18 clinical settings around the world	543	CIDI (DSM-III)	1-month: 21.0 6-month: 23.5 Lifetime: 27.7	See also Witchen et al. (1991)

Note: ADIS = Anxiety Disorders Interview Schedule; CIDI = Composite International Diagnostic Interview; DSM = Diagnostic and Statistical Manual of mental disorders; SCID = Structured Clinical Interview for DSM.

Exceptionally, the National Comorbidity Survey (NCS) studied a sample representative of the population of the USA (Kessler, McGonagle, Zhao, Nelson, Hugues, Eshleman, Wittchen, & Kendler, 1994). Another noteworthy study (issued from the WHO/ADAMHA joint project; Lépine, Wittchen, Essau, et al., 1993) involved representative samples of patients seeking treatment from 18 countries worldwide. Table 5.8 summarizes all available studies known to me.

In summary, this survey of national, community, and clinical samples highlights a bewildering variability of prevalence rates of social phobia – viewed narrowly as a distinct entity. Admittedly the surveys were not exclusively of social phobia; such a study does not exist. The typical epidemiological investigations cast their nets wide and trawl through a vast psychiatric expanse by means of structured interviews designed for the purpose, administered by lay-interviewers. As seen in an earlier section concerning reliability, the results of such procedures may be open to some doubt.

As it is, in various advocacy writings concerning social phobia, the higher prevalence rates or the most recent publications seem to hold sway (e.g. Moynihan, 2002). If all available studies are examined simultaneously – as they are here – the great variability in prevalence rates undermines confidence in all.

Although various methodological differences in the studies either in assessment (the instruments measuring social phobia, the lay research assistants administering them) or equally important the sampling (recruitment, size, representativeness) doubtless all account for some of the variation in prevalence rates, it is difficult to accept that these methodological and sampling differences adequately make sense of ranges such as between 0% for men in Seoul (Lee, Kwak, Yamamoto, Rhee, Kim, Han, Choi, & Lee, 1990a) and 16% (Wacker, Müllejans, Klein, & Battegay 1992) in Basel or the still higher 44% (Pakriev, Vasar, Aluoja, & Shlick, 2000) in Russia. Among patients seeking treatment the variability is as high (see Table 5.9 for a selective list of countries around the world). Faced with such disparities one must first conclude that the construct of social phobia is not easily transposed (i.e. generalized) from its place of origin to other settings. Second, at the present it is unjustifiable to speak of a rate of prevalence of social phobia in the general population.

Furthermore, even within one country – although a sizeable one – the USA, prevalence rates differ extremely. In two studies: (ECA – Schneier, Johnson, Hornig, Liebowitz, & Weissman, 1992 and NCS – Kessler et al., 1994), although admittedly involving two different representative samples and using slightly different criteria (i.e. DSM-III and III-R), prevalence rates were 2.4% and 13.3% respectively. Were the two studies identifying individuals exhibiting the same psychological pattern? Could the anchoring definitions have possibly referred to the same phenomena? This can only be doubted; we are clearly not standing on firm ground.

Generalizability of Co-occurring Patterns of Psychopathology

If Goldenberg, White, Yonkers, Reich, Warshaw, Goisman, & Keller (1996) are to be believed, social phobia in its pure form is the rarest of occurrences. However that may be, a comprehensive and more true-to-life test of what social phobia is like in different countries and settings must be widened to include related patterns of psychopathology. These were described in some detail in the convergent validity section (see Table 5.6).

In summary, similarly to what we have seen earlier in our survey of the generalizability of social phobia itself, rates of prevalence of co-occurrence are inconsistent between studies. The variability diminishes somewhat when odd ratios (OR) or degrees of risk are considered. Nevertheless, the differences in the results were far greater than what might be expected bearing in mind the various methodological idiosyn-crasies of each individual study. It must be concluded again that the con-struct of social phobia – this time viewed broadly as stretching in time and also involving a host of associated patterns – generalizes poorly.

External – Ecological Validity

The underlying assumption in all studies reviewed so far was that answering an interviewer's questions in an office reveals something valid about the subject's conduct (i.e. various specific behaviors or involved tactics within an overall organizing strategic pattern) in a mul-titude of real-life situations and extended in time.

Furthermore, most studies seem to regard social phobic responses as little short of a monolith (i.e. as unitary), expressed in a general (trait-like) tendency to anxious distress, applied evenly across "phobic" situations.

As seen in chapter 1, there are grounds to doubt such a view from a conceptual standpoint. Furthermore, clinical experience (e.g. studies of single cases) lend it little support (Stravynski et al., 2000b). No systematic investigation providing a well-modulated description of social phobic conduct extended in time and ranging over various areas of social life (e.g. enacting social roles, friendship, intimacy) has been published so far. It is an important gap that needs to be filled.

The ecological perspective on external validity could be gauged from estimating variations and nuances in the generalization of conduct from the experimental setting to real-life situations. The kind of evidence of generalization we would be seeking to document, could be twofold.

First, to what extent might the behavior studied be said to reflect the manifestation of actual conduct in real-life situations? Two aspects of behavior could be considered: its constituents and, more importantly, its functional role. Second, to what extent are the situations recreated experimentally representative (qualitatively as well as quantitatively) of their real-life counterparts?

What kind of experimental evidence could be used to answer the questions raised above? Our choices are limited. The only studies actually observing behavior as opposed to querying subjects about how they might behave elsewhere are those using behavioral assessment (i.e. role-play) tests — BAT. These typically involve the simulation of behavior (e.g. public speaking) and measurement of its various facets in a laboratory context. The BATs have commonly been used to gauge improvement following therapy or to highlight differences between sub-groups (e.g. Holt, Heimberg, & Hope, 1992; Turner et al., 1992; Tran & Chambless, 1995; Brown, Heimberg, & Juster, 1995; Hofmann et al., 1995b — descriptions of the above studies may be found in the discriminant validity section).

As the above studies actually took pains to observe the behavior of social phobic participants (although contrived for being simulated), their results could potentially lend themselves to an "ecological" reading. Unfortunately (from our point of view), the behavior itself — although observed — was not actually measured in these studies; the subjects — while making a speech or approaching a stranger — rated their experience in terms of subjective anxiety or were rated on this dimension or that of social skills (e.g. in Turner et al., 1992) by others.

Other shortcomings are also inherent in the BAT methodology. The situations studied, although seemingly straightforward (e.g. giving an impromptu speech of 3 min.) were so contrived by laboratory experimental demands (e.g. electrodes to measure heart-rate were attached, base-rates were taken, cue-giving red lights went on, etc.) that their relevance to the social phobic subjects' lives is hard to imagine.

In summary, this aspect of external validity, whose importance cannot be overstated, remains unexplored.

Are there typical social phobic actions and reactions to a variety of trigger situations or do idiosyncrasies predominate? Are they best analyzed topographically, in terms of their constituting elements, or functionally, in terms of their impact? Are there typical adjustment tactics to wrenching environmental pressures as well as attempts to transform the social environment(s) that might be considered proper to it? These questions still await empirical answers. Perhaps other approaches (e.g. ethological) developed for the study of other animals or ethnographic data developed by anthropologists for describing (cultural) patterns, could prove to be more productive in this context.

General Conclusion

This survey was conducted so as to test the proposition that social phobia might be an entity characterized by a consistent and highly defined pattern of conduct.

The search for relevant evidence was framed by the proviso that the hypothetical construct of social phobia is whatever is measured by the most widely accepted definitions, those of the DSM-III onwards and ICD-10; all were considered equivalent.

It is worthwhile to recall at this juncture that these definitions are anchored in three features: anxious reactivity to, and avoidance of, social situations in fear of embarrassment, and disruptions of social functioning. These are presumed to be the chief indicators of the social phobic pattern of conduct.

The results of numerous uncoordinated investigations published in scientific/professional journals and driven by their own imperatives were selected and organized as having a bearing on three kinds of validity: content, criterion, and construct.

Large gaps in the various strands of evidence were found and the information available was not necessarily evenly distributed, so as to answer all queries. In part, this is the natural upshot of the unrelated efforts of many individual researchers and research groups guided mostly by the implicit assumption conveyed by diagnostic manuals that social phobia might be a disease entity of sorts. In another sense, this reflected an unseen hindrance, namely the absence of a coherent theory or better still theories of what social phobia is, to propel and structure research effort.

I shall recapitulate the main conclusions of this survey by weighing and sifting them into three categories: supporting the entity-hypothesis, ambiguous, and undermining it.

Supporting Evidence

A self-reported social phobic pattern of responding can be fairly accurately agreed on from interviewing the subject by either unstructured (as typical to clinical practice) or structured interviews incorporating standard questions based on the defining criteria found in manuals. This fulfills an important necessary condition for further investigations.

As a construct, social phobia was consistently associated with difficulties in more social situations with more severe anxiety reactions to them regardless of measuring instrument.

The social fears characterizing social phobia are in varying degrees widely shared with normal individuals and other anxiety disorders, especially agoraphobia. All the same, these are highly distinguishable not only in degree but as a kind whose configuration of fears represents a pattern. This is the strongest unequivocal single finding.

As expected, lower employment and marriage rates and fewer friends characterize social phobia; these are the gross features of an unsatisfactory pattern of social functioning. In the past lurk more than common difficulties at school.

Some socially phobic individuals come from socially anxious families; first-rank relatives are more likely to be socially phobic. This seems particularly true at the more severe (i.e. generalized) end of the spectrum; it is not entirely clear who among the relatives is particularly at risk.

Social phobia has a fairly distinctive age range of onset (15 to 18) and equal sex distribution; it usually precedes other anxiety, affective, and alcoholism disorders with which it has affinities.

Ambiguous Supporting Evidence

Disconcertingly, concordance rates between different ways of identifying social phobia (e.g. clinical interview vs. structured interview) are rather modest.

Similarly, the accuracy in identifying social phobia over time was less than that obtained by two interviewers operating simultaneously. Although acceptable, this is worrisome. This inconsistency might indicate an error of measurement. Alternatively, it might raise a question mark over the received view of the stability of social phobic features or the social phobic pattern altogether. A clue to this may be found in the difference between present and lifetime rates of prevalence. The far greater rate over the life span would imply that there are numerous former social phobic individuals. The process that led them to overcome their handicap or outgrow it may yet be profitably studied.

Furthermore, the accuracy of observation of specific facets of social phobia (as opposed to gross patterns) was rather low. In actual fact, very few studies have concerned themselves with the finer topographical features of social phobia so far. None have grappled with the functional role of what social phobic individuals do. Both deficiencies in research are likely to stem from the fact that — with the exception of avoidance as the commonplace parameter studied — it was conceptually unclear what kind of behavior social phobia would entail.

The social phobic pattern, or its main features, have close links with other hypothetical constructs with pronounced anxious features (e.g. agoraphobia/panic) as well as those of alcoholism and depression. It is important to emphasize that these inter-relationships obtain both with individuals seeking treatment and with those in the general populations, who do not. These findings could be interpreted as suggesting that the social phobic construct might be an element in an even larger pattern also encompassing, for example, other anxieties, depression, and wider interpersonal difficulties (e.g. general neurotic syndrome; Tyrer, 1985). Another speculative possibility, not based on the assumption of stable multiple independent entities inherent in the DSM (III, III-R and IV), might be that social phobia is a loosely defined multi-tiered protean pattern extended in time, sometimes fading out of existence and reincarnated in various guises in particularly evocative circumstances.

While social phobia is distinguishable from normality, it is typically only in terms of a (higher) degree of distress in certain situations or dimensions of experience. It remains yet to be shown that the social phobic pattern is not an exacerbation of, say, normal social anxiety.

Of some practical value is the fact that social phobia responds well to a range of treatments be they psychological or pharmacological. Both approaches to treatment produce equivalent improvements in the short-term; these maintain over the long haul for patients who underwent psychological treatment. Patients taking medication, however, tend to relapse when it is stopped. None of these treatments are specific to social phobia.

Finally, no feature or construct of childhood predicted social phobia specifically.

Undermining Evidence

Social phobia cannot be separated from the (clearly related) hypothetical entity of APD. On the face of it, this fact undermines the validity of social phobia (or APD) as currently conceived. It may, however, be interpreted as questioning the distinction between phobic and inter-personal difficulties that in theory belong to two different realms of psychopathology expressed in Axes I ("performing in situations") and II ("relating to persons") of the DSM-III and upwards (Millon & Martinez, 1995, p. 222). Subversively, social phobia straddles both; it is simultaneously an anxiety and a personality disorder.

It seems unadventurous, therefore, to suggest that the two (or three, if social phobia is separated into the specific and generalized subtypes) hypothetical constructs are degrees of severity of the same pattern. The relationships that social phobia might have to other personality disorders await investigation.

Of considerable importance by its absence is the fact that no specific factors on any level of analysis (social, psychological, biological) have been firmly established as characterizing the social phobic pattern despite considerable research effort. This issues, by implication, a chal-lenge to the unspoken assumption inherent in the classification schemes such as DSM-IV, that social phobia is clearly marked off from normality.

Large discrepancies in the prevalence of social phobia reported by various studies cast a serious doubt on what is being measured by the defining criteria. Regarding social phobia as a natural entity would lead us to expect a certain (rather high given the definition) prevalence rate that would fluctuate to a degree in view of the somewhat different life-demands that various cultures make on members in terms of the social roles they fulfill. International and same-country (e.g. USA) discrepan-cies, however, are of such magnitude as to question altogether what is being measured each time. Similar problems were encountered when co-occurring constructs were delineated. The variability and incompa-rability of rates of prevalence across studies throw into doubt the very measurement and ultimately the meaningfulness of the construct of social phobia.

Disappointingly, neither studies documenting actual social phobic behavior in real-life situations, nor delineating the social phobic pattern of behavior extended in time and ranging over various areas of social functioning were to be found. Although we presume it does obtain nat-urally – hence the hypothetical construct – and believe we detect it through interviews, it has not been as yet shown independently. The hypothetical construct of social phobia may stand or fall on this latter direct test of it.

In summary, this overview of the process of construct validation of social phobia has ended inconclusively. It has answered some questions while raising yet more queries to be grappled with.

Some evidence such as inter-rater reliability and especially the demonstration that social phobia has definable qualities well distinguishable from those of other phobias with which it stands in close relationship, firm up the validity of the construct.

Other results, especially those concerning generalizability, are so inconsistent as to seriously undermine our confidence both in what we are searching for, as well as in the means available to identify it (defining indicators anchored in structured interviews administered by lay-interviewers). The remaining results are of a middling kind, pointing in the right direction, but rather tentatively; they do not contribute meaningfully to strengthening the validity of our construct-in-the making.

Perhaps of equal importance is the fact that much of the evidence needed to reach an informed decision is as yet unavailable. To fill these gaps should be a priority. A serious obstacle to progress is the absence of a theory of what social phobia is, let alone what may cause it. For the most part, this stems from the fact that social phobia has been investigated as if it were a disease entity. Consequently, putative anomalies or breakdowns in various hypothetical mechanisms purportedly explaining what makes social phobia tick have been put forward. On current evidence, the support for these is frail at best (see part III; chapters 6–9). If – as argued in chapter 4 – the disease analogy were inappropriate, social phobia as malfunctioning clockwork and, by extension, social phobic individuals as passive sufferers – would become ill conceived and misleading. In that case, a theory of social phobia might profitably recast phobic individuals as agents of their own lives, who – however inadequately – pursue purposeful goals. I shall attempt this in chapter 11.

Part III

What Causes Social Phobia?

6　Social Phobia as a Consequence of Brain Defects

Individuals complaining of social phobia often provide vivid accounts of their distress in terms of various physical sensations (e.g. sweating, blushing, tachycardia, and tremulousness) they experience when, for example, entering a cafeteria, a classroom or meeting strangers at a party or imagining an interview lying ahead. At their peak, a vast range of somatic reactions include, among others: (1) palpitations and cool extremities and pallor (peripheral vaso-constriction); (2) respiratory difficulties; (3) the urge to urinate, intestinal cramps and alternating diarrhea and constipation, and vomiting; (4) muscle tension in the face, trembling, and incoordination of the hands; (5) speech difficulties due to troubled breathing and incoordination of muscles involved in articulation ("tongue-tied"). These are also accompanied by blunted perceptiveness and diminished responsiveness.

Although reported subjectively, these are not confabulations; many of these somatic responses can be independently measured. What could account for these very physical reactions experienced powerfully and bafflingly in seemingly anodyne circumstances?

A possible account could be that the brain processes involved in the regulation of the above reactions are defective. It has been suggested in this vein, that, "it is tempting to speculate that social phobics either experience greater or more sustained increases or are more sensitive to normal stress-mediated catecholamine elevations" (Liebowitz, Gorman, Fyer, & Klein, 1985, p. 729).

Background

With the exception of the brief statement of Liebowitz et al. (1985) a neurobiological formulation of social phobia has – to our knowledge – never been published. Nevertheless, its (unstated) principles and unarticulated theses hold sway over a considerable number of researchers and clinicians who give them their allegiance and uphold them in practice.

A biomedical outlook concerning the etiology of psychiatric disorders inspires this account of social phobia in general, that — in its search for explanatory models — accords ontological primacy to biological structures and physiology. Such a perspective, in turn, is the logical extension of the disease model (see chapter 4).

Its principles may be summarized in the following propositions:

1. The social phobic pattern of behavior is the result of (molecular or cellular) events in particular brain regions of the individual exhibiting it. These events may be localized and are associated with quantitative changes in particular neurobiological or biochemical substances. In other words, both morphological (structural) and physiological (functional) abnormalities (both unspecified) ought to be detected in the brains of individuals identified as social phobic. This, however, begs a related question: how do the above abnormalities come into being? The answer is found in the next proposition:

2. Something coded in the genes of the individual displaying the social phobic pattern predisposes him/her to the above brain abnormalities and hence to social phobia.

Overall then, this implicit model presumes that social phobia is something as yet unspecified — on the biological level of analysis — which the afflicted individual actually and concretely carries within. Materially and figuratively, social phobia — as construed within the biomedical model — is something that one has (or lacks).

In the following pages we shall review the available evidence providing a test of the above propositions.

Neurobiological Abnormalities

A research program seeking to show that the social phobic pattern of behavior and experience is the consequence of brain abnormalities has first to identify the brain abnormalities, theoretically and then experimentally. A subsequent demonstration of their causal role needs to be carried out independently.

Practically speaking, the main research efforts have been directed towards identifying biological correlates of social phobia. In the absence of a theoretical framework to guide these, what could be the foundations of this line of research?

The general premise of these studies has been that a quantitative difference (i.e. one of degree) between a group of social phobic subjects and a matched control group on a neurobiological parameter might hint at an underlying abnormality (i.e. neurobiological imbalance) characteristic of social phobia. In order to identify such disparities, the bulk of the studies under review took one of three approaches:

1. measuring (either directly or indirectly) neurotransmitter or hormone responses;
2. measuring brain function (by means of brain-imaging techniques);
3. considering responses to pharmacological treatment as indications of underlying neurobiological mechanisms.

Direct and Indirect Measurement of Neurotransmitter Systems and Neuroendocrine Function

Direct Measurements

Direct measurement of peripheral receptor and transporter functions is a paradigm that has been commonly used in the study of anxiety and mood disorders as a means to assess indirectly the less accessible central neurotransmission. The rationale of extending this general approach to social phobic individuals is based on the expectation that they would display similar alterations in markers of monoaminergic function that are known to be present in other conditions with prominent anxious components such as mood, panic, and generalized anxiety disorders (Millan, 2003). Studies using this paradigm are summarized in Table 6.1.

Their results indicate that the binding parameters for platelet 5-HT transporter (Stein, Delaney, Chartier, Kroft, & Hazen, 1995), 5-HT2 receptors (Chatterjee, Sunitha, Velayudhan, & Khanna, 1997), or for lymphocyte beta adrenergic receptors (Stein, Huzel, Delaney, 1993) observed in social phobic individuals do not differ from those observed in controls. Similar negative results were obtained for the platelet vesicular monoaminergic transporter (Laufer, Zucker, Hermesh, Marom, Gilad, Nir, Weizman, & Rehavi, 2005) – the carrier responsible for the uptake of different types of monoamines (5-HT, DA and NE) from the cytoplasm into intracellular storage vesicles.

In contrast, a lower density of peripheral benzodiazepine receptors on platelets was found in generalized social phobic patients than in controls (Johnson, Marazziti, Brawman-Mintzer et al., 1998). The theoretical meaning of this finding is murky since the central and peripheral benzodiazepine receptor sites are structurally and functionally different. A reduced density of the peripheral sites has no clear implications for the central nervous system.

Table 6.1. *Direct and indirect measures of neurotransmitter systems*

Study	Subjects	Monitored variable	Observation
Direct Measurements			
Chatterjee et al., 1997.	20 CTL 20 SP	[^{3}H]ketanserin binding parameters to 5-HT2 receptor (Kd and Bmax) in platelets	5-HT2 receptor in platelets: CTL = SP. Association between 5-HT2 receptor density and severity of disorder.
Stein et al., 1995.	23 CTL 18 SP 15 PD	[^{3}H]paroxetine binding parameters to 5-HT transporter (Kd and Bmax) in platelets	5-HT transporter in platelets: CTL = SP = PD
Stein et al., 1993.	17 CTL 17 SP	[^{125}I]pindolol binding parameters (Kd and Bmax) to beta adrenergic receptors in lymphocytes	Beta adrenergic receptors in leukocytes: CTL = SP
Laufer et al., 2005.	15 CTL 20 SP	[^{3}H]dihydrotetrabenazine binding parameters (Kd and Bmax) to vesicular monoaminergic transporter in platelets	Vesicular monoaminergic transporter in platelets: CTL = SP
Johnson et al., 1998.	53 CTL 53 SP	[^{3}H]PK11,195 binding parameters (Kd and Bmax) to peripheral benzodiazepine receptor in platelets	Bmax for peripheral benzodizepine binding site: SP > CTL
Tiihonen et al., 1997.	11 CTL 11 SP	Striatal density of DA transporters as measured using the transporter radiotracer [^{123}I]b-CIT and SPECT	Striatal density of DA transporters: SP < CTL
Schneier et al., 2000.	10 CTL 10 SP	D2 receptor binding capacity in striatum measured using D2 receptor radiotracer [^{123}I]IBZM and SPECT	Striatal density of D2 receptor: SP < CTL
Indirect Measurements: Challenge Studies ***Pharmacological challenge paradigms***			
5-HT system			
Shlik et al., 2004.	18 CTL 18 SP	Neuroendocrine response measured by: *prolactin plasma levels *cortisol plasma levels	Increase in prolactin and cortisol plasma levels following acute, single dose of citalopram (20 mg/kg, i.v.): CTL = SP.

Study	Subjects	Monitored variable	Observation
Hollander et al., 1998.	21 CTL 21 SP 42 OCD	Neuroendocrine response measured by: *prolactin plasma levels *cortisol plasma levels	Increase in prolactin plasma levels following acute challenge with 5-HT partial agonist *m*CPP (0.5 mg/kg; p.o.) CTL = SP = OCD. Increase in cortisol plasma levels: SP > CTL > OCD. (Note: pair-wise comparisons among each group yielded no significant differences).
Tancer et al., 1994.	22 CTL 21 SP	Neuroendocrine response measured by: *prolactin plasma levels *cortisol plasma levels	Increase in prolactin plasma levels following acute challenge with fenfluramine: CTL = SP. Increase in cortisol plasma levels SP > CTL.
DA system			
Condren et al., 2002a.	14 CTL 14 SP	Neuroendocrine response measured by: *prolactin plasma levels	Prolactin suppression following acute challenge with D2 agonist *quinagolide* (0.5 mg, p.o.): CTL = SP.
Bebchuk & Tancer, 1994–95.	21 CTL 22 SP	Neuroendocrine response measured by: *prolactin plasma levels	Prolactin suppression following acute challenge with DA precursor levodopa CTL = SP.
NE system			
Tancer et al., 1993; 1995.	31 CTL 16 SP 13 PD	Neuroendocrine response measured by: *growth hormone plasma levels	Increase in growth hormone plasma levels following acute, intravenous α2A agonist clonidine: SP = PD < CTL. (Note: CTL=SP using oral clonidine as challenge).

Table 6.1. (cont.)

Study	Subjects	Monitored variable	Observation
Papp et al., 1988.	11 SP	Anxious response defined by autonomic symptoms, fear of embarrassment or humiliation. Assessment of cardiovascular and respiratory activity	Intravenous infusion of adrenaline provoked observable anxiety only in one subject. Ventilatory indexes correlated with self-rated anxiety during infusion, no correlation with cardiovascular indexes.

Physiological challenge paradigms

Coupland et al., 2003.	56 CTL 28 SP	Heart beat and blood pressure.	Supine blood pressure: SP > CTL Heart rate in supine position: SP = CTL Blood pressure change following orthostatic challenge: SP < CTL Heart rate change following orthostatic challenge: SP = CTL
Stein et al., 1994a.	15 CTL 14 SP	Heart beat, blood pressure, NE and E plasma levels.	Supine blood pressure: SP = CTL Heart rate in supine position: SP = CTL Blood pressure change following orthostatic challenge: SP = CTL Heart rate change following orthostatic challenge: SP = CTL Change in plasma NE and E concentrations following orthostatic challenge: SP = CTL
Stein et al., 1992.	15 CTL 15 SP	Heart beat, blood pressure, NE and E plasma levels.	Supine blood pressure: SP = CTL Heart rate in supine position: SP = CTL Blood pressure change following orthostatic challenge: SP > CTL Heart rate change following orthostatic challenge: SP > CTL

Study	Subjects	Monitored variable	Observation
			Change in plasma NE and E concentrations following orthostatic challenge: SP = CTL
Social challenge paradigms			
Gserlach et al., 2004.	32 CTL 32 SP	Heart rate, self-reported anxiety and worry about anxiety symptoms when exposed to public broadcasting of cardiac beat.	Measured heart rate during challenge: SP > CTL Increase in heart rate induced by social challenge: SP > CTL Worry about heart rate increase: SP > CTL Perceived anxiety and worry about anxiety symptoms: SP > CTL
Gerlach et al., 2003.	14 CTL 30 SP	Heart rate and self-reported anxiety while watching an embarrassing video.	Measured heart rate during challenge: SP > CTL Increase in heart rate induced by social challenge: SP > CTL Anxiety before and during challenge: SP > CTL Embarrassment during challenge: SP > CTL
Davidson et al., 2000.	10 CTL 18 SP	Self-reported anxiety and heart rate elicited by public speech.	Measured heart rate before social challenge: SP > CTL Measured heart rate during social challenge: SP > CTL Reported anxiety before social challenge: SP > CTL Reported anxiety during social challenge: SP > CTL

Note: CTL: control; SP: social phobia; PD: panic dissorder; OCD: obsessive-compulsive disorder.

More recently, the use of sophisticated neuroimaging methods such as single photon computed tomography (SPECT) has allowed visualizing neurotransmitter receptors and transporters in the living human brain. This is achieved by using non-toxic chemical agents that selectively bind to a designated molecule of interest (e.g. a specific receptor) in the central nervous system. Neuroimaging allows tracing the distribution of the compound marking the molecule of interest.

This technique has shown that generalized social phobic patients display a low density of DA transporter sites (Tiihonen, Kuikka, Bergstrom, Lepola, Koponen, & Leinonen, 1997) and D2 receptors in the striatum (Schneier, Liebowitz, Abi-Dargham, Zea-Ponce, Lin, & Laruelle, 2000). Given that radiotracer binding is highly influenced by extra-cellular levels of the endogenous neurotransmitter, it is difficult to say whether these changes reflect a real decrease in binding sites or an increase in synaptic availability of DA. Thus, the significance of the observed difference between controls and social phobic patients remains obscure. Moreover, the specificity of these associations is uncertain since a reduction in striatal DA transporters (Tiihonen, Kuikka, Bergstrom, Hakola, Karhu, Ryynanen, & Fohr, 1995) or D2 receptors (Hietala, West, Syvalahti, Nagren, Lehikoinen, Sonninen, & Ruotsalainen, 1994) also has been observed in clinical populations (e.g. substance abusing) quite different from the socially phobic.

Indirect Measurements

Pharmacological Challenge Paradigms This approach investigates the involvement of specific neurotransmitter systems through their activation by means of a pharmacological agent. This is commonly referred to as a "challenge," defined as "the hormonal or physiological response to probes mediated by the neurotransmitter systems under investigation – the magnitude of the response providing a relative measure of the activity of the system" (van Praag, Lemus, & Kahn, 1987; see also Uhde, Tancer, Gelernter, & Vittone, 1994).

A number of studies have made use of the pharmacological challenge paradigms to investigate the possible malfunctioning of the NE, DA and 5-HT systems in social phobia. In the case of the 5-HT system, challenges have included: the selective serotonin reuptake inhibitor (SSRI) citalopram (Shlik, Maron, Tru, Aluoja, & Vasar, 2004); 5-HT receptor agonist methyl-chloro-phenyl-piperazine (m-CPP; Hollander, Kwon, Weiller, Cohen, Stein, DeCaria, Liebowitz, & Simeon, 1998) and 5-HT releasing agent fenfluramine (Tancer, Mailman, Stein, Mason, Carson, & Goldeen, 1994). The NE system has been probed by administration of the α2A (alpha2A) agonist clonidine (Tancer, Stein, & Uhde, 1993; Tancer, Lewis, & Stein, 1995) and the hormone adrenaline (Papp, Gorman, Liebowitz, Fyer, Cohen, & Klein, 1988). The activity of the DA system has been assessed either by using the D2 receptor agonist quinagolide (Condren, Sharifi, & Thakore, 2002a) or the DA precursor levodopa (Bebchuk & Tancer, 1994–95). The responsiveness of postsynaptic receptors to pharmacological challenges has been assessed by measuring changes in plasmatic levels of prolactin and cortisol.

Results obtained by means of these approaches appear in Table 6.1 where they are subdivided by neurotransmitter systems. Our comments follow the same order.

First, considering the 5-HT system's responsiveness of post-synaptic hypothalamic 5-HT1A receptors that regulate prolactin, secretion was compared in social phobic and normal subjects. If the 5-HT1A reactivity in social phobic individuals were different from that of controls, one would expect the prolactin responses in the two groups to differ. Such an effect was not observed in any of the studies analyzed.

In studying anxiety, the cortisol response to pharmacological 5-HT challenges has been commonly used as an index of postsynaptic 5-HT2 receptor reactivity (Newman, Shapira, & Lerer, 1998). Within this context, enhanced cortisol responses to fenfluramine and m-CPP such as the ones observed in social phobic patients have been interpreted as an indication of increased postsynaptic 5-HT2 receptor sensitivity. This interpretation must be treated with caution since cortisol secretion is a complex response modulated by different 5-HT receptor subtypes at distinct levels of the adreno-pituitary-hypothalamic axis (Contesse, Lefebvre, Lenglet, Kuhn, Delarue, & Vaudry, 2000). Moreover, the specificity of the association of enhanced cortisol responses with social phobia is doubtful. Similar challenges of the 5-HT system in quite dissimilar conditions such as panic disorder (Wetzler, Asnis, DeLecuona, & Kalus, 1996; Vieira, Ramos, & Gentil, 1997), depression (Maes, Meltzer, D'Hondt, Cosyns, & Blockx, 1995; Ghaziuddin, King, Welch, Zaccagnini, Weidmer-Mikhail, & Mellow, 2000), and pedophilia (Maes, van West, De Vos, Westenberg, Van Hunsel, Hendriks, Cosyns, & Scharpe, 2001), resulted in high cortisol secretion.

Second, pharmacological challenges of the DA system indicate that hypothalamic postsynaptic D2 receptors that regulate prolactin secretion are equally sensitive in social phobic and normal individuals (Bebchuk & Tancer, 1994).

Third, in keeping with the same principle as above, reactivity of post-synaptic adrenergic α2 (alpha2) receptors has been studied by assessing changes in growth hormone (GH) secretion. The results have been inconsistent, with intravenous but not oral administration of clonidine resulting in abnormal growth hormone response in social phobic individuals (Tancer et al., 1993, 1995). The difference in outcome was put down to the fact that the oral route of administration was less effective than the intravenous one. Clonidine, however, did decrease plasma noradrenaline levels in 53–54% of controls regardless of its route of administration, suggesting that sufficient drug was in fact absorbed in all cases. The blunted GH response to clonidine has been interpreted as a possible manifestation of global decrease in GH function in social phobic individuals (Uhde, 1994). The fact that there are no documented differences in height between social phobic individuals and normal controls makes this interpretation untenable.

Finally, a study, using the hormone adrenaline as probe, has shown that its intravenous administration stimulates cardiovascular and respiratory responses in social phobic subjects. Since this study did not include a control group, it is difficult to judge whether autonomic reactivity to the challenge was abnormal. Interestingly, though subjects in this study were aware of the cardiovascular and respiratory effects of adrenaline, only one described experiencing sensations similar to those experienced in real-life social situations. This is puzzling given the prevailing notion that excessive awareness of physical sensations induced by sympathetic activation (sweating, blushing, increased heart rate) is one of the abnormal cognitive processes presumed to underlie social anxiety (Liebowitz et al., 1985; Spurr & Stopa, 2002).

Physiological Challenge Paradigms In this type of approach, biochemical and physiological changes related to a postural "challenge," i.e. moving from a supine to a standing position, are used as an indirect measure of the activity of the autonomic nervous system. The main underlying rationale for this approach is the attempt to associate specific physical signs with imbalances in autonomic neurotransmission. In this formulation, the physical complaints typical of social phobia, are associated with rapid release of catecholamines (noradrenaline, adrenaline, and/or dopamine) and are assumed to reflect a pronounced and persistent increase in sympathetic activity. Studies reporting performance-related elevations in noradrenaline and adrenaline levels in normal individuals (Dimsdale & Moss, 1980; Neftel, Adler, Kappeli, et al., 1982; Taggart, Carruthers & Summerville, 1973) lend some support to this assumption as circumstantial evidence for the role of these amines in social phobia.

Studies testing the effects of orthostatic challenge on two cardiovascular variables (heart rate and blood pressure) and modifications in catecholamine plasma levels appear in Table 6.1. In most studies, social phobic and normal groups were similar (Stein et al., 1994a). When differences were detected, these were not consistent across studies (Stein et al., 1992, 1994a; Coupland, Wilson, Potokar, Bell, & Nutt, 2003). This failure to replicate results was put down to the use of different social phobic populations in the various studies. An alternative interpretation might be that the lack of reproducibility stems from drawing an analogy between a simple physical exertion and a highly complex reaction to perceived danger embedded in interpersonal relationships. Such misleading oversimplifications throw into doubt the adequacy of physiological challenge as an approach for the study of the neurobiology of social phobia.

Social Challenge Paradigms When exposed to "socially challenging" (i.e. threatening) situations, social phobic individuals report a heightened awareness of physical sensations elicited by the activation of the sympathetic nervous system (blushing, sweating, increase in heart rate). Thus, a number of studies compared the correlation between self-reported and objectively measured intensity of physical reactions in control and social phobic individuals; the results are summarized in Table 6.1. In these studies, that do not focus on any specific neurotransmitter system, social phobic individuals when simulating social activities (e.g. making an impromptu speech in the laboratory) displayed both enhanced sympathetic activation during social challenge and worried more about their sensations than did the controls (Gerlach, Wilhelm, & Roth, 2003; Gerlach, Mourlane, & Rist, 2004; Davidson, Marshall, Tomarken, & Henriques, 2000). Interestingly, differences, while significant on the continuum of subjective anxiety, tended to blur (e.g. Gerlach et al., 2001) or vanish altogether (e.g. Edelmann & Baker, 2002) on the physiological indices of anxiety measured objectively.

Altogether, this information adds little to our understanding of what provokes both the enhanced sympathetic responses and the exaggerated perception of physical sensations characteristic of social phobic individuals. If anything, it suggests that the social phobic reactions might be an exacerbation of normal fear responses.

Metabolic, Respiratory and Peptide Probes

Various chemical agents including sodium lactate, CO_2, caffeine, and activators of cholecystokinin receptors, have been shown to elicit "panic" in individuals meeting criteria for different anxiety disorders. Despite the popularity of this approach, the theoretical implications of the results have been limited. This is in consequence of the fact that little is known about the processes by which the different agents induce panic (Davies, 2002; Klein, 2002; Geraci, Anderson, Slate-Cothren, Post, & McCann, 2002) and the fact that from a theoretical standpoint, the studies did not test any definite hypotheses. Additionally, the confounding effects associated with elevated levels of anxiety and expectancy induced by the prospect of an impending "panic attack" are the major drawbacks of this approach. These difficulties notwithstanding, a number of research groups have used different challenge agents to study social phobia, justifying the use of the paradigm on the grounds of the clinical, demographic, and therapeutic similarities between social phobia and panic disorder (e.g. Caldirola, Perna, Arancio, Bertani, & Bellodi, 1997).

a. Lactate-dependent "panic": Lactate sensitivity in social phobia was tested by Leibowitz et al. (1985); 1 out of 15 social phobic subjects reported panic in response to lactate as compared to 10 out of 20 phobic and 4 out of 9 agoraphobic subjects. Remarkably, the complaints induced by the challenge were atypical of social phobia. As the study did not include a control group, the rate of panic response in social phobic subjects could not be compared to that of non-phobic individuals.

b. Caffeine-dependent "panic": Caffeine has been shown to induce panic and greater increases in blood lactate and cortisol levels in panic disorder patients than in controls. Caffeine by contrast, did not lower the threshold for panic in social phobic subjects and only cortisol − but not lactate levels − were increased by the challenge (Uhde, Tancer, Black, & Brown, 1991).

c. Cholecystokinin (CCK)-dependent "panic": CCK is an octapeptide found in the gastrointestinal track and limbic areas of the brain, where it contributes to the regulation of emotion. It is accepted that intravenous administration of CCK receptor agonists like CCK-4 or pentagastrin precipitate a full-blown panic or some of its complaints in panic disorder patients (Bradwejn, Koszycki, & Shriqui, 1991). Since many of CCK-related complaints such as severe anxiety, blushing and abdominal discomfort are features of social anxiety it was "considered of interest to determine whether the effects of CCK-agonists generalize to patients with social phobia" (McCann, Slate, Geraci, Roscow-Terrill, & Uhde, 1997).

Table 6.2. *Panicogenic challenges: peptides probes*

Study	Subjects	Monitored variable	Results
Katzman et al., 2004.	12 CTL 12 SP	Panic symptoms following administration (20 mg, i.v.) of CCK-4	Induction of panic (4 or more symptoms): SP = CTL Number of panic symptoms: SP = CTL Intensity of panic symptoms: SP = CTL Induction of embarrassment, blushing: SP = CTL Increase in heart rate and blood pressure: SP = CTL Increase in ACTH and cortisol: SP = CTL
Geraci et al., 2002.	4 SP	Panic symptoms following administration (0.6 mg/kg, i.v.) of pentagastrin.	2 out of 4 patients developed panic attacks during sleep, accompanied by increase in plasma ACTH and cortisol levels.
McCann et al., 1997.	19 CTL 19 SP 11 PD	Panic symptoms following administration (0.6 mg/kg, i.v.) of pentagastrin.	Induction of panic (4 or more symptoms): SP = PD > CTL Induction of anxiety in social interaction task: SP = PD > CTL Induction of self-consciousness during social interaction: SP = PD > CTL Increase in heart rate and blood pressure: SP = PD > CTL Increase in ACTH and cortisol: SP = PD = CTL
van Vliet et al., 1997b.	7 CTL 7 SP	Panic symptoms following administration (0.6 mg/kg, i.v.) of pentagastrin.	Total score in panic symptom scale: SP > CTL

Note: CTL: control; SP: social phobia; PD: panic disorder.

Results (summarized in Table 6.2) have been variable. In some studies the panic-triggering threshold of social phobic subjects to CCK derivatives was similar to that of panic disorder patients (McCann et al., 1997). In others, social phobic participants did not differ from controls in number and duration of induced anxious complaints (van Vliet,

Westenberg, Slaap, den Boer, & Ho Pian, 1997b; Katzman, Koszycki, & Bradwejn, 2004). As in other such challenges, the anxious complaints reported by the subjects during the study were unlike their experiences during real threatening social situations.

Additionally, many studies (Katzman et al., 2004; Geraci et al., 2002) created a confound by including social phobic patients with a history of panic in their samples. Although the lack of differences between social phobic and panic disorder patients has been hopefully interpreted as evidence of shared neurobiology, such a view overlooks the many studies in which social patients reacted similarly to controls. Finally, it is not clear where CCK receptors for panic responses are located, but it is unlikely that pentagastrin enters the CNS to produce its effects. It has therefore been suggested that CCK receptors on the vagus nerve may convey information to the brain (Katzman et al., 2004). This interpretation ought to be viewed with caution since several studies have failed to show a link between social phobic complaints and vagal tone dysregulation (Coupland et al., 2003; Gerlach et al., 2003; Nahshoni, Gur, Marom, Levin, Weizman, & Hermesh, 2004).

d. CO_2-dependent "panic": Inhalation of 35% CO_2 and 65% O_2 tends to elicit panic reactions in panic disorder patients (van Den Hout & Griez, 1984), due perhaps to a false feeling of suffocation that in turn triggers an autonomic and anxiety reaction (Klein, 1993). Studies looking at hypersensitivity to CO_2 inhalation in social phobia, have consistently reported higher rates of panic in social phobic compared to normal subjects (Gorman et al., 1990; Papp, Klein, & Martinez, 1993; Caldirola et al., 1997). CO_2-induced panic was slightly higher in panic disorder than in social phobic subjects, although Caldirola et al. (1997) found no significant differences between the two. Besides demonstrating some possible differences between control, social phobic and panic disorder subjects, the neurobiological significance of these findings is not clear.

Measurements of Neuroendocrine Function

Hypothalamic-Pituitary Adrenal Axis (HPA)

Various stress-related conditions (e.g. psychosomatic; Ehlert & Straub, 1998), post-traumatic stress (Yehuda, 1998) and affective disorders (Gold & Chrousos, 2002; Parker, Schatzberg, & Lyons, 2003) have been associated with a dysregulation of the HPA axis. It is part of a system that controls the endocrine response to stressful situations.

The HPA has also been assessed in social phobia, most of the studies focusing on cortisol secretion. The results are summarized in Table 6.3.

Irrespective of whether hormonal levels were established from urinary, salivary or plasma samples (Uhde et al., 1994; Martel, Hayward, Lyons, Sanborn, Varady, & Schatzberg, 1999; Furlan, DeMartinis, Schweizer, Rickels, & Lucki, 2001; Condren, O'Neill, Ryan, Barrett, & Thakore, 2002b), all studies assessing basal cortisol production failed to observe a difference between control and social phobic participants, indicating that their basal HPA function is normal.

Several studies assessed HPA reactivity to social challenge with ambiguous results. While in Martel et al. (1999) no difference between patients and controls was found, the cortisol response of social phobic patients was enhanced following exposure to a social stress paradigm in Condren et al. (2002b). Similarly, Furlan et al. (2001) found that some of the social phobic participants had an exaggerated cortisol response. However, the proportion of such social phobic subjects was almost 4 times lower than that found among the control subjects. While it could be argued that this lack of response is an indication of HPA axis desensitization in chronic patients, no correlation could be established between the duration of social phobia and cortisol response (Furlan et al., 2001).

Hypothalamic-Pituitary Thyroid Axis

While patients with hyperthyroidism report experiences of anxiety, overall, patients with primary anxiety disorders do not have higher rates of thyroid dysfunction (Simon, Blacker, Korbly, Sharma, Worthington, Otto, & Pollack, 2002). Tancer, Stein, Gelernter, & Uhde (1990b) have specifically compared thyroid function in social phobic and control individuals finding no differences in plasma levels of T3, T4, free T4 and TSH. Similarly, Simon et al. (2002) examined thyroid histories and serum levels of thyroid hormones in 48 social phobic patients, confirming the absence of biochemical anomalies and reporting a prevalence of thyroid dysfunction among social phobic patients similar to that prevailing in the general population.

Neuroimaging Studies

Advances in magnetic resonance imaging (structural MRI; functional MRI and spectroscopy) and radionuclide imaging (Positron Emission Tomography – PET – and Single Photon Emission Computed

Table 6.3. *Measurements of neuroendocrine function*

Hypothalamic-Pituitary-Adrenal (HPA) Axis

Study	Subjects	Monitored variable	Results
Condren et al., 2002b.	15 CTL 15 SP	Plasma cortisol and ACTH levels following: Social challenge consisting of mental arithmetic and short memory tests done in public	Basal cortisol levels: SP = CTL Basal ACTH levels: SP = CTL Increase in cortisol following social challenge: SP > CTL Increase in ACTH following social challenge: SP = CTL
Furlan et al., 2001.	17 CTL 18 SP	Salivary cortisol levels following: Social challenge (text reading) Physical exercise (ergometry)	Responder versus non-responder ratio in social challenge: SP < CTL Increase in salivary cortisol of responders during text reading: SP > CTL Perceived anxiety during text reading: SP > CTL All individuals were responders in physical challenge Increase in salivary cortisol during ergometry: SP = CTL Increased anxiety during exercise: SP = CTL
Martel et al., 1999.	21 CTL 27 SP	Salivary cortisol levels: Daily pattern of secretion following Trier social stress test	Daily pattern of cortisol secretion: SP = CTL Cortisol levels during anticipation of social stress: SP = CTL Increase in cortisol during social stress: SP = CTL
Potts et al., 1991.	15 CTL 11 SP patients	24 hour cortisol secretion assessed by measuring urinary free cortisol	Free cortisol present in urine collected during 24 hs: SP = CTL

Note: CTL: control; SP: social phobia.

Tomography – SPECT) allow direct, non-invasive, measurement of activity in the living human brain. This technology has been recently applied to study structural and functional neural correlates of social phobia.

In a study of brain structure Potts, Davidson, Krishnan, & Doraiswamy (1994) found that social phobic individuals show a greater age-related decrease in putamen volume than do controls. In Tupler, Davidson, Smith, Lazeyras, Charles, & Krishnan (1997) the same research group, using spectroscopy, found that social phobic individuals displayed increased choline and myo-inositol levels in cortical and subcortical gray matter (including putamen). These changes in brain metabolites were interpreted as possible evidence of increased phospholipase C activity and altered 5-HT or DA receptor signaling. Though in keeping with previous findings of altered striatal DA function (see section on neurotransmitter systems), this interpretation remains speculative since myo-inositol levels are only partially regulated by monoaminergic receptors. As it stands, these studies await independent replication.

From a functional point of view, imaging studies of social phobia have explored changes in regional cerebral blood flow (rCBF) at rest or following stimulation with different types of activation paradigms (summarized in Table 6.4). The only report concerning resting metabolism found no differences in baseline blood flow between social phobic and normal individuals (Stein & Leslie, 1996).

A more common approach to study brain metabolism in social anxiety has been the use of activation paradigms such as face recognition, fear conditioning or simulation of public speaking. Regardless of the approach used, the majority of such studies have shown that rCBF changes within the cortico-limbic circuit (amygdala, hippocampus, insula, temporal lobe as well as anterior cingulate, medial, orbito, and dorsolateral prefrontal cortices) of social phobic patients are greater than those of controls. While, these structures are also activated in normal subjects in a state of anticipatory anxiety (e.g. fear conditioning: Benkelfat, Bradwejn, Meyer, Ellenbogen, Milot, Gjedde, & Evans, 1995; Chua, Krams, Toni, Passingham, & Dolan, 1999; Irwin, Davidson, Lowe, Mock, Sorenson, & Turski, 1996; Schneider, Grodd, Weiss, Klose, Mayer, Nagele, & Gur, 1997), levels of activation of the amygdala, hippocampus, and parahippocampal cortices were consistently higher in social phobic individuals (e.g. Straube, Kolassa, Glauer, Mentzel, & Miltner, 2004; Lorberbaum, Kose, Johnson, Arana, Sullivan, Hamner, Ballenger, Lydiard, Brodrick, Bohning, & George, 2004; Stein, Goldin, Sareen, Zorrilla, & Brown, 2002d; Veit, Flor, Erb, Hermann, Lotze, Grodd, & Birbaumer, 2002; Tillfors,

Table 6.4. *Neuroimaging studies*

Functional Studies

Study	Subjects	Monitored variable	Results
Resting State Studies			
Tupler et al., 1997.	10 CTL 19 SP treatment free	Brain metabolites (choline, creatinine, mio-inositol, N-acetyl aspartate) in cortical, subcortical gray matter and white matter measured by magnetic resonance spectroscopy (MRS).	Choline and mio-inositol in cortical gray matter SP > CTL. Mio-inositol in subcortical gray matter SP > CTL. Differences were unaffected by treatment with clonazepam.
	15 SP following clonazepam		White matter metabolites SP = CTL.
Stein & Leslie, 1996.	11 CTL 11 SP	Resting state rCBF in interior frontal cortex, anterior cingulate, caudate and thalamus by SPECT.	Cerebral blood flow in all regions of interest; SP did not differ from CTL.
Face Recognition Studies			
Straube et al., 2004.	10 CTL 10 SP	Recognition of angry or neutral facial expressions accompanied by evaluation of: *Task performance*: recognition of type of emotion present in stimulus. *Stimulus rating* for valence and arousal.	*Task performance:* Accuracy of emotion labeling. SP = CTL. *Valence:* SP and CTL groups similarly perceived angry faces more unpleasant than neutral faces. *Arousal:* Angry faces were more arousing than neutral ones: SP > CTL. *rCBF implicit task:* insula, amygdala, parahippocampal gyrus activated in SP not in CTL. Dorsomedial prefrontal cortex more activated in SP.

Study	Subjects	Monitored variable	Results
		rCBF during implicit task no reference to emotional contents of stimulus made, consisted in identifying a sketch or a photograph. *rCBF during explicit task* recognition of emotional contents of stimulus, fMRI study.	*rCBF explicit task:* Dorsomedial prefrontal cortex, insula more activated in SP than CTL. No difference in other regions affected by implicit task.
Stein et al., 2002.	15 CTL 15 SP	Recognition of facial expressions depicting distinct emotional states: negative (angry, contemptuous), positive (accepting) and neutral accompanied by evaluation of: *Task performance:* recognition of type of emotion present in stimulus. *rCBF during recognition of different face expressions,* fMRI study	*Task performance:* Accuracy of emotion labeling. SP = CTL. *rCBF, contrast between accepting and negative expresssions:* activation in amygdala, hippocampus, parahippocampal gyrus, medial temporal lobe, dorsomedial prefrontal cortex, and orbitofrontal cortex SP > CTL. No group differences observed for neutral expressions.
Birbaumer et al., 1998.	5 CTL 7 SP	*Stimulus rating for:* valence, arousal and intensity. *rCBF measured in:* thalamus and amygdala, following presentation of two different type of stimuli: neutral face or aversive odor. fMRI study.	*Subjective rating of stimuli:* valence, arousal, and intensity GSP = CTL. *rCBF in thalamus:* activation with both types of stimuli, GSP = CTL. *rCBF in amygdala:* activation to aversive odor GSP = CTL, activation to neutral faces GSP > CTL.

Table 6.4. (*cont.*)

Study	Subjects	Monitored variable	Results
Emotional Conditioning Studies			
Veit et al., 2002.	4 CTL 4 SP	Classical aversive conditioning paradigm: *Conditioned stimulus (CS)*: face with or without moustache. *Unconditioned stimulus (UCS)*: painful pressure. *Presentation of stimuli*: face no moustache followed by non painful pressure, face with moustache followed by painful pressure. *rCBF evaluated during*: habituation, acquisition and extinction of conditioned response, fMRI study.	*rCBF during habituation*: activation of orbitofrontal cortex, dorsomedial prefrontal cortex and amygdala to both faces SP > CTL. *rCBF during acquisition and extinction*: activation of orbitofrontal cortex, dorsomedial prefrontal cortex, amygdala, insula and anterior cingulate cortex SP > CTL.
Schneider et al., 1999.	12 CTL 12 SP 6 SP: CBT	Classical aversive conditioning paradigm: *Conditioned stimulus (CS)*: neutral face *Unconditioned stimulus (UCS)*: aversive odor. *Stimulus rating for*: valence and arousal. *rCBF evaluated during*: habituation and acquisition of conditioned response, fMRI study.	*Subjective rating of CS and UCS*: SP = CTL. Conditioning effect more pronounced in SP than CTL. *rCBF during habituation*: Following CS, no change: SP = CTL. Following UCS, activation of amygdala, thalamus, dorsolateral prefrontal cortex anterior cingulate, orbito frontal cortex, occipitalcortex: SP = CTL. *rCBF during acquisition*: Amygdala and hippocampus inactivated in CTL but activated in SP.

Study	Subjects	Monitored variable	Results
Anxiety Provocation Paradigms: Public Speaking			
Lorberbaum et al., 2004.	6 CTL 8 SP	Anxiety rating and rCBF measurements: at rest during anticipation of public speaking fMRI study.	*Anxiety rating at rest*: SP > CTL. *Anxiety rating during anticipation*: SP > CTL. Contrast between rest and anticipation, rCBF: Amygdala, hippocampus, insula, temporal lobe activated in SP not CTL. Prefrontal cortex activated in CTL but inactivated in SP.
van Ameringen et al., 2004a.	6 SP	Assessment of: Perceived anxiety and physical symptoms of arousal Similarity between spontaneous and provoked symptoms rCBF; PET during exposure to public speaking under scrutiny or during baseline (watch someone else give the speech). PET study.	Exposure to public speaking induced: SP-like emotional response and reduction in CBF in ventro-medial frontal cortex.
Furmark et al., 2002	6 SP: no treatment 6 SP: citalopram 6 SP: CBT	Assessment of public-speaking and social anxiety measurements before, immediately after, and one year after different treatments. Assessment of rCBF during exposure to public speaking after having completed treatment. PET study.	After nine weeks of treatment: Both treatment groups improved public-speaking and social anxiety measurements. No change for non-treated. Both treatment groups showed attenuated activation of amygdala, hippocampus, anterior and medial temporal cortex as compared to non-treated patients. Favorable outcome one year after end of treatment was correlated with degree of attenuation of rCBF responses.

Table 6.4. (*cont.*)

Study	Subjects	Monitored variable	Results
Tillfors et al., 2002.	18 SP	Comparison of perceived SP, heart rate and rCBF (PET) before exposure to public performance (n = 9) and before speaking alone (n = 9). PET study.	Those anticipating to speak in public had: Higher perceived anxiety and heart rate. Enhanced CBF in amygdala, hippocampus, inferior temporal cortex, and dorsolateral prefrontal cortex. Reduced CBF in temporal pole as compared to the group of subjects who knew they would speak by themselves.
Tillfors et al., 2001b.	6 CTL 18 SP	Perceived anxiety, heart rate and rCBF during public speaking or speaking alone. PET study.	Public speaking was associated with: Increase in heart rate SP > CTL Increase in perceived anxiety SP > CTL Increase in CBF in the amygdala SP > CTL Reduced CBF to orbitofrontal cortex, insula, and temporal pole in SP patients but increased perfusion in CTL group. Increased perfusion of perirhinal and retrosplenial cortices in CTL but not in SP participants.

Note: CTL: control; SP: social phobia; CBT: cognitive–behavior therapy.

Furmark, Marteinsdottir, Fischer, Pissiota, Langstrom, & Fredrikson, 2001b).

Activity changes in the lateral paralimbic belt (insula, temporal pole, orbitofrontal cortex), medial and dorsolateral prefrontal cortices, have also been reported, but results across studies were inconsistent, showing both increases and/or decreases in the same structure. While some studies highlighted hyperactivity of fronto-temporal cortical regions (Straube et al., 2004; Stein et al., 2002d; Veit et al., 2002) others reported hypofunction (Loberbaum et al., 2004; van Ameringen, Mancini, Szechtman, Nahmias, Oakman, Hall, Pipe, & Farvolden, 2004a; Tillfors et al., 2001b).

Electrophysiological studies have not helped in resolving the above seeming contradictions, since available information lends support to both sets of observations. On the one hand, social phobic participants have been shown to display temporal and prefrontal EEG activation before public speaking (Davidson et al., 2000) consistent with metabolic hyperactivity in the region. On the other hand, verbal learning difficulties and anomalies in intensity and latency of evoked potentials (electric activity in the brain; Sachs, Anderer, Margreiter, Semlitsch, Saletu, & Katschnig, 2004), are in keeping with cortical hypoactivity (i.e. reduced cerebral flow to the frontal lobe).

Taken as whole, neuroimaging findings have been interpreted as characterizing social phobia with a predominantly subcortical/automatic pattern of emotion processing with insufficient cortical control (Tillfors, 2004). This interpretation raises a number of difficulties. Firstly, the experiments do not allow us to tell whether the enhanced amygdala activity is a consequence of an inadequate cortical control, or whether it reflects a primary hyperactivity of this subcortical structure with the consequent insufficiency of an otherwise normal cortical function? Secondly, hyperactive amygdala and cortical dysfunction have been observed in other anxiety disorders including panic (Eren, Tukel, Polat, Karaman, & Unal, 2003), generalized anxiety disorder (Bremner, 2004; Thomas, Drevets, Dahl, Ryan, Birmaher, Eccard, Axelson, Whalen, & Casey, 2001) and post-traumatic stress disorder (Shin, Wright, Cannistraro, Wedig, McMullin, Martis, Macklin, Lasko, Cavanagh, Krangel, Orr, Pitman, Whalen, & Rauch, 2005; Liberzon & Phan, 2003). This, if anything, suggests that amygdala hyperactivity is a common thread of fear states. The neurobiological substrate specific to social phobia, if such occurs, remains to be determined first conceptually and then experimentally.

Pharmacological Treatments and the Neurobiology of Social phobia

The demonstrated efficacy of various pharmacological compounds reducing distress and avoidance has been on occasion invoked as evidence for a neurobiological mechanism underlying – as it were – social phobia. For instance, Nutt, Bell, & Malizia (1998, p. 7) have expressed the opinion that "the clinical effectiveness of SSRIs in the treatment of social anxiety disorder indicates that serotonin (5-HT) has a role in the etiology of social anxiety disorder." Even if serotonin might play such a role, response to treatment cannot be regarded as providing evidence for it as it must be remembered that social phobic patients also respond to other classes of medication, to alcohol as well as various psychological treatments in like manner (see overview of treatment in chapter 10).

Overall, 4 different classes of pharmaceutical agents with different molecular targets have been extensively evaluated for their anxiety-reducing properties in the treatment of social phobia. These are:

I. Monoamine oxidase inhibitors (MAOI); these block the metabolism of the catecholamines and serotonin through inactivation of their catabolic enzyme: monoamine oxidase. A refinement within the same class is the reversible inhibitors of monoamine oxidase (RIMAs). Both target the catabolic enzyme: while the MAOIs bind permanently, the RIMAs do so reversibly. Practically, this broadens the restrictive diet required under the MAOIs. A typical use for this type of medication (e.g. moclobemide) is for the treatment of depression.

II. Selective serotonin reuptake inhibitors (SSRIs); these inhibit the transport of serotonin back into the neuron where it is subsequently stored, thus increasing the synaptic concentration of this neurotransmitter. Today this type of medication is considered first-choice treatment for depression and most of the anxiety disorders.

III. Other regulators of monoaminergic synaptic activity (e.g. buspirone). This type of medication is used occasionally as an anxiolytic; however olanzapine is primarily used as an antipsychotic.

IV. Suppressants of neural excitability that regulate gabaergic transmission:

   a. agonists of aminobutyric acid (GABA) receptors (e.g. benzodiazepines). This type of medication is commonly used as a treatment of anxiety and insomnia.

   b. stimulators of GABA release (e.g. gabapentin). This type of medication is used as an anti-convulsant and more recently as a mood stabilizer.

Despite their distinct molecular targets, most pharmacological treatments are of equivalent efficacy, and result – in the short-term and/or as long as the treatment lasts – in a similar degree of improvement. Additionally, psychological therapies result in rather similar outcome in the short run while maintaining gains subsequently, after treatment has stopped. Thus, the generalized decrease in anxiety observed as a result of a diversity of pharmacological and psychological treatments cannot be seen as providing evidence for the involvement of any one of the putative processes invoked by each theoretical approach. Furthermore, placebo also has not negligible therapeutic effects in social phobia. For example in two out of four controlled studies of moclobemide, its effects were equivalent to those of placebo.

In summary, the inference of malfunctioning neurobiological processes allegedly implicated in social phobia from pharmacological treatments, is unwarranted. The unspoken assumption that the pharmacological agent directly affects a putative biological substrate of social phobia is highly speculative, since the therapeutic response measured might be in all likelihood only a facet of a wider underlying neurobiological activity. On current evidence, it is probable that pharmacological treatment results in functional improvement by dampening the activity of the systems involved in emotional regulation and therefore without actually influencing any putative underlying neurobiological defect. This is quite likely to be the case in social phobia since pharmacological agents with very different pharmacological profiles have been shown to be equipotent in reducing anxious distress.

Conclusions

In the face of sustained efforts yielding a large body of research, the potential neurobiological malfunctioning underpinning social phobia has remained elusive. Overall, research has been exploratory in nature and its results inconclusive at best. With the possible exception of some functional imaging findings (Straube et al., 2004; Lorberbaum et al., 2004; Stein et al., 2002d; Veit et al., 2002; Tillfors et al., 2001b), inhalation of 35% CO_2 (Gorman et al., 1990; Papp et al., 1993; Caldirola et al., 1997) and pentagastrin-induced panic (McCann et al., 1997; van Vliet et al., 1997b), no other reports highlighting significant differences from normal subjects have withstood replication. Moreover, the implications of the observed differences and their integration into a comprehensive theoretical framework of the neurobiology of social phobia are not obvious.

Overall, and on current evidence, we reach the conclusion that no major structural, neurochemical or endocrine abnormalities are in evidence in social phobia as such. This conclusion is in agreement with earlier reviews (Tancer et al., 1995; Nickell & Uhde, 1995). It is also consistent with the normal biological functioning of social phobic individuals in evidence in various areas (e.g. general psycho-physiological responding: see chapter 5; sleep: see Papadimitriu & Linkowski, 2005).

Functional neuroimaging studies have repeatedly shown that the activation of the amygdala is stronger in social phobic than in normal individuals. Whether this is an exacerbation of the normal fear response − as is most likely − or evidence of a qualitative difference, remains to a certain extent an open question. In the absence of any other abnormality, however, a structural defect or a malfunctioning of the brain seems highly implausible.

To sum up, the literature on the neurobiology of social phobia has on the whole failed to highlight systematic, specific abnormalities in social phobic individuals. This might be the outcome of both a general absence of hypotheses to be tested as well as the types of experimental designs in use. Of the two, the lack of a neurobiological theory of social phobia is in our view the main liability; this dictates to a large extent the rather haphazard quest for some abnormality characteristic of the current investigations in the area. Ultimately, the results of this survey convey the likelihood that there is in fact no specific neurobiology of social phobia. An intense reactivity of the "fear-network" is after all within normal range; it is hardly specific to social phobia (see Gorman et al., 2000). Such a state of over-excitement of the brain would be associated with social phobia not specifically, but indirectly − as an instance of fearfulness. An intensified brain activity is involved in and sustains the active process of fearing of the whole living organism in the face of threat, be it phobic or not.

Genetic Transmission of Social Phobia

In principle, the most satisfactory demonstration of the hereditary nature of social phobia would have been the identification of a gene controlling it. All other methods are by contrast speculative estimates. These indirect approaches to show genetic heritability attempt first to demonstrate that social phobia runs in families. This is a precondition for a further search for supporting evidence in favor of genetic inheritance. As usual in scientific practice, it has to be done while simultaneously controlling for rival explanations, such as that family agglomeration is due to environmental processes.

Does Social Phobia Run in Families?

In the first of such attempts, Reich & Yates (1988) compared relatives of social phobic (n = 76), panic disorder (n = 476) and normal participants (n = 46). The prevalence of social phobia among relatives of social phobic participants was 6.6% and significantly higher than the rate found in the panic disorder group (0.4%). There were 2.2% of relatives who met criteria for social phobia in the normal group; although lower, it was not significantly different from that found in the social phobia group. The highest prevalence of disorder among relatives in the social phobia group, however, was major depression (13.2%).

In a similar study carried out in Pisa (Italy), Perugi et al. (1990) found no significant difference in the prevalence of social phobia in the first-degree relatives of three groups of probands (recruited from an outpatient clinic): primary social phobia, agoraphobia with secondary social phobia and agoraphobia/panic disorder (DSM-III). Prevalence rates were: 4%, 0% and 2.4% respectively.

In both studies then, having a relative with social phobia did not necessarily put one at a greater risk of it.

In Fyer et al. (1993) first-degree relatives (n = 83) of 30 social phobic probands (without other lifetime anxiety disorders) and 77 normal controls (n = 231) were directly interviewed by means of a semi-structured interview (SADS-LA) and lifetime diagnoses established.

Relatives of the social phobic participants had significantly greater rates of social phobia (16%) than those of the normal group (5%). The relative risk (RR) was established at 3.1. The presence of social fears without "impairment or distress" (i.e. that do not meet a necessary criterion for social phobia), however, were "neither familial nor associated with an increased familial risk for social phobia" (p. 289).

The social phobia group was associated with a significantly higher propensity towards major depression (27% vs. 15%) and drug abuse (5% vs. 2%) among its relatives.

In a further analysis of the above study, Manuzza et al. (1995b) found a greater family aggregation among probands of social phobia of the generalized subtype (16%) than among the relatives of the specific (6%) and normal (6%) participants.

A test of the degree of specificity of the family aggregation of all types of phobia was performed by Fyer et al. (1995). First-degree relatives of panic/agoraphobic (131 relatives; 49 probands), social (105; 39) and simple phobic (49; 15), and normal controls (231; 77) were interviewed and incidence of lifetime diagnosis of types of phobia established blindly.

Incidence of social phobia among the relatives of social phobic probands were 15% compared with 10% for those of simple phobic, 8% for panic with agoraphobia and 6% in those of normal subjects. The magnitude of the risk for a relative of a social phobic proband was 2.4.

Typically then, "relatives of each of the three phobic disorders proband groups had higher rates of the proband's disorder than did relatives of the other phobia probands" (Fyer et al., 1995, p. 569). A tendency towards specific agglomeration, however, did not imply homogeneity within each proband group.

Stein et al. (1998a) replicated Manuzza et al.'s (1995a) focus on generalized social phobia (n = 23) probands who designated 106 relatives. 24 normal controls identified 74 relatives. Prevalence among relatives was subdivided into discrete (performance), nongeneralized (limited interactional) and generalized subtypes. Whereas no significant differences were found in prevalence of the discrete (14.2% vs. 14.9%) and nongeneralized subtypes (22.6% vs. 17.6% among the relatives of the social phobic and normal probands, they were observed in relation with the generalized subtype (26.4% vs. 2.7%). This yielded an RR = 9.7 implying that being a member of a family with a generalized social phobic (in this study) increased one's risk of generalized social phobia about 10 times. Conversely, there was also a greater risk of avoidant personality disorder (19.8% vs. 0%) emphasizing the close resemblance between the two.

As no theoretical rationale has been offered to account for the expectation of the above distinction (between the prevalence of like-morbidity among the first-degree relatives of the two subtypes of social phobia) at the outset, the meaning of the findings is difficult to interpret. Incidentally, it is the only empirical support available for the distinction between specific and generalized social phobias.

In an attempt to test whether there is anything specific in the family history of social phobic individuals (among others), Fyer et al. (1995) evaluated 105 first-degree relatives of 39 social phobic, 49 first-degree relatives of 15 simple phobic and 131 first-degree relatives of 49 agoraphobic participants. 77 controls with 231 first-degree relatives were also recruited. The designation was established from multiple sources of information in a discussion ("best-estimate diagnosis").

In terms of prevalence, 15% of the relatives of social phobic patients fulfilled criteria for social phobia, against 10% among relatives of simple phobic patients, 8% in relatives of panic with agoraphobia and 6% in those of control subjects. The differences in prevalence rates between relatives of social phobic compared with control subjects were statistically significant.

When prevalence of social phobia was calculated on the basis of percentage of "families affected," (i.e. at least one relative corresponding to the criteria) it was 31% of the families of social phobic, 20% both of the families of agoraphobics and simple phobic and 19% of the families of normal control participants.

As can be seen from the prevalence rates, relatives of social phobic individuals carried twice the risk (RR = 2.4, p < 0.05) for a social phobia than those of normal controls. This was not true of the relatives of the other phobic participants compared with those of controls, hence the conclusion that the results "indicate specific but moderate familial aggregation" (1995, p. 571) of each phobic disorder.

While a significant difference in the risk of meeting criteria for social phobia between the relatives of social phobic and agoraphobic patients (RR = 2.3) was detected, none was observed when relatives of social phobic and simple phobic subjects were compared.

By contrast, a study from Germany (Bandelow et al., 2004) comparing 50 social phobic to 120 normal participants, found that agglomeration of social phobia among first-degree relatives although significant (8% vs. 0%) was the smallest. Relatives meeting criteria for generalized disorder (58% vs. 2.5%) or depression (56% vs. 12%), for example, were more prevalent by far.

All told, although the conclusion of specificity of moderate family aggregation seems justified statistically, it is not clear how meaningful it is. Given the wide confidence intervals (95%) and the rather low RRs (2.3−2.4), the predictability of social phobia in relatives of social phobic patients is muted. Furthermore, although statistically significant, in absolute terms the rates were low and the greatest association was typically with depression − not social phobia. The contrary results reported by Bandelow et al. (2004) give further pause.

High-Risk Children

The question of family agglomeration was tested rather more directly with high-risk children in an uncontrolled study by Mancini et al. (1996). 26 (of 36 contacted) families of social phobic patients had between them 47 children between 12 and 18 years of age. Of these

23 (49%), met (lifetime) criteria for an anxiety disorder; 11 (23%) that of social phobia. The significance of the latter finding is not clear, as there was no contrast group in the design. However that may be, the rate exceeds the prevalence in the general population of similar age (cf. Anderson, Williams, McGee, & Silva, 1987; Kashani & Orvaschel, 1988).

In a controlled study (Beidel & Turner, 1997) prevalence of psychopathology among children (age range 7−12) of 4 groups of parents: normal controls (n = 48), an anxiety disorder (n = 28, of which 4 of social phobia), depression (n = 24) and mixed anxiety/depression (n = 29) were studied.

Contrary to what might have been expected, the only group to have no social phobic children was that of the anxious parents. Rates of social phobia were established as follows: 2% − control, 13% − depression and 7% − mixed anxiety/depression. This more direct and probing test − albeit lacking a group of social phobic parents − puts somewhat in doubt the family agglomeration of social phobia suggested in the earlier studies framed by the rather more ambiguous and ill-identified notion of first-degree relatives.

In summary, some of the above reviewed studies suggest that social phobia − only when considered over the lifespan − might run to a certain extent in families (defined somewhat ambiguously as first-degree relatives). The prevalence of social phobia in them is at any rate significantly higher than the morbidity in the families of normal individuals: 2.2%, 5%, 6%, and 2.7% for generalized and 14% for discrete social phobia in Stein et al. (1998a). With the exception of the latter, these prevalence rates are in line with the known range of estimates of prevalence of social phobia within the general population in the USA.

Studies looking either at relatives in general, or as in Beidel et al. (1997) specifically at children of parents with anxiety disorders, however, contradict the above conclusion.

The highest estimate puts over a quarter of family members at risk but the actual rates varied greatly: 6.6%, 15%, 16%, and 26.4%. This fact − if anything − would tend to question all 4 rather than corroborate any as the true estimate.

It is methodologically intriguing that the lowest rate was reported in a study using the widest definition of "family members" and an all-inclusive definition of social phobia, while the highest was reported in a study of first-degree relatives while attending only to the generalized subtype of social phobia.

Furthermore, samples were small (e.g. 23 social phobic subjects in Stein et al., 1998a) and one wonders to what extent the social phobic subjects in these studies are representative, as they were drawn from units recruiting patients for the pharmacological treatment of social phobia (e.g. Reich & Yates, 1988; Fyer et al., 1993) and may therefore have been self-selected.

Genes vs. Environment

While it might be tempting to see genetic factors at work in the results reviewed above (e.g. Gelder, Gath, Mayou, & Cowen, 1996, p. 172), nothing much may be concluded as yet about such inheritance, as members of a family not only share genes, but also share and have a hand in creating the family environment as well, as they also do – but to a lesser extent – the world outside it.

One way around this difficulty would be to differentiate family members according to their genetic similarity or closeness and to demonstrate that liability to social phobia increases with genetic likeness.

An additional scientific constraint when wishing to highlight heritability is somehow contriving to keep the influence of environment and experience from confounding the results. Can this be done?

There are two schools of thought on the matter. One, a minority view (e.g. Rose, Kamin, & Lewontin, 1984) would argue that the social phobic pattern of conduct is an ongoing process that has been fusing (and is continuing to do so) certain genetically determined characteristics with inputs from the environment. As a result of that historic process – still operative in the present – linking interactively genetic capabilities and environmental influences, the two are inextricably intertwined and would prove as impossible to disentangle, as, say, the ingredients of a cake and the ambient heat. All attempts to separate the constituent elements of an interactive process at a particular point in time are bound to fail to convince and, in the final analysis, futile.

The second, by far the received point of view at this time (e.g. Plomin, DeFries, & McClearn, 1990; Dawkins, 1976), closely allied with the disease model, regards certain (all??) abnormalities as fixed in the gene – manifesting themselves according to a rather implacable logic and to which the environment serves at most as backdrop or as evoking opportunity. As such, the effects of both factors are assumed to be rather independent of each other and therefore, in principle, quantifiable and amenable to being parceled out according to certain statistical models resting on numerous assumptions (e.g. Kendler, Neale, Kessler, Heath, & Eaves, 1992).

Demonstration of Genetic Transmission

In principle, had we been able to assume that the social phobic pattern of conduct is under complete genetic control, the most powerful and convincing way to demonstrate it would be to identify the genetic markers that correlate perfectly with the presence of social phobia and then, armed with this knowledge, predict which member(s) of a family would develop the disorder in adolescence or young adulthood.

As the above assumption would be in all likelihood unwarranted and, furthermore, as the relevant technical knowledge is lacking (the steps entailed are discussed in Rutter & Plomin, p. 215), such demonstrations are, for the time being at least, beyond our reach.

What additional (lesser) kind of evidence could be invoked to help to settle the matter? Table 6.5 provides a summary of the main approaches.

Twin Studies

Four twin studies have been reported; all compared concordance rates of social phobia between monozygotic (MZ) and same-sex dizygotic (DZ) twins.

The rationale of this particular paradigm rests on the fact that the MZ twins are genetically identical whereas the DZ twins − like other siblings − share (on average) 50% of their genes.

The fact that DZ twins are only half as similar as the MZ twins would imply that the resemblance of any trait in the MZ twins ought to be far greater than in the DZ twins. The comparisons typically are restricted to same-sex DZ twins since MZ are all of the same sex.

Table 6.5. *Approaches to the study of genetic transmission and respective quality of evidence*

Approach	Design	Quality of evidence
Study of twins	Monozygotic (MZ) vs. dizygotic (DZ) same-sex twins	Inconclusive
	Concordance rates for MZ twins reared apart	Impressive but impractical
Genetic marker studies	Association of a genetic marker with social phobia	Impressive
	Presence of marker in childhood successfully predicts social phobia in adulthood	Conclusive

The degree of heritability, in theory, might be estimated from the magnitude of the difference between the MZ and the DZ correlation (see Plomin et al., 1990, pp. 207–253).

Let us now turn from theory to evidence. The first two studies use countrywide samples of patients treated in psychiatric institutions. Torgerson's (1983) study involved a sample of adult same-sex twins treated for neurotic disorders in a psychiatric institution in Norway. A structured interview and a developmental history were used as the basis for establishing a lifetime (i.e. not current) DSM-III diagnosis. Zygosity was determined by blood analysis of 10 genetic markers (in three quarters of the sample) and by questionnaire (all subjects).

85 (out of 318) met criteria for various anxiety disorders; 1 pair of identical (MZ) twins and 3 pairs of fraternal (DZ) twins met criteria for social phobia. The analysis (following the "proband concordance-wise method" whereby the number of twins both satisfying criteria for social phobia is divided by the total number of pairs – also used in all other studies) found that no MZ pairs had the same anxiety disorder and that no twin pairs were concordant for social phobia.

In a similar study from Norway, (Skre, Onstad, Torgersen, Lygren, & Kringlen, 1993), subjects were recruited from the same source (i.e. mostly psychiatric inpatients). In addition to the sample of probands with anxiety disorders, there was also a contrast group of probands with other conditions (e.g. mood and substance abuse disorders). Lifetime diagnoses (DSM-III-R) were determined following a structured interview and zygosity by means of a questionnaire with the assessors aware of who the subjects were.

As to social phobia, there were 2 identical (MZ) pairs of twins compared to 4 fraternal (DZ) pairs of twins among the anxiety disorders probands in comparison to no MZ and 3 DZ pairs of twins in the comparison group. No significant difference was found between the 2 sets of twins and similar prevalence of social phobia was found in anxiety and comparison co-twins. The authors' conclusion that "the predisposition to social phobia is caused by environmental experiences" (1993, p. 91) illustrates a dichotomy pervading much of the theorizing in this area – if the cause is not to be found in the genes, it must reside in the environment.

Studies drawing on twin registries from the general population established for research purposes (i.e. subjects who are not individuals seeking help) end this survey. Such studies are of great importance as they allow a far greater scope for drawing general conclusions.

The first (Andrews, Stewart, Morris-Yates, Holt, & Henderson, 1990) from Sydney, interviewed 462 pairs. Lifetime diagnosis (DSM-III) was established by means of a structured interview while zygosity was determined by questionnaire. The final sample included the following 5 groups of twins: 104 MZ-female, 82 MZ-male, 86 DZ-f, 71DZ-m and 103 DZ-opposite sexes. This is another strength of this exemplary study, as typically – because of the need to compare same-sex twins – only women or men would be included (see next study). The results showed that MZ twin-pairs were no more concordant than the DZ pairs for either social phobia or, for that matter, any other category of anxiety disorders.

In the second study (Kendler et al., 1992) from Virginia (USA), of 2,163 female twins, 654 met DSM-III-R criteria for phobias. The probandwise concordance for social phobia was 24% for MZ twins compared with 15% for DZ; the concordance for a lifetime diagnosis was identical in both sets of twins – 12%. The probandwise concordance rates, although different, were not significantly so for either social or any other phobia.

In a subsequent and complex statistical analysis, heritability and environmental influences were partitioned off (see Brown, 1996, p. 393 for a critical assessment of this procedure). Heritability for social phobia was estimated at 31%; 68% was put down to environmental influences of a "traumatic conditioning" rather than that of a "social learning" (i.e. in the family environment) kind.

Genetic contributions (i.e. liability) were then separated into specific (i.e. social phobia alone) and common (i.e. any phobia). Specific genetic factors were estimated to contribute 21% of the variation in liability to social phobia and the common factors 10%.

The latter results (and theoretical logic) are contradicted by Fyer et al. (1995) who found a rather moderate but specific agglomeration of social phobia in families of social phobic probands, but without an increased liability for other types of phobia. Behind the dazzling statistical apparatus deployed in this oft-quoted aspect of the study, various perplexing features may be found.

First, it is not clear what evidence supports the conclusions concerning the environment. Neither the individual and family environment – keys variables in the study – are given an operational definition, nor are the corresponding measurements that quantify them described. That factors of such complexity are actually validly summarized by a single valuation (a score) needs to be demonstrated (see Medawar, 1977). The failure to provide a description of the conception guiding the measurement of the environment, as well as some proof of the validity of the measuring instruments in use, is a serious flaw limiting the drawing of any conclusions from this study.

Second, dichotomies are created (e.g. traumatic conditioning vs. social learning, heredity vs. environment), that rely on an a priori assumption of the independence of each factor. Whether such assumptions are warranted is doubtful. For, "this procedure is only satisfactory if there is no gene-environment interaction" (Brown, 1996, p. 393). Even if the case for interaction is not ironclad, it is the likelier assumption for humans (see Mayr, 1974 on "open" vs. "closed" genetic programs). The notion of independence of genes and environment in the case of social phobia seems implausible in the extreme and needs – if one wishes to assume it – to be at the very least systematically defended. These aspects of the results, however, are presented as naturalistic observations rather than theory-driven.

Third, an alternative statistical model resting on quite different assumptions fits the results just as well (p. 280) but was little made of.

Fourth, the meaning of the very notion of heritability and consequently the figure attached to it remain shrouded in obscurity.

Fifth, the relationship of the degree of heritability (whatever it may mean) to the finding that the prevalence rates of social phobia are not significantly different in both groups of twins, is of the greatest theoretical importance, and yet was not explicitly discussed in the paper. Moreover, it is not entirely clear what is the value of estimating a somewhat abstract notion of heritability, while the rather similar rates of morbidity in the two groups of twins do not support the hypothesis of a greater liability for social phobia due to genetic influences.

The case that the somewhat recondite statistical approach, although not as intuitively graspable as is the relatively simple comparison of the degree to which MZ and DZ twins share the disorder, affords greater or different insights, has not been made.

Finally, the general notion of heritability itself surely refers to an abstract underlying liability to a certain and unspecified behavioral disposition (trait); it is not necessarily to the disorder as such.

It is therefore all the more important to remember in interpreting the results that these calculations do not highlight universal characteristics of the trait in question, because inheritance is not fixed. Rather, it says something about the specific population investigated under a very specific set of circumstances. If these were to change, so would the result.

To paraphrase Rutter & Plomin (1997, p. 209–210), the true meaning of heritability is that the estimate indicates how much of the individual liability to a social phobic trait (whatever this might be) in a particular population at a particular time, is due to genetic influences. Crucially, if circumstances change, so will the heritability.

Genetic Marker Studies

Whereas the previous studies are inconclusive at best, a more impressive demonstration of the possibly hereditary nature of a disorder would be correlating a genetic marker with the presence of social phobia. For such a type of investigation to be meaningful (i.e. driven by a clear hypothesis), prior knowledge of the neurobiology of the disorder as well as a familial pattern of transmission is necessary. As we have seen earlier, neither is available in social phobia.

Nevertheless, two different exploratory approaches have been used in order to identify potential genes for social phobia: linkage analysis and association studies (summarized in Table 6.6).

Close proximity of genes on a chromosome ensures that they are passed on together from generation to generation. This fact is exploited by "linkage analysis" so as to study the association between the presence of a given phenotype – in our case social phobia – and a marker gene whose location on a given chromosome is accurately known.

Technically, the term "linkage" refers to alleles (forms of a gene) from two different loci (locations of the gene in the chromosome) passed on as a single unit from parent to child. Consequently, genetic linkage requires family studies. Thus, if the frequency with which the association between a given marker and social phobia manifest in family members is higher than what would have been expected from both genes being located in completely different chromosomes, one could conclude that it is likely that the gene for the phenotype (i.e. social phobia) is in close proximity to the marker.

In an elegant study using this method, Gelernter, Page, Stein, & Woods (2004) highlighted evidence linking social phobia to markers in chromosome 16. That would imply that if social phobia is genetically determined, a contributing gene (for the time being unknown) is located in this chromosome.

Other studies of a similar nature have assessed linkage between social phobia and the DA transporter, the 5-HT transporter or different subtypes of monoaminergic receptors, all yielding negative results (Kennedy, Neves-Pereira, King, Lizak, Basile, Chartier, & Stein, 2001; Stein, Chartier, Kozak, King, & Kennedy, 1998c).

The second approach towards identifying potential genes for social phobia compares the incidence of social phobia in people with distinct

Table 6.6. *Studies of genetic transmission*

Study	Subjects	Monitored variable	Results
Linkage Studies			
Gelernter et al., 2004.	17 families each with at least 3 members with an anxiety disorder (Total of 163 subjects)	Genome-wide linkage scan using 422 markers to identify genetic locations harboring susceptibility loci for social phobia	Evidence of suggestive linkage to social phobia for chromosome 16 markers. Gene encoding the NE transporter maps to this region.
Kennedy et al., 2001.	39 SP, 27 PD and corresponding family members (Total of 122 subjects)	Linkage of SP or PD to DA system genes: DA transporter, D2; D3 and D4 receptor genes.	Linkage was excluded for all genes in the three conditions.
Stein et al., 1998c.	17 SP and corresponding family members (Total of 76 subjects)	SP linkage to 5-HT2A receptor gene SP linkage to 5-HT transporter gene	Linkage was excluded for 5-HT2A and 5-HT transporter genes. Power analysis excluded the possibility that negative results were due to inadequate statistical power.
Association Studies			
Samochowiec et al., 2004.	202 CTL, 101 anxiety disorders	Association between specific polymorphisms for the the 5-HT transporter gene, the MAO-A gene and COMT gene	No differences between patients and controls in allele frequency for 5-HT transporter and COMT gene polymorphism. Frequency of long MAO-A alleles (more than 3 repeats) was higher in females with panic and generalized anxiety disorders, but not social phobia.

Table 6.6. (*cont.*)

Study	Subjects	Monitored variable	Results
Furmark et al., 2004.	18 SP	Presence of short or long alleles in promoter region of 5-HT transporter gene	Individuals with one or two copies of short alleles exhibited increased levels of anxiety-related traits, state anxiety and enhanced right amygdala response to anxiety provocation than individuals homozygous for long alleles.

Note: CTL: control; SP: social phobia; PD: panic disorder.

forms of a candidate gene thought to have the potential to contribute to it. This allows establishing an association between social phobia and the presence of a specific allele. The 5-HT transporter, for example, is encoded by a polymorphic gene that has a short and a long allele (Heils, Teufel, Petri, Stober, Riederer, Bengel, & Lesch, 1996; Lesch, Bengel, Heils, Sabol, Greenberg, Petri, Benjamin, Muller, Hamer, & Murphy, 1996). The presence of the short allele is associated with reduced transporter expression and 5-HT uptake (Lesch et al., 1996). Individuals in the general population with a short polymorphism for the 5-HT transporter gene display higher anxiety measures than those with long forms of the gene (Melke, Landen, Baghei, Rosmond, Holm, Bjorntorp, Westberg, Hellstrand, & Eriksson, 2001). This observation has prompted several studies evaluating the association between the short allele and anxiety disorders such as panic disorder (Ishiguro, Arinam, Yamada, Otsuka, Toru, & Shibuya, 1997) and social phobia (Samochowiec, Hajduk, Samochowiec, Horodnicki, Stepien, Grzywacz, & Kucharska-Mazur, 2004). As with findings from linkage analysis, no associations between 5-HT transporter polymorphisms and social phobia were found.

However, a study of social phobic individuals in which the short allele genotype was associated to state or trait anxiety showed that individuals homozygous for this form of the gene reported higher levels of both types of anxiety (Furmark, Tillfors, Garpenstrand, Marteinsdottir, Langstrom, Oreland, & Fredrikson, 2004). This is in keeping with the fact that in the general population short alleles are related to increased self-reported anxiety (Melke et al., 2001). Unfortunately, the lack of a control group in Furmark et al. (2004) prevents us from ascertaining whether the frequency of association between anxiety levels and short alleles in social phobic individuals is different from that of normal controls. Associations between social phobia and polymorphisms for monoamine degradation enzymes like MAO-A and COMT have also been sought, but no specific genotype for either of these enzymes was associated with social phobia.

In summary, the studies under review have failed to establish a clear association between genes encoding for functional proteins of different monoaminergic systems and social phobia. These findings are consistent with results from neurochemical studies reviewed earlier, in which no major abnormality in monoaminergic function could be found.

Conclusions

No systematic evidence supporting the hypothesis that social phobia (as a full-fledged pattern of conduct) might be genetically transmitted has been brought to light. As the number of studies to have looked at the question was limited and the chosen paradigms of the bulk, not the most powerful, corroboration, if obtained, would have been in any case inconclusive. Furthermore, the fact that social phobia is to a high degree associated with numerous co-occurring disorders (see chapter 5), makes the hypothesis that all are under specific and separate genetic control even less plausible. In the final analysis, it is unlikely that the hypothesis of the genetic transmission of social phobia has bright prospects.

Broad propensities manifested in universal phenomena, such as fear of strangers (Marks, 1987, p. 133–147), emotionality (Gray, 1970) or "temperament" (Kagan & Zentner, 1996) are highly likely to be in some sense inherited. One or more of these factors might speculatively be considered a necessary condition for social phobia. It would still constitute only one of the risk factors for it, as "expression of a genetic program depends on the environment" (Marks, 1987, p. 110).

The reason for this is made forcefully clear by Rose et al. (1984, p. 95):

The critical distinction in biology is between the *phenotype* of an organism, which may be taken to mean the total of its morphological, physiological, and behavioral properties, and its *genotype*, the state of its genes. It is the genotype, not the phenotype, that is inherited. The genotype is fixed; the phenotype develops and changes constantly. The organism itself is at every stage the consequence of a developmental process that occurs in some historical sequence of environments. At every instant in development (and development goes on until death) the next step is a consequence of the organism's present biological state, which includes both its genes and the physical and social environment in which it finds itself.

The other forces involved in shaping the individual might be generally termed developmental (Sroufe, 1997, p. 253–255), that is, embedded in a historic process that the organism undergoes – simultaneously biological and social.

Kagan & Zentner's (1996, p. 347) hypothesis illustrates the crucial role of the environment. It argues that the emergence of social phobia requires at least three independent factors: a particular inhibited (timid) "temperament" (assuming this to be a pure expression of the genotype), an environment that continuously amplifies the psychological vulnerability associated with that temperament, and consistent social demands eliciting the pattern.

To paraphrase Sapolsky (1997, p. 40) and Rose (1995, p. 382) the shorthand gene "for" a condition is profoundly misleading – after all there aren't even genes for blue or brown eyes, let alone such complex historically and socially shaped features of human existence as shyness or (the probably not unrelated) social phobia. The process that leads to social phobia (and away from it, as in cases of therapeutic or marital success) clearly involves genes (e.g. Shumyatsky, Malleret, Shin, Tokizawa, Tully, Tsvetkov, Zakharenko, Joseph, Vronskaya, Yin, Schubart, Kendel, & Bolshakov, 2005) but cannot be regarded abstractly as embodied in them.

General Conclusion

The biomedical outlook on social phobia was represented in this review by two interlinked propositions postulating that: (1) The social phobic pattern of behavior is caused by unspecified (molecular or cellular) events in particular brain regions of the individual exhibiting it; (2) Something coded in the genes of the individual displaying the social phobic pattern predisposes him/her to social phobia.

Both general propositions but especially the first have proven a great stimulus to research; this makes them valuable. The findings they gave rise to, however, provide little support for either thesis. Consequently, the possibility that social phobic conduct is hereditary and the consequence of a malfunctioning in the brain is unlikely; it has not made social phobia more intelligible. Knowing more, has not necessarily — as is often the case — resulted in understanding better.

It is possible that this rather unsatisfactory record may be the upshot of various methodological shortcomings; these may be overcome in time. Another possibility is that this disappointing outcome was fore-shadowed in the absence of a neurobiological theory of social phobia and hence the lack of specific hypotheses to guide research. In that case, the formulation of such a theory, or better still theories, is of the highest priority.

Over and above methodology and theory, a more substantive alternative must not be overlooked. Likely, no defects or anomalies in the brain have been highlighted or patho-physiology delineated because there are none to be found. The bulk of the results surveyed are consistent with the fact that, on any measure, social phobic individuals are more like their normal counterparts than different from them. Startlingly, this state of affairs has neither thrown into doubt the view of social phobia as a neurological disease of sorts, nor diminished its influence. Rather, it seems acceptable in this field of inquiry to be following the inferential logic that if hypotheses have not been conclusively refuted, then there is no pressing need to question them.

The reason for this might be found in the fact that the biomedical outlook also fulfills an important extra-scientific function. It provides the justification for the pharmacotherapy of social phobia in lockstep with the marketing efforts of the pharmaceutical companies. The circular logic underlying this activity seems to be: if social phobia responds to medication, something biological must be the matter; since it is "biological," it should be treated pharmacologically.

Thus, the commercial availability of an ever expanding number of classes of psychotropic medications shown capable of lessening anxious distress is in itself impetus enough to drive an incessant intellectual effort to rationalize their use. The wider disease model, with its biological deterministic perspective in which this effort is embedded, continues to provide the concepts and their logical organization for the task of rationalization.

7 Social Phobia as a Consequence of Cognitive Biases

When encountering individuals complaining of social phobia one is rapidly disconcerted by the eerie strangeness of what they are saying about seemingly mundane events. A former military officer describes an oral examination at university as worse than going into battle. A landscape designer is convinced that an unsteady grip on a cup of coffee will give away how mentally unsound he is ("they'll think I'm a former alcoholic"). A few words of criticism addressed to a physiotherapist by a colleague are portrayed as "being slaughtered," leaving her with only one way out: resigning. Which she did, explaining: "I could not face her again."

Betraying disarray (e.g. losing one's train of thought) is viewed with great alarm. Admitting to being anxious is considered inconceivable as others are taken to be implacably stern judges bound to regard anyone with less than perfect poise – a disgraceful failure. Predictions of imminent doom are stated with great assurance: "I know I'll panic the moment I'll step into that room."

The oddness of it all is compounded by the fact that the situations described (e.g. speaking in front of a group of people or courting someone) as well as the sentiments (e.g. trying to make a good impression while fearing a slip-up) are so familiar and common.

What could account for these individuals' peculiar outlooks? And what possible relationship does it have with the social phobic pattern of behavior? Assuming that these narratives reflect faithfully what the social phobic individuals perceive and believe, a possible account for it is that the thought processes of these individuals are distorted and that their social behavior and suffering are their ultimate consequence.

Aim and Method

My main goal in this chapter is to sift and assess the evidence having a bearing on such a cognitive account of social phobia. Before reaching that stage, however, I shall have to take several intermediate steps.

Firstly, it is necessary to inquire into the specific meaning of the notion of "cognition" in general and its application to social phobia in particular.

Subsequently, as psychological concepts cannot exist apart from the way they are measured, it is important to examine the validity of tests devised to identify and quantify thought processes in general and their value in social phobia in particular. As in many psychological processes, measurement is easier to imagine than to carry out, for thinking is imperceptible and cannot be readily detected.

The various cognitive concepts and the measures purporting to assess them are indispensable to the practical testing of the hypothesis of "cognitive biases" and its other theoretical ramifications. Once the matter of their validity has been dealt with, we should be free finally to tackle more specific questions. For example, is the thinking of social phobic and normal individuals altogether different? And what of other contrast populations? Do sub-groups of social phobic individuals differ in this respect?

The demonstration of such differences is a necessary (but not sufficient) condition for the ultimate query: do cognitive distortions (biases) play a causal role in the social phobic pattern of behavior?

Finally, I shall examine the value of the cognitive approach indirectly, by studying the effects of therapies implementing its principles.

The Notion of Cognition

The somewhat arcane (see Malcolm, 1977, p. 385) but today rather familiar-sounding philosophical term "cognition" is defined by the *Concise Oxford Dictionary* as the faculty of knowing, perceiving, and conceiving in contrast, for example, with emotion and volition – a distinction inherited from Plato.

Its general modern use is in reference to the experimental study ("cognitive science") of reasoning on its own terms (e.g. memory, decision-making), often with a view to duplicating these processes by machines. Such an approach is in contrast to considering the person as a whole – involved in a dynamic relationship with a social and physical environment.

A particular, clinical, use of the term originated with Beck (1976) who came to advocate a psychotherapy he branded cognitive, as aiming at correcting certain faulty hypothetical structures or operations of the mind of patients. This analysis, which was first applied generally and in the abstract to a broad range of psychopathology, has been subsequently refined and extended to social phobia as well (Beck, Emery, & Greenberg, 1985, pp. 146–164).

It is curious that there is little meeting of minds between the two cognitive domains (the "science" and the "therapy"). Both methodology and theory divide them (McFall & Townsend, 1998, pp. 325–327). Whereas cognitive science uses mostly objective measures (i.e. acts of choice, classification, detection, etc.) the therapy relies on introspection via subjective questionnaires. Even the notion of cognition is not necessarily a shared one (Looren de Jong, 1997). Attempts to reconcile the two have recently been made (e.g. McFall, Treat, & Viken, 1998).

The historic impetus to the emergence of the cognitive model appears to have been dissatisfaction in the ranks of the behavior therapists with behaviorism as too narrow in outlook. This widely held view seems to have originated in a misunderstanding of the behaviorist school of thought by identifying it narrowly with ("mindless") conditioning. In that sense, the cognitive approach may be viewed as an attempt to reform behaviorism from within, as it were, by making it more thoughtful.

Although numerous other "cognitive" models have been put forward (e.g. Meichenbaum, 1977), most have been ultimately eclipsed by that of Beck and his collaborators (e.g. Clark, 1999).

The Cognitive Model of Social Phobia

Despite numerous statements of the cognitive outlook while laying stress on its therapeutic implications, the key term "cognition" remains undefined (e.g. Beck et al., 1985). It is typically used either as a label for a hypothetical information-processing system or the product of such a process, or both. A lay interpretation of the word might be that it refers to that misty region of our consciousness in which the kind of thinking that may be put into words takes place. Some of the theorizing in this area, however, is gradually creeping towards notions tantalizingly suggestive of the unconscious (e.g. "automaticity", McNally, 1995).

Proponents of the cognitive school hold the view that faulty thinking results in emotional distress (anxiety) and inadequate behavior. This in turn generates more distress. Although they take pains to point out that "the cognitive model does not postulate a sequential unidirectional relationship in which cognition always precedes emotion" (Clark & Steer, 1996, p. 76), it is plain that for all intents and purposes the cognitive perspective is mostly interested in precisely this sort of causal relationship. Fodor (1983), a foremost proponent of cognitivism, puts it unequivocally: "the structure of behavior stands to mental structure as an effect stands to its cause" (p. 8). The assertion that "social phobics become anxious when anticipating or participating in social situations *because* they hold beliefs (dysfunctional assumptions) which *lead them to*..." (my italics; Stopa & Clark, 1993, p. 255), serves as a case in point. Cognition, as a generic description of mental structures with agency, is at the center of the theoretical universe of cognitive therapy (hence the name). It is for this reason that cognitive factors are regarded as "maintaining" social phobia (e.g. Hackmann, Surway, & Clark, 1998, p. 9) as its efficient cause. They are therefore its linchpin and are considered as providing the necessary leverage for therapeutic change.

On the most simple level, faulty thinking ("cognitions"; e.g. Clark & Steer, 1996, p. 79) implies various kinds of irrational inference drawing, such as exaggerating, or ignoring counter-evidence as gathered from the justifications patients offer for what they did or felt. On a somewhat loftier plane, inadequate thinking implies broad beliefs ("schemas") expressing a whole outlook (e.g. the ultimate dangerousness of losing face or the viciousness of others). Finally, various cognitive processes are said to be operative (e.g. focus on self), presumably driven by overarching cognitive structures.

According to this [the cognitive] model, social phobics become anxious when anticipating, or participating in, social situations because they hold beliefs (dysfunctional assumptions) which lead them to predict they will behave in a way which results in their rejection or loss of status. Once triggered, these negative social evaluation thoughts are said to contribute to a series of vicious circles which maintain the social phobia. First, the somatic and behavioral symptoms of anxiety become further sources of perceived danger and anxiety (e.g. blushing is interpreted as evidence that one is making a fool of oneself). Second, social phobics become preoccupied with their negative thoughts, and this preoccupation interferes with their ability to process social cues, leading to an objective deterioration in performance. Some of the changes in the social phobic's behavior (for example, behaving in a less warm and outgoing fashion) may then elicit less friendly behavior from others and hence partly confirm the phobic's fears. Third, an attentional bias towards threat cues means that when not preoccupied with their internal dialogue, social phobics are particularly likely to notice aspects of their behavior, and the behavior of others, which could be interpreted as evidence of actual, or impending, negative social evaluation. (Stopa & Clark, 1993, p. 255)

An elaboration of the above outline may be found in Clark & Wells (1995, pp. 69–93).

An immediate problem in this line of theoretical analysis is the nature of thought. Although our own consciousness is accessible to us to some extent, that of others is obviously (and frustratingly for any model relying on it) only accessible in a limited way, if at all. Therefore, whatever we may hazard to say about it must be derivative and tentative, reliant on whatever the patients choose to say, as well as inferred from their general account of their way of being.

Moreover, as is always the case with hypothetical constructions, there is the danger of reifying "cognitions." Whatever they are, these have to be viewed as structures to be found within the individual or as hypothetical mental constructs standing for predispositions to act in a certain way. In other words, these constructs represent an underlying principle that may be said to manifest itself in, or may be inferred from, actual behavior.

The main theoretical value of such point of view is in the kind of explanation it offers: the mental construct within drives hypothetically the action without. In such quest, however, lurks the danger of tautology. If cognitions and beliefs are inferred from what the individual says and does, this behavior cannot be seen as resulting from the operations of dysfunctional cognitions or assumptions. An inferred mental structure from a certain conduct could hardly be invoked as a causal explanation for the same behavior. For a hypothetical structure to be considered as endowed with explanatory power, it has to be shown to be valid (i.e. to make a difference and to have a myriad of predictable consequences) in a series of independent studies.

Before being able to survey the studies that have been carried out, however, we must now turn to the intricate issue of how to assess and quantify thought (dysfunctional or otherwise).

Measuring Dysfunctional Thought

Despite the staggering conceptual, and to a lesser extent practical, difficulties in measuring thought processes, a number of scales have been developed, all boldly assuming, for all intents and purposes, that what people say about themselves reflects "cognitions." I shall examine this underlying assumption at some length in the discussion.

The various proposed methods to assess cognitions have been reviewed by Heimberg (1994) and others. Typically, the measures have attempted to quantify either enduring cognitive dispositions (traits) or thoughts that happen to occur through either endorsement of readymade statements, or the listing by the subjects of idiosyncratic thoughts they experienced on occasion.

In what follows, the psychometric characteristics of the measurement devices I have selected will be summarized in their application to social phobic subjects whenever available. It must be remembered, however, that most instruments have been developed using student subjects. For the purpose of illustration of issues involved in the measurement of thought, I have selected three scales commonly used with social phobic subjects as well as the availability of some background research to document their psychometric characteristics.

Self-Report Instruments

The Social Interaction Self-statement Test (SISST – Glass, Merluzzi, Biever, & Larsen, 1982)

This is a 30-item self-report scale rated for frequency of occurrence of thoughts the subjects may have had. Half of the statements are negative and half are positive. Occurrence is rated on a 1 to 5 continuum ranging from "hardly ever had the thought" to "very often had the thought." Correspondingly, the results are summarized in two scores: positive and negative.

This test is typically used to assess thoughts before, during, and after a role-play test with members of the opposite sex.

Reliability This refers to the accuracy of measurement, conceived of as agreement between occasions of testing or between different items and the overall score.

1. *test—retest* – Zweig & Brown (1985) tested the stability of the scale on 86 students who repeated assessments after 2 and 3 weeks. Coefficients ranged between 0.72 and 0.76 for the positive self-statements and 0.73 to 0.89 for the negative ones.
2. internal consistency – the same study reported an alpha for the different situations ranging between 0.85 to 0.89 for the positive score and 0.91 to 0.95 for the negative score.

Convergent Validity This type of validity concerns the degree of correspondence between measurement of the kind of process under investigation and other measures of similar factors.

In Glass et al. (1982), 80 students role-played interactions with a member of the opposite sex and filled out a battery of tests. The resulting SISST scores were factor analyzed: 4 factors emerged contrary to the original structure of 2 factors of 15 items each that might have been expected. Furthermore, 11 out of 30 items did not contribute to the factors. Despite these challenging results, the test was kept unchanged.

In another study (Glass & Furlong, 1990), 101 community residents who responded to an offer of treatment for shyness filled out a battery of tests. The SISST negative score correlated 0.54 with SAD (Social Avoidance and Distress) and 0.37 with FNE (Fear of Negative Evaluation), the correlations with the positive score were much lower. Associations with the IBT (Irrational Beliefs Test) were small (e.g. 0.22 with the total score).

The correlations obtaining between spontaneous thought listing by the subject and the SISST were 0.28 with the negative score and −0.23 with the positive score. Interestingly, thought-listing − the only individual measure of consciousness − also correlated poorly with other measures such as the SAD and FNE.

In Dodge, Hope, Heimberg, & Becker (1988) 28 social phobic individuals filled out the SISST in retrospective fashion (i.e. without role-plays).

The negative score correlated significantly 0.35 with the SAD and 0.39 with the FNE. Unlike in Glass & Furlong (1990), there was a good correlation (0.59) between the percentage of negative thoughts (compiled from a period of thought listing) and the negative score of the SISST.

Discriminant Validity   This type of validity concerns the degree to which the measure under investigation is distinguishable from other measures assumed to be different or whether it is able to differentiate two groups assumed to be different.

In Glass et al. (1982) described earlier, 80 students were divided into "high" and "low" socially anxious (the grounds were left unspecified). The two groups had significantly different SISST scores. The anxious sub-group was characterized by lower positive scores and higher negative scores than the non-anxious group. In an additional analysis of the same sample, two groups of subjects were created: the highly anxious/poorly skilled and the little anxious/highly skilled. Significant differences were found between the groups in terms of both positive and negative scores of the SISST. This observation was strengthened through similar results reported by Zweig & Brown (1985). In the absence of normative scores, it is difficult to interpret these differences in degree.

In summary, although the test has acceptable accuracy, evidence that it measures thought processes is rather weak. Its most firm support is in the association between the negative score of the SISST and thought listing. Another lies in the distinction between subject groups representing degrees of severity.

Other aspects of the results raise some problems. First, a test of the measure's theoretical structure by means of factor analysis does not confirm it. Second, although significant correlations between the negative score of the SISST and various (cognitive?) scales of anxious distress were found, these were quite modest. Ultimately, what the SISST does measure remains uncertain for the time being.

The Cognitive and Somatic Anxiety Questionnaire
(CSAQ – Schwartz, Davidson, & Goleman, 1978)

This is a self-report questionnaire of 14 items describing somatic (7 items) and mental (7 items) features of an anxious state. Each item is rated on a 1 (not at all) to 5 (very much so) continuum of agreement. The test yields two scores: somatic and cognitive; each the sum of ratings of the relevant items. The authors also suggest that a summation of the two may be used to produce a total score.

Reliability   The only form of reliability investigated so far was that of internal consistency.

In Delmonte & Ryan (1983) 100 subjects drawn from a local hospital (no other details given) took the test. Alphas were 0.81 for the somatic and 0.85 for the cognitive subscales.

Similar results were also reported in DeGood & Tait (1987). In this study, when the total score was used to calculate internal consistency, the resulting alpha coefficient (0.86) was higher than that obtained for each subscale: somatic 0.76; cognitive 0.81. This is awkward, as the coefficient should in principle have been lower. It might suggest, in fact, that far from being distinct, some items in the two subscales overlap.

Convergent Validity   In DeGood & Tait (1987) 109 students filled out a battery of tests including the CSAQ and the SCL-90 (general psychopathology). The cognitive subscale of the CSAQ correlated significantly with the obsessive subscale of the SCL-90. This particular result was singled out by the authors as vindicating the cognitive nature of the subscale. Confusingly, the very same obsessive scale of the SCL-90 also correlated significantly with the somatic subscale. More obviously, the somatic subscale was also found to correlate significantly with the somatization scale of the SCL-90. The latter, however, was also significantly associated with the cognitive subscale of the CSAQ, albeit to a smaller degree.

In Heimberg, Gansler, Dodge, & Becker (1987), 50 social phobic participants simulated a social interaction and filled out a battery of questionnaires. The cognitive subscale of the CSAQ correlated significantly (0.4) although modestly with subjective ratings of distress. This was seen as evidence of the cognitive nature of the distress. The somatic subscale was similarly correlated (0.4) with heart rate; but the latter had no association with the cognitive subscale.

Heimberg et al. (1987) found that the cognitive subscale of the CSAQ was correlated (0.52) with the FNE and (0.48) with (negative) thought listing. This lends weight to the claim that the cognitive subscale is measuring something in common with other cognitive scales. However, it also correlated to a similar degree with several anxiety scales (SAD, STAI). It is either the case that all measure a cognitive construct, or conversely an anxiety construct. This cannot be determined from the present study.

In Crits-Cristoph (1986), 227 students filled the questionnaire and the results were submitted to factor analysis. Although two factors (cognitive and somatic were identified, many items had high associations with both. For example, the item of "becoming immobilized" was originally designated as somatic but actually weighed more in the cognitive factor (0.41) than in the somatic one (0.26). Similarly "imagining terrifying scenes" loaded higher on the somatic factor (0.35) than the cognitive one (0.30). The author concluded that there is a considerable overlap between the two subscales. This conclusion is supported by further studies.

In Freedland & Carney (1988), 120 inpatients filled out the CSAQ. 4 factors emerged, each a mixture of cognitive and somatic items. The authors concluded that the items probably also tap other features of anxiety in addition to the cognitive and the somatic chosen as the main dimensions. DeGood & Tait (1987) reported similar results.

In Tamaren, Carney, & Allen (1985a) 22 students enrolled in a course on anxiety filled out a battery of tests. The cognitive subscale of the CSAQ was found to correlate 0.46 with the irrational belief test (IBT). In contrast, the somatic subscale did not correlate with it.

Predictive Validity   This aspect of validity relies on the ability of the measure to predict aspects of behavior.

In Tamaren, Carney, & Allen (1985b) 24 students were selected out of 42 as primarily cognitive or somatic on the basis of a higher score on one of the subscales of the CSAQ. Subjects were assigned to two treatments of anxiety: cognitive and relaxation (i.e. somatic). Half of the subjects were matched with the treatment, and the other half mismatched. The hypothesis suggested that group membership (e.g. cognitive) would predict a better response to appropriate (i.e. cognitive) treatment.

Treatment outcome (measured by the total CSAQ score) seemingly favored the matched group. The authors, however, ignored the significant difference in the total CSAQ scores between matched and mismatched groups before treatment. Therefore, significantly worse results for the mismatched group could simply reflect the greater severity of their distress before treatment began. Furthermore, as only total scores were used, we do not know whether improvement actually occurred in the specific feature of anxiety targeted by the treatment. Because of the above methodological flaws, it is impossible to see evidence in this study of predictive validity for the subscales of the CSAQ.

In summary, the subscales of the CSAQ have good internal consistency and its cognitive subscale correlates positively with other instruments regarded as measuring cognitive activity. In one study, the original two factors were recreated; these however were largely found to overlap.

Unfortunately, the most basic measures of the accuracy of this questionnaire are unavailable, as are most elements of validity. For now, it is hard to tell what exactly the CSAQ is a measure of.

Fear of Negative Evaluation (FNE: Watson & Friend, 1969)

As the SAD (reviewed in chapter 3), with which it is commonly administered, this is a self-report of 30 items rated as true or false, concerning mostly thoughts and worries about social life but also including some items about subjective distress. This questionnaire is therefore aiming at tapping inner experience rather than overt behavior.

Reliability

1. *test–retest* – In Watson & Friend (1969), 154 students took the test twice over a one-month period. The correlation between the two moments was r = 0.78.
2. *internal consistency* – This was 0.79 with a sample of 205 students, r = 0.96 with another sample of 154 students (Watson & Friend, 1969) and r = 0.94 with a sample of 265 (of which 35 social phobic) patients with various anxiety disorders (Oei et al., 1991).

Predictive Validity   High FNE scores did not predict avoidance of disapproval in students (Watson & Friend, 1969). In Friend & Gilbert (1972), 77 women undergraduates were divided into high or low FNE scorers. High FNE subjects tended to compare themselves to people who were less good than they were in threatening conditions.

Convergent Validity   In Watson & Friend (1969), the FNE correlated as follows with other constructs: Taylor's Manifest Anxiety −0.6 (n = 171), Audience Sensitivity Index −0.39 (n = 42) and Jackson's Personality Research Form (social approval) −0.77 (n = 42), and Marlowe-Crown Social Desirability Scale −0.25 (n = 205).

Discriminant Validity   In Turner et al. (1987), FNE scores did not distinguish social phobia from most other anxiety disorders (e.g. agoraphobia, panic, OCD, GAD) save specific phobia, in a study of 206 outpatients. A similar result was reported in Oei et al. (1991).

In summary and taken together, the psychometric characteristics of the cognitive measures surveyed leave much to be desired. This state of affairs might not have to do only with measurement narrowly construed but possibly also reflect the nebulous validity of the mental constructs that the instruments supposedly tap. As seen earlier, we have only the faintest notion of what terms like cognition mean. This may be sufficient for loose speculative theorizing but fails to provide the basis from which to draw sufficiently well-defined hypothetical structures and allow a proper process of validation of both construct and measurement.

Are Social Phobic Individuals Characterized by Different Cognitive Processes to Those of Normal Individuals?

The mental processes of social phobic individuals are held by the cognitive model to be systematically and typically dysfunctional. The following section reviews the relevant available studies grouped in several processes.

Negative Self-Appraisal

Rapee & Lim (1992) compared the evaluations of 28 social phobic (DSM-III-R) participants and 31 normal controls (staff and their friends who never sought help) of their social performance. The performance consisted of making a brief speech in front of a small audience (6 other subjects). Each subject rated their own performance and that of the other participants.

In both groups, self-appraisal was lower than appraisal by others; the tendency was more pronounced in the social phobic group. The difference however obtained only in the global judgments (e.g. "generally spoke well"); ratings of specific dimensions of performance (e.g. tone of voice) were comparable. Walters & Hope (1998), in their study of 22 social phobic (DSM-III-R) and non-anxious individuals reported similar findings.

Alden & Wallace (1995) compared 32 "generalized" social phobic (DSM-III-R) and 32 normal individuals drawn from the general community, in an experiment studying self-appraisal through a task of "getting acquainted." Subjects were randomly assigned to either a positive (were given encouragement and asked questions every 15 sec.), or a negative condition (less encouragement, fewer questions).

As in the previous study, self-appraisal tended to be less favorable than the appraisal of others. While being more pronounced in the social phobic group, negative self-appraisal was not influenced by the experimental condition (i.e. it was neither enhanced nor diminished by it). Furthermore, social phobic participants tended to give more credit to the performance of the confederates whereas the control subjects tended to diminish it.

In a further refinement of the above study, Wallace & Alden (1997) studied perceptions of success. Social phobic subjects rated themselves both as less successful and as appearing less successful than the controls. However the groups changed their judgments differently in light of feedback. Whereas the social phobic individuals' self-appraisal improved under the positive condition while the self-appraisal of control subjects remained unchanged, that of the latter worsened under the negative condition. Surprisingly, the social phobic participants remained unmoved.

In Stopa & Clark (1993), 12 social phobic participants (DSM-III-R), 12 subjects with other anxiety disorders and 12 normal controls had to engage in role-plays of a conversation, new job meeting, getting acquainted, and returning a defective product. All subjects evaluated their performance in several ways: thinking aloud, rating a "thoughts (positive and negative) questionnaire," rating their behavior, and completing memory (recall and recognition) tests. Globally, social phobic individuals tended to have more negative thoughts and worse self-evaluation than both control groups.

In Hofmann et al. (1995b) 14 social phobic, 16 social phobic with an additional avoidant personality disorder, and 24 normal controls (DSM-III-R) role-played giving a speech. Both social phobic groups reported higher scores of negative thoughts compared to the controls;

no differences however were found regarding positive thoughts. Both groups of social phobic subjects also spoke less than the controls.

In Woody & Rodriguez (2000) 20 social phobic and 20 normal subjects gave a speech in front of a small audience. Measures included self-reported subjective anxiety and ratings of performance by the subject as well as by trained judges.

In terms of performance, social phobic subjects rated themselves as lower than did the controls. However, the judges rated both groups of subjects equivalently (as neither very good nor very bad). Interestingly, the judges' ratings of skillfulness corresponded closely to those of the social phobic subjects but were significantly lower than those that the control subjects ascribed to themselves. This study highlighted the normal subjects' inflated assessment of their abilities compared to the soberness and realistic self-assessment displayed by the social phobic subjects.

In summary, with the exception of Woody & Rodriguez (1968), social phobic subjects exhibited an exaggeration in a general tendency toward self-depreciation also in evidence in normal subjects. It is best, however, to put this conclusion in perspective as this tendency is not reflected in other aspects of evaluation. Social phobic individuals showed similar rates of positive thoughts, similar ideas of other people's perception of their performance and similar appraisals of other people's performances. One would expect a powerful bias to exercise a decisive influence over many cognitive processes and not to be limited to a subjective evaluation only. The lack of converging evidence and the fact that only a difference in degree between social phobic and control subjects was in evidence, does not lend support to the hypothesis of an abnormal kind of thinking possibly characterizing social phobic individuals.

The only qualitative differences were those reported in Wallace & Alden (1997) who found that social phobic self-appraisal was more responsive to positive influences from the environment than that of normal individuals, who however were more responsive to negative feedback. This is a startling result as social phobic individuals are typically exquisitely sensitive to a critical stance from others. That social phobic individuals displayed a better ability to disregard negative feedback than normal subjects is nothing short of astonishing, as well as being inconsistent with everything we know about social phobia.

Memory Biases

In a study from Australia, Rapee, McCallum, Melville, Ravenscroft, & Rodney (1994) reported four studies attempting to delineate memory processes specific to social phobia. In the first study, 32 social phobic participants (DSM-III-R) were compared to 21 controls on a recall and recognition task of words projected on a screen that either conveyed a "threat" (either social or physical) or not.

The typical tasks were: "recall" during which subjects wrote down the words they remember after a screening; and "recognition" during which they had to identify the words they had seen projected earlier on a screen. No differences between the two groups of subjects were observed on either recall or recognition.

In the second study, 20 social phobic subjects were compared to 40 undergraduate students subdivided into sub-groups of the highly anxious (n = 19) and the low in anxiety (n = 21) according to their FNE scores.

The subjects were presented with words (on cards), which they had to recall, as well as having to complete words based on the first three letters. Additionally, subjects had to complete words they had not seen before – again based on the first three letters. This was considered a measure of "implicit memory," whereas the recall tasks are regarded as measuring "explicit memory."

No differences were found on any task between the three experimental groups, suggesting "that social phobics do not preferentially remember threat information" (1994, p. 94).

In an attempt to render the experimental task more realistic, subjects were given feedback concerning an imaginary speech someone as well (i.e. in the same group) as themselves had given. Against expectation, the recall of negative elements of feedback was greater among control subjects (n = 21) than among the social phobic subjects (n = 33) in this study.

The same participants as above were asked to remember a real event during which they received negative feedback from someone they knew. This "more realistic" procedure still failed to highlight a greater propensity of social phobic individuals to remember negative words.

As a summary, it is best to quote the authors: "The four studies consistently failed to demonstrate a memory bias for social threat information for social phobics" (1994, p. 98). This conclusion is strengthened by results reported by Stopa & Clark (1993) highlighting similar lack of differences concerning memory between social phobic subjects and those with other anxious disorders and normal controls.

In a similar study (carried out in Sweden) by Lundh & Ost (1997), implicit and explicit memory biases were studied in 45 social phobic (11 specific, 34 generalized) outpatients who were compared to 45 control subjects. Overall, no differences were found between social phobic and control subjects on either task. There was, however, a difference between 2 sub-groups of social phobic individuals on the "completion" task; specific social phobic participants completed more social-threat and more positive words than did the generalized. Bafflingly, this is in contradiction to the results of Rapee et al. (1994). Finally, the latter partial results are difficult to interpret, especially in light of the fact that social phobic participants as a group had better "completion" rates than the controls.

In a variation on the previous studies, Lundh & Ost (1996a) investigated non-verbal aspects of memory. 20 social phobic individuals were compared to 20 normal subjects (matched on sex and age) in terms of their responses to a recognition task. The task consisted of:

1. rating 20 photographs of faces on a 5-point continuum ranging from "very accepting" (1) to "very critical" (5);
2. completing words based on their first 3 letters (distraction phase);
3. recognizing the 20 persons appearing in the original photographs among 80 photographs.

Contrary to prediction, no differences between the 2 groups of subjects were observed in their tendency to rate the individuals in the photographs as either accepting or critical (phase 1), nor in terms of recognition of previously presented persons (phase 3).

In a further attempt to test their hypotheses, the authors: (1) eliminated photographs rated neutral and kept only those rated purely critical and purely accepting, (2) eliminated 3 social phobic subjects who had previously correctly recognized all 20 persons in the original batch of photographs (no explanation was given). Although, as before, no straightforward differences between the groups were in evidence, the remaining social phobic subjects recognized critical-appearing faces significantly more than the accepting-looking ones. The obverse was true of the control group. A correlation analysis, however, indicated that subjects of both groups tended to recognize more the critical faces to a similar degree.

In light of these results, it is surprising to find the authors reaching the conclusion that "The social phobics in the present study showed a clear bias for 'critical' vs. 'accepting' faces on the recognition task, whereas the control Ss had a tendency in the opposite direction" (p. 792).

Foa, Gilboa-Schechtman, Amir, & Freshman (2000) reported two studies. In the first, 14 generalized social phobic subjects were compared to 12 non-anxious controls in terms of their responses to 48 slides showing individuals with happy, angry, or neutral emotional expressions. The names of the individuals had to be learned first and the emotion identified later. Social phobic subjects did better than the controls in overall free-recall of names and corresponding facial expressions. Specifically, social phobic subjects recalled better angry (vs. happy or neutral) facial expressions.

In a second experiment 15 generalized social phobic subjects were compared to 16 non-anxious controls in terms of their responses to the same images described above but displayed on computer. The task in this experiment was to decide whether images had already been viewed or not. Overall the phobic subjects displayed better recall. Furthermore, social phobic subjects recalled better negative than non-negative facial expressions while taking longer to do it. No such differences were found among the normal controls.

In Perez-Lopez & Woody (2001) 24 social phobic subjects were compared to 20 non-anxious controls in terms of their responses to photographs displaying disgust, anger, surprise, and happiness. Half of the photographs were presented on a computer screen first. In a second phase all photographs were shown. Contrary to Foa et al. (2000) recognition of threatening faces was the same by both groups.

To sum up, in light of the above and with the exception of Foa et al. (2000), no memory bias specific to a social phobia concerning "social threat" information was in evidence in the studies surveyed.

Attention Bias

The failure to detect memory biases nevertheless raised the possibility of a bias operating only in the present. Several studies attempted to identify it.

Cloitre, Heimberg, Holt, & Liebowitz (1992) compared the responses of 24 social phobic (DSM-III-R) and 24 control subjects to a series of projected words that had to be rated in multiple ways. Globally, social phobic and normal subjects were alike in terms of their performance on lexical tasks for positive and neutral stimuli. Only one difference was observed: social phobic subjects responded more slowly than the controls to threat stimuli. This is consistent with other reports (e.g. Hope, Rapee, Heimberg, & Dombeck, 1990); its meaning remains obscure.

In Mattia, Heimberg, & Hope (1993) 28 social phobic subjects were compared to 47 normal volunteers in terms of responses to the modified Stroop task. The proper Stroop test consists of the presentation of colored cards with the color name typed in. The color name could match or not the color of the card. The subject has two tasks: first to name the color of the card while ignoring the typed name, second to read the color name while ignoring the color of the card. The test is scored in terms of the latency of the response. The modified version used in the present study (and others described below) had colored cards but in addition to color names, used 4 categories of meaningful words conveying either social (e.g. stupid) or physical threat (e.g. illness) or neutral words (e.g. leaning) that served as controls. Response latency is normally the variable of interest while assuming that the longer delay reflected interfering cognitive processes (e.g. vulnerability to social threat).

Social phobic participants exhibited significantly longer latencies (albeit in terms of fractions of seconds) than the normal ones in pronouncing the name of the color overall (i.e. regardless of whether the word was neutral, or implying a physical or social threat), but more so to social words (e.g. boring).

The same test was administered pre- and post-treatment to 29 social phobic patients who were being treated by "cognitive behavioral group therapy," medication or placebo (it was not reported how many were in each condition). Responders (defined by a clinician), regardless of experimental condition, took significantly less time to respond to social threat words after treatment as well as responding quicker than non-responders who did not change (although the groups were equivalent at baseline).

Lundh & Ost (1996b) compared the responses of 42 social phobic participants to those of 42 matched controls on the Stroop task. Social phobic subjects took significantly longer (in terms of seconds) to name the color of the cards on which social threat words were written (but not other kinds of words) than did the control subjects. The meaningfulness of this finding is not clear.

However that may be, the above findings were contradicted by those of Amir, McNally, Riemann, Burns, Lorenz, & Mullen (1996). In this study, the responses of 14 social phobic participants and 14 controls on the modified Stroop task were compared. This was done however under various levels of presumed discomfort induced by the "threat" of having to simulate an impromptu speech that will be videotaped.

No differences in time latencies in response to the Stroop between the two groups — regardless of levels of anxiety or degrees of threat — were detected.

The social phobic subjects reacted more anxiously to the threat of public speaking. Subsequently, when they were divided in two subgroups based on the above score, the more anxious subjects were faster in their responses to social threat stimuli.

In terms of what the authors construe as "cognitive interference," social phobic subjects exhibited significantly more of it than did the controls in the condition before the "threats" were made. Oddly, the threat of public speaking affected the normal subjects more (in terms of responses to social-threat words) than it did the social phobic ones. The most meaningful finding of this study is that social phobic individuals are more like normal controls than different from them in respect to whatever the "modified Stroop" task is measuring.

In Amir, Foa, & Coles (1998a), 22 generalized social phobic participants and 22 normal controls (SCID; DSM-IV) underwent a lexical task requiring interpretation of words with a multiple meaning (homographs).

Both groups did better on non-homographic tasks. The only significant difference found was that social phobic subjects took longer to respond to a short exposure than to the longer one of the socially relevant homograph. The meaningfulness of this finding is obscure as it is in contradiction to the hypotheses predicting a shorter response time for the social phobic subjects – regardless of time of projection (p. 286). Furthermore, the validity of this lexical task in the way it was used in the study remains unclear.

As such, the authors' conclusion that "the findings regarding socially relevant homographs suggest that generalized social phobics are characterized by an autonomic activation of threat relevant information, but controlled strategies are used to inhibit threat meanings" (p. 289) has very little to support it.

In Gilboa-Schechtman, Foa, & Amir (1999) 16 generalized social phobic and non-anxious control subjects were instructed to identify the presence of a discrepant face among 12 appearing on the screen that were either happy, angry or neutral; time latencies were recorded.

Angry faces were identified faster than happy faces by both groups of subjects. However social phobic subjects were quicker (the differences were 2.1 vs. 2.7 secs.) to detect angry faces than happy ones in contrast with the normal subjects. This held however only on the background of a neutral group; the effect was no longer significant with a crowd of happy faces in the background.

In another subset of the experiment involving only crowds of faces with similar expressions, social phobic subjects' response latencies increased more than those of the control subjects when angry faces were compared to neutral ones. The difference, however, no longer held when angry faces were compared to happy ones. Despite these and previous disconfirming results, the authors nevertheless concluded that social phobic subjects display an attention bias for angry faces.

In an experiment carried out in Belgium (Philippot & Douilliez, 2005) involving 21 social phobic, 39 normal, and 20 subjects with other anxiety disorders, responses to threatening facial expressions displayed on computer were compared. No differences between the groups were found in terms of the decoding accuracy, attributed emotion intensity or the reported difficulty of the task.

In summary, social phobic individuals have been found in some (but not all) studies to respond somewhat more slowly (typically in terms of fractions of seconds) than control normal subjects. The meaningfulness of this statistically significant difference in degree is not clear. However tempting it may be for those so inclined, it is difficult to consider it as compelling evidence pointing to the influence of some cognitive structure.

Judgment Biases

In Lucock & Salkovskis (1988) 12 social phobic subjects and an unspecified number of control subjects rated 4 categories of events (social negative and positive, and non-social negative and positive) on a measure of "subjective probability scale." Social phobic subjects rated significantly higher than the controls the likelihood of social negative events. Differences in probabilities were significant but in the opposite direction of what might have been expected as far as positive social and non-social events were concerned. No differences were observed in relation to non-social negative events.

The authors rather hastily conclude that the results highlight the cognitive biases inherent in social phobia, ignoring an alternative possibility that the differences in subjective estimates might reflect a different pattern of social and non-social events as lived and realistically estimated by both groups of subjects.

Foa, Franklin, Perry, & Herbert (1996) compared the responses of 15 generalized social phobic individuals to 15 non-anxious controls to the "Probability cost questionnaire" (PCQ) constructed for the study. The PCQ consists of 20 negative social events and 20 negative but non-social events, rated by the subjects for the likelihood that these events, might happen to them as well as how bad it feels (construed as "cost").

The social phobic subjects rated significantly higher than the controls the likelihood of negative social events happening to them as well as feeling worse about this. As to the non-social negative events, all subjects rated the likelihood of these happening to them alike; the social phobic ones, however, expected to feel worse about it.

In a similar study (Gilboa-Schechtman, Franklin, & Foa, 2000) involving, in addition to social phobic and non-anxious control subjects, also obsessive-compulsive patients, the earlier results (Foa et al., 1996) were replicated. An additional difference to emerge was that social phobic subjects reported an anticipated emotional reaction to negative events to last days whereas normal subjects expected it to last 2 hours (and 13 hours by obsessive compulsives). Although these estimates might reflect reality, the authors put the differences down to a cognitive bias.

Stopa & Clark (2000), rather than using negative and positive social and non-social events, investigated the responses of 20 social phobic subjects, 20 non-anxious controls, and 20 subjects with other anxiety disorders to ambiguous situations.

They found that social phobic subjects interpreted social situations (but not non-social ones) more negatively than did the other groups. Social phobic subjects tended to describe the meaning of negative social events to them in more apocalyptic terms ("catastrophizing") than the other subjects.

Roth, Antony, & Swinson (2001) compared the responses of 55 social phobic and 54 non-clinical control subjects to a questionnaire listing 8 possible explanations to a variety of social phobic (observable) features. Half of the subjects in each group rated an "observer" (how one views others) version and half an "actor" (how one is viewed by others) version.

Only 3 out of the 8 explanations elicited differential responses. Social phobic subjects were more likely to endorse the view that others will consider observable features of social phobia as due to intense anxiety or some other type of disorder. Normal subjects tended to endorse the view that it is likely to be considered a normal physical state (e.g. shivering when cold). Social phobic subjects, however, consistently tended to attribute to others (rather than themselves) any explanations, be they in term of disorders or normal physical states. Although the latter finding stands in contradiction to the proposition that social phobic subjects would tend to see themselves in the worst possible light, the authors considered their hypotheses as being corroborated.

To sum up, although the above studies highlighted differences between social phobic and other control (normal, anxious) subjects, it is not clear why the authors treat their own interpretation of the source of variance, namely a built-in social phobic judgment bias, as self-evident. An alternative interpretation might be that social phobic subjects are frank and self-observant and that their responses to the different self-report instruments fairly reflect how their lives are different from those of normal individuals.

Imagery

In Hackmann et al. (1998), 30 social phobic and 30 control participants were asked to recall a recent episode of social anxiety and to describe it in detail ("as a film-scenario"). Subjects also had to rate to what extent they saw themselves through their own eyes on a 7-point scale. Such perspective taking is theoretically important within the cognitive model. The "observer perspective is problematic in that it is likely to be distorted and interfere with the individual's ability to process information from the environment contrary to her or his beliefs" (Coles, Turk, Heimberg, & Fresco, 2001, p. 662). Social phobic subjects reported more images and rated them more negatively. They described themselves more from an "observer" vantage point than did controls. In contrast, social phobic participants realized as clearly as did the control subjects the distortions in their scenarios. Similarly, an interviewer rated scenarios from both groups equally. These are consistent with Lundh & Ost (1997) in which social phobic individuals displayed better recall than normal controls.

In Coles et al. (2001) subjects were asked to generate social situations on 3 levels of anxiety (low, moderate, and high) and to rate the degree to which they were observing themselves through their own eyes or rather viewing themselves from an external point of view.

The main finding was that social phobic subjects tended to view themselves more externally with the increase of the anxiety level of the situation. However, the difference between social phobic and normal subjects was in evidence only when high anxiety situations were rated. Despite the quantitative difference, this finding failed to demonstrate qualitative differences (observer vs. one's own perspective; i.e. the social phobic typically seeing himself/herself from the outside).

In a study investigating a similar hypothesis by similar measures, Wells & Papageorgeiou (1999) compared 12 social phobic, 12 agoraphobic, and 12 blood-injury phobic subjects to 12 non-patient controls. The situations however were classified as neutral as opposed to social.

In this study a change of perspective occurred in the social group from a field perspective in neutral situations (similarly to the other subjects) to an observer perspective in social situations (in contrast to blood-injury phobic and normal subjects). Agoraphobic subjects maintained an observer perspective throughout; it was smaller, however, than the ratings of the social phobic subjects.

In summary, in this study social phobic individuals tended to report "more imagery," recalling events in more vivid detail. The meaningfulness of this finding is not clear. The contention of Hackman et al. (1998), therefore, that "negative self-imagery plays an important role in the maintenance of social phobia" (p. 9) seems unjustified. Similarly in imagining anxiety-evoking social events social phobic subjects tended to view themselves in a disembodied way as if through the eyes of an observer. Again, it is difficult to grasp the meaningfulness of this finding, let alone as evidence of a bias. However that may be, this putative "bias" is assigned a role of some importance as it is proclaimed to necessitate a correction by means of cognitive therapy (Wells & Papageorgiou, 1999, p. 658) further assuming that this brand of therapy actually effects such corrections. I shall return to this point in a further section dealing with the claim that cognitive factors are the efficient (immediate) cause of social phobia.

Is There a Link Between Levels of Social Anxiety and Cognitive Processes?

Although not concerning social phobia in the formal sense, this study might be useful in shedding light on this subject. Moreover, it is likely that some of the highly anxious participants in the study would fulfill the requisite criteria for social phobia if these had been applied.

In Eckman & Shean (1997) student subjects were divided into highly anxious (n = 29) and little-anxious (n = 26) groups based on their responses to the Brief social phobia scale – BSPS (Davidson, Potts, Richichi et al., 1993b). Subjects completed the SISST after three simulations of impromptu speeches of 3 min. each.

In both groups of subjects, there were significant decreases of negative self-statements with subsequent role-plays; the decreases, however, were significantly greater among the less-anxious subjects. Conversely, there was no change in the positive self-statements in either group in time. It is not clear from the results whether the two groups differ on either positive or negative self-statements (most studies do not report any differences for the positive).

In summary, there seems to be little link between degree of social anxiety and frequency of either negative or positive thoughts as measured by self-statements.

Do Subtypes of Social Phobia Differ in Their Cognitive Processes?

Possible differences between sub-groups of social phobic individuals might be masked if social phobia is prematurely assumed to be a unitary pattern. The following studies attempted to compare cognitive responses (measured by self-reports) of social phobic individuals subdivided into specific and generalized categories.

In Holt et al. (1992) social phobic participants divided into 10 specific, 10 generalized, and 10 generalized with an additional avoidant personality disorder – APD (DSM-III-R) were compared in terms of results on the Cognitive-Somatic Anxiety Questionnaire (CSAQ). No significant differences in scores between the subtypes were found. As no values for each group were reported, it is not possible to tell if the various subtypes reported particularly anomalous "cognitions."

In another study of subtypes of social phobia (Turner et al., 1992), 27 specific, 61 generalized (15 also met criteria for APD), were asked to give a 10-minute speech in front of a small audience. Subjects rated the "negative thoughts" subscale of the SISST.

As in Holt et al. (1992), and while using different measures, no significant differences between the subtypes emerged; all groups were characterized by a high rate of negative thoughts.

Herbert et al. (1992) have compared two groups of generalized social phobic individuals: 9 without and 14 with additional APD, in terms of the frequency of positive and negative thoughts during role-play.

As in previous studies, no differences were found in ratios of positive to negative thoughts. It is impossible to say whether these were abnormal in any way.

In Hofmann, Newman, Becker, Barr, Taylor, & Roth (1995a) 8 generalized social phobic individuals, who also met criteria for APD, were contrasted to 8 specific ones on a cognitive scale administered after a 10-minute simulated speech in front of a small audience. Consistently with previous results, no differences in the thinking self-reported by the two groups of subjects were detected.

Several studies, however, did report some statistically significant differences. In Brown et al. (1995), 36 specific social phobic subjects were compared to 36 generalized without and 28 generalized social phobic participants with APD on the cognitive subscale of the CSAQ. Significant differences were found between the extremes of the continuum of subtypes, namely between the specific and the generalized with APD. What this difference in degree of severity represents qualitatively speaking remains unclear.

In Hofmann & Roth (1996) 15 generalized, 9 non-generalized social phobic participants (n = 9), 12 anxious, and 10 normal controls were compared. In contrast with the other groups, the generalized social phobic individuals reported higher scores on the negative subscales of the SISST. As in other studies, no differences were observed on the positive subscales.

In an earlier study, Heimberg et al. (1990b) compared 35 generalized to 22 specific (public speaking) social phobic subjects (DSM-III) in terms of a role-play test and the thoughts this brought into play. The generalized group had to simulate initiating a conversation with a member of the opposite sex, going to a party, or talking to a co-worker; the specific social phobic subjects had to simulate a presentation. After that, all subjects listed their thoughts, which were classified as positive, negative, or neutral.

The generalized subjects rated higher on the negative subscale of the SISST and lower on its positive subscale. But, when the rating of severity of social phobia (from the intake interview) was taken into account, the differences on the positive subscales were no longer significant. Almost the opposite was observed with thought listing: the generalized group had a lower proportion of positive thoughts but no differences were found in the proportion of negative thoughts. If anything, these contradictory results raise doubts about the measurement of cognitive processes among social phobic individuals.

In summary, most studies do not provide evidence of different cognitive processes among subtypes of social phobia.

Do Social Phobic Individuals Differ from Those with Other Disorders in Terms of Cognitive Processes?

According to cognitive theory, different disorders ought to be characterized by specific cognitive distortions and overarching beliefs (see Clark, 1999, p. S5). In this section, the available evidence will be reviewed.

Rapee, Mattick, & Murrell (1986) compared the thoughts listed by 16 panic disorder (PD) participants to those of 16 social phobic (without panic) subjects, after an experience of panic provoked by CO_2 inhalation.

The social phobic subjects reported a much lower proportion of "catastrophic thoughts" than did the PD ones. The rates of "catastrophic thoughts" reported by social phobic participants − unlike those of the PD subjects − were not influenced by reassuring instructions.

These results seem to question the received view holding social phobic individuals as particularly vulnerable while being in a state of high anxiety (see Amir, Foa, & Coles, 1998b).

Hope et al. (1990) compared the responses of 16 social phobic subjects to a modified Stroop task described earlier with those of 15 PD (without agoraphobia) subjects. Social phobic participants took longer to read the social "threat" (compared to control) words, than did those in the panic group. The latter by contrast, took longer to read words describing physical threat. No differences in reaction to the unmodified part of the test (color naming) were observed.

Altogether, these results are somewhat questionable as they were obtained by multiple statistical comparisons (t-tests) rather than by a single analysis of variance. Even if the statistical analyses were beyond reproach, the fact that social phobic individuals take somewhat longer (about 8 secs.) to read words of "social threat" than "control" words hardly bears out the authors' conclusion (p. 185) that a specific cognitive process purported to explain this rather anodyne fact has been revealed.

In Harvey, Richards, Dziadosz, & Swindell (1993), social phobic and panic disorder subjects were compared to controls (12 subjects each) in terms of their interpretation of ambiguous stimuli.

The experiment required the rating of 14 brief scenarios in terms of harmfulness and anxiety, the underlying assumption being that the higher score reflects a bias in interpretation. The 2 clinical groups had higher scores than the controls but (with the exception of one result) did not differ from each other.

Although the conclusion that the anxious patients tend to interpret ambiguous events in a more alarming fashion seems uncontroversial, the overall interpretation that "These results lend support to the theory that interpretive biases are a function of schema which require activation by salient stimuli" (p. 246), has nothing in the study to support it.

In Amir et al. (1998b) 32 generalized social phobic subjects were compared to 13 obsessive-compulsive patients and 15 normal controls. The propensity to negative interpretation was studied by the responses of the subjects to social and non-social ambiguous scenarios. The questionnaire had a forced choice between positive, negative, and neutral interpretations that the subjects had to rank in terms of plausibility. Participants were also asked to rate the questionnaire twice: as concerning them personally and in general.

When subjects rated the questionnaires as if it concerned them, generalized social phobic individuals interpreted social situations more negatively than the other two groups; there were, however, no differences on the non-social situations. When rating the situations in general there were no differences between the groups regardless of scenario (either social or not).

The authors concluded from this that generalized social phobic individuals have a negative bias in interpreting social situations in which they are involved. This conclusion is rather doubtful for several reasons. First, the unknown validity of its scenarios and the limited comparisons with other pathologies leaves us uncertain as what is actually being measured.

The statistical analysis in this study further undermines the credibility of its conclusions. Ranking order results are transformed into a score by summation and the data are subsequently treated as if originating in a scale of equal intervals. This violates the basic postulates of the analysis of variance. The relevant data should have been properly treated through some form of non-parametric ranking analysis.

In summary, with the possible exception of having less catastrophic thoughts induced by CO_2 inhalation than did PD participants, there seems to be little that is specific and distinct in the cognitive processes of social phobic individuals on current evidence.

Do Cognitive Factors Maintain Social Phobia?

Two recent studies have advanced the claim of having uncovered cognitive factors implicated in the causal control of social phobia. Amir et al. (1998b) for example have reached the conclusion that "The results of the present study are consistent with studies implicating cognitive biases in the maintenance of social phobia and lends support to the presence of yet another bias in generalized social phobias, interpretation bias" (p. 956). If "maintenance" is taken to mean acting as the controlling factor, or the immediate or proximate (as opposed to the final) cause(s), the above-mentioned studies presume to have unveiled something of the etiology of social phobia. Such claims bear a deeper examination.

In the first study I shall consider (Hackmann et al., 1998), 30 social phobic participants and 30 controls were asked to recall a recent episode of social anxiety and to describe it in detail ("as a film-scenario"). Subjects also had to rate to what extent they saw themselves through their own eyes on a 7-point scale. Social phobic subjects reported more images and rated them more negatively. They described themselves more from an "observer's" vantage point than did controls. In contrast, social phobic subjects realized as clearly as did the control subjects the distortions in their scenarios. Similarly, an interviewer rated scenarios from both groups equally.

Although clearly, in this study, social phobic individuals tended to report "more imagery," (i.e. imagine or recall events in more vivid detail) than did the control subjects, the meaning of the above finding is for the time being obscure. How this difference in degree between groups of experimental subjects supports the inference of the causal implication of cognitive factors in social phobia remains baffling. After all, the same cognitive quality is found in both groups albeit to a somewhat higher degree among social phobic individuals. The contention of the authors therefore, that "negative self-imagery plays an important role in the maintenance of social phobia" (p. 9) seems wholly unjustified.

The second study (Amir et al., 1998b) to be considered in this section was already described previously in another context. It concerns a comparison of the responses of (generalized) social phobic subjects to the Interpretation Questionnaire (IQ) to those of two other groups of subjects (obsessive-compulsive disorder and normal controls).

The IQ is made up of 15 scenarios depicting direct social interactions and 7 not requiring it. 3 alternative outcomes/interpretations are provided and designated by definition as positive, negative, and neutral. The subjects were asked to rank the likelihood that such an interpretation would come to mind in similar situations, as well as to rate on a 7-point scale how positive or negative such an outcome would be for them. Two versions of the questionnaire were filled out: when thinking about oneself or when imagining a typical person.

Social phobic individuals were predicted to be more likely to choose the negative possibility in social situations.

When the participants rated the questionnaires as if it concerned them, social phobic individuals interpreted social situations more negatively than did the other participants; there were no differences regarding non-social situations. When rating the situations in general, no differences between the groups came to light, regardless of scenario (social or not).

Although on the face of it − given its elegantly controlled design − the study appears methodologically sound, some concerns about the nature of the data must be raised. The most pressing is that despite its reassuring name, we do not know what the IQ is actually measuring.

Let us overlook, for the sake of discussion, both the uncertainty as to what psychological quality the results (1998b, p. 950) actually express, and the reservations about the transfigurations they underwent (subjects' rankings were transformed into interval or ratio-like scores and subjected to analysis of variance, followed by t-tests, 1998b, p. 950). Let us then say that the social phobic subjects have significantly more of this (hypothetical) quality than do the OCD and the normal subjects. Is one justified to speak of bias then? On what grounds? What is the normative unbiased response? Is it that of the normal subjects? After all they too exhibit the very same negative interpretations, although admittedly to a smaller degree. So do the OCD subjects, who report a similar tendency but to a higher degree without turning into social phobic individuals.

In the final analysis, characterizing social phobic individuals as tending to view social situations through the prism of a "negative interpretative bias," is no more than saying – figuratively – that they fear them or that ultimately – they are socially phobic. As to the proposition that these "biases" are the proximate cause of social phobia, if maintenance were to be defined as the effect exercised by a controlling factor, no support for it was in evidence in the experiments under review as all participants – not just the socially phobic – displayed it to some extent.

Does Cognitive Therapy Result in Different Cognitive Changes Than Other Treatments?

All available controlled studies of the psychological treatment of social phobia were surveyed and their effects in terms of cognitive variables compared. 16 studies were selected. Of these, 6 studies concerned a variant of cognitive modification (e.g. cognitive restructuring, rational emotive therapy) that was compared to behavioral therapy (exposure) or control conditions. These studies allowed us to gauge the effects of the cognitive treatment in a relatively pure condition on cognitive variables.

In the remaining 10 studies, the cognitive modification technique was either an element in a package (e.g. a cognitive-behavioral therapy or CBT) or a phase in a treatment made up of a sequence of various techniques with outcome assessed only at the end of the overall treatment. The implications of results reported in these studies are less obvious. Nevertheless, comparisons between packages with a cognitive modification ingredient and those without it allow us to draw some tentative conclusions.

In addition to the most frequently used questionnaires (e.g. FNE, reviewed in the assessment section), many cognitive measures described in the studies, were made up ad hoc. Although their psychometric qualities are not known, I shall assume for the sake of discussion that indeed they measure literally what their name indicates.

Table 7.1 describes the cognitive outcome of cognitive modification compared to behavioral treatments or control conditions. Out of 6 studies, 3 showed the same cognitive outcome regardless of therapy, while 3 showed significantly better results in favor of the cognitive treatment. Typically, outcome at the end of treatment remained stable at follow-up where available. In summary, the available evidence does not corroborate the premise that cognitive therapies systematically result in greater or better cognitive changes than do alternative treatments.

Table 7.2 describes the cognitive outcome of various CBT packages (i.e. including a cognitive modification technique) compared to

Table 7.1. *Comparative cognitive outcome of exposure and cognitive modification*

Study	Treatment conditions	Outcome Post-treatment	Follow-up	Comments
Emmelkamp et al. (1985)	1. Exposure 2. Cognitive restructuring: self-instruction variant 3. Cognitive restructuring: rational–emotive variant	1 < 2 = 3	Improvement stable at 1 month; further improvement for rational emotive variant	Results revealed specific effect of cognitive therapy on cognitive measures.
Mersch et al. (1989)	1. Cognitive restructuring 2. Social skills training	1 = 2	Improvement stable at 6 weeks and 14 months	
Mattick et al. (1989)	1. Exposure 2. Cognitive restructuring 3. Exposure + cognitive restructuring 4. Waiting list	1 = 4 < 2 = 3	Improvement stable at 3 months; further improvement for cognitive restructuring alone	Results revealed specific effect of elements of cognitive therapy on cognitive measures.
Scholing & Emmelkamp (1993a; 1996a)	1. Exposure (followed by cognitive restructuring) 2. Cognitive restructuring (followed by exposure) 3. Combination of both 4. Waiting list	1 = 2 = 3 = 4 (all improved)	Improvement stable at 3 and 18 months	Cognitive restructuring alone, exposure and the combination of both are effective to the same extent in changing cognitions.

Scholing & Emmelkamp (1993b; 1996b)	1. Exposure (followed by exposure) 2. Cognitive restructuring (followed by exposure) 3. Integrated exposure + cognitive restructuring 4. Waiting list	1 = 2 = 3 = 4 (all improved)	Improvement stable at 3 and 18 months	Exposure induced faster cognitive change than did cognitive restructuring.
Taylor et al. (1997)	1. Cognitive restructuring (followed by exposure) 2. Associative therapy (followed by exposure)	1 > 2	Improvement stable at 3 months	Cognitive restructuring had greater effects than the control condition.

Table 7.2. *Comparative cognitive outcome of treatment packages with a cognitive component and other treatments*

Study	Treatment conditions	Outcome Post-treatment	Follow-up	Comments
Stravynski et al. (1982b)	1. Social skills training 2. Social skills training + cognitive restructuring 3. No treatment (phase)	1 = 2 > 3	Improvement stable at 6 months	Cognitive restructuring does not enhance the extent of change; further improvement during follow-up for some measures.
Mattick & Peters (1988)	1. Exposure 2. Exposure + cognitive restructuring	1 = 2	Improvement stable at 3 months	Both groups improved significantly.
Heimberg et al. (1985); Heimberg et al. (1993)	1. CBGT 2. Discussion + lectures + group support (control)	1 > 2 (FNE) 1 = 2 (thought listing)	Improvement stable at 6 months (FNE); 1 > 2 (thought listing); 1 = 2 at 5 years (negative thoughts came back in the CBGT condition)	Only half of the original sample was reassessed at 5 years, difficult to compare data.
Bruch et al. (1991)	1. CBGT 2. Discussion + lectures + group support (control)	1 = 2 (both improved) (thought-listing)	1 > 2 at 6 months	The control group returned to pretreatment levels of dysfunctional thoughts; the treated group progressed further and achieved a functional percentage of positive vs. negative thoughts.

Mersch (1995)	1. Exposure 2. A sequence including cognitive restructuring, social skills training and exposure 3. Waiting list	1 = 2 > 3	Improvement stable at 3 months; further improvement at 18 months on one measure
Hope et al. (1995a)	1. CBGT 2. Exposure 3. Waiting list	2 > 1 = 3	1 = 2 Improvement stable at 6 months
Salaberria & Echeburua (1998)	1. Exposure 2. Exposure + cognitive restructuring 3. Waiting list	1 = 2 > 3	Further improvement at 6 months, relatively stable at 12 months	Overall and in the longer term both treatments resulted in equivalent cognitive change. Between 6 and 12 months, the exposure group revealed a slight worsening while the combined group showed further improvement but the 2 groups were still not significantly different.

Note: FNE = fear of negative evaluation; CBGT = cognitive–behavioral group therapy.

packages without them. Out of 7 studies selected, 5 showed equivalent cognitive change. In one study a package including cognitive therapy induced superior change and in one study exposure resulted in greater cognitive change than a package including cognitive modification.

In 3 of the studies described above, results at the end of treatment or short-term follow-up were no longer the same at long-term follow-up. In Heimberg, Salzman, Holt, & Blendell (1993) greater cognitive change disappeared at a 5-year follow-up, while general clinical improvement maintained. In Bruch, Heimberg, & Hope (1991) by contrast, equivalence at the end of treatment was overturned; at 6-months follow-up the cognitive treatment resulted in greater cognitive change. In Hope et al. (1995a) exposure led to greater cognitive change at the end of treatment, but at 6-month follow-up the cognitive improvement induced by the CBT package caught up with it.

Table 7.3 describes 3 studies of packages of CBT (i.e. including a cognitive modification technique) compared to pharmacotherapy.

In Heimberg et al. (1998) phenelzine gave rise to a greater cognitive change than did the CBT at the end of a 12-week treatment; the follow-up being unavailable at the present. In Gelernter et al. (1991) the CBT and exposure combined with medication led to equivalent cognitive change. Finally, in Clark & Agras (1991) two different cognitive packages resulted in similar cognitive change, as did the contrast experimental conditions.

Overall then, there is no evidence supporting the hypothesis that cognitive therapies or techniques are able to effect cognitive changes better (either quantitatively or qualitatively) than other approaches. Rather, it seems that what may be considered cognitive factors change hand in hand with other features of psychopathology in an overall improvement during or after effective therapy, regardless of therapeutic approach.

This premise is also supported by studies summarized in Table 7.4. This describes 6 studies of pharmacotherapy compared to placebo that included a cognitive measure (typically the FNE). Differences or equivalence in the cognitive feature measured by the FNE parallel exactly the efficacy of the medication in contrast to placebo. FNE improves hand in hand with other measures of outcome in all studies reporting useful improvement and remains at the same level as in placebo when the medication (e.g. atenolol) has little additive effect (Liebowitz et al., 1992).

Discussion

The inquiry into social phobia from the perspective of cognitive processes has not deepened our understanding of it. An obvious stumbling

Table 7.3. *Comparative cognitive outcome of cognitive and pharmacological therapies*

Study	Treatment conditions	Outcome		Comments
		Post-treatment	Follow-up	
Clark & Agras (1991)	1. CBGT + placebo pill 2. CBGT + buspirone 3. Buspirone alone 4. Placebo pill alone	1, 2 = 3, 4 (no improvement) (self-statement)	1, 2 > 3, 4 (1 month)	The specific effects of CBGT and drug treatments are difficult to separate.
Gelernter et al. (1991)	1. Exposure + cognitive restructuring (CBGT) 2. Exposure + phenelzine 3. Exposure + alprazolam 4. Exposure + placebo pill	1 = 2 = 3 = 4 (FNE)	Improvement stable at 2 months	The specific effects of CBGT and drug treatments are difficult to separate from the effect of exposure that was an integral part of the 4 conditions.
Heimberg et al. (1998) Liebowitz et al. (1999)	1. CBGT 2. Phenelzine 3. Placebo pill 4. Educational supportive therapy	2 > 1 = 4 > 3 (FNE)	2 (further improve) > 1 deteriorate	The follow-up was in phases: 6 months off maintenance (support) and 6 months no treatment.
Otto et al. (2000)	1. Exposure + Cognitive restructuring 2. Clonazepam	1 = 2 (FNE)	Not available	Both groups improved significantly.

Note: FNE = fear of negative evaluation; CBGT = cognitive–behavioral group therapy.

Table 7.4. *Cognitive effects of pharmacotherapy (FNE*)*

Study	Treatment conditions	Outcome	
		Post-treatment	Follow-up
Versiani et al. (1992)	1. Moclobemide 2. Phenelzine 3. Placebo	1 = 2 > 3 (8 weeks)	not available
Liebowitz et al. (1992)	1. Phenelzine 2. Atenolol 3. Placebo	1 = 2 2 = 3 1 > 3 (8 weeks)	not available
Davidson et al. (1993b) Sutherland et al. (1996)	1. Clonazepam 2. Placebo	1 > 2 (2, 4, 6, 8, 10 weeks)	Improvement stable at 2 years
Lott et al. (1997)	1. Brofaromine 2. Placebo	1 > 2 (10 weeks)	not available
Schneier et al. (1998)	1. Moclobemide 2. Placebo	1 = 2 (8 weeks) (no improvement)	not available
Allgulander (1999)	1. Paroxetine 2. Placebo	1 > 2	not available
van Ameringen et al. (2001) Walker et al. (2000)	1. Sertraline 2. Placebo	1 > 2	1 > 2

Note: FNE = fear of negative evaluation.

block on this path is the elusive nature of mind and the difficulty of making its hidden processes plain. I shall return to these rather philosophical issues later.

Despite the formidable appeal of the cognitive perspective in terms of generator of research, it has not given rise to more accurate predictions concerning social phobia nor to more potent treatment methods (see review of treatment outcome in chapter 10).

Several questions were raised at the outset. Are individuals identified as social phobic characterized by cognitive processes typical to them? Comparatively speaking, are such hypothetical processes different in degree or in kind? Finally, could such differences constitute the cause of social phobia at the present (without necessarily accounting for its origins)?

The main theoretical stumbling block on the way to answering such questions is the absence of a formal definition of the main terms used within the context of the cognitive perspective.

What are cognitions in cognitive therapy? Whereas cognitive science construes cognition as "information-processing" (McFall & Townsend, 1998, p. 526) inferred from actions such as classification and detection, cognitive therapy represents cognition either as a thing (something that one has) or a subjective mental experience (1998). Cognitions are conceived of as accessible and quantifiable by introspective self-report methods. Thus, the uncertainty arising from measuring cognitive content or processes in such a way compounds further the theoretical ambiguity noted earlier. Moreover, many such self-reported introspective instruments, (e.g. the Interpretation Questionnaire: IQ – Amir et al., 1998b and the "Probability Cost Questionnaire": PCQ – Foa et al., 1996), were constructed ad hoc. What do they measure?

Psychological measurement, especially with a new instrument, is by necessity an attempt to validate both the instrument as well as the underlying construct it is meant to assess. While the theoretical construct is never defined, the participants' responses to the IQ – to take it as an example – are taken to be self-evidently as revelatory of their thinking. Whereas only the responses (in this case presumably the act of writing) can be observed, it is the thinking "behind" them – as it were – that is constantly alluded to in the text of the article. But responses to the IQ might be meaningful in different ways. An alternative interpretation could be that it is a social behavior in a particular and circumscribed social situation. Typically, the social phobic individual is eager to satisfy important people (or anxious at the very least not to provoke their displeasure). In this case, the experiment could be an exercise in self-description in reference to past and future actions, in terms molded by the social context of the experiment and constrained by the limited options provided by the experimental task.

Real-life experience, unlike laboratory tasks (e.g. responding hypothetically to written inventories of faintly outlined situations), is not neatly laid out. It presents a fluid situation providing a continuous flow of information, some of considerable ambiguity, from which the individual has to extract the relevant bits. Furthermore, the relationship between the laboratory task where the participants indicate (e.g. on the PCQ) what they might do and what actually takes place in their ordinary lives (external or ecological validity), remains to be determined.

In a similar vein, although the term is invoked frequently, no definition of what a "cognitive bias" might be was to be found in the numerous articles under review. Is bias defined relatively, in comparison to some standard (embodied by whom?) or absolutely, defined by formal rules of logic? Is a theoretical perspective or a philosophical outlook a bias? What of religious beliefs such as reincarnation or Judgment Day – to the pious as manifest as the seasons – are these biased? Is the well-documented (Baron, 1988) willingness of most people to generalize from small unrepresentative samples or make spurious predictions (e.g. about future conduct) from irrelevant bits of information (e.g. impressions during a brief interview) and other widespread irrationalities (Gardner, 1993), the norm or a bias?

In general, the term has been used interchangeably with cognitive distortions, dysfunctional thoughts or assumptions or beliefs, cognitive structures or schemata, associative networks or encoding bias. Rough equivalents unfortunately do not make up for the lack of definition of "cognitive bias," for the theoretical meaning of these terms is just as ambiguous.

As to the specific queries raised earlier, I will summarize the results in accordance with the kinds of measures in use. The first – the objective ones – are those that allow an objective quantification of performance, such as used in the experiments of "cognitive science." The second – the subjective ones – are those that rely entirely on self-report questionnaires. These attempt to quantify subjective estimations by the subjects of some features of their own state of consciousness (e.g. occurrence of negative thoughts) quantified in terms such as "very often" or "hardly ever" to which a numerical value is attached.

Do specific cognitive processes, then, characterize social phobic individuals? In terms of the objective measures, the results are equivocal. First, social phobic individuals perform no differently from control subjects in terms of memory. Second, in terms of attention, social phobic individuals were either no different than controls (homographs) or showed a *slightly* delayed response (modified Stroop task) in comparison to that of normal and panic disorder subjects.

Overall, in some experiments social phobic subjects showed responses that differed – to some degree – from those of other subjects. The source of this difference remains obscure. There is no evidence however to support the claim that it reflects a "cognitive bias" that is inherently socially phobic. In fact, no "cognitive" activity – objectively measured – inherently and exclusively typifies social phobia.

As to the results obtained by means of self-reported subjective estimates of uncertain validity, these seem to be no more than various ratings of anxious distress, expressed by the social phobic participants within the constraints of the metaphors imposed on them by different questionnaires. These point for instance to the fact that under certain conditions social phobic individuals tend to depreciate themselves more than controls. Ultimately these measurements are no more revealing than a casual interview. What they highlight of alleged cognitive processes remains uncertain at best. In most studies under review, social phobic subjects' responses to experimental tasks were indeed somewhat different from those of contrast subjects. However, since all subjects in those studies seem to be exhibiting the hypothetical cognitive quality to some extent, these results cannot be regarded as compelling proof of specific social phobic cognitive processes in play.

Altogether, assertions that cognitive biases (whatever they are) cause (maintain) social phobia, rest on most shaky foundations. If maintenance were defined as the effect exercised by a controlling factor, no support for it was in evidence in the experiments under review. As seen previously, in all studies making such claims, social phobic individuals showed to a greater extent (i.e. to a greater degree) the "cognitive process" allegedly being measured. Thus, although Amir et al. (1998b) for example claimed that social phobia results from faulty cognitive processes, all participants in their study, not just the social phobic participants reported them to varying degrees (1998, Fig. 2, p. 951).

Similarly, while the social phobic participants in Hackmann et al. (1998) did report "more imagery" (i.e. imagine or recall events in more vivid detail than did the control subjects) the control participants reported it too. Thus, the same cognitive quality was found in both groups albeit, on average, to a somewhat higher degree in social phobic participants.

How would such a difference in scale between experimental groups square with the propositions that: (1) it reflects a cognitive "bias" and furthermore, (2) it plays a causal role in social phobia? Need not effect be present when the cause is manifest (and vice versa)? In light of the above, why were only the social phobic participants socially phobic? Perhaps a counterargument to the objection could be that only a certain critical threshold of this factor is causal, but then what is it? Given the great individual differences found on every dimension of social phobia, it is highly likely that some of the social phobic participants would fall below such a hypothetical threshold while some of the controls would score above it. Thus, the likelihood that some participants in all experimental groups overlap to some extent further undermines the possibility that a cognitive factor − "bias," if that is what it is − plays a causal role in social phobia.

Bias in this context, rather than referring to any activity characterizing social phobia, fits much better the systematic singling out of one group of individuals for basically a universal trait, subjectively reported.

Thus, while reading the literature under review, one gradually forms the impression that "the cognitive-behavioral clinician merely assumes causality, without a quantitative theoretical model or empirical evidence; whatever behavior is observed must have resulted from a person's cognitions" (McFall & Townsend, 1998, p. 325).

Indirect evidence (drawn from clinical trials) does not offer much support to the cognitive perspective either. "Cognitive" treatments neither affect hypothetical cognitive processes in a specific way nor more so, than supposedly non-cognitive treatments. Moreover, the kind of cognitive changes observed in these studies seemed to be a facet of a general improvement in psychopathology, rather than the cause of it.

Regardless of its scientific status, the hypothesis of the cognitive causation of social phobia has a powerful appeal as a rationale for the "proper" kind of treatment. In keeping with this, cognitive approaches to treatment are seen as fixing the cognitive "apparatus" within the patient. Such a construal of treatment (i.e. as an antidote to a presumed "etiology") follows an idealized pattern established by the medical model of disease. It is interesting that the two interlocking notions – etiology and treatment – are presented at the early stages simultaneously, although the relevant evidence for either is unavailable. Later on, outcome studies demonstrating promising efficacy are somehow construed as evidence supporting the causal hypothesis. At the present however, with sufficient evidence at our disposal, such a reading is no longer tenable.

Why has this highly productive research program yielded rather disappointing results with social phobia?

Several possibilities need to be considered. First, it may well be that no typical "social phobic" cognitive structure or process has been identified within the individuals complaining of "it," because there are no inherently social phobic structures or processes "within" the individuals exhibiting the broad social phobic pattern of conduct. This would imply that social phobic characteristics – cognitive and otherwise – are exacerbations of fundamentally normal responses occurring within normal range (see also chapter 6). Ultimately – although this may not be entirely obvious at the present – there might be no social phobic entity to be found in nature. As we have seen previously (in chapter 5) and although some of the evidence is encouraging, we do not know with all certainty that social phobia is a distinct psychological pattern; it may well be an aggravation of common shyness – with admittedly rather dire consequences.

Second, it is possible that despite the insightful theoretical speculation, the methods available for the teasing out of cognitive processes are not equal to the task. The fact that it is difficult to imagine alternative methods gives us a measure of the practical difficulties inherent in the cognitive outlook.

Third, it is possible that the conceptual or indeed the philosophical foundations (e.g. Cartesian dualism – summarized in chapter 3) of this approach are problematic. I shall briefly examine some of the conceptual assumptions under-girding the cognitive research program.

In the cognitive perspective, words are used to denote an intangible reality. For instance, its central tenet is that people act on beliefs. But what is belief? Within the cognitive approach, it is by definition an inner state. But what could possibly be its referents (see McFall & Townsend, 1998, p. 317) to allow measurement?

A "belief can be articulated in words; it can be open to the bearer's awareness; and it can be manifested in action" (Lacey, 1995, pp. 70–71). None of these is of course the belief itself; this – if it may be said to exist other than metaphorically – remains inaccessible. Furthermore, the conviction that we have a direct and unencumbered perception of our minds that can readily be articulated may be an illusion (see Gopnik, 1993; Sampson, 1981).

If belief, by contrast, were defined as an extended pattern of behavior (i.e. an intricate process of acting *as if*) the postulated but intangible inner state becomes redundant (see Rachlin, 1992).

Nevertheless, in the cognitive approach such inner states are abstracted from the living human organism taking part in dynamic relations with the (social) environment. Mental states are seen as elements in a self-contained structure of causes and effects with conduct as its output. Agent and environment are seen as separable, with the environment as a kind of stage on which a plot dictated from within unfolds. "The knower's psychological states, the ideas in his or her head, are held to be more important, more knowable, and more certain than any underlying material interests, social practices or objective properties of the stimulus situation" (Sampson, 1981, p. 731).

The practice of setting up a dichotomy between the actual display of behavior and/or the manner of the quality of its organization (thoughtfulness) has been criticized on philosophical grounds as an instance of a "category mistake." According to Ryle (1949) this logical fallacy consists of treating the label for a class of events as if it were a member of that class. From this vantage point the distinction between conduct and its organization might be likened to attempting to separate the choreography of a ballet (the complex interlocking sequence of steps) from the movements of the dancers or the strategy from the actual armed forces striving to implement it.

The Cartesian philosophy in which the cognitive program is embedded accords a central role to mind while separating it from the body (dualism). In contrast, a key doctrine in Hume's philosophy is the primacy of feeling – a quality undeniably embodied. In his *Treatise of Human Nature* (1739/1961), Hume famously asserted that "Reason is and ought only to be the servant of the passions and can never pretend to any other office than to serve them" (Kemp Smith, 1941, p. 144). In this view, reasoning is limited to propositions that represent something else and may be true or false. Actions, by contrast, do not represent something else; they exist only by dint of being carried out. Conclusions and actions are therefore ontologically different; this is why "reason can never be a motive to an action" (1941, p. 144).

Wittgenstein (1958) raised even wider objections, from the perspective of the analysis of linguistic practices (known as analytic philosophy); these cannot be treated in full here (see Williams, 1985 for a comprehensive summary). Suffice it to say that Wittgenstein called into question the notion that introspective practices penetrate some hidden inner realm. He held that invoking inner processes provides at best pseudo-explanations for conduct (Parker, 1996, p. 367). Rather, he considered the metaphorical descriptions of "inner states" as the presentation of criteria for further action (embedded in a certain cultural pattern of life). "Because life is lived *in advance of itself*, it is more plausible to understand talk of inner world as oriented towards impending action than as predications based on reference to internal states. In this way ... language, as verbal gesture, grounds experience" (Davis, 1996, p. 95). Similarly, Quine (1960) argued that language was crucial in establishing private experience and self-awareness, while being tied inextricably to the culture of the community of its users. Marx (quoted in Chalmers, 1976, p. 136) put it thus: "It is not the consciousness of men that determines their being, but, on the contrary, their social being that determines their consciousness."

These philosophical views, presented as an antidote to the conceptual confusions generated by Cartesian dualism, do not so much diminish thought as attempt to widen our conception of it, by anchoring it in social life.

Jones & Nisbett (1971) found that actors in situations believed that conjunctures of circumstances determined how they behaved. Observers, however, tended to impute the actors' behavior to innate characteristics and habit. When trying to understand individuals we know little about for lack of information or curiosity, we tend to attach inner causes to behavior. This is part of "folk psychology." Perhaps this practice has been elevated into the cognitive approach (Stich, 1983).

8 Social Phobia as a Consequence of Inadequate Social Skills

On first encounter social phobic individuals stand out as remote and self-involved. Although on duty (e.g. about to present) or in attendance (e.g. Christmas party), they hardly participate in the ongoing social activity (e.g introducing themselves to others, exchanging pleasantries, dancing), being apart — sometimes literally. When engaged by others, they remain passive, reply tersely and appear distracted, liable to lapse into embarrassing silences or become overtalkative. Physically, they keep a distance and look away, stiff rigidity alternating with noticeable agitation (tremors, perspiration, blushing, faltering voice).

Extended in time and ranging over numerous social occasions, the social phobic pattern of conduct is strongly characterized by self-protective evasion of challenging encounters, flight for safety and avoidance — if possible — of situations in which one might be carefully scrutinized and found wanting or altogether undesirable. As a manner of speaking, social phobia might be typified by what such individuals fail to do (e.g. take a stand, initiate, take charge) and achieve socially (e.g. associates, friends, spouses).

Many activities essential to normal life (e.g. presenting, negotiating, courting) are struggled with tentatively or given up in despair — with serious consequences. Possibilities of promotion, forging partnerships, and making new friends are often forgone. In the limited number of encounters they participate in, such individuals say little, hardly expressing feelings or opinions. Their very suffering is usually kept hidden; the state of apprehension they usually experience is typically dissembled. What might account for this unusual pattern of reticence?

One possibility is that social phobic individuals are deficient in or lack altogether the social skills necessary in order to function proficiently (Curran, 1979, p. 319, Stravynski & Greenberg, 1989, p. 208, Marks, 1985, p. 615). Their anxious distress might be considered from such a perspective as arising from the inability to act effectively, while forseeing — realistically — its social consequences.

Aim and Method

My main goal in this chapter is to consider the evidence having a bearing on the "skill-deficits" account of social phobia. Before doing that, however, several intermediate steps need to be taken.

I will first inquire into the notion of "social skills" generally and its application to social phobia specifically. Subsequently, as psychological concepts cannot exist independently from the methods of their measurement, I will look into the validity of the corresponding tools devised to identify and to quantify social skills deficits generally and their value in social phobia in particular.

If validity is acceptable, more important questions may be dealt with, namely whether the socially phobic differ in their social skills from normal individuals and/or other contrast populations. The demonstration of such differences is a necessary (but not sufficient) condition for the ultimate query: do skills deficits play a causal role in the social phobic pattern of behavior?

Finally, I shall examine the value of the construct of "skills deficits" indirectly, by considering the effects of a therapy designed to remedy them.

What are Social Skills and their Deficits?

The hypothesis of skills deficits is obviously reliant on the notion of social skills. The hypothetical construct of social skills arises from attempts to provide an explanatory framework for normal social behavior. A possible way of studying social behavior is to construe it as analogous to a motor skill (e.g. using chopsticks, swimming). It involves acting according to pre-established rules in pursuit of certain goals (Argyle & Kendon, 1967). This underlines the tightly conventional (i.e. rule-bound) aspect of social behavior (e.g. first meeting someone) as well as its dynamism (i.e. constantly undergoing revisions in light of signals originating in the social environment). A failure to perform proficiently is by analogy accounted for in terms of lack of requisite skills (Trower, Bryant, & Argyle, 1978).

"Deficient social skills" provide a concept accounting for the observation that certain individuals are socially inept either because they tend to bungle common social encounters, shirk them or fail to realize normal achievements (e.g. finding a mate).

As all psychopathologies unfold on the backdrop of social relations, this explanatory hypothesis has had a wide influence. Among others, it has been applied to: schizophrenia (Wallace & Lieberman, 1985), depression (Lewinsohn, 1974), sexual dysfunctions in men (Lobitz & LoPiccolo, 1972), and social phobia (Stravynski & Greenberg, 1989). Such an account hypothetically associates certain social skills deficits with membership in various diagnostic categories (Hersen, 1979). The breadth of application, however, raises the question of whether the construct of "social skills deficits" has any precise meaning.

This compels us to clarify the concept of skill. The term itself, despite frequent use and wide-ranging application, has proved to be exceedingly difficult to define (see Adams, 1987).

Libet & Lewinsohn (1973) provided one of the first and oft-quoted definitions of social skills being "the complex ability to maximize the rate of positive reinforcement and to minimize the strength of punishment from others" (p. 311). This functional definition, does not pinpoint specific behaviors, but considers any social success to be necessarily the result of skill. This definition is problematic. First, desired social outcomes may result from circumstances rather than skill. Second, this definition also includes conduct considered inappropriate (e.g. temper tantrums), or even morally repugnant (e.g. shifting the blame). Finally, it does not provide the unskilled performer with any guidance as to what he or she could do to improve their lot.

Another functional definition stresses control over others: "a person can be regarded socially inadequate if he [sic] is unable to affect the behavior and feelings of others in the way he intends and society accepts" (Trower, Bryant, & Argyle, 1978, p. 2). The same critique as above applies here.

A different kind of definition altogether seeks to provide details of the essential elements of skillful performance. Eye contact, appropriate content of speech, and reciprocity, among others, are mentioned (see Curran, 1979 and McFall, 1982 for overviews). Lists of elements, however concrete or comprehensive, cannot be taken for a definition. Nor is it clear why the listed elements have been singled out while potential others have been left out.

Other definitions still (e.g. Bellack, 1979, p. 98), argue for the integration of cognitive factors (e.g. social perception) to the behavioral elements of social skills. Such splitting of constituting elements may pose a risk of diluting the construct of social skills through its expansion to the extent of encompassing almost all behavior.

As may be gathered from this brief survey, no satisfactory definition of social skills, and by implication their absence or inadequacy, is available today. Nevertheless, the term has wide currency perhaps because it seems endowed with a certain concrete obviousness in the eyes of its users. Bolstering this face validity seems to be the sense that "deficient social skills" are a set of behaviors or characteristics and therefore, pal-pably recognizable.

In Wlazlo, Schroeder-Hartig, Hand, Kaiser, & Münchau (1990), for example, clinicians had little trouble separating skill-deficient patients from others on the basis of information from their clinical notes. Similarly, Juster, Heimberg, & Holt (1996a) maintain: "in our clinic most social phobic persons are found to possess adequate social skills but are inhibited when it comes to applying their skills in social situa-tions" (p. 84). What is the conceptual and empirical basis for both sets of observations? Does the term "skill" denote similar psychological qualities in both cases?

In conclusion, Curran's (1979, p. 321) remark that "everyone seems to know what good and poor social skills are" but "no one can define them adequately" still holds today. Putting the frustrating quest for definitions aside, I shall now consider how the construct of social skills has been assessed in research.

Assessment of Social Skills of Social Phobic Individuals

As the assessment of social skills had to be fashioned out of the concep-tual imprecision of the fundamental notion of "social skills," two basic orientations have evolved.

The first might be termed, an *intra-personal* approach. Within this, social skills are most commonly treated as a hypothetical mental con-struct denoting certain mental processes assumed to predispose a person to act in a particular way. Being "socially unskilled" in the intra-personal sense is not an observable performance. Rather, it is an underlying qual-ity that manifests itself in or may be inferred from, actual behavior. Trower (1995, p. 55) for example distinguishes between the components of social skills, (i.e. behaviors or repertoires of actions) and social skill (i.e. the process of generating skilled behavior). The mental construct (or process) is the driving force within that gives rise to the action with-out. As a trait, social skills are attributes of persons, not something they do.

Such a construal brushes against the risk of tautology. Inadequate social skills are inferred from an inept performance. Yet the very same lackluster performance will be put down to deficient skills.

For a hypothetical mental structure to be endowed with explanatory power, it must be shown to be valid in a series of independent studies (i.e. that it makes a difference and that it has a myriad of predictable consequences). Such independent demonstrations are scarce.

The advantage that the trait approach brings to the study of social skills is that it does not require a specific definition of such skills; such a definition is after all unavailable. As it is an abstraction, it is sufficient that such a construct meets certain psychometric criteria to be considered useful. The drawback is that as with all trait conceptions, social skills are assumed to be stable in time and across situations and therefore can be summed up in a score; this is very doubtful. Self-rating scales illustrate the intra-personal approach to assessment.

The second approach might be termed *inter-personal*. Within this conception, social skills are considered a function of given situations. Moreover, "social skills are an attribute of a person's situation-specific behavior, not of the person per se" (McFall, 1982, p. 7). It follows that "no particular behavior can be considered intrinsically skillful, independent of its context" (1982, p. 7). While highlighting the failings inherent in the trait approach, the interpersonal perspective is not free of shortcomings. It is not clear, for example, what are the key units of behavior to consider (constituent structures of behavior) and how to measure their effects on others. Nor is it obvious what makes a performance satisfactory.

The implication of this approach for assessment is that behaviors must always be seen in the context of situations. The most radical implication, by far, is that social skills are idiosyncratic and cannot be measured by some general test. Simulations of behavior observed by assessors illustrate this approach to assessment of social skills. However, the manner of reporting results with scores generalized across situations ignores the interpersonal principles and draws close to the intra-personal conception.

As carrying out a comprehensive review would not serve our purpose (McNeil, Ries, & Turk, 1995 provide one), I shall limit myself to several instruments with some background research to document aspects of their psychometric characteristics with social phobic subjects.

Self-rating

Scale for Interpersonal Behavior (SIB) (Arrindell & van der Ende, 1985)

This is a multidimensional self-report scale (originally in Dutch) measuring 4 domains rated for performance and distress. These are:

1. display of negative feelings (15 items)
2. expression of personal shortcomings (14 items)

3. display of assertion (9 items)
4. expression of positive feelings (8 items).

Distress is rated on a 5-point dimension ranging from 1 = not at all to 5 = extremely. Performance is quantified in terms of frequency ranging from 1 = never do to 5 = always do. Each domain has a score: a general score (separate for distress and performance) is the summation of the scores of all domains. The evidence regarding the soundness of the test is summarized in Table 8.1.

In summary, the accuracy of this instrument is satisfactory. However, it is not altogether certain what it ultimately measures as its (convergent)

Table 8.1. *Psychometric characteristics of the Scale for Interpersonal Behavior (SIB)*[1]

Reliability		Validity	
Test−retest	Internal consistency	Concurrent	Convergent
interval = 22 to 40 days	α (distress) = from 0.95 to 0.97 (**)	r (SIB distr./FQ[a]) = from 0.53 to 0.73 (**)	r (SIB distr./SIB perf.) = −0.53 (**)
r (distress) = 0.85	α (perform.) = from 0.91 to 0.97 (**)	r (SIB perf./FQ[a]) = from −0.15 (ns) to −0.38 (**)	r (SIB distr./FSS[b]) = 0.65 (**)
r (performance) = 0.73			r (SIB distr./SCL-90[c]) = 0.62 (**)
			r (SIB distr./STAI-s) = 0.27 (**)
			r (SIB distr./STAI-t) = 0.36 (**)
interval = 41 to 93 days			
r (distress) = 0.70	similar results for the English version		r (SIB perf./SCL-90[c]) = −0.13 (ns)
r (performance) = 0.80	(α = from 0.92 to 0.95)		r (SIB perf./STAI-s) = −0.07 (ns)
			r (SIB perf./STAI-t) = −0.18 (*)

FQ[a] = social phobia subscale of the Fear Questionnaire; FSS[b] = social fear items of the Fear Survey Schedule; SCL-90[c] = social inadequacy subscale of the Symptom Checklist (SCL-90); SIB = Scale for Interpersonal Behavior; STAI = State-Trait Anxiety
[1]Based on the following studies: Arrindell & van der Ende (1985); Arrindell, Sanderman, van der Molen et al. (1988); Arrindell, Sanderman, Hageman et al. (1991b); Bridges, Sanderman, Breukers et al. (1991); Mersch, Breukers, & Emmelkamp (1992b). (ns)= non significant; (*)= p < 0.05; (**)= p < 0.01.
NB: There are no *p* values given for test−retest correlations.

validity rests on moderate correlations with other instruments. The relationship of the SIB with the social behavior of social phobics in their own lives remains for the time-being unknown.

Role-play Tests

The construction of most role-play tests flows from the interpersonal view of social skills, namely as being situation-specific and rather individual. For this reason, most role-play tests are ad-hoc creations. Additionally, most tend to widen the narrow behavioral focus on conduct by adding ratings of subjective assessment of anxiety during it. A key issue in role-play tests is how to analyze and make sense of the performance displayed by the participants. As only theory can offer guidance, the definitions of social skills acquire a high practical importance. In practice, two perspectives are taken.

The first, "molecular," focuses on various verbal (i.e. speech) content and para-linguistic dimensions (e.g. intonation, length of speech, pauses) and non-verbal (e.g. gaze, posture, hand-movement) elements of social performance. These are sought across behaviors. The elements are in all likelihood chosen because they have an intuitive appeal (as seeming building blocks) and easy to "make sense" of as there is no theoretical grounding to this practice.

The second, the "molar," focuses on global behaviors in key domains (e.g. assertion, courtship) deemed to be essential to social functioning. The assessors' ratings (on Likert-type scales) reflect their intuition as to what constitutes a skillful performance. Although such practice seems to yield good reliability, "it is not clear precisely what these ratings actually reflect" (Bellack, 1979, p. 168).

These two levels of assessment are not mutually exclusive and have been used simultaneously in some studies. By way of illustration I chose the most psychometrically elaborate and sophisticated role-play test:

The "simulated social interaction test" (SSIT) – Curran (1982)

The SSIT provides descriptions of 8 short situations described by a narrator. These are: criticism, being the focus of attention, anger, meeting someone of the opposite sex, expression of warmth, conflict with a close relative, interpersonal loss, and receiving compliments. These themes were selected on the basis of previous factor-analytic investigations aiming to identify the most common difficulties (e.g. Richardson & Tasto, 1976; Goldsmith & McFall, 1975). At the end of each description, the subject is prompted to respond. The role-plays are intended to be short but no specific duration is suggested. All proceedings are videotaped.

The simulation is rated for performance and anxiety on an 11-point Likert-type scale ranging from "not at all skillful" (1) to "extremely skillful" (11) and "extremely anxious" (1) to "not at all anxious" (11).

Two key features of the test give rise to some concern. First, a global (and molar) approach to the rating of social skills was adopted because the authors "have not yet empirically determined the components of social skills for our criterion situation" (Curran, 1982, p. 363). That such a decision was guided by nothing more meaningful than the lack of a better option, gives pause.

Second, the training of the assessors involved 6 senior clinicians reaching agreements on ratings of performance of bogus patients. These ratings then become the criterion (i.e. the proper normative) response. The process of training consisted in "recalibration" of the assessors' judgments (correlation coefficients had to reach r = 0.8 at the least) to conform to those on which the senior clinicians had agreed.

Although this procedure guarantees agreement (i.e. reliability) among assessors, it may, paradoxically, through enforcing conformism, compromise the validity of what constitutes skillful behavior. The evidence regarding the soundness of the test is summarized in Table 8.2.

In summary, the strengths of this test reside in it having a representative selection of difficult situations, a high rate of inter- and intra-assessors reliability. Furthermore, it distinguished psychiatric patients from normal control participants.

Its weaknesses consist of poor accord with independent ratings performed in other settings and with non-trained observers (nurses, research assistants). Interestingly, assessors' agreements varied despite the setting of a high threshold by the experimenters. The greatest shortcoming of this test, however, is the absence of any evidence of its generalizability, namely that it provides information that may be considered as equivalent to observing what people do in actual life. Being on the ward can hardly be considered representative of routine social life. The author of the test concedes that "we are still not content with the information yield from such ratings" (Curran, 1982, p. 371). Overall, then, this one device for measuring social skills has, accuracy aside, few sound psychometric characteristics to recommend it.

To sum up, in view of the vagueness of the construct of social skills, it is not entirely surprising that its measurement leaves something to be desired. This is especially disappointing in the case of the role-play as its appeal lies precisely in the promise of being an economical substitute for

Table 8.2. *Psychometric characteristics of the Simulated Social Interaction Test (SSIT)*[1]

Reliability		Validity	
Inter-rater agreement	Internal consistency	Convergent	Discriminant
with mixed psychiatric patients	α (skills) = 0.69	*SSIT skills/SIB perform.*	
r (skills) = from −0.59 to 0.76 (*)	α (anxiety) = 0.96	r = 0.27 for men (ns)	national guardsmen
r (anxiety) = from 0.45 to 0.68 (*)		r = 0.41 for women (*)	
when raters = nurses	ICC (skills) = 0.22	*SSIT anxiety/SIB distress*	psychiatric outpatients
r (skills) = 0.51 (**)	ICC (anxiety)= 0.73	r = −0.01 for men (ns)	
when raters = research assistants		r = −0.48 for women (*)	
r (skills) = 0.64 (**)		*SSIT/behaviors on the ward*	
when raters = interviewers		r = from 0.51 to 0.94 (*)	
r (skills) = 0.62 (**)			
when raters = video judges			
r (skills) = 0.94 (**)			
with social phobic patients			
r (skills) = 0.91 (***)			
r (anxiety) = 0.70 (***)			

[1]Based on the following studies: Curran (1982); Curran, Wessberg, Monti et al. (1980); Curran, Wessberg, Farrel et al. (1982); Mersch, Breukers & Emmelkamp (1992b). SIB = Scale for Interpersonal Behavior; (ns) = non significant; (*)= p < 0.05; (**)= p < 0.01; (***)= p < 0.001.

observation of real social conduct in natural settings. Unfortunately, it is not (see McNamara & Blumer, 1982, p. 545 and Bellack, 1979, p. 167).

Finally, a framework for analyzing the performance displayed in role-play tests is sorely lacking. This is yet another consequence of the fact that no theoretical or operational definition of social skills is available. In practice, the analysis of performance is done in ways that generally preclude comparisons and, paradoxically, diminish the likelihood of identifying elements of convergent validity.

Strictly speaking, this survey ought to end at this stage for, lacking a clear theoretical vision of what social skills (and conversely their deficit or deficiencies) are, as well as meaningful means to identify and quantify them, how can we hope to answer the more complex question of whether social phobia is characterized by deficient social skills, let alone if these are its cause? Nevertheless, as there is something to be said for pursuing the exploration as instructive in itself, I shall carry on as if the conceptual/measurement drawbacks were not there.

Are there Social Skills Deficits Characteristic of the Socially Phobic?

Direct Evidence: Laboratory Simulations

The Socially Phobic Compared to Normal Individuals   Unfortunately, it is impossible to answer this question satisfactorily as neither norms of social skills nor of their deficiencies have been established. A roundabout way of attempting to answer it is to compare the social skills of the socially phobic to those of normal control individuals, the latter presumed to personify skillful social conduct. Although this precludes the drawing of absolute conclusions, it casts some light on the relative standing of social phobic individuals. As usual, the large variety of operational definitions of social skill used in different studies makes comparisons inherently difficult.

Rapee & Lim (1992) compared the enactment of a brief speech in front of a small audience by 28 social phobic individuals (13 generalized, 15 specific) to that of 31 control subjects. The performance was analyzed in terms of

1. specific elements of behavior (e.g. eye contact, clarity of voice) and
2. global quality of performance (e.g. subject's capacity to arouse interest) and rated on 5-point Likert scales by observers and the subjects themselves.

While no differences in terms of specific behaviors were reported, differences emerged in comparisons of the amalgamated scores of both specific and global aspects of performance. In light of the above, the meaning of the association between lesser skill and social phobia remains obscure. Subjects' self-ratings of performance tended to be lower than those of the observers, especially for the social phobic subjects.

In Alden & Wallace (1995), simulations of "getting acquainted" for 5 minutes by 32 generalized social phobic individuals were compared to those of 32 control subjects. Half the participants from both groups were assigned to a "positive" (e.g. the confederate was friendly and encouraging) and half to a "negative" (e.g. the confederate was cool and allowed silent pauses) condition.

Both groups did better with an encouraging than with an unresponsive confederate. Social phobic participants were more visibly anxious, spoke less and were not found to convey as much warmth and be as likeable as the controls. The meaning of these statistical differences is not entirely clear. Although we ignore what constituent elements of skill were rated or how any of this relates to the subjects' conduct in real-life, the authors nevertheless concluded that "the social phobic patients in both conditions were less skillful than control subjects."

Hofmann, Gerlach, Wender, & Roth (1997) compared 24 social phobic and 25 normal individuals in terms of speaking with the interviewer, telling the interviewer what they did the day before, preparing a talk with the interviewer, sitting in front of 2 persons (all 3 min. each) and role-play giving a speech prepared earlier (10 min.).

The participants' performances in all 5 situations were analyzed in terms of gaze, while the first 2 min. of the speech were also rated for speech disturbances defined as silent pauses, errors and dysfluencies.

No differences between the experimental groups were found in terms of gaze across situations, however calculated. As to speech disturbances, social phobic participants showed mostly less fluidity, although the generalized sub-group took more time pausing.

These results, although suggesting that social phobic individuals experience some difficulties in conversation, do not allow the drawing of general conclusions as to the state of their social skills.

Fydrich, Chambless, Perry, Buergener, & Beazley (1998) compared 34 socially phobic to 28 normal and 14 participants with other anxiety disorders who simulated initiating and maintaining a conversation with a confederate instructed to be passive. Overall, social phobic participants rated lower than the 2 control groups on several non-verbal and paralinguistic parameters.

In Baker & Edelmann (2002) 18 "generalized" social phobic and 18 normal participants interacted briefly with a confederate of which a 1-minute segment was analyzed. Social phobic subjects made less eye contact while talking and displayed more manipulative gestures. All subjects, however, spent equal amounts of time talking, being silent or smiling. Despite a considerable overlap between the groups, judges found social phobic subjects less adequate in their performance.

Walters & Hope (1998) compared the simulation of an impromptu speech and conversations with same- and opposite-sex confederates of 22 social phobic subjects and 21 non-anxious controls. As the study tested hypotheses derived from Trower & Gilbert's (1989) model of social anxiety, the videotaped role-plays were rated for behaviors deemed to reflect the domains of cooperation, dominance, submissiveness and escape/avoidance.

Social phobic subjects faced their interlocutors less and expressed less praise (construed as cooperation) and engaged less in bragging and commanding (construed as dominance). They were not, however, different in other respects. Crucially, social phobic participants were neither more submissive nor more avoidant than the non-anxious controls.

This study, like those that preceded it, shows that social phobic subjects behave somewhat differently from controls in simulated social interactions. Whether and to what extent these behaviors are indicators of the studied theoretical constructs remains an open question. How these constructs reflect adequate social behavior and what this might possibly be (optimally equidistant between dominant vs. submissive and cooperative vs. avoidant?) remains to be justified.

In summary, the few studies available do not allow the question I have raised to be addressed directly. For the most part, social skill remains undefined and the performance in role-playing, as its measure, is analyzed in ways that do not allow the integration of the fragmented bits into meaningful behavior (i.e. as a mean to an end).

Specifically, the results were mixed and did not systematically point to definite deficiencies in social skills, however broadly construed. Moreover, many elements of performance of the two experimental groups largely overlapped. Thus the statistically significant differences seem more indicative of differences in degree rather than in kind of skillfulness. Nevertheless, social phobic individuals were perceived during the simulations as functioning less adequately than their normal counterparts.

Are Social Skills Deficits Characteristic of a Subtype of Social Phobia? Are social skills deficits typical of a certain subtype of social phobia, rather than social phobia as such? No studies to my knowledge addressed this question directly; I shall therefore seek to answer it indirectly. This is feasible since several studies, while in pursuit of other purposes (typically seeking to tease out subtypes of social phobia), have used role-plays as a measure of social skills or social anxiety.

In Turner et al. (1992), 88 social phobic participants were divided into specific (n = 27) and generalized sub-groups (n = 61). They were required to: (1) make a 10-minute speech that had to last "at least 3 minutes" (2) pretend engaging in conversation with a first date and with a new neighbor of the same sex. These were rated for a number of molecular components of behavior (e.g. gaze, voice tone, number of verbal initiations, and duration of speech) and overall impression of skill.

No differences between experimental groups were noted on any element of skill. In a subsequent analysis of the subjects within the generalized group that took into account the fact that some also met criteria for avoidant personality disorder (APD), nothing differentiated the two subsets.

In a similar study, Herbert et al. (1992) compared the simulation of making an impromptu speech (3 min.), initiating a conversation and maintaining it by 23 "generalized" social phobic participants 14 of whom also met criteria for APD.

The performances were analyzed in terms of overall skill, paralinguistic aspects of speech, speech content, and non-verbal behavior while subjects rated their subjective anxiety. As in the earlier study, no differences in behavior were found between the two groups although those with APD rated themselves as more anxious before simulating the speech, but not afterwards.

These results were further reanalyzed, in light of a more stringent definition of the generalized subtype of social phobia, proposed by Heimberg & Holt (1989). After reclassification, it was found that this more severe group of generalized social phobic individuals were rated as significantly less skilled on an overall composite score than their reclassified counterparts; however, no specific differences in either behavior or thought were observed.

Tran & Chambless (1995) had 16 specific, 13 generalized, and 16 generalized social phobic/APD participants simulating three 4-minute role-plays: impromptu speech and conversations with individuals of the same and the opposite sex.

Assessors behind a one-way mirror rated performance for general impression of social skill. Simultaneously the subjects rated their impression of their own skill as well as the subjective anxiety they experienced. Specific social phobic individuals gave a better impression of skill than did the generalized/APD subjects. These results were found consistently with self-ratings and observer ratings across role-plays.

In summary, the comparisons of individuals from several subtypes of social phobia provide little systematic evidence to suggest that despite apparent differences in severity, one subtype is particularly deficient in social skills — however measured.

Indirect Evidence: Outcome of Clinical Trials

Are Social Skills Acquired through Social Skills Training?   A round-about way to probe the validity of the construct of social skills in social phobia would be to study what happens to it after a course of therapy (i.e. social skills training: SST) aiming specifically to improve it. As it is crucial to establish whether changes in social skills result exclusively from SST, only controlled studies will be considered.

In Wlazlo et al. (1990), 167 patients (generalized social phobia/APD) were treated by either group SST or exposure in vivo — administered individually or in a group. SST was administered over 25 sessions of 1.5 hours each. Group exposure involved a total of 34h. of treatment, whereas the individual format included 12h. 103 patients completed treatment and 78 were followed-up for 2.5 years on average. At the end of treatment, the 3 regimens brought about significant and equivalent improvement in terms of social anxiety and tendency to avoid. These gains maintained and slightly strengthened over the follow-up period. For the sake of analysis, the sample was subdivided into two groups: those with primary "skills deficits" and those with primary "social anxiety." Overall, those classified as "skill deficient" did less well in treatment. Most importantly from our point of view, no evidence was found of a better response to matching type of problem with kind of treatment (e.g. SST for patients identified as skill deficient). The internal validity of this study, however, is somewhat compromised by the fact that the exposure condition also included some training in social skills as well as in "social perception."

Skills deficits were said to be measured in this study by a self-report scale (UF-questionnaire). However, judging from the examples given, this seems to be doubtful as this measure (in German) listed fears (e.g. of failure and criticism) and guilt as well as abilities (e.g. making requests, refusing). On the strength of changes observed in this scale, patients in all treatment conditions (i.e. also in exposure) were said to have acquired social skills.

Subsequently, patients were divided into primarily "social phobic" (anxious) or "skill deficient" by experienced clinicians based on case records. It is not clear what was the basis of this subdivision as neither independent definition nor its anchoring points were provided. On the evidence of treatment outcome, it seems likely that the patients labeled "skill deficient" were the most severely phobic.

In Mersch et al. (1989) and Mersch, Emmelkamp, & Lips (1991), SST was compared to cognitive restructuring while also testing the value of matching treatment with patients' patterns of fear. Based on extreme responses to a role-play and a "rationality" test, 39 patients were classified as either predominantly behavioral (unskilled but rational) or cognitive (irrational but skillful). Half of each category of patients was assigned to SST and half to the cognitive treatment. Both treatment conditions resulted in significant and equivalent improvement on all measures. There was no support, however, for the notion that a match between predominant feature and treatment results in greater therapeutic gains. Nor did a significant lessening of social anxiety in this study lead to increased social activity.

Social skills were measured in this study by the SSIT described earlier (Curran, 1982). Patients' (classified as behavior reactors) skills improved following social skills training or a cognitive therapy (only on patients' self-ratings). This is an important finding being the only demonstration of improvement in skills following SST. However, as a similar improvement (patients' self-rating) occurred following a cognitive therapy, the construct of skill deficits as well as its improvement following a specific matching treatment (SST) are both weakened.

In summary, some evidence documents significant improvement in social skills following SST. This however is not exclusive to SST; statistically significant changes in social skills were also noted in patients receiving other treatments. How meaningfully these changes contribute to remedying deficient social skills remains unknown.

Is Improvement in Social Functioning Related to Skill-acquisition?
Stravynski, Marks, & Yule (1982a) assigned 27 patients identified (in today's terminology) as generalized social phobia/avoidant personality disorder to 12 1.5-hour sessions of either SST alone or SST combined with cognitive restructuring. 22 patients completed treatment. In each treatment condition patients improved significantly and equally on all measures of outcome (i.e. decrease in subjective anxiety, increased social activities, a corresponding improvement in social functioning with friends and at work). Only behaviors targeted for treatment improved, little meaningful generalization to other behaviors occurred. During an initial no-treatment phase, no improvement was observed. At 6-month follow-up, improvement remained stable.

Although changes in social skills were not measured in this study, it did document functioning in real-life through self-monitoring by the patients. A subsequent reanalysis of this data (Stravynski, Grey, & Elie, 1987) revealed that treatment had a sequentially diminishing impact on trained behavior. In other words, the greatest improvement in terms of frequency of performance was found in the first target; it gradually diminished with the introduction of treatment to each new target. The sequentially diminishing impact of treatment did not seem to be compatible with "a skills-acquisition process that might be reasonably expected to take the form of gradual competence building and similarly gradual and steady improvement" (1987, p. 228).

Is Social Skill Training Essential to Improvement in Social Functioning? As we have seen earlier, there are few convincing demonstrations that SST actually improved the social skills of social phobic patients (e.g. Wlazlo et al., 1990; Mersch et al., 1991). Moreover, the outcomes of SST and two contrasting anxiety reduction methods in the above studies were comparable either in terms of anxiety reduction (to an equal degree) or social functioning (unchanged).

This raises a further question: is SST necessary for a beneficial improvement in social functioning to occur? The answer to this query is of considerable theoretical and practical interest.

In an early study (Stravynski, Lesage, Marcouiller, & Elie, 1989) 28 generalized/avoidant personality disorder patients were assigned to two combined treatment conditions each consisting of 5 sessions of SST plus homework (social assignments) and 5 sessions of group discussion plus homework, administered in a different order in keeping with a crossover design.

Equivalent and significant improvements in social functioning and social skills were observed in both treatment conditions (combining each of the two modalities in reverse order). Most importantly from our point of view, no differences in outcome were found between the treatment modalities (i.e. SST and discussion during the sessions and homework in between them).

In Stravynski, Arbel, Bounader, Gaudette, Lachance, Borgeat, Fabian, Lamontagne, Sidoun, & Todorov (2000a) the same hypothesis was put to another test. This study compared two treatments aiming both at the improvement of social phobic patients' social functioning, one including SST (modeling, role rehearsal, feedback) and the other without it. In both treatment conditions, the patients had predetermined individual behaviors targeted for treatment that came in equally for attention in the clinic and as homework tasks to be practiced in-between sessions.

The regimen without SST promoted improvement in social functioning by means of practicing the targeted behaviors during the session and assigning these tasks to be performed in-between sessions. Unlike the SST, no attempts were made to improve upon how the patient enacted the targeted behavior spontaneously; nor were the staple ingredients of SST (modeling, role-rehearsal, feedback) used. This condition took the form of SST, but without its essence.

Both treatment conditions (with 30 patients completing treatment in each) resulted in highly significant reductions in the level of subjective anxiety and in improvements in social functioning in most areas of social life (e.g. work, friends). Furthermore, 60% of patients in each condition no longer met DSM-IV criteria for social phobia at 1-year follow-up.

In summary, while it remains uncertain whether SST corrects the social skills of social phobic patients, it is clear that the social functioning of these individuals can be improved by various methods not involving SST.

Discussion

The attempt to better understand social phobia by means of the construct of social skills deficits has not fulfilled its promise. Although deceptively palpable, the master-concept has proven elusive and attempts to define it, unsatisfactory. Inevitably, this had crippling implications for measurement. Any attempt to establish normative social skills and conversely deficiencies in those must founder for lack of anything firm to lean on. This state of affairs is, figuratively speaking, in the image of social phobic individuals, reticent, elusive and given to dissembling.

No evidence has emerged to link social phobia consistently with "deficits of social skills" of any sort. Simulated social phobic performance did not differ markedly or systematically from that of normal subjects on any specific parameters. It was either undistinguishable or overlapped to a large degree when statistically significant differences between the averages of both groups emerged. Since many normal individuals were as skillful or even less so than those who were socially phobic, without being socially phobic themselves, this makes it highly unlikely that "deficient" social skills could in principle even play a causal role in social phobia.

Additionally, SST – the method presumed to improve deficiencies in social skills – has not been shown to produce such outcomes with social phobic individuals consistently. At most, it yielded results not dissimilar from those obtained by other methods (e.g. cognitive modification;

Mersch et al., 1991) that have not sought to improve social skills. Furthermore, when change in social behavior following SST was measured (Stravynski et al., 1987), improvement was not found to follow a skill-acquisition pattern. Finally, an approach that aimed at improving the social functioning of social phobic patients without SST resulted in clinically meaningful improvement equivalent to that obtained with SST (Stravynski et al., 2000a).

In light of the above, social skills deficits in social phobia remain for the time being a manner of speaking; a metaphor for something else.

Social Phobia as a Problem in Social Functioning

While no specific deficits in the social skills of social phobic individuals have been identified, social phobic individuals were nevertheless perceived during the simulations as functioning "less adequately" than their normal counterparts. Over and above what takes place in the confines of the artificial experimental settings, the way these individuals live socially, be it in limited (e.g. public speaking) situations or generally, is troubled. The grievous repercussions of this way of being in various spheres of their lives are unmistakable.

How can the overall ostensible normalcy of the social behavior of social phobic individuals be reconciled with the inadequacy of their social functioning? For this an alternative perspective to that of skills deficits is called for.

First, it is possible, that contrary to theory, social phobic individuals are not failing to realize conventional social goals, but are primarily in pursuit of different goals altogether. If that were true, their overt behavior would neither be a defective performance nor express an inability. Instead, it would be meaningful and purposeful in the sense of reflecting different priorities (i.e. the same means directed to different ends). Indeed, the social functioning of social phobic individuals is not monolithic; rather it is highly differentiated. Many are highly successful in some spheres of social life (e.g. friendship, intimacy) while functioning adequately but with great strain in others (e.g. occupational, extended family, community).

Furthermore, social phobic individuals are highly skillful for instance at being self-effacing and pleasing others, or at the very least, not annoying and provoking them by being unreliable, demanding, and critical. Regarding such diffidence as a deficiency in or lack of skills is by anology the equivalent of considering lying an inability to be truthful. It overlooks the purpose of the action and the dynamic social and interpersonal context into which it is embedded.

Attempting to deflect attention from oneself and being eager to please, for example, gain in meaningfulness by being construed as facets of a wider pattern of insufficiency of power (see chapter 3). As such, these become elements in a purposeful and integrated defensive pattern of interpersonal behavior whose chief function is to minimize the danger of confrontation and ultimately of being hurtfully treated.

Second, if we shift perspective by stepping back – figuratively speaking – so as to take in a broader view, over time larger and more meaningful units of behavior – recurring patterns – will emerge. Thus, the social behavior of social phobic individuals observed in *one situation* at *one point in time* while carrying out an artificially structured task, is indeed not dissimilar from the range of conduct exhibited by normal persons in similar circumstances. By contrast, some differences would become apparent if observation were *extended in time* and participants were left to their own devices. Moreover, the natural social functioning of social phobic individuals, involving numerous patterns of behavior extended in time and ranging over various situations, is likely to be wholly different from that of normal persons. Such a wider pattern of patterns for instance, might include in addition to typical ways of behaving (e.g. pliant and ingratiating: acts of commission), also failures to act (e.g. initiate contact with an attractive person) or outright avoidance (e.g. ignore invitations: acts of omission) combined with tentative wavering between various courses of action without committing definitively to any. It is the larger pattern in which numerous sub-patterns are embedded – although varying in particulars from individual to individual – that would characterize social phobia. Consequently, the overall social phobic pattern is likely to be distinct from normal functioning both in degree (e.g. fewer job interviews or attempts to establish an enterprise), and in kind (e.g eagerness to please, appeasement), for self-protection from loss of face occasioned by failure or ridicule is its paramount goal and most activities – social and otherwise – are geared towards achieving it. I shall elaborate on this outline in the integrative section of chapter 11.

Most research on social phobia takes a social phobic pattern for granted while assuming that it is the consequence of an inner malfunction and attempting to account for it in terms of hypothetical constructs (e.g. anxiety). The merit of the skills-deficit hypothesis, not specifically but as expressing an outlook, was that it attempted to characterize social phobia in terms of (observable) social actions. Its potential was undercut, however, by the conventional construal of social phobia as the consequence of an inner disability.

This way of conceiving of social phobia fits the biomedical mold of separating the putative disease (that the individual carries within) from the resulting social impairment displayed in the environment. Whether a reified social phobia may be separated from the problematic social functioning can be doubted on an observed level (as opposed to a speculative one), for social phobia – as a pattern – is about how such individuals act socially and live their lives.

The alternative to such a reductive view – already outlined earlier – would be to consider social phobia not as a breakdown in social ability but as emerging out of a pattern of meaningful actions that constitute a means to an end. Although not necessarily abnormal in themselves, in time and ranging over numerous social occasions, these self-protective actions combine to create an intricate pattern, reliant mostly on defensive tactics that conflict with and undermine normal social functioning.

On this view, better understanding social phobia implies studying the social life of the socially phobic in its own right; various patterns unfolding over numerous situations and life circumstances, carefully established from observations and individual life-stories. This remains to be done.

Social Skills Training for Deficient Social Skills

One of the chief functions of an etiological hypothesis such as that of "skills deficits" (its scientific merits notwithstanding) is to provide a rationale for a certain approach to treatment. Thus, SST is construed as remedying the deficient repertoire of social skills of socially phobic patients. Although plausible in theory, this symmetry is not necessarily borne out by the facts, for the record is ambiguous.

As we have seen earlier, there is hardly proof that SST actually improves social skills (e.g. Wlazlo et al., 1990; Mersch et al., 1991), however defined. Moreover, although anxiety reported by social phobic patients lessened, their social functioning remained unchanged.

This is in contrast with the outcome reported in Stravynski et al. (2000a, 1982a) in which SST resulted in less anxiety and in improved social functioning.

What accounts for the difference in outcome? Perhaps the better social functioning obtained in the latter approach was due to the fact that its content of treatment was not driven by the strategy of building up generic hypothetical skills deemed necessary for social functioning be they molecular (e.g. appropriate eye contact, timing) or not. In other words, it did not seek to build up deficient social skills. Rather, individual patients were trained to develop *non-defensive* personal ways of dealing with their real-life social/interpersonal circumstances and to use them in situations very much a part of their daily lives. Admitting to being uncertain or flustered, making requests, initiating contact, and accepting invitations are examples of behaviors targeted in such a therapy (see Stravynski et al., 2000b for descriptions of single cases). These promoted participation and enhanced the patient's interpersonal power while at it.

As we have seen earlier (Stravynski et al., 2000a) SST is not necessary for improvement in the social functioning of social phobic patients to take place, for a similar improvement was obtained by a therapy promoting better social functioning without the benefit of SST. Morover, fully 60% of patients in each condition no longer met DSM-IV criteria for social phobia at 1-year follow-up.

These outstanding outcomes illustrate the promise of treating the difficulties of social functioning (i.e. social participation, fitting in, and assuming social roles) of the socially phobic in their own right, freed from the intertwined notions of skills deficits corrected by SST.

9   Social Phobia as a Consequence of Individual History

Many individuals consulting for the constellation of problems we call social phobia mention (often unprompted) having "always been that way": wary of unknown people, unobtrusive, and timid. Similarly tempered members of the family (a mother, an uncle) are pointed out for good measure, implying "it is in the blood." Other individuals clearly relate current problems, to vividly remembered and rather dramatic triggering events (typically) in early adolescence (e.g. DeWit, Ogborne, Offord, & MacDonald, 1999). Peeing in terror while waiting in line for confession, standing beet-red, drenched in sweat, heart pounding, mind blank (but hearing the laughter of derision of the other pupils) after being singled out in class and asked by the teacher to rise and recite a poem, are remembered as watersheds.

These examples draw our attention both to the ostensible stability of the problems as well as to the time-contingent nature of their coming into being. Specifically, as we seek explanations for the origins of social phobia, we might wonder whether the full-blown pattern is already prefigured in certain features of the young organism expressing genetic imperatives, or whether social phobia emerges gradually, and not inevitably, through processes and circumstances unique to an individual.

In contrast to other accounts we have encountered in previous chapters, a truly developmental outlook would not seek to pinpoint the figurative "mechanisms" (neurophysiological, psychological) allegedly controlling social phobia at the present (e.g. due to either genetic defects or environmental "pathogens"). Rather, it would attempt to look at the past as key to present manifestations.

Broadly, such an historic outlook as a still-unfolding process could be portrayed as seeking to study the interplay between the biological nature (e.g. genetic endowment) of the organism and the environmental conditions molding it. As seen in chapter 6, certain approaches regard these two influences as separable and therefore neatly apportioned through mathematical models and related formulas; others consider organism and context interwoven and therefore inseparable as a matter of principle. On that view, development implies, in addition to the interaction between the organism (with its genetic potential) and the environment that molds it, also a learning process of incorporating experience: "the history of adaptation of the organism to that point" (Sroufe, 1997, p. 252).

Aim and Method

My main goal in this chapter is to assess the evidence for and against the developmental perspective of social phobia as expressed in specific hypotheses drawing mostly on two available models. At its most rudimentary, it concerns either features of the organism (e.g. temperament) or environmental influences, assuming the two may be kept apart. Other hypotheses (e.g. attachment) draw on a conceptualization of a relationship and as such abolish the dichotomy between organism and other and emphasize the historical pattern of interactions between a particular caregiver and a child. I shall examine each of these in turn. In the interest of clarity of exposition, the chapter is divided into constitutional and environmental factors.

Constitutional Factors

Temperament

Certain psychological features of the infant are taken by some as early expressions of an inborn propensity to shyness or overall timidity. It is an attempt to account for considerable individual differences in regards to (low) levels of social and non-social activity and (heightened) emotionality, for example. Such presumably enduring characteristics are considered as indicative of temperament. What then is temperament?

The most prominent perspectives on the matter are summarized in Goldsmith, Buss, Plomin, Rothbart, Thomas, Chess, Hinde, & McCall (1987). A rather abstract definition would be that of a hypothetical construct linking early appearing and enduring complex patterns of behavior to regulating systems in the brain (Reiss & Neiderhiser, 2000, p. 360).

An illustrative operational definition of temperament might be found in the seminal work of Chess & Thomas (1987). In their original study 9 variables (based on parental reports, not observation) were rated: activity level, regularity of biological functions, tendency towards approach or withdrawal, adaptability (over time; not a response to the new), intensity of reaction, threshold of responsiveness, distractibility, attention span, and perseverance.

This multidimensional assessment gave rise to 4 temperamental categories. These were: (1) an "easy" temperament – positive in mood, regular in bodily functions, quick to adapt; (2) a "difficult" temperament – negative in mood, irregular bodily functions, slow to adapt, tends to withdraw from new situations, reacts with high emotional intensity; (3) a "slow to warm up" temperament – similar to the latter but more placid; and (4) a "mixed" temperament – an undifferentiated category. The finding that parents of the difficult children in that study were on the whole no different from parents of the other children sums up the "temperamental" perspective.

Thus, the hypothetical tendency to reticence in encounters with unfamiliar individuals and unusual situations (so prominent in social phobia) has been put forward as such a temperamental trait. This trait, labeled "behavioral inhibition" (probably an equivalent of withdrawal, in the Chess & Thomas, 1987 terminology), has been postulated to be a reflection of a lowered threshold to fearful stimuli in limbic and hypothalamic structures (see Kagan, Reznick, & Snidman, 1987), themselves under genetic control.

Social Phobia and "Behavioral Inhibition" Several authors (e.g. Rosenbaum, Biederman, Hirshfeld, Bolduc, & Chaloff, 1991b) postulated a link between anxiety disorders overall (social phobia amongst them), and the temperamental construct of "behavioral inhibition." I shall first examine the theoretical underpinnings of this construct and the evidence concerning its validity. This will be followed by an overview of the studies relating it to social phobia.

"Behavioral inhibition" – the temperamental construct – was investigated in a series of four studies (Garcia Coll, Kagan, & Reznick, 1984; Kagan, Reznick, & Snidman, 1987; Kagan, Reznick, & Snidman, 1988; Kagan, 1989) all carried out in the Boston area. Garcia Coll et al. (1984) is the seminal study highlighting "behavioral inhibition." It has involved 305 21–22-months-old children (all born in 1978) selected after a brief telephone interview with the mother either because of their pronounced tendency to withdraw from or conversely, to seek out, encounters with unfamiliar children and adults. Based on these telephone interviews, 56 children (of 305) were classified as *inhibited* and 104 as *uninhibited*; 145 of the middling kind (therefore unclassifiable) were excluded.

Of these, the mothers of 117 children agreed to be tested with their offspring in the laboratory. After further observations, 33 were reclassified as inhibited and 38 as uninhibited and 47 as neither. It is noteworthy that only the most extreme cases were selected for study (see 1984, p. 1018). I shall return to this point later.

Two "coders" (positioned behind a one-way mirror) observed mother and child during several "episodes":

1. warm-up: the subjects were greeted and briefed;
2. free-play: the mother was instructed neither to prompt the child to play nor to initiate interactions with him or her;
3. reaction to modeling: the experimenter, enacted several scenarios (talking on toy phone, a doll cooking food and serving it to other dolls, three animals walking through a rain-storm);
4. reaction to an unfamiliar adult: an unfamiliar woman entered the room and sat down for 30 seconds without initiating contact; then she called the child by name and asked him/her to perform 3 items taken out of Bailey's scale of mental development and left the room;
5. reaction to an unfamiliar object: the experimenter drew the curtains to reveal a robot; the child was encouraged to explore the robot and was shown how to switch on/off the lights fixed in its head; the experimenter switched on a recording and the voice came through a speaker in the robot's mouth; the child was again encouraged to explore the robot.
6. separation from the mother: the mother was motioned to leave the room (when the child was playing) for 3 minutes or came back immediately if the child started crying.

Throughout these scenarios, ratings were made of: latency of the approach to the stranger or the robot, clinging to the mother, crying, fretting, withdrawal, and vocalization of distress. Additional measurements such as inhibition of play, apprehension, and facial expressions were taken without being further defined. This is rather problematic as these measures are less obvious indicators of inhibition or lack thereof.

Based on the number of inhibited behaviors, the index of "behavioral inhibition" (IBI) was created; the children were classified as inhibited (9 and more), uninhibited (2 or less) and neither (3 to 8). These predetermined cut-off points were based on a pilot study.

The experiments were carried out again after 3 to 5 weeks with an overall reliability of 0.63. It is surprising in light of this figure to find that the stability for the inhibited sub-group was 0.56 but only 0.33 for the uninhibited. Nonetheless, most children – 68% of the inhibited and 82% of the uninhibited – retained their classification at the second testing.

Parental ratings of the toddler's temperament were correlated with the IBI; these were: mother 0.54, father 0.49. The correlations across episodes were on average a rather low 0.27; while subsequent testing tended to be even less consistent.

A second study (Kagan et al., 1987), this time including 120 children (21 months and 31 months old) of which 60 were classified as inhibited and 60 uninhibited, overall replicated the results of Garcia Coll et al. (1984). The latter study, however, expanded physiological measurements (only heart rate was monitored in first study). Larger pupil diameters, elevated levels of (morning) salivary cortisol and greater muscle tension (inferred indirectly from the evidence of less variability in the pitch periods of single words utterances spoken under stress) characterized the inhibited children.

These physiological peculiarities were essentially replicated in a third study (Kagan et al., 1988) including 58 subjects (28 inhibited, 30 uninhibited) 21 months old, 49 (26 inhibited, 23 uninhibited) 31 months old and 100 unselected subjects 14 months old.

The fourth study (reported piecemeal in Kagan, 1989; Kagan & Snidman, 1991a,b) concerned the all important question of whether inhibited and uninhibited profiles may be predicted from certain features of the infant's behavior, observed at 2 and 4 months of age, in various assessment situations. These included: one minute quiet with mother smiling, presentation of three-dimensional images, presentation of three movable toys, and playing a record with a female voice at different loudness levels. The variables rated were limb movement (flex – extend), arching of the back, tongue protrusions, motor tension in hands or limbs, and crying. 4 groups (94 subjects in total) were created on the basis of combinations of levels of motor activity and crying. The 2 contrast groups were made up of subjects high in motor activity and crying vs. low in motor activity as well as in crying.

The children were reassessed at 9, 14 and 21 months for reactions to 16 situations representing unfamiliarity (see above) with fretting and crying as indices of fearful behavior. With the exception of crying, the whole gamut of behaviors presumably assessed was not reported in the results. This limits considerably the conclusions that can be drawn from them.

The main finding established links between a high degree of motor activity and crying on the one hand and fearful behavior (defined by crying and fretting again) on the other hand. These, however, seem to be more demonstrations of the stability of the same behavior rather than the prediction of a type of conduct from altogether different features of behavior one might have expected. The fact that the inhibited and uninhibited profiles seemed to be stable over time cannot be seen as establishing them necessarily as predictors of "behavioral inhibition"; no evidence for this has been reported so far. These studies stimulated a series of other investigations (to be detailed below) that expanded but also challenged aspects of the construct. Having considered the construct of "behavioral inhibition," I shall now cast the net wider in an attempt to determine how valid it is.

Supporting Evidence   (1) The construct of "behavioral inhibition" has been highlighted in studies issued from various countries and carried out across cultures. Using overall the same measures described above, "behavioral inhibition" has been highlighted in children from North-America: USA (Garcia Coll et al., 1984), Canada (Rubin, Hastings, Stewart, Henderson, & Chen, 1997), Western Europe: Germany (Kagan et al., 1987), Sweden (Kerr, Lambert, Stattin, & Klackenberg-Larssen, 1994), Africa: Mauritius (Scarpa, Raine, Venables, & Mednick, 1995) and Asia: China (Chen, Hastings, Rubin, Chen, Cen, & Stewart, 1998).

The study from China, by stressing the importance of the cultural context, cautions against defining certain characteristics as inherently problematic a priori. First, the Chinese children were on average more inhibited than Canadian children (from London, Ontario) who served as contrast. Not only did Chinese mothers accept their child's inhibition relatively better than Canadian mothers, their view of their child's inhibition was positive in an absolute sense as a sign that the child was well brought up. By contrast, Canadian mothers' attitudes to their children's inhibition were wholly negative and of concern, as if facing a looming problem.

On this view, "behavioral inhibition" is not problematic in itself, its significance as a psychological pattern depends mostly on the meaning attached to it by the culture in which it is displayed. Thus, "Asian cultures strongly value the need for behavioral and emotional control and the restriction of emotional expression during interpersonal interactions; highly expressive individuals are often regarded as poorly regulated and socially immature" (Chen et al., 1998, p. 682).

Western (and especially US) culture, by contrast, values sociability and engaging spontaneity greatly. This value finds expression in the very operational definition of "behavioral inhibition." Thus, in Kagan et al. (1988), for example, children were rated for spontaneous smiles and interactions with an adult stranger who entered the laboratory as if these were a natural occurrence; their absence was interpreted psychologically (as an intra-personal deficiency) rather than a cultural product (as a means towards different cultural goals).

(2) Reliability of the construct: the degree of agreement between measurements is the most basic characteristic; although good agreement does not guarantee validity, poor reliability undermines it.

a. Stability over time: Garcia Coll et al. (1984) reported a coefficient of stability 0.56 over 1 month for the inhibited group (in contrast with 0.33 for the uninhibited). Over a much longer period of approximately 3.5 years, the coefficient held good at 0.52 (Kagan et al., 1987). Surprisingly it increased to 0.67 after 5.5 years. Over a similar period of time (but with a different cohort), the coefficient was a more disappointing 0.39 (Kagan, 1989). Hirshfeld, Rosenbaum, Biederman, Bolduc, Faraone, Snidman, Reznick, & Kagan (1992) addressed this question in creating 4 groups of children on the basis of the stability of their "behavioral inhibition." To be included in a stable group (inhibited or uninhibited) a child had to be identified consistently in one way at 21 months and 4, 5, and 7.5 years. Strikingly, 83% among the stable – inhibited group (n = 12), were girls. The proportion was reversed in the stable – uninhibited group (n = 9) 78% of which were boys. As the numbers of subjects were rather small, these results need to be replicated.

b. General trends over time: there was a greater trend towards the disinhibition of inhibited children than the other way around; differences between girls and boys in this respect remain a matter of controversy.

c. Agreement between observers: the agreement between coders of the subjects' behavior in the laboratory were consistently very high e.g. 95% agreement in Garcia Coll et al. 1984, perhaps the outcome of training. In contrast, correlations between mothers' observations at home and (the coders') observations in the laboratory were more modest (i.e. 0.42 to 0.52 (Kagan, Reznick, Clarke, Snidman, & Garcia Coll, 1984)).

(3) Correlates of "behavioral inhibition": Such correlates are important elements of (concurrent) validity in that they associate reliably a hypothetical construct with certain features of the organism.

a. Physiological: behaviorally inhibited children were found to have a higher pulse rate, a low inter-beat variability, higher muscular tension (as measured by the vagal tone), larger pupil diameters, and higher morning level of salivary cortisol as compared to uninhibited subjects (Garcia Coll et al., 1984; Kagan et al., 1984, 1987, 1988).

b. Psychological: 75% of the inhibited children showed pronounced fears (e.g. speaking voluntarily in front of the class, attending summer camp, staying at home alone) in contrast to 25% of the uninhibited children (Kagan, 1989).

(4) Features predictive of "behavioral inhibition": A history of various "illnesses" (e.g. colic, sleeplessness, irritability) during the first year of life (Kagan et al., 1988) predicted "behavioral inhibition."

(5) "Behavioral inhibition" was predictive of a lesser tendency to play with another child: 0.46 – 0.51 (Kagan et al., 1984) at the age of 4. Similarly "behavioral inhibition" was predictive of the "total fears" at the age of 4 (ranging 0.33 to 0.41). Inhibition at 21 months predicted (0.34) greater loneliness and fewer social interactions (Kagan et al., 1987) in the school setting at the age of 6.

(6) Discriminant validity: "Behavioral inhibition" was neither confounded by activity level and persistence (Garcia Coll et al., 1984); nor was it related to cognitive performance (Kagan et al., 1984, 1987) or to parental depression (Kochanska, 1991).

(7) Convergent validity: "Behavioral inhibition" is closely associated with a similar construct of social fear (Rubin et al., 1997) as reported by the mother of the child.

(8) Heredity: Something about "behavioral inhibition" might be said to be inherited as the correlations between the scores of identical twins (0.6) were significantly stronger than those between fraternal twins (0.03) in Plomin & Rowe (1979). Comparable results were reported by Matheny (1989), Robinson, Kagan, Reznick, & Corley (1992) and DiLalla, Kagan, & Reznick (1994), who, although using different methods of determining heritability (statistically it refers to the variance that can be attributed to shared genes) came to roughly similar conclusions. While such suggestive results provide food for thought, the ultimate evidence – specific genetic mechanisms at the molecular level – have yet to be identified.

Contrary Evidence (1) The unitary construct of "behavioral inhibition" as originally formulated by Kagan, has not held up under closer scrutiny. Kochanska (1991) and Kochanska & Radke-Yarrow (1992), for example, have highlighted a distinction between social and non-social inhibition. In the latter study, 107 children were assessed over a period ranging between 1.5 to 3.5 years (between the ages of 1.5 to 3 and 5). Methods were similar to those used in the studies described earlier. Overall, social "behavioral inhibition" at first assessment was associated (r = 0.33) with shy and inhibited behavior at second assessment. This however, was not the case with non-social inhibition that was unrelated to inhibited behavior. Strikingly, it was inversely related to solitary play (r = −0.24). These results question the monolithic unity typically attributed to the construct of "behavioral inhibition."

In a similar vein, Asendorf (1990) has found distinctions between familiar and non-familiar situations (peers and settings) and has separated the "social unfamiliar" situations into those concerning peers and adults.

Finally, Rubin et al. (1997) have differentiated peer-social inhibition and adult-social inhibition from non-social inhibition. Correlations between the latter and the other two indices were mostly low or non-significant. All these elements in the hypothetical wider construct might have been expected to correlate.

Contrary to Kagan's view of "behavioral inhibition" (but rather consistent with the results), 69% of the most extremely inhibited subjects in Rubin et al. (1997) did not necessarily act alike either in altogether non-social situations or in adult-social and peer-social situations. In other words, the rather stereotyped extreme reactions were not observed as a general trend. The latter findings, as well as results from previously mentioned studies, tend to cast a doubt over the status of "behavioral inhibition" as a unitary construct and raise the next question.

(2) Is "behavioral inhibition" an artifact of the method used in teasing it out?

It is worthy of note that, statistically, "behavioral inhibition" stood out as a construct only when extreme scoring individuals from both ends of the distribution (10% each) were compared. In contrast, when the whole cohort was used, the main composite measure − IBI − was found to be unrelated at several points in time − especially at the longer (e.g. 34-month) intervals (see Kagan, Reznick, & Gibbons, 1989). Furthermore, neither the strongest correlates (e.g. heart rate), nor all other differences were replicated with the next 20% of subjects at each end of the distribution.

Ultimately, one might ask what is the point of singling out a temperamental trait (inhibition) apparent only in contrast with its opposite? The demonstration would obviously have been much more convincing had the characteristic in question held up in comparison with the norm (average) characterizing the cohort. For example, are inhibited children characterized by more fears than the average? So far, the answer to this query remains unknown. What is known in this respect is that 75% of the inhibited vs. 25% of the uninhibited children, manifest some fears (Kagan, 1989). It is not inconceivable, however, that it is the uninhibited children who might be outstandingly abnormal, with the inhibited children closer to the norm. However that may be in reality, such comparisons have not been reported to my knowledge. The omens in this respect, however, are not good since the typically available study including the whole sample found none of the significant correlations that come up only when comparing the most extreme 20% of the subjects, found on both ends of the distribution.

In summary, behavioral inhibition is an interesting and heuristically, a useful construct. But, while having some evident strength in terms of validity, it is nevertheless not as solid as it appears. First, some evidence suggests that it is not a uniform construct. Second, over a third of the children identified as inhibited at 21 months turn less inhibited in time. Third, the behavioral tendency associated most closely with the construct is evident only in a small fraction of the children, exhibiting the worst psychological and physiological features.

Nevertheless, this intimates the possibility that social phobia might have a very early (e.g. 21 months) temperamental predisposition. I will now turn to the studies that have investigated such possible links.

"Behavioral Inhibition" and Childhood Social Phobia/Avoidant Disorder

Before approaching the possible link between behavioral inhibition and social phobia/avoidant disorder in childhood, the latter constructs are in need of clarification.

First, what is the meaning of social phobia so far as children are concerned? Beidel et al. (1999) compared 50 children (mean age 10; range 7 to 13) meeting DSM-IV criteria (established in an interview of both child and parents) for childhood social phobia to 22 normal children (mean age 12; range 9 to 14). In contrast to their ease with familiar members of the family, children identified as socially phobic experienced at least moderate distress in the following situations: reading aloud in front of the class, musical or athletic performances in which they had to take part, and joining a conversation, among others. Overall such children reported a higher number of distressing social events (over a fixed period of 2 weeks) and only they reported difficulties of reading aloud (Beidel, 1991). 35% of these children resorted to avoidance in response to these situations. Similarly they rated their distress as significantly higher than the normal children.

In simulations of social situations (reading aloud, interactions with a child) social phobic children were rated as more anxious and as less skilled compared to normal children. Unfortunately, despite using normal control subjects, this study failed to provide descriptive results concerning them. These could have served as a norm that would have allowed a better perspective on the behavior of the socially phobic children either as exhibiting an exacerbation of normal social anxiety and behavior or as being qualitatively apart.

Second, how does social phobia relate to avoidant disorder in children? To answer this question Francis, Last, & Strauss (1992) compared children (between the ages of 6 to 17) meeting criteria (DSM-III-R) for social phobia (33), avoidant disorder (19), a mixture of the two (12), and 32 normal controls. No significant difference between the groups in terms of overall anxiety ratings was observed. Social phobic subjects however reported a significantly higher fear of criticism and failure than the normal controls. Overall, the authors failed to distinguish social phobia from avoidant disorder. Rather, the core of avoidant disorder (i.e. fear of strangers at the age when the child is mostly at home) is transformed into a more involved pattern, (i.e. social phobia) when the older child has to confront the wider demands of school both formal and social. Avoidant disorder was removed from DSM-IV in recognition of this redundancy.

After these preliminary definitions, I shall now turn to studies of behavioral inhibition and childhood social phobia. The main study exploring the link between "behavioral inhibition" in young children and anxious disorders in general (manifested by the subjects at an older age) was reported in Biederman, Rosenbaum, Hirshfeld, Faraone, Bolduc, Gersten, Meminger, Kagan, Snidman, & Reznick (1990).

The children-subjects were drawn from three sources: (1) The cohort from the Garcia Coll et al. (1984) (so-called "epidemiologic" as it used subjects from the general population) studies previously described (originally classified as inhibited n = 22, uninhibited n = 19; age 7−8 at the time of the study); (2) Children of a group of patients treated for panic disorder/agoraphobia (classified as inhibited n = 18 or not inhibited n = 12 at the age 4−7); (3) Children consulting the pediatric care service (undifferentiated n = 20 at the age 4−10) whose parents − it was assumed − were normal. Diagnoses (lifetime) were arrived at on the basis of interviews with the mothers.

No differences in prevalence rates of avoidant disorder were found between the groups. However, when all anxiety disorders were lumped together, a link between this wide category and "behavioral inhibition" was found in the sample of children whose parents met criteria for panic/agoraphobia but not in the "epidemiologic" (Garcia Coll et al., 1984) sample. A study testing this link in children of social phobic parents remains to be carried out.

From a different perspective, Rosenbaum, Biederman, Hirshfeld, Bolduc, Faraone, Kagan, Snidman, & Reznick (1991a) tested whether the family members (parents as well as siblings) of behaviorally inhibited subjects had a stronger propensity towards social phobia (and anxiety disorders in general).

The samples described in the previous study (Biederman et al., 1990) were amalgamated to create three groups: inhibited, uninhibited, and normal controls. Parents of inhibited children had greater rates of (lifetime) adult social phobia (17.5%) compared with parents of uninhibited subjects (0%) and those of normal controls (3%). Conversely, parents of inhibited children also reported significantly higher rates of childhood avoidant disorder (15%), compared to none reported in the other groups.

The results regarding siblings, however, were disconcerting. Contrary to what might have been expected, none of the siblings of the inhibited subjects met criteria for avoidant disorder (this was also the case with the siblings of the normal controls) while 17% of the siblings of children in the uninhibited group did.

In a further analysis, (Rosenbaum, Biederman, Bolduc, Hirshfeld, Faraone, & Kagan, 1992) the combination of both "behavioral inhibition" and an anxiety disorder in a child were found to be highly associated with a parent's anxiety disorder (88% vs. 32%). Statistically, however, the rate of anxiety disorders in parents of children, inhibited or uninhibited, was similar. In the case of (parental) social phobia, 50% of the inhibited children meeting criteria for anxiety disorders had such parents as compared with 9% in children classified only as behaviorally inhibited, and 0% for the uninhibited children without anxiety disorders. These results, if anything, seem to diminish the role of "behavioral inhibition" in the development of social phobia as such.

This particular question was addressed specifically in Biederman, Rosenbaum, Bolduc-Murphy, Faraone, Chaloff, Hirshfeld, & Kagan (1993). For this end, inhibited children with parents free of anxiety disorders (from the Kagan study) were compared to inhibited children whose parents met criteria for various anxiety disorders.

Overall, the results showed that a greater proportion of inhibited children, whose parents fulfilled criteria for anxiety disorders, tended to meet criteria for anxiety disorders themselves (22% vs. 14%). Limiting this to avoidant disorder, the rates, although lower, were still in the same direction (17% vs. 9%). In a subsequent 3-year follow-up, the rate of inhibited children who developed avoidant disorder increased (from 9 to 28%). A similar trend (from 17 to 27%) was observed in the group of inhibited children whose parents fulfilled criteria for anxiety disorders. No such trend was observed among the uninhibited children.

Specific results concerning social phobia as such at the end of the follow-up, however, showed a different picture. 17% of the inhibited children in the "epidemiologic" sample (Garcia Coll et al., 1984) met criteria for social phobia but so did 20% of the uninhibited children. In contrast, 23% of the inhibited children whose parents met criteria for panic/agoraphobia were classified as socially phobic, compared with 6% of the uninhibited children (1984, p. 817, Table 2). These results suggest that the clinical status of the parents – more than any other factor – acts as a powerful liability towards the social phobia of a child.

In a study testing whether behavioral inhibition predisposes specifically to social phobia or avoidant disorder of childhood (among other specific anxiety disorders) Biederman, Hirshfeld-Becker, Rosenbaum, Hérot, Friedman, Snidman, Kagan, & Faraone (2001), compared 64 inhibited children to 152 non-inhibited children aged 2 to 6. Correspondence to defining criteria was established by means of the Schedule for the affective disorders and schizophrenia for school-age children; epidemiologic version (Orvaschel, 1994) completed by the mother.

The prevalence of social phobia and avoidant disorder among the inhibited group was found to be significantly higher at 17% than that of the non-inhibited group at 5%, suggesting that behavioral inhibition may be associated with problems of social anxiety in early childhood. Statistical significance notwithstanding, it is difficult to imagine the meaning of designating a 4 or 5 year old as socially phobic. The typical onset of social phobia is in adolescence; prevalence rising with age, as social demands increase (from 0.5% in 12–13 year olds to 4% in 14–17 year olds in Essau et al., 1999 for example). The astonishing above result could be an artifact of the fact that the mothers filled out the "diagnostic" instrument, perhaps misidentifying a pre-existing tendency to withdrawal (i.e. behavioral inhibition) as a pattern of social phobia.

It is difficult to draw a general conclusion from these studies for, with the exception of Biederman et al. (2001), they are marred by several important methodological flaws. First, most studies in this series deal with aggregates of multiple anxiety disorders (e.g. Biederman et al., 1990; Rosenbaum et al., 1991a, 1992) as a meaningful single variable. This seems to be in part the direct consequence of the inadequacy of the sample size (e.g. n = 31) that is often too small to enable meaningful distinctions between categories of anxiety disorders. The upshot is that the statistical analyses were often carried out on percentages calculated from small cells of subjects, e.g. 50% = 2 subjects out of 4. Although this masks the underlying problem, the difficulty in drawing meaningful conclusions remains.

Second, and most important, all longitudinal studies have made use of the same original sample (of 41 subjects) described in Biederman et al. (1990). Thus, despite numerous publications and a variety of control-groups, all have used the same experimental cohort (Garcia Coll et al., 1984). One would be hard put in such circumstances to talk of independent replication. Third, whether the operational definition of "behavioral inhibition" was equivalent (they were clearly not the same) throughout the various studies is uncertain. Finally, the parents in the control groups are assumed to be without mental health problems, because they have not sought help (pediatric vs. psychiatric clinic). No screening was carried out to make sure that this was the case.

Possible Precursors to the Construct of
"Behavioral Inhibition"

A longitudinal study of social anxiety, although not making use of the modern category of social phobia as it was carried out between 1929 and 1959 (Kagan & Moss, 1962), seems most relevant as the descriptions of the children resemble the main features of the socially anxious (1962, p. 174 and Appendix 2, p. 296).

The main objective of this study (the Fels longitudinal program) was to ascertain the stability of certain psychological characteristics, one of them being passivity in the face of frustration. Passivity in this study (1962, p. 51), in terms of its psychological content (defined as "the degree to which the child acquiesced or withdrew in the face of attack or frustrating situations"), appears to be the rough equivalent of the construct of "behavioral inhibition" developed later on (Kagan, 1989, p. 668).

The subjects (45 girls and 44 boys, offspring of 63 families) were recruited into the study between 1929 and 1939 during the last trimester of the mother's pregnancy. Both children and mothers were observed in various situations (at home, at school, and at day camp) between the ages of 3 months and 14 years. The information was extracted from detailed observation diaries. The remaining 71 subjects were reevaluated as adults (between the ages of 19 to 29) by means of interviews and administered tests.

The most important finding was that passivity between the ages of 3 to 6 and 6 to 10 was significantly associated with social anxiety in adulthood (r = 0.41 and 0.46 respectively), but for men only. The same results emerged when childhood behaviors (e.g. sudden crying, withdrawal from social interactions, seeking proximity to the mother) were related to adult social anxiety in men (the only exception being withdrawal from social interaction for women). Conversely, social spontaneity (laughing, smiling, displaying eagerness to interact) at childhood was inversely related to social anxiety in adulthood ($r = -0.45$).

In conclusion, the studies under review establish a relationship between early manifestation of reticence and seeking safety at an early age, and social anxiousness in adulthood for men.

Retrospective Studies of "Behavioral Inhibition"

Retrospective studies of "behavioral inhibition," although perhaps more questionable methodologically speaking, are still of interest. Mick & Telch (1998) divided 76 undergraduate psychology students in 4 groups: highly socially anxious, highly generally anxious, a mixture of the two, and a control group of subjects scoring below cut off in both respects, and each filled out a retrospective self-report questionnaire of inhibition.

Contrary to prediction, the socially anxious students did not report a history of "behavioral inhibition" that would distinguish them from the other anxious subjects. The socially anxious subjects, however, reported a significantly greater history of "behavioral inhibition" than the non-anxious subjects.

Muris, Merckelbach, Wessel, & van de Ven (1999) studied the link between "behavioral inhibition" and various anxiety disorders in high-school students (age $12-15$) from Holland. It is noteworthy that the questionnaire measuring "behavioral inhibition" in that study in fact concentrated mostly on social inhibition (i.e. difficulties interacting with strangers). It is therefore hardly surprising that a correlation of 0.78 was found between this measure and a self-reported social phobia score. Conversely, lower correlations were found with scores measuring panic disorder (0.46) and generalized anxiety disorder (0.3).

Van Ameringen, Mancini, & Oakman (1998) studied 225 patients seen in an anxiety disorders clinic of which 48 were diagnosed as social phobic. A "Retrospective self-report of behavioral inhibition" (RSRI) was administered from which, following a factor-analysis, social inhibition and non-social inhibition factors were extracted. A correlation of 0.5 was found between the social inhibition score and the social phobia subscale of the Fear Questionnaire; the coefficients were 0.45 with the total "behavioral inhibition" score and 0.28 with non-social inhibition. These correlations were consistently higher for social phobia than for other anxiety disorders.

It is of interest that social phobic subjects were undistinguishable from other anxiety disorders in terms of their total "behavioral inhibition" score, but had significantly higher social inhibition scores, although other subjects reported social fears too.

In Hayward et al. (1998) 2,242 high-school students had a diagnostic interview administered 4 times at 1-yearly intervals from grade 9 (average age 15) to 12. The subjects also filled the RSRI. An analysis yielded 3 factors: social avoidance, fearfulness, and illness behavior.

Social phobia overall could be predicted from social avoidance scores; their combination with fearfulness scores further increased the predictive power. For example, 23% of those who reported social avoidance and fearfulness in childhood met criteria for social phobia at adolescence in contrast with 3.5% of the subjects who fulfilled criteria for social phobia while reporting little avoidance and fearfulness in childhood.

Schwartz et al. (1999) studied 79 subjects remaining from their original cohort (who had been followed between either 21 months or 31 months and the age of 13). The category of social anxiety was established by means of the DIS-children, while a criterion of social impairment was added to bring it closer in line with the definition of social phobia.

Among the inhibited in young childhood, 44% of the girls at the age of 13 met the definition of generalized social anxiety compared with 22% of the boys. In contrast, only 6% of the uninhibited girls fulfilled the definition compared with 13% of the boys. Unfortunately, no information was provided concerning the majority of the children who were not in the extremes. I have already alluded to this shortcoming when discussing the validity of the construct of "behavioral inhibition."

In conclusion, a link between "behavioral inhibition" in childhood and various anxious conditions in adulthood seems on the face of it to have been established through retrospective recollections. However, the RSRI is a rather problematic instrument in terms of validity. Whether it measures what was painstakingly observed in the original studies remains uncertain. However this may be, this link has not been unequivocally and specifically demonstrated for social phobia as such. A longitudinal study aiming specifically at social phobia in adulthood is long overdue.

Overall and bearing in mind the various methodological weaknesses and contradictory findings, at this point it cannot be maintained that a clear link between "behavioral inhibition" and social phobia in adulthood has been established. This conclusion is consistent with the findings of Caspi, Moffitt, Newman, & Silva (1996) who have failed to find a link between inhibited temperament as established at the third year of life and anxiety disorders at the age of 21. A particular significance attaches to the results of this longitudinal study of a cohort from Dunedin, New Zealand for being an independent investigation unrelated to the project from Boston. Furthermore, temperament in this study was treated as a continuum and as a consequence may have included subjects who were less extreme exemplars of inhibition, questioning thereby the findings issued from studies defining inhibition in the most restrictive way while using as contrast the most extremely uninhibited subjects.

Potentially more interesting however – if fears rather than diagnostic entities are considered – was the observation by Garcia Coll et al. (1984) that "behavioral inhibition" is clearly associated with social fears. The stability of this association was much later demonstrated in a prospective study (Schwartz et al., 1999) of 13 year olds (drawn from the same original two cohorts) classified 12 years earlier as inhibited (n = 44) and uninhibited (n = 35). A significantly higher percentage (61% vs. 27%) of inhibited subjects reported a general discomfort in various social situations and interactions. Incongruously, inhibited subjects were no different statistically from the uninhibited subjects in their concerns about performance in front of groups (e.g. public speaking).

In summary, on current evidence, there is little clear-cut evidence to support the proposition that "behavioral inhibition" is a genetically transmitted trait leading to anxiety states culminating in social phobia. In any case, "behavioral inhibition" can neither be considered a sufficient condition nor a necessary one for the emergence of social phobia. As seen earlier, the link held true for only a fraction of inhibited individuals while many uninhibited ones also developed social phobia.

Perhaps, "if behavioral inhibition is a constitutional variable it might be more appropriately considered a behavioral propensity towards social introversion" (Turner, Beidel, & Wolff, 1996a, p. 168). Possibly, "behavioral inhibition" is a facet – albeit considered in an extreme degree – of a common psychological or personality feature (or dimension) such as introversion (Eysenck & Eysenck, 1969). Introverted individuals have, by definition, a stronger propensity to behave defensively and react with greater alarm (i.e. anxiously: Gray, 1970). It must also be remembered, however, that uninhibited children have also fulfilled criteria for anxiety disorders (e.g. Biederman et al., 1990).

However that may be, it stands to reason that this propensity to engage people defensively or withdraw from social contacts altogether, would need a social environment in which such individuals over time repeatedly fail to adapt, for the maladjusted pattern of functioning to crystallize. It is therefore the social environment (in the sense of social practices and cultural demands) in which the individual lives — rather than the temperamental propensity — that would likely be the determinant factor in the emergence of the full-blown disorder.

Environmental Influences

Environmental influences that have been studied in relation to the development of social phobia have been mostly those of the parents and the family and to a lesser extent peers and adverse life-events.

Family Environment

Child Rearing and Other Parental Characteristics Viewed Retrospectively and Prospectively in Relation with Social Phobia/Avoidant Personality Disorder Several studies attempted to learn about the family environment of social phobic individuals by querying them (retrospectively) about their parents on instruments issued from various theoretical perspectives. The main thrust of this line of research was Parker's (1979) model situating parental influences on two dimensions: control and caring. Its main hypothesis combining "overprotection" with "low-care" is that "by restricting the usual developmental process of independence, autonomy and social competence might further promote any diathesis to a social phobia" (1979, p. 559). This was tested either by contrasting social phobic and control groups (e.g. normal subjects) or by calculating correlations. The results of the relevant studies are summarized in Table 9.1.

Overall, in 9 studies out of 12, all types of socially anxious subjects tended to describe at least one of their parents as overprotective; this was not exclusive to social phobia (Grüner, Muris, & Merckelbach, 1999). The above self-reported results have been reconfirmed through observation of child — parent interactions by Hudson & Rapee (2001). Moreover, overprotection was found a stable parental characteristic, equally true of mothers and fathers, applied equally to all siblings Hudson & Rapee (2002).

This is confirmed in the only longitudinal study available (Kagan & Moss, 1962) that has the additional merit of being based on observation rather than retrospective recall on the part of the subjects.

Table 9.1. *Family characteristics and their relationship with social phobia, avoidant personality disorder and social anxiety*

Study	Construct (design)	Overprotection (control)	Hostility/ criticism	Less caring/ rejection	Less emotional warmth	Guilt-engendering	Favoring other siblings	Social isolation	Concern over the opinions of others	Sociability as a family	Less comfortable in social situations	Less encouragement to socialize	Shaming
Kagan & Moss (1962)	SP (L)	+	−										
Parker (1979)	SP (R)	+		+									
Arrindell et al. (1983)	SP (R)	+		+	+								
Daniels & Plomin (1985)	SA (C)									+			
Arrindell et al. (1989)	SP (R)	+		+	+								
Stravynski et al. (1989)	APD (R)	x	+	+	+	+	+						
Bruch et al. (1989)	SP (R)							+	+	+			
Klonsky et al. (1990)	SA (C)	x		+									
Eastburg & Johnson (1990)	SA (C)		x	+		+							

Study							
Arbel & Stravynski APD (R) (1991)			x	+		+	+
Bruch et al. SP (R) (1994)				+	+	+	+
Leung et al. SP (R) (1994)				+	+	+	+
Juster et al. SP (R) (1996b)		+					
Rapee et al. SP (R) (1997)	+		+	+	x	+	
Caster et al. SA (C) (1999)				+	+	+	+
Whaley et al. SP (C) (1999)	+	+	+				
Lieb et al. SP (L) (2000)	+	+	x				
Hudson & Rapee SP (C) (2001)	+	+	+				
Hudson & Rapee SP (C) (2002)	+						
Woodruff-Borden et al. (2002) SP (C)	−						

Note: C = concurrent; L = longitudinal; APD = avoidant personality disorder; R = retrospective; SA = SA; SP = SP; − = inverse relationship; + = positive relationship; x = no relationship.

Overprotectiveness on the part of mothers towards girls between the age of 0 to 3 and boys between the ages of 6 to 10 were associated with social anxiety in adulthood.

Similarly, in 9 out of 10 studies, socially anxious subjects identified their parents as less caring or outright rejecting (parents were also described as shame or guilt-engendering). In the dissenting study (Arbel & Stravynski, 1991) of that series, social phobic/avoidant personality disorder participants stood out from the control group in mostly lacking positive experiences with their parents, rather than the extent of feeling rejected. This observation is bolstered by 6 studies reporting less emotional warmth on the part of the parents of social phobic individuals.

The findings stressing the absence of positive experiences are to some extent contradicted by some results reported in Kagan & Moss (1962). In this study hostility (including rejection) on the part of mothers towards girls at the age of 0 to 3 and boys between the ages of 6−10, was negatively associated with social anxiety in adulthood.

Another important factor prominent in most studies is the relative isolation of the parents and the low sociability of the family (all of 7 studies). Similarly, in 4 out of 5 studies testing this, parents were perceived as greatly concerned about the opinion of others.

In Juster, Heimberg, Frost, Holt et al. (1996b), social phobic individuals reported higher parental criticism but were similar to normal controls in terms of parental expectations while growing up.

In summary, there was a fairly consistent link between social phobia and the retrospective perception of parents as being on the one hand overanxious and overprotective, and on the other hand rather little or only intermittently involved with their child. The implications of such environmental features on the shaping of the social phobic pattern (e.g. through modeling and encouraging self-protective patterns of behavior) are still to be elucidated. The haphazard care given often in response to self-dramatizing expressions of distress on the part of the child are well-known features of the anxious pattern of attachment. Finally, social phobia seems rather consistently linked to a membership in a family that is both rather isolated and mindful of proprieties in relations with others.

Child Rearing and Other Characteristics of the Family Viewed Retrospectively in Relation to Social Anxiety/Shyness Although not concerning social phobia as such, these studies might shed some light on the (not unrelated) link between social anxiety and parental behavior. Typically, volunteer subjects (college students) reporting high degrees of social anxiety were contrasted in terms of their perception on the rearing practices prevalent in their families of origin with the perceptions of subjects reporting low levels of social anxiety.

Highly socially anxious subjects perceived parental attitudes rather similarly (see Table 9.1). In Caster, Inderbitzen, & Hope (1999), the highly socially anxious subjects perceived their family as tending toward being less sociable, to isolate the child, and being preoccupied with the good opinion of others. Although there was a positive correlation between the subjects' perceptions and those of their parents (who were also interviewed), these correlations were fairly low.

In a similar study carried out by Klonsky, Dutton, & Liebel (1990), of a wide array of perceptions of parental attitudes measured, only perceptions of rejection and stern discipline on the part of the father and neglect (by both parents) characterized the reports of the highly anxious students.

In a study of university students, Eastburg & Johnson (1990) found that the degree of "shyness" tended to correlate with a perception either of the parents as having been inconsistent in enforcing discipline or tending to control through guilt by means of a threat or an actual withdrawal from the relationship.

In a study concerned primarily with the inheritance of shyness (Daniels & Plomin, 1985) 3 groups of parents were investigated regarding the sociability of their children. These were: biological parents who raised their children, biological parents who gave their children up for adoption, and the adoptive parents who raised these children. The first and the third groups of parents were asked to rate the sociability of their children at the age of 12 and 24 months.

The involvement of parents in social life and openness to novelty was correlated inversely to the children's shyness. This was true of the adoptive parents and, even more so, of the biological parents who raised their own children. This finding underscores the importance of the family environment in fostering or leading away from shyness in children. The stronger correlation in the biological parents who raised their own children may allude to genetic predisposition at play. Few associations, however were found between the biological parents' (who gave their children up for adoption) sociability and the children's shyness. This indirectly underscores again the importance of the environmental experience provided by the parental home to the child. The importance of the family environment was emphasized again in Bögels, van Oosten, Muris, & Smulders (2001) who found that socially anxious children rated it as less sociable than did normal children.

In summary, these studies dovetail broadly (but not in all particulars) the findings concerning social phobic subjects. The findings imply indirectly that social phobia is not so much a distinct entity sharply distinguished from normality, but rather an exacerbation of a general trend of common fears extant in social life.

Social Phobic Parents   Several studies reported that compared to a normal control group, a statistically significant (ranging from 15% to 26%) proportion of social phobic individuals seen in the clinic (i.e. self-selected) had social phobic parents (e.g. Fyer et al., 1995). A similar proportion was reported in a small sample (n = 25) drawn from an epidemiological study carried out in Sweden (Tillfors, Furmark, Ekselius, & Fredrikson, 2001a; see chapter 6 for a complete review).

Growing up in such a household doubtlessly will have its implications for upbringing. How parents might transmit their own patterns of behavior either directly (e.g. serving as an example, encouraging and discouraging certain behaviors) or indirectly (e.g. inculcating certain rules) remains an important research question. Woodruff-Borden, Morrow, Bourland, & Cambron (2002), for example, have found that parents with anxiety disorders tended to agree and praise their children less and ignore them more frequently than normal parents.

Furthermore, mothers with anxiety disorders granted less autonomy to their children. A gradation was found: anxious mothers with anxious children restricted their autonomy more than did anxious mothers with non-anxious children who resembled the normal mothers in this respect (Whaley, Pinto, & Sigman, 1999).

However that may be, only a fraction of social phobic individuals had grown up with such parents; the notion of familial transmission (of the full-blown pattern) fails to account for the bulk of cases of social phobia.

Parental Influence Facilitating the Development of "Behavioral Inhibition" or Moving Away from It   Kagan et al. (1987) reported that inhibited children (at the age of 21 months) who became uninhibited later on (between the age of 3.5 and 5.5 years) had mothers who introduced peers at home and encouraged their child to face up to stressful situations. Conversely, uninhibited children who became inhibited later on had mothers who encouraged greater caution. Unfortunately, no definite rates of switching from "behavioral inhibition" to a lack of it, and vice versa, in relationship to the encouragement of sociability or social prudence (on the part of the mother) were reported. These would have allowed the testing of the hypothesis of an enduring maternal influence on what is regarded by the authors as an innate (biological) temperamental characteristic of the child ("behavioral inhibition").

In Chen et al. (1998) "behavioral inhibition" observed at 25 months was inversely correlated with acceptance and encouragement towards achievement and positively with protection and concern, in a sample of (non-Chinese) Canadians. Surprisingly, the correlations were in the opposite direction in a sample of Chinese from Mainland China. For instance, whereas punishment was positively correlated with "behavioral inhibition" in the Canadian sample, it was inversely correlated in the Chinese sample. These cultural differences might in actual fact question the importance of specific parental characteristics. As suggested by Leung, Heimberg, Holt, & Bruch (1994), the sociability of the family (i.e. what is being done about the "behavioral inhibition") rather than various general parental attitudes towards the child, may be the key determinant environmental factor in "behavioral inhibition."

Parental Influences on the Development of Social Behavior In a study of 42 grade 1 children, Putallaz (1987) examined a possible link between the behavior of mothers and the social behavior and status of the children at school (defined as three positive nominations and ratings). After observing interactions of the children and their mothers, pairs of children and their mothers were created and the children observed at play together.

A positive association was found between a mother being disagreeable and demanding towards her child and the child exhibiting a similar pattern of conduct towards his/her mother and the playmate.

Hypothetical social situations (e.g. trying to enter a group, bullying) were then presented to the subjects who had to say what they would do and then to the mothers who had to say what advice they would give to their child.

Mothers of higher-status children tended to advise their children to be more assertive in the face of teasing, for example, whereas the mothers of low-status children tended to advise them to seek the assistance of an adult. Similarly, higher-status children responded that they would join a group of unknown children during recess, whereas low-status children answered that they would play by themselves. Interestingly, an association was found between the mothers' advice and that of the children's hypothetical behavior in only 1 out of 4 experimental situations.

In a study from Australia (Finnie & Russell, 1988), 40 pre-school children (5 year olds) were observed at play by themselves. Then the mothers were instructed to bring their child to a room where 2 children were at play and help their child join in, in whatever way she or he can. The mothers of high-social-status children encouraged them to join in, stimulated exchanges between the children, and integrated the child without disrupting the ongoing play. Mothers of low-status children tended to interact more with their own child while ignoring the others and allowing negative behavior on the part of their child.

In a similar study (Russell & Finnie, 1990) of 49 5 year olds, children were divided (by their teachers) into popular, rejected, and neglected categories. A mother would be asked to help their child to join 2 children already at play. Mothers of popular children were found to give more suggestions as to how to integrate the play activity, compared to mothers of rejected or neglected children. During the play period, mothers of popular children interfered less, whereas mothers of the other children tended to be more directive, authoritarian, and disruptive. It appears that distinct patterns of behavior characterized the mothers of children belonging to different status categories.

Homel, Burns, & Goodnow (1987) investigated the associations between parental membership in social networks and the children's friendship networks among 305 families from Sidney with 5- to 9-year-old children.

Overall, the more friends the parents had, the more sociable the children and the greater the number of their playmates. Furthermore, the subjects knew many children who were not acquainted with each other.

Family Influences on Social Phobic Children   In the only such study (carried out in Australia; Craddock, 1983) highly socially anxious undergraduates (whom the authors considered socially phobic) were compared to normal subjects in terms of the family systems in which they lived. A greater rate of families of socially anxious subjects, compared to those of normal controls, were characterized by high cohesion (strong bonding, limited autonomy) and high rigidity (enforced by authoritarian and rule-bound leadership), resulting in limited flexibility in terms of role-relationships and shifts in power structure.

In a study investigating parental influences (Barrett, Rapee, Dadds, & Ryan, 1996; Dadds, Barrett, Rapee, & Ryan, 1996), 150 anxious children between the ages of 7 to 14 (31 considered socially phobic), were compared to normal children. The children, as well as their parents, were presented separately with various (mostly social) scenarios and their responses regarding the behavior of the child in them were recorded. This was followed by a joint family discussion regarding what were the appropriate responses to the situation that was observed.

The socially phobic children did not give more avoidant responses to hypothetical social situations than did the other children in the anxious group; but the anxious group overall reported a greater tendency to avoid than did the normal subjects.

The mothers and fathers of socially phobic children, however, tended more than other parents to foresee avoidance of social situations on the part of their child. Following the family discussion, the rate the children in the anxious group who predicted that they would tend to avoid threatening social situations more than doubled, from 30% to 68%. In the normal group joint family discussions resulted in the opposite trend; responses involving avoidance dropped from 17% to 6%.

Both results powerfully illustrate the influence of parents in molding child responses. Unfortunately, distinct results for social phobic individuals were not provided, nor do we know how the verbal reports relate to what the participants actually do.

In summary, socially phobic individuals tended to originate from rigidly rule-bound families that hampered autonomy and bolstered (or at least did not discourage) avoidance.

Peer Environment

Socially Anxious Children and Their Peers   A question of interest in the developmental study of social phobia is whether typical relationships characterize the contact of social phobic/socially anxious children. As no relevant studies with socially phobic subjects have been carried out, I will survey the available research with either socially anxious children or such adults describing their childhoods retrospectively.

In Gilmartin (1987) 2 age groups (19–24 and 35–50) of individuals described as "shy with the opposite sex" were compared to a group (19–24) of self-confident subjects.

Shy subjects (of both age groups) reported a greater incidence of bullying by peers in childhood and adolescence than did the self-confident (94% and 81% vs. 0%) as well as being left out of sports activities at school and a dislike for rough games. Although this retrospective study cannot clarify whether the withdrawn behavior of the shy or the rejecting behavior of the peers comes first, it does highlight the vicious circle that characterizes such a relationship.

Two studies looked at this question. In the first (La Greca, Dandes, Wick, Shaw, & Stone, 1988), children aged 8 to 12 were assessed in terms of their social anxiety and their "sociometric status." Children who were ignored by their peers were more socially anxious than children labeled "popular" and, crucially, in some ways were more anxious than children who attempted to socialize but were actively rejected.

In the second study (Walters & Inderbitzen, 1998) 1,179 adolescents were investigated. Those classified as submissive (i.e. easily pushed around) by their peers were characterized by the highest levels of social anxiety. Conversely, lower but equivalent levels of social anxiety characterized all other children, cooperative as well as dominant.

Social Anxiety and Status Within Peer Groups (Longitudinal Studies)   In Hymel, Rubin, Rowden, & LeMare (1990), 155 8 year olds (from Waterloo, Ontario) were followed and reassessed after 3 years. Measures included both observation of the child at play in the laboratory, assessment of classroom (shy, anxious) behavior by the teacher as well as peer assessment of social behavior (popularity, aggression, and isolation) at school.

At the age of 8 no association was found between shy and anxious behavior and isolation, as determined by peers or observation. At the age of 11, however, an association between the above factors did emerge; teachers perceived as shy and anxious children ignored by peers (e.g. not chosen as playmates).

Solitary play at the age of 8 did not predict shyness and anxiousness at the age of 11, but isolation at the age of 8 predicted (albeit weakly, $r = 0.34$) isolation at the age of 11 as well as shy and anxious behavior. Under regression analysis, however, none of these associations held. But being shy and anxious at the age of 8 predicted isolation at the age of 11. This is suggestive that the process of isolation starts with shyness and not the other way around.

In Vernberg, Abwender, Ewell, & Beery (1992) 68 12 to 14 year olds who had just moved to a new neighborhood were assessed at the beginning of a new school year in September, and then reassessed in November and May the following year. Self-report by the children of being rejected was correlated with self-reports of social anxiety. Social anxiety at the beginning of the study predicted (-0.4) less companionship in subsequent assessments.

The above studies are contradicted to some extent by the findings of Olweus (1993) who focused on 15 out of a 71-strong sample of 16 year olds who had been victimized by their peers at school. Victimized children were considered those identified (by both teachers and peers) as being persistently aggressed. No sequels to victimization in terms of differences in social anxiety at the age of 23 were found. Given the small number of subjects and the possibility of insufficient statistical power, these results must be approached with caution until further replication.

Social Anxiety, Social Phobia and Victimization   Slee (1994) administered questionnaires concerning bullying and social anxiety to

114 children 11 years of age on average. Being a victim of bullying correlated significantly with fears of negative evaluation (0.31 for boys and 0.41 for girls).

Crick & Grotpeter (1996) studied the link between victimization and adjustment in terms of loneliness and social anxiety in 474 children (grades 3 to 6). Social anxiety, avoidance, and loneliness could be predicted from self-reports of exclusion from groups or being belittled and denigrated. Being the target of overt aggression however did not increase predictive power. Lack of positive peer treatment was related to loneliness and social avoidance but not social anxiety. Similar results were reported by Storch, Brassard, & Masia-Warner (2003). Altogether, it is possible that victims exhibit a perceptible vulnerability and defenselessness that excites verbal, or physical aggression in some children.

Craig (1998) studied 546 (grade 5 to 8) children who were divided into bullies, victims, bullies and victims, and comparison subjects according to cut-off scores on scales. Victims of bullying had the highest social anxiety scores.

In a meta-analytic study (Hawker & Boulton, 2000) the association between being victimized and social anxiety has been reconfirmed. However, the larger framework of this study put this link in a proper perspective. The statistical size of effect for social anxiety was the smallest whereas the size of effect of the association between victimization and depression came out as the highest.

McCabe, Antony, Summerfeldt, Liss, & Swinson (2003) asked social phobic, obsessive-compulsive, and panic disorder patients (26 of each) whether they were ever bullied or severely teased. Fully 92% of the social phobic individuals reported such experiences, compared with 50% of the obsessional subjects and 35% panic disorder subjects.

In summary, social anxiety is strongly associated with various behavioral strategies aiming at self-protection; avoidance, passivity, and especially submission are prominent. Whether victimization leads to anxiety or something in the (e.g. defenseless) behavior of the victim provokes aggression remains unclear. It is possible that victimization is a spiraling process, stemming from a failure to integrate into a group and achieve standing amongst its members.

Adverse Life-Events During Childhood

In this section, I will consider retrospective studies in which social phobic individuals were queried about various adverse events in their childhood.

Separation or Loss of Parent

In three studies (David, Giron, & Mellman, 1995; Arbel & Stravynski, 1991; Tweed, Schoenbach, George, & Blazer, 1989) no greater association between separation and loss experiences for social phobic participants compared to control groups was reported. Bandelow et al. (2004), however, found more instances of social phobic individuals being raised by foster parents as compared to controls.

Interestingly, Arbel & Stravynski (1991) found a greater fear of abandonment without the actual event ever taking place reported by social phobic/avoidant personality disorder subjects compared to normal controls. This was perhaps the outcome of an insufficiency of positive interactions rather than of actual threats of abandonment.

Strife Between Parents

Magee (1999) found that witnessing chronic hostility and verbal aggression between parents was associated with higher risk of social phobia. Moreover, Bandelow et al. (2004) reported a considerable degree of actual violence (e.g. father beating mother − 18% vs. 2.5%) in families of social phobic individuals. Such familial context, where it occurs, might be related to the tendency towards appeasement and avoidance of conflict typical of social phobic individuals.

Parental Alcoholism

David et al. (1995) found an association between parental alcoholism and phobia (both social and agoraphobia); 35% of phobic subjects reported parental alcoholism compared with 8% in normal controls. Unfortunately, the results were not broken down and the rate among social phobic individuals alone was not given. A comprehensive study of this kind with social phobic participants remains to be done.

Sexual and Physical Abuse

In 4 out of 6 studies available (Dinwiddie, Heath, Dunne, Bucholz et al., 2000; Magee, 1999; David et al., 1995; Pribor & Dinwiddie, 1992) an association between some form of sexual coercion in childhood and adult social phobia was reported. Sexual abuse was detected by questions such as "Were you ever forced into sexual activity including intercourse?" Conversely, social phobic individuals were less likely to have been sexually abused than those identified as panic disorder (Safren,

Gershuny, Marzol, Otto, & Pollack, 2002), while avoidant personality disorder was less associated with sexual abuse than all other personality disorders (Rettew, Zanarini, Yen, Grilo, Skodol, Shea, McGlashan, Morey, Culhane, & Gunderson, 2003).

In a similar vein, Mancini, van Ameringen, & MacMillan (1995) and Ernst, Angst, & Foldenyi (1993) failed to find such an association. The latter finding has the advantage of according with clinical experience.

Mancini et al. (1995) have also failed to find a link between physical mistreatment while growing up and social phobia. In contrast, Bandelow et al. (2004) found a significant level of physical violence directed at the social phobic individual from members of the family when compared with normal controls (e.g. father 50% vs. 29% or siblings 26% vs. 5%). A similar link was reported by Chartier, Walker, & Stein (2001). These findings go against the grain of clinical experience.

In summary, it is exceedingly difficult to give due weight to the relative importance of these disparate developmental factors. Studies investigating the links between them and a variety of psychiatric problems (social phobia included), however, set these in perspective. In Kessler, Davis, & Kendler (1997), for instance, almost all types of childhood adversities predicted social phobia. However, the same types of adversities also predicted many other disorders equally well or better. Furthermore, none of the adversities resulted in the highest associations with social phobia. The presence of multiple adversities was interactive rather than additive and resulted in a greater association. This finding might imply that the adverse factors are not discrete features but, rather, elements that combine (partially or in totality) to form a general pattern of the environment in interaction with which the child develops. I shall now turn to a research program exploring such a social interactive view of the development of social phobia from the perspective of attachment.

The Attachment Relationship

A crucial point about attachment in its modern formulation by Bowlby (1981a) is that it is defined in relational terms (i.e. of a dyadic behavioral system). Previous definitions, by contrast, considered attachment a trait of the infant that was driven by primary motives (e.g. feeding). Furthermore, Bowlby's theory was anchored from the outset in an evolutionary outlook and relied also on observations of non-human animals (comparative ethology).

The attachment theory maintains that the human infant has a set of preadapted behaviors that will unfold with maturation. These behaviors will be elicited when a suitable context (certain adults) will be available. Adults, in turn, are predisposed to respond to the infant by nurturing, vocalizing, and touch. The attachment relationship organizes the infant's attachment behaviors (e.g. smiling, vocalizing, and seeking closeness) around the caregiver. By 12 months, these behaviors are well established and are used towards maintaining and reactivating contact with the caregiver. The attachment relationship remains as a backdrop even when the infant directs its attention elsewhere (e.g. exploration). When detecting a potential threat, the infant will seek safety (physical and/or emotional) with the caregiver. While delineating the interpersonal and emotional vicissitudes of the attachment relationship, Bowlby (1981a) repeatedly emphasized its main function: survival, not psychological well-being. He regarded human infants especially (but also primates in general) as being primed and driven to make such relationships.

To sum up, attachment is conceived as a behavioral system ensuring proximity to caregivers and by consequence their protection. Its main function is protection from danger. Attachment therefore is not a quality that an infant is endowed with, nor does it drive the infant to do anything. Attachment – the relationship – was presumably selected for the reproductive success of individuals in the environment in which they evolved.

Furthermore, attachment as a relationship between an infant and a caregiver is the product of a history of interactions between the two participants who, by means of this process, become emotionally *tied* to one another. For example, for those so involved, even brief separations are upsetting. Both separation anxiety as well as stranger anxiety – becoming rather pronounced in the second half of the first year of life – might be construed as part of the process of attachment, organized around a particular (usually mothering) figure.

It is noteworthy that the response to separations is patterned and highly organized, not haphazard. A typical sequence is a period of protest, followed by a period of despair culminating in detachment (Sroufe & Waters, 1977). A prolonged separation, however, has a highly upsetting (i.e. disorganizing effect) on the infant; this highlights the emotional importance of the attachment relationship.

A paradigm of assessment (the Strange Situation) to assess the attachment relationship was developed by Ainsworth, Blehar, Waters, & Wall (1978) (see Sroufe, 1996, pp. 180–182 for a detailed description).

The procedure involves 8 episodes:

1. A caregiver and an infant enter a room containing various toys (1min.);
2. The infant is allowed to play while the caregiver is seated in a chair nearby (3 min.);
3. A stranger comes in and sits quietly (1 min.), chats with caregiver (1 min.), engages the infant in play;
4. The caregiver leaves (3 min.) unless the stranger cannot calm down the upset infant;
5. The caregiver returns and the stranger leaves (3 min.);
6. The caregiver leaves the infant alone (3 min. or less);
7. The stranger returns and attempts to comfort the infant, if needed (3 min.);
8. The caregiver returns (3 min.).

Various doubts have been raised about the extent to which observations gathered by this method reflected behavior in a natural (i.e. home) environment (see Lamb, Thompson, Gardner, Charnov, & Estes, 1984 for a critique). Nevertheless, the Strange Situation seems to have withstood the test of time through extensive use (see Karen, 1998 for a survey of its use in various studies). Moreover, the fact that this method of assessment conflates both stranger and separation (steps 3 and 4) anxieties (see chapter 3; Marks, 1987, p. 142) constitutes a serious flaw in the procedure.

Based on observations during the Strange Situation assessment, 3 patterns of attachment relationships have been proposed: secure, anxious, and avoidant (the following descriptions rely on Sroufe, 1996, pp. 182–185).

The *securely* attached infants willingly separate from the caregiver to become involved in play activities. They are not too apprehensive of a stranger. If distressed, they seek contact with the caregiver and recover smoothly from a heightened and disorganized emotional state in her/his presence. The *anxiously* attached infants by contrast, are reluctant to explore and are wary of a stranger. They are quite upset by separations and find it difficult to settle down even when reunited with the caregiver. The *avoidantly* attached infants separate rather easily to play. They are upset only when left alone and, significantly, take little notice of the caregiver upon reunion and are not responsive to her/him.

Bowlby's central hypothesis was that the availability and responsiveness of the caregiver (i.e. quality of care) are strong determinants of the kind of resulting attachment relationship. Theoretically, securely attached infants would have had histories of caregiver availability and responsiveness; avoidant infants, histories of unavailability, and rejection on the part of the caregiver; while anxiously attached infants, histories of haphazardly available care and intermittently effective interventions on the part of the caregiver.

According to Bowlby (1981b) the intense separation anxiety and other fears exhibited by these infants are a reaction to the uncertainty of the availability of the caregiver in the face threat. Anxiety signals and proximity seeking have also a communicative function in alerting the caregiver to the distress of the infant and elicit its reassurance and assistance in calming the infant (emotional regulation in Sroufe's, 1996 terminology). Given that the caregiver cannot be counted on to attend to the needs of the infant when they arise, the infant will tend to intensify the signals in response to lower and lower thresholds of possibility of threat. As a consequence the infant would be easily aroused, frequently distressed and not easily reassured.

Interestingly, infant temperament has not been shown to affect attachment directly, while seeming to influence the relationship in interaction with certain caregiver characteristics (e.g. maternal tendency to control – see Mangelsdorf, Gunnar, Kestenbaum, Lang, & Andreas, 1990).

Is a particular pattern of attachment in infancy enduring? What are its long-term implications? Clearly, a particular pattern of attachment in infancy does not directly lead to specific outcomes in adolescence or adulthood. Secure attachment does not ensure life without difficulties, but in the face of such difficulties, securely attached children tend to display more resourcefulness, resilience, and relational abilities. Conversely, anxious attachment in infancy does not by necessity result in an anxiety disorder later on. Such a complex disordered pattern of behavior would depend, in Bowlby's (1981b) formulation, "on an interaction between the organism as it has developed up to that moment and the environment in which it then finds itself" (p. 364). Theoretically, this implies that with the rise of new circumstances, past experiences would not simply vanish without trace, but would leave their mark on the process of adaptation through the remnants of the behavioral patterns that have been forged previously.

Validating Research

The main ideas embedded in attachment theory were examined in an admirable longitudinal study carried out by the "Minnesota group for research on attachment." For descriptions of it, I rely mostly on Sroufe,

Carlson, & Shulman (1993) and Sroufe (1983). Two specific hypotheses were put to a test. First, that the psychological availability and responsiveness of the caregiver determines the quality of attachment; and second, that the quality of attachment in turn influences the way a person deals with intimate relationships (e.g. dependency, nurturing, separations, and loss; p. 47) and participates in social life.

Subjects were recruited before birth in 1974–1975 relying on 267 expectant mothers who were high risk for difficulties in caregiving (low socioeconomic status, high-school dropouts, unmarried, unplanned pregnancy). In this ongoing longitudinal study the quality of attachment relationship was determined by the Strange Situation paradigm at the age of 12 and 18 months. Observations in the home were carried out in the first 6 months. Subsequently, the children were observed with their parents in the laboratory on several occasions as well as in various other environments (e.g. school, summer camp) during childhood, adolescence, and adulthood.

In what follows, I will single out examples of behavior typical of the anxiously attached children (classified as such at 12 and 18 months) as they grew up because of the striking resemblance of their conduct with features of social phobia. A comprehensive overview of this pattern of attachment may be found in Cassidy & Berlin (1994).

For example, as a group, anxiously attached 4-year-old girls were particularly withdrawn, passive, submissive, and neglected by their peers. Furthermore, anxiously attached 4 year olds were found to participate less socially and, when they did, were less dominant (the index included verbal and non-verbal observed behaviors) than the securely attached children.

In another study, however (Renken, Egeland, Marvinney, Mangelsdorf, & Sroufe, 1989), a strong link between anxious attachment and passive withdrawal was established for 6- to 8-year-old boys in a school context. Thus, 58% of the passively withdrawn children were previously categorized as anxiously attached.

At summer camp anxiously attached 10 to 11 year olds spent less time in group activities, and rarely initiated and structured group activities themselves. Groups of mostly securely attached children were involved in more elaborate play activities. When 3 or more anxiously attached children congregated, their activities had to be structured by a counselor. Left to their own devices, they would revert to uncoordinated and solitary types of activities performed in parallel (e.g. play on a swing). This illustrates the difficulties such children had in managing important aspects of social functioning such as fitting in and establishing one's status (Sroufe et al., 1993, pp. 330–331).

A sense of the tendency towards submissiveness of the anxiously attached children might be conveyed by observations of exploitative behavior among children attending the summer camp. In 5 dyads out of 19 observed, there was evidence of victimization (repetitive pattern of exploitation or physical or verbal abuse) of one child by another. In all cases the victim was an anxiously attached child whereas the bullies were all avoidant; none of the bullies were anxiously (or securely) attached children.

Both examples illustrate to some extent how the complex pattern of behaviors of the anxiously attached children helped to shape the social environment in which they found themselves. For example, teachers tended to be nurturing and controlling with the obedient and retiring anxiously attached children. By contrast, they were rejecting and punitive with avoidant children who tended towards defiance.

Anxious Attachment, Social Anxiety, and Social Phobia

Although not concerning social phobia as such, a study of social functioning and attachment (Bohlin, Hagekull, & Rydell, 2000) carried out in Sweden found that social anxiety was more severe among the anxiously attached than among securely and avoidantly attached 8 to 9 year olds.

Only one study to my knowledge has linked anxious attachment in early childhood to anxiety disorders – with social phobia amongst them – at the age of 17.5 (Warren, Huston, Egeland, & Sroufe, 1997). The subjects were 172 17.5 year olds, diagnosed by means of a structured interview (the interviewers being blind to their attachment status that was determined at the age of 12 months by means of the Strange Situation 16 years earlier). In the final sample, 32 subjects were anxiously attached, 95 securely and 37 avoidantly attached.

The main finding was that more children fulfilling criteria for anxiety disorders were, as infants, classified anxiously attached. The most prevalent anxiety disorder observed in that group was indeed social phobia (10), followed by separation anxiety disorder (8) and over-anxious disorder (8). 28% of the anxiously attached infants developed anxiety disorders in adolescence compared to 13% of the children who were not anxiously attached in infancy. However, far more (40% vs. 28%) of the anxiously attached infants had no clinical problems when interviewed in adolescence. Perhaps the most theoretically meaningful result was that only anxious attachment (but not avoidant or secure attachment) in infancy was associated with social phobia (and other anxiety disorders) in late adolescence.

Remarkably, nurses' ratings of the newborn's temperament (defined as newborn crying, motor activity and relaxation when held) significantly predicted anxiety disorders (undifferentiated) in late adolescence. In a study investigating the relationship between insecure attachment and temperament (Manassis, Bradley, Goldberg, Hood, & Swinson, 1995), the subjects were 20 children (age 18 to 59 months) of 18 mothers meeting criteria for various anxiety disorders. They were assessed for "behavioral inhibition" as well as "type of attachment" using the original assessment procedures described earlier. While 16 out of 20 children were insecurely attached and 15 were behaviorally inhibited, no relationship was found between the 2 constructs. Only 1 of the children, however, met DSM-III-R criteria for avoidant disorder.

In summary, anxious attachment (and significantly, only anxious attachment) at the age of 12 months was associated with anxiety disorders, (with social phobia prominent amongst them) in late adolescence (17.5 years). In regression analysis, anxious attachment in infancy predicted anxiety disorders (not specifically social phobia) in adolescence over and above other variables such as maternal anxiety and an array of variables indexing temperament. Nonetheless, it must be borne in mind that an even greater proportion of infants classified as anxiously attached did not develop an anxious disorder of any description by late adolescence.

Discussion

The Role of "Behavioral Inhibition" and "the Attachment Relationship" in Social Phobia

Neither the constitutional feature of temperament defined as "behavioral inhibition" nor the "attachment relationship" have been shown to be the determining factor in the genesis of social phobia in otherwise admirable longitudinal studies, spanning almost two decades. This also applies to environmental features such as style of parenting. None have been linked directly and specifically to social phobia nor associated to all or most cases of social phobia.

The temperamental perspective on development regards temperament as expressing the innate and enduring properties of the individual central nervous system. As such it has strong inherent appeal. It seems uncontroversial to postulate an individual innate substratum (i.e. the genotype) constituting the core raw material as it were, subsequently fashioned or even perhaps transformed in the course of development by environmental events.

Practically, however, it has proved exceedingly difficult to translate this abstract idea into concrete formulations. First, there are numerous perspectives about how to conceive temperament (e.g. categories, dimensions). Second, since temperament (being a hypothetical construct) cannot be measured directly, the behavioral indices which might best express it remain a matter of debate (see Goldsmith et al., 1987). Third, with time, numerous patterns of behavior manifest in specific contexts (i.e. the phenotype) will be overlying, as it were, the temperamental substratum, thereby making the gauging of temperament more and more difficult. Ultimately, this process will render its very meaning as an independent feature uncertain. This is well illustrated by the fact that in Kagan et al. (1987), some of the children classified as inhibited and uninhibited (both at the opposite ends of the distribution of temperament) no longer fitted their original classification between the ages of 2 to 5. Moreover, in light of parental influences these children changed to such an extent that they now corresponded to the opposite category (i.e. from behaviorally inhibited to uninhibited and vice versa). Although undocumented, this is likely to apply with at least equal force to the unstudied 80% of the children that mass between the two extreme ends of the distribution. Furthermore, as "behavioral inhibition" in most studies was established at the age of 21 months, it is difficult to see how pure temperament might have been distinguished from environmental influences of almost 2 years' duration.

Development seen through the perspective of the "attachment theory" ignores in its theorizing the presumably innate individual characteristics highlighted earlier and instead lays stress on how these unarticulated characteristics coalesce in the crucible of the "attachment relationship" with the principal caregiver into a pattern of relating to others. Presumably an "insecure attachment relationship" expresses a mismatch between certain characteristics of the infant and those of the caregiver who fails to satisfy the needs of the infant. A parent might respond in various ways to attention seeking or other forms of fearfulness on the part of their child: patient reassurance on occasion but for example increasing frustration or anger at other times or subsequently. Who of the two participants has the greater influence on the shaping of the anxious attachment relationship is difficult to say. This is typically ascribed to the caregiver, but certain propensities of the infant might be said to increase the likelihood of eliciting particular responses from the parent.

However that may be, according to Sroufe (1996), attachment captures the quality of the relationship as opposed to temperament.

According to Warren et al. (1997), indices of temperament may be related to attachment behaviors (e.g. crying at separation) but not to a pattern of attachment. Although, it is a matter of controversy at this time whether insecurity of attachment might be predicted from temperamental and other characteristics of the child (see Cassidy and Berlin, 1994), enough examples are available to give pause. For instance, in Warren et al. (1997) nurses' ratings of temperament of a newborn (crying, motor activity, and relaxation when held) together with anxious-attachment-predicted anxiety disorders in adolescence.

Although seemingly denoting somewhat different phenomena construed from varying perspectives (intra-personal as opposed to inter-personal), there is much that the actual behavioral patterns involved in "behavioral inhibition" and "anxious attachment" have in common (see Stevenson-Hinde, 1991). First, they share a common function of protecting from harm; the one through fear of unfamiliar surroundings and the other of being left alone. Second, although the integrated patterns begin to appear in the second half of the first year of life, the common behavioral elements such as clinging, smiling, crying, and startle responses occur from birth. Third, both patterns are evoked first rather indiscriminately, with a gradual narrowing and fine-tuning of what elicits fear or who is the preferred attachment figure. Finally, social influences and other circumstances mold both. In the course of life both attachment figures (e.g. from parent to friend to spouse) and objects of fear (e.g. from peers to persons in positions of power) evolve.

Theoretically speaking, both models share the common goal of attempting to explain the rise of anxiety and disorders of anxiety. On the one hand, the temperamental viewpoint of Kagan et al. (1987) is that the anxiety experienced by the "behaviorally inhibited" stems from an innate lower threshold of excitability in limbic structures. Another possibility consistent with the temperamental point of view might be a difficulty in *modulating* arousal rather than excess in arousal as such (see Lader & Marks, 1971). On the other hand, the attachment viewpoint regards the distress of separation as "the earliest form of anxiety experienced by children" (Warren et al., 1997, p. 638). Anxiety is viewed as becoming fully fledged through a process during which the child insistently dramatizes its appeals to the caregiver and remains perpetually aroused and vigilant in the face of care lacking in sensitivity and responsiveness (anxious attachment).

Unfortunately, as argued in chapter 3, anxiety is a rather ambiguous concept. Although "it" might be experienced powerfully, it is difficult to define, and, unsurprisingly, difficult to measure. Although often invoked in reference to an inner state it does not have a more precise meaning than "fearful discomfort." How the anxious state relates to what socially anxious or phobic individuals do in various spheres and phases of life remains unexplained by both approaches.

Neither "anxious attachment" nor "behavioral inhibition" is in itself a manifestation of abnormality. Rather they might be seen as the kernel of a developmental construct the outcome of which is dependent on subsequent experiences. For example, Kagan & Zentner (1996, p. 347) argue that the emergence of social phobia requires at least 3 independent factors: first, a particular inhibited (timid) "temperament" (assuming this to be a pure expression of the genotype); second, an environment that continuously amplifies the psychological vulnerability associated with that temperament; and third, consistent social demands eliciting the pattern. A similar outlook in principle characterizes attachment theory, with anxious attachment replacing behavioral inhibition as the linchpin.

Both "anxious attachment" and "behavioral inhibition" have been shown to represent a potential towards, rather than the actuality of, social phobia. Crucially, neither constitutes a necessary condition for social phobia. The external conditions aggravating the risk or attenuating it, are therefore of the utmost importance.

Environmental Conditions

Are any particular environmental conditions propitious for the development of social phobia? Most research has been concentrated on parents; perhaps a vestige of psychoanalytic teaching that accords the utmost importance to family life. As a matter of principle, parental influence is doubtlessly important. Parents inculcate rules of social behavior (e.g. the importance of propriety) and examples of social life (e.g. relative isolation). They encourage and reward certain behaviors but perhaps more importantly ignore most and punish others. The latter point may be relevant to the failure of extinction of social fears. Thus, little is known of particular patterns of punishment (e.g. types of punishment, their proportionality) and intimidation in the process of socialization of social phobic individuals and the pattern of relationship (say between parent and child or certain peers) in which it is embedded (Kemper, 1978, pp. 237–262). Furthermore, how much of this is generalized outside the home, and how lasting such influences are, is largely unknown.

However that may be, the validity of the results of most of the research reviewed earlier is uncertain in that it was organized by rather ambiguous concepts (see Masia & Morris, 1998) and draws on retrospective recollections. It is rather doubtful that these reflect specific parental practices. Irrespective of methodology, however, this line of research perhaps accords too much importance to parental influences at home altogether while neglecting the exceedingly important area of group socialization outside the home (see Deater-Deckard, 2001). Arguably (see Harris, 1995), children learn separately how to behave at home, how to behave outside it, and how to discern acutely the differences between the two. The consequences of behavior in each environment are plainly different. At home the child might be shown gratuitous signs of affection at times, praised for what is considered praiseworthy occasionally, and scolded for misbehaving most of the time. Out of the home, most appropriate behavior is ignored, misbehavior is at times rewarded, and mistakes magnified and ridiculed. It is likely that much of the socialization in terms of enacting social roles and the transmission of culture are done outside the home and take place in peer groups (1995). We need to turn our attention to these environmental factors in seeking a better understanding of the development of social phobia.

In the final analysis, however, no single all-important factor, no one particular experience, unsettling as it might have been, leads inexorably towards social phobia. Neither temperament nor parent – child relationships lead irreversibly to the development of social phobia – although they might constitute a serious liability towards it. As we have seen earlier, some of the children identified as the likeliest candidates did not become social phobic, whereas some of those considered least likely to develop social phobia ultimately did.

What is the alternative? The overall findings reviewed in this chapter fit best with the proposition that the development of a social phobic pattern is the product of widely extended process punctuated by ceaseless demands placed by a certain social environment on an individual with a specific endowment and a certain history of (mal)adjustment. Ultimately, social phobia starts to develop (from the raw material of normal social anxiety) through an extended process of learning that, in dealings with powerful others, one does not count for much, as one's wishes and feelings are mostly ignored. Moreover, when at odds with such individuals, one is usually defeated or outdone. While engaging in such struggles, one's weaknesses (real and imaginary) are magnified and ridiculed, while strengths and achievements are ignored and belittled. Naturally, such possibilities are viewed with increasing alarm and self-protective measures, aiming at minimizing the risks of being coerced or otherwise mistreated, emerge. When these stabilize or broaden, the embryonic social phobic pattern begins to crystallize. Such an historic process is simultaneously social (interpersonal) and biological (fearful), literally incorporating experience. It is consolidated when an individual systematically and repeatedly fails to engage various aspects of the social life of his or her community in a participatory and assertive manner and instead responds both fearfully and defensively. This theoretical outlook will be further elaborated in the integrative section of chapter 11.

Part IV

What Helps Social Phobic Individuals?

10 The Treatments of Social Phobia: Their Nature and Effects

If "epidemiological" studies are to be believed, estimated rates of prevalence of social phobia at the present are generally lower than those over the "lifetime." Natural social processes (e.g. meeting an enterprising admirer, a sympathetic but demanding teacher) leading to remission would account for the difference. Little evidence of such benign processes can be seen however in the lives of patients seeking help, perhaps because these are for the most part little capable of taking advantage of naturally occurring social opportunities. Social phobia typically crystallizes as a pattern in the face of the increasingly insistent social and interpersonal demands of adulthood made on adolescents, and remains among the most chronic problems seen in the clinic (see chapter 5). Help is often sought long after the onset of problems. What of proven value can be offered such patients?

An attempt at the valuation of treatments of social phobia requires establishing boundaries as to what claims to consider and which to dismiss outright or ignore. What are the possibilities? One end of a continuum of strictness might be defined as an indulgent approach relying on the self-valuation of the proponents of various treatments. The other end might be designated as a discerning approach demanding relatively high quality of evidence. Immoderately, I shall opt for the latter for it seems to me that the most meaningful answer will arise from the careful selection of the best available studies, methodologically speaking. This provides as much guarantee as can be had for the relative soundness of the results, but not necessarily of the conclusions drawn from them. These must be judged on their own merits.

Studies included in this review had to satisfy the following requirements:

1. The sample had to admit only social phobic participants; in the interest of clarity, mixed samples were excluded. As the onset of social phobia is typically in late adolescence, all studies concern adult patients.

289

2. Clinical status had to be determined by publicly recognized defining criteria e.g. DSM-IV.

3. The assessment battery had to use multiple measures of outcome; given that the psychometric characteristics of individual measures often leave much to be desired, a convergence of outcome of all or most measures enhances confidence in the validity of the results.

4. The study design had to involve more than one experimental condition (and therefore random assignment of patients to them). Consequently, this survey was limited to "controlled" studies that contrast the experimental treatment with either a well-established treatment of known outcome or an experimental condition that simulates a treatment without offering its substance (e.g. "placebo"). Placebo (from the Latin *placere*, literally, *I shall be pleasing*) controls are desirable because dealings between individuals recognized as healers and cure-seeking sufferers are known to stimulate self-healing and might therefore constitute a confound. Such simulation of treatment, to have an effect, must be culturally sanctioned in the terms of reference of the patient (see Moerman, 2002). Shamanic rituals aiming to appease offended spirits (incantations, amulets, potions) for example, would be meaningless to the western patient. This, on the other hand, responds powerfully to medical authority and hopefully to its healing rituals (establishing diagnosis, prescribing pills, performing surgery), embedded in a shared outlook ("science"), construing the living organism as a machine and inadequate functioning as its breakdown (in this case, of the brain or the mind).

Three potential strands of outcome were considered:

1. Reduction in subjective distress in and avoidance of anxiety-evoking situations; this was taken as the main measure of improvement owing to its adoption as such by most studies. It is the natural upshot of the commonly held view that social phobia is a "disorder" of social anxiety. This aspect of outcome will be summarized throughout.

2. Improvement in social functioning (i.e. the manner in which the patient participates in social life, assumes roles, and fits in; see Beattie & Stevenson, 1984). Relatively few studies measured this effect of treatment although impaired social functioning is at the heart of social phobia and one of the defining criteria in DSM-IV. Consequently, it will be summarized only when available.

3. Improvement in clinical status (i.e. remission). As the best result possible it sets an absolute standard. Improvements in social anxiety and social functioning, by contrast, are relative to pretreatment levels. Although ostensibly "significant" by statistical standards, such gains might be modest from the point of view of the difference they make to patients' lives. Rates of remission will be reported only when available.

Current Contents, Medline, and PsychInfo electronic databases were systematically searched in order to increase the likelihood of including all relevant publications. The selected studies broadly fell into 3 categories of treatments: the purely psychological, the purely pharmacological, and the combination or comparison of both.

Psychological Treatments

Two broad strategies have emerged in the psychological treatment of social phobia: anxiety reduction and improvement in social functioning.

Anxiety Reduction

Exposure and cognitive restructuring are the main tactics used within the broad anxiety-reduction strategy.

In principle, *exposure* is the therapeutic application of the well-demonstrated fact (Marks, 1987, pp. 457–494) that repeated and prolonged exposure to the anxiety-evoking social setting results in significant reduction in anxiety. It is arguably the methodical application of the principle of habituation, documented in various studies (e.g. Mauss, Wilhelm, & Gross, 2003). Exposure is particularly useful when a strong tendency to avoid is manifest. Practically, a graded hierarchy of increasingly difficult situations might be devised. Starting at the lower end of the hierarchy, the patient will be induced to face up to the feared situation (perhaps simulated) in the clinic and remain in it until distress subsides. Later on (or immediately) exposure will be extended to real-life situations among others by means of self-exposure assignments to be performed in-between sessions.

In theory, *cognitive restructuring* (a generic term for different models of cognitive modification) rests on the assumption that erroneous thinking, fed by mistaken beliefs, generates social anxiety. The clinician practicing this sort of therapy first identifies presumed systematic errors in thinking (i.e. irrational inference drawing; e.g. exaggerating, ignoring counter-evidence) as inferred from the narrative of the patient. Second, in addition to these, putative underlying organizing broad beliefs ("schemas") expressing a whole outlook (e.g. being above reproach guarantees safety), similarly inferred, are challenged. Between sessions, patients are sent to confront anxiety-evoking encounters and asked to identify their anxiety-generating thoughts as they arise and rebut them using methods taught during sessions. Although cognitive restructuring might be used as a technique in an otherwise behavioral treatment, it is typically the organizing principle of a therapy relying on (exposure-like) graduated social tasks, construed as experiments in putting patients' assumptions to a test. Such a regimen is known as cognitive behavior therapy (CBT).

The evaluation of anxiety reduction by means of either exposure or cognitive restructuring as a general orientation to the treatment of social phobia has generated most research. It is the natural outgrowth of the construal of social phobia as a "disorder" of anxiety. Anxiety in turn is conceived of *intra-personally* (i.e. as an enduring quality of the individual generated from within; see chapter 3 for a detailed discussion of the term). In addition to this primary effort, a good proportion of the research attempted to gauge the relative effects of exposure and cognitive restructuring. The backdrop to this line of research is a theoretical clash between two rival outlooks: behaviorism and cognitivism.

The design and outcome of the studies assessing exposure and cognitive restructuring are displayed in Table 10.1.

Overall exposure and CBT are of value for both single- (usually public-speaking) and multi-situation (generalized) social phobia, yielding clinical improvement in distress and avoidance either in a group or individual format. Statistically significant improvements from pretreatment levels are achieved in between 8 to 12 sessions with up to 15% dropping out. These gains do not obtain in control conditions, and tend to be maintained at 6−18 month follow-up, with one report of gains maintained till 5−6 years follow-up.

Although it is widely assumed that reduced (presumably more manageable) levels of social anxiety lead automatically to meaningfully improved social functioning, there is little evidence to support this. Better-focused research is needed to clarify this important point. Conversely, the addition of social skills training to CBT enhanced its effects in terms of anxiety reduction and improved social functioning (Herbert, Gaudiano, Rheingold, Myers, Dalrymple, & Nolan, 2005).

Table 10.1. *Comparative outcome of psychological approaches – anxiety reduction*

Study	Treatment conditions	Outcome				Comments
		Social Avoidance	Subjective Distress	Social Functioning	Follow-up	
Exposure alone vs. waiting list						
Mattick et al. (1989)	6 sessions × 2 h 1. CR (G); n = 11 **2. EXP (G); n = 11** 3. EXP + CR (G); n = 11 **4. WL; n = 10**	(1 = 2 = 3) > 4 2 not improved	(1 = 2 = 3) > 4 2 not improved	—	Exposure improved only at follow-up. Improvement stable at 3 months for other conditions.	Exposure improved only at follow-up.
Scholing & Emmelkamp (1993a)	8 sessions × 1h (4 weeks) **1. EXP (I); n = 10** 2. CR (I); n = 10 3. EXP + CR (I); n = 10 **4. WL**	1 = 2 = 3 = 4 (all improved)	—	—		
Newman et al. (1994)	8 sessions × 2 h **1. EXP (G); n = 18** **2. WL; n = 18**	—	1 = 2 (no improvement)	—	—	Exposure superior on some measures.
Hope et al. (1995a)	12 sessions × 2 h **1. EXP (G); n = 11** 2. EXP + CR (G); n = 18 **3. WL; n = 11**	1 = 2 > 3	1 > 2, 3	—	Improvement stable at 6 months (1 = 2).	Responders 1. 70% 2. 36% 3. 0% **1 = 2 > 3**

Table 10.1. (*cont.*)

Study	Treatment conditions	Outcome Social Avoidance	Subjective Distress	Social Functioning	Follow-up	Comments
Mersch (1995)	14 sessions × 1 h **1. EXP (I)** 2. CR⇨SST⇨EXP (I) 1 + 2; n = 17 **3. WL; n = 17**	(1 = 2) > 3	(1 = 2) > 3	(1 = 2) > 3	—	
Salaberria & Echeburua (1998)	8 sessions × 2.5 h **1. EXP (G); n = 24** 2. EXP + CR (G); n = 24 **3. WL; n = 23**	—	(1 = 2) > 3	—	—	
Cognitive restructuring alone vs. waiting list						
Mattick et al. (1989)	6 sessions × 2 h **1. CR (G); n = 11** 2. EXP (G); n = 11 3. EXP + CR (G); n = 11 **4. WL; n = 10**	(1 = 2 = 3) > 4 2 not improved	(1 = 2 = 3) > 4 2 not improved	—	—	
Scholing & Emmelkamp (1993a)	8 sessions × 1 h (4 weeks) 1. EXP (I); n = 10 **2. CR (I); n = 10** 3. EXP + CR (I); n = 10 **4. WL**	1 = 2 = 3 = 4 (all improved)	—	—	—	

Study	Treatment					
Taylor et al. (1997)	8 sessions × 1.5 h 1. CR (I); n = 32 2. NSP (control) (I); n = 28	1 > 2	1 > 2	—	—	Responders 1. 14% 2. 7% 1 = 2
Cottraux et al. (2000)	6 weeks 1. CR (I) (8 × 1 h); n = 31 2. NSP (control) (I) (3 × 30 min); n = 32	1 > 2	1 = 2 (?)	—	Improvement stable at 6 months.	
Stangier et al. (2003)	15 weeks 1. CR (G: 15 × 2 h); n = 26 2. CR (I: 15 × 1 h); n = 24 3. WL; n = 21	—	1 = 2 > 3	—	Further significant reductions for the individual modality.	Remitters 1. 14% 2. 50% 2 > 1 Significant results obtained only on one of six measures.

Exposure vs. cognitive restructuring

Study	Treatment					
Emmelkamp et al. (1985)	6 sessions × 2.5 h 1. EXP (G) 2. CR (self-instruction variant) (G) 3. CR (rational-emotive variant) (G) n = 38	1 = 2 = 3 3 not improved	1 = 2 = 3 (all improved)	—	Improvement stable at 1 month. Exposure showed further improvement on the avoidance and anxiety measures.	Patients were on various medications.

Table 10.1. (cont.)

Study	Treatment conditions	Outcome			Follow-up	Comments
		Social Avoidance	Subjective Distress	Social Functioning		
Mattick et al. (1989)	6 sessions × 2 h **1. CR (G); n = 11** **2. EXP (G); n = 11** 3. EXP + CR (G); n = 11 4. WL; n = 10	(1 = 2 = 3) > 4 2 not improved	(1 = 2 = 3) > 4 2 not improved	—	Exposure improved only at follow-up. Improvement stable at 3 months for other conditions.	
Scholing & Emmelkamp (1993a)	8 sessions × 1 h (4 weeks) **1. EXP (I); n = 10** **2. CR (I); n = 10** 3. EXP + CR (I); n = 10 4. WL	1 = 2 = 3 = 4 (all improved)	—		—	
Exposure vs. exposure combined with other ingredients						
Butler et al. (1984)	7 sessions × 1 h **1. EXP + AM (I); n = 15** **2. EXP + NSP (control) (I); n = 15** 3. WL; n = 15	1 = 2 > 3	1 > 2 = 3	**1 = 2 = 3** 3 not improved	At 6 months, a significant difference appeared on the avoidance measure (1 > 2)	Although anxiety management made some contribution to outcome, it was not meaningful
Mattick & Peters (1988)	6 sessions × 2 h **1. EXP (G); n = 26** **2. EXP + CR (G); n = 25**	1 = 2 (both improved)	1 = 2 (both improved)	—	Improvement stable at 3 months	The combined group was superior to exposure alone on some measures of avoidance

Study	Design				Follow-up / Comments	
Mattick et al. (1989)	6 sessions × 2 h 1. CR (G); n = 11 **2. EXP (G); n = 11** **3. EXP + CR (G); n = 11** 4. WL; n = 10	(1 = 2 = 3) > 4 2 not improved	(1 = 2 = 3) > 4 2 not improved	—	Exposure improved only at follow-up Improvement stable at 3 months for other conditions	
Scholing & Emmelkamp (1993a)	8 sessions × 1 h (4 weeks) **1. EXP (I); n = 10** 2. CR (I); n = 10 **3. EXP + CR (I); n = 10** 4. WL	1 = 2 = 3 = 4 (all improved)	—	—	—	
Hope et al. (1995a)	12 sessions × 2 h **1. EXP (G); n = 11** **2. EXP + CR (G); n = 18** 3. WL; n = 11	1 = 2 > 3	1 > 2, 3	—	Improvement stable at 6 months (1 = 2)	
Mersch (1995)	14 sessions × 1 h **1. EXP (I)** **2. CR ⇨ SST ⇨ EXP (I)** 1 + 2; n = 17 3. WL; n = 17	(1 = 2) > 3	(1 = 2) > 3	(1 = 2) > 3	Improvement stable at 18 months (1 = 2) Further improvement on the avoidance measure from 3 months	Avoidant personality disorder patients responded equally well to all treatments, but functioned less well at 3 months follow-up Responders **1.** 70% **2.** 36% 3. 0% **1 = 2** > 3

Table 10.1. (*cont.*)

Study	Treatment conditions	Outcome				Follow-up	Comments
		Social Avoidance	Subjective Distress	Social Functioning			
Salaberria & Echeburua (1998)	8 sessions × 2.5 h **1. EXP (G); n = 24** **2. EXP + CR (G);** **n = 24** 3. WL; n = 23	——	(1 = 2) > 3	——		Improvement stable at 12 months (1 = 2) Further improvement for both groups between post-test and 6 months follow-up	The distribution of a self-help manual has not contributed to outcome Remitters Post-test 1. 44% 2. 44%: (**1 = 2**) 12 months 1. 66% 2. 61%: (**1 = 2**)

Note: AM: Anxiety management; CR: Cognitive restructuring; EXP: Exposure *in vivo*; G: Group modality; I: Individual modality; NSP: Non specific psychotherapy; SST: Social skills training; WL: Waiting list; +: combined with; ⇨: followed by; **Highlighted areas** = treatments compared.

Clinically and practically, exposure, cognitive restructuring, and their combination as CBT produced equivalent effects. Theoretically, however, the fact that cognitive restructuring or therapy do not affect cognitive processes more or differently than exposure is of greater moment. This point is discussed in great detail in chapter 7.

Improving Social Functioning

Two approaches towards improving social functioning have been developed. Although often using rather similar methods of inducing behavior change, the two differ radically in the manner of construing the content of treatment.

The first — I shall name it *structural* — attempts to improve social functioning somewhat indirectly, by means of correcting deficient social skills or problems in the *structure* of the social behavior of social phobic patients, deemed necessary for proper social functioning. The structural deficiencies could be located at the molecular (e.g. averted gaze, poor timing) or molar (e.g. assertion) levels of behavior.

Social anxiety might be regarded in such a theoretical framework as a realistic recognition of inadequacy on the part of the patients foreseeing failure in achieving their social aims.

The second approach by contrast, de-emphasizes the formal/structural aspects of the proper performance of social behavior. Instead, it lays stress on the *function* of social behaviors or patterns of behavior. Practically, it attempts to train the fearfully self-protective social phobic patients to develop non-defensive interpersonal ways of dealing with their real-life social circumstances, and to use them in situations very much a part of their daily lives. The emphasis in therapy is on finding ways of behaving that will enable patients, for example, better fitting in, participating in various social activities, and enacting social roles within the social context of their community. For instance, patients are trained and encouraged to admit to being flustered or wrong, while making requests, initiating contact, and being firm or in charge, or assuming the role of an educator while presenting. Such a functional approach takes the view that there are many ways of achieving social goals (e.g. speaking in public or approaching a relative stranger) each potentially useful. Setbacks are not necessarily fatal; another one better suited for the circumstances can replace a behavior proven unsatisfactory. Conversely, even a flawless execution of certain behaviors would not have the intended effect under certain circumstances (e.g. when the goals of the participants are not aligned).

Ultimately, this approach to therapy seeks to erode the overall pattern of fearful self-protective and defensive tactics that constitute social phobia and turning it around. Positively stated, that means enhancing the participation of the individual in the social life of the community of which he or she is a member in the pursuit of personal goals. Such therapy construes social anxiety relationally, as arising from the defensive interpersonal pattern of which it is a facet, evoked by social transactions characterized by insufficiency of social power (see chapter 3). In therapy, social anxiety is therefore likely to subside hand in hand with the dissolution of a defensive overall pattern and the gradual emergence of a participatory one, allowing the patient to pursue desired social goals more effectively.

Whereas the structural approach tends towards a generic view of social skills applicable to all, the functional approach views social behavior as idiosyncratic and firmly embedded in a specific social context. It attempts to devise appropriate behaviors for the achievement of specific social goals of definite individuals living in concrete social circumstances, and relentlessly encourages them to put these to use.

The structural approach uses social skills training to effect behavior change in treatment. Conceptually, "social skills training" is complementary to the notion of "social skills deficits" that it is meant to redress. Practically, it is a sequence of behavior-change techniques usually including modeling, role-play, and feedback, used during training and homework assignments to be carried out in-between sessions. The functional approach might use a similar sequence of behavior change techniques during training sessions. These however are neither conceptually nor practically necessary. The functional approach yields similar results with or without modeling, role-play, and feedback (Stravynski et al., 2000a). The practice of targeted behaviors between sessions, however, is indispensable (Stravynski et al., 1989).

Such therapy approaches social phobia (in DSM terms) as a disorder of personality and anxiety rolled in one. This follows the logic of construing social anxiety *interpersonally* (see chapter 3) as having a dual locus: self-protective interpersonal maneuvering in threatening circumstances and a somatic state of alert in its support.

The treatment of social phobia envisaged as an improvement in social functioning is a less common approach. The design and outcome of the studies assessing the two variants of regimens seeking to improve social functioning are described in Table 10.2.

Overall, improving-social-functioning approaches yielded results superior to waiting lists. Moreover, a smaller number of studies

Table 10.2. *Comparative outcome of psychological approaches – improving social functioning*

Study	Treatment conditions	Outcome				Comments
		Social Avoidance	Subjective Distress	Social Functioning	Follow-up	
Improvement in social functioning (functional) vs. waiting list						
Stravynski et al. (2000a)	12 sessions × 2 h **1. ISF (G); n = 36** 2. ISF + SST (G); n = 32 **3. WL**	1 = 2 > 3	1 = 2 > 3	1 = 2 > 3	Improvement stable at 12 months	Remitters Post-test **1**. 25% **2**. 32% Follow-up **1**. 62% **2**. 61%
Stravynski et al. (2006)	12 sessions **1. Discussion + home-work (G: 2 h); n = 38** 2. ISF + SST + homework (G: 2 h); n = 35 **3. Review/assign homework (I: 20 min); n = 29** **4. WL**	1 = 2 = 3 > 4	1 = 2 = 3 > 4	1 = 2 = 3 > 4	Improvement stable at 12 months	Remitters Post-test **1**. 9% **2**. 22% 3. 29%: **1** = **2** = **3** Follow-up **1**. 43% **2**. 52% 3. 67%: **1** = **2** = **3** There was a significant drop in the number of patients still considered socially phobic between the end of treatment and 12 months follow-up for all treatment conditions

Table 10.2. (cont.)

Study	Treatment conditions	Outcome			Follow-up	Comments
		Social Avoidance	Subjective Distress	Social Functioning		
Improvement in social functioning (structural) vs. anxiety reduction						
Mersh et al. (1989)	8 sessions × 2.5 h					A match between type of patient (e.g. cognitive or behavioral responders) and type of treatment (e.g. CR or SST) did not result in better outcome
Mersch et al. (1991)	1. **CR (G); n = 37** 2. **SST (G); n = 37**	1 = 2 (no meaningful improvement)	1 = 2 (both improved)	1 = 2 (no meaningful improvement)	Improvement stable at 14 months (1 = 2)	
Wlazlo et al. (1990)	1. **SST (G); n = 54: 37.5 h** 2. **EXP (I); n = 41: 12 h** 3. **EXP (G); n = 52: 34 h**	1 = 2 = 3 (all improved)	1 = 2 = 3 (all improved)	—	Improvement stable at 3 months Further improvement after 2.5 yr (range 1–5.5 yr) on social anxiety and avoidance	No advantage in matching types of problem (e.g. phobic or deficit) and corresponding treatment (e.g. anxiety reduction or SST). "Skill-deficient" patients did less well Group and individual exposure were equivalent

Study	Treatment				Improvement	Findings
van Dam-Baggen & Kraimaat (2000)	17 sessions × 1.5 h 1. **SST (G); n = 24** 2. **CR (G); n = 24**	1 > 2	1 > 2	——	Improvement stable at 3 months	Social anxiety and social skills scores of the SST group at follow-up reached the level of a normal reference group; this was not the case for the CR participants
Improvement in social functioning (functional) with or without other treatment modalities						
Stravynski et al. (1982b)	12 sessions × 2 h 1. **ISF; (I: n = 4)** **(G: n = 7)** 2. **ISF + CR;** **(I: n = 4) (G: n = 7)**	1 = 2 (both improved)	1 = 2 (both improved)	1 = 2 (both improved)	Improvement stable at 6 months	CR did not enhance SST; only treated interpersonal behaviors changed.
Stravynski et al. (2000a)	12 sessions × 2 h 1. **ISF (G); n = 36** 2. **ISF + SST (G);** **n = 32** 3. **WL**	1 = 2 > 3	1 = 2 > 3	1 = 2 > 3	Improvement stable at 12 months	Remitters Post-test **1.** 25% **2.** 32% Follow-up **1.** 62% **2.** 61%
Stravynski et al. (2006)	12 sessions 1. **Discussion + home-** **work (G: 2 h); n = 38** 2. **ISF + SST + home-** **work (G: 2 h); n = 35** 3. **Review/assign homework** **(I: 20 min); n = 29** 4. **WL**	1 = 2 = 3 > 4	1 = 2 = 3 > 4	1 = 2 = 3 > 4	Improvement stable at 12 months	Remitters Post-test **1.** 9% **2.** 22% **3.** 29%; **1 = 2 = 3** Follow-up **1.** 43% **2.** 52% **3.** 67%: **1 = 2 = 3**

Note: CR: Cognitive restructuring; EXP: Exposure in vivo; G: Group modality; I: Individual modality; ISF: Improving social functioning; SST: Social skills training; WL: Waiting list; +: combined with; **Highlighted areas** = treatments compared.

has found this strategy to be as effective as exposure and cognitive restructuring in reducing anxiety and avoidance with both specific and generalized social phobia/avoidant personality disorder. In one study, SST resulted in significantly better improvement (van Dam-Baggen & Kraimaat, 2000). Three studies applying the functional variant (Stravynski, Arbel, Chenier, Lachance, Lamontagne, Sidoun, & Todorov, 2006; Stravynski et al., 1982b, 2000a) have shown such treatment to lead to significant improvements in social functioning. Outstandingly, Stravynski et al. (2000a) reported a remission rate of 60% in the patients who completed therapy at 1-year follow-up. Equivalent results are reported in Stravynski et al. (2006).

Treatment was usually administered in small groups (5−7) and tended to last 12−25 sessions for up to 37 hours. The efficiency gained through group treatment was somewhat offset by a higher drop-out rate (20−25%). Gains have been shown to maintain up to 2.5 years.

Psycho-Pharmacological Treatments

Whereas individuals devising psychological therapies are driven mostly by theoretical concerns (and doubtless personal ambition), psycho-pharmacological treatments have different origins altogether. These need to be elucidated and put in proper context.

Practically, pharmacological treatments are made possible by the availability of new compounds, created typically by the pharmaceutical industry. Psychotropic compounds commonly have a broad impact on the brain and, correspondingly, an exceedingly wide range of effects (Janicak, 1999). None of the effects are self-evidently therapeutic; these need to be singled out with a certain potential application in mind. In consequence of such choices, some of the effects become desirable; many others − although unwanted − occur all the same. None is inherently primary or secondary.

It is a commercial decision, made by marketing departments, that creates a new drug as "an antidepressant rather than an anxiolytic or a treatment for premature ejaculation" (Healy & Thase, 2003, p. 388). A similarly commercial decision designates a medication previously established as an "anti-depressant" or as "anti-convulsant" as one that will become "indicated" for social phobia. Furthermore, marketing departments orchestrate and fund the many activities, not least clinical trials, analysis and publication of the results, that create the necessary evidence in support of a certain use of the drug (2003, p. 388). Equipped with these considerations, we shall now turn to the studies themselves.

Overall, 4 different classes of pharmaceutical agents with different molecular targets have been extensively evaluated for their anxiety-reducing properties in the treatment of social phobia. These are:

1. Monoamine oxidase inhibitors (MAOI); these block the metabolism of the catecholamines and serotonin through inactivation of their catabolic enzyme, monoamine oxidase. A refinement within the same class concerns the reversible inhibitors of monoamine oxidase (RIMAs). Both target the catabolic enzyme; while the MAOIs bind permanently, the RIMAs do so reversibly. Practically, this broadens the restrictive diet required under the MAOIs. A typical use for this type of medication (e.g. moclobemide) is for the treatment of depression.

2. Selective serotonin reuptake inhibitors (SSRIs); these inhibit the transport of serotonin back into the neuron where it is subsequently metabolized, thus increasing the synaptic concentration of this neurotransmitter. Today this type of medication is considered first-choice treatment for depression and most of the anxiety disorders.

3. Other regulators of monoaminergic synaptic activity (e.g. buspirone). This type of medication is used occasionally as an anxiolytic; olanzapine however is primarily used as an anti-psychotic.

4. Suppressants of neural excitability that regulate gabaergic transmission:

   a. agonists of aminobutyric acid (GABA) receptors (e.g. benzo-diazepines). This type of medication is commonly used for the treatment of anxiety and insomnia.

   b. stimulators of GABA release (e.g. gabapentin). This type of medication is used as an anti-convulsant and more recently as a mood stabilizer.

The design and outcome of the studies within each class of medication are summarized in Table 10.3.

Overall, to date the above classes of psycho-pharmacological medications have been shown to yield effects that supersede placebo. All the same, in 5 studies medication within these categories (the SSRI fluoxetine, the RIMA moclobemide, the monoaminergic modulators – buspirone, olanzapine and St John's Wort) did not produce effects that exceeded placebo.

Although not all possible comparisons have been performed, as can be seen in Table 10.4, overall the various classes of medication appear to result in similar outcomes, with phenelzine showing a slight advantage over moclobemide and a significant superiority over the beta-blocker atenolol.

Although the bulk of samples included generalized social phobic patients, similar results also obtain with specific (i.e. usually public-speaking) socially phobic patients. While the reduction of subjective anxiety and the tendency to avoid was worthwhile, the medications also induce adverse effects, the nature and the extent of which vary. The main ones are typically selected in relevant publications by the following combined standards: having been reported by at least 10% of the patients on medication, while simultaneously being at least twice the rates reported by patients receiving placebo. The latter standard seems arbitrarily high and results in a narrowing of reported adverse effects. However that may be, these are summarized in Table 10.5. Related or not, the rates of patients on medication dropping out of treatment varied between 0% to 74%.

As can be seen in Table 10.3, the response to the placebo pill prescribed by authoritative figures (i.e. specialist physicians) operating in an awe-inspiring medical setting – although varying in degree – is powerful. In Stein, Pollack, Bystritsky, Kelsey, & Mangano (2005) for example, 33% of the patients on placebo (vs. 58% on venlafaxine) were considered improved or much improved. Moreover, 16% of patients on placebo were in remission (vs. 31% of patients on medication) after the end of treatment. Considering this, the effect of medication is overvalued. If the net effect of a medication were to be estimated, the placebo effect ought to be subtracted from the overall response.

The link between becoming less anxious and less handicapped and being more and better socially active remains uncertain. Similarly, no studies to date have systematically observed the relapse rate on and after stopping medication. In an approximation, 36% of the patients relapsed after 20 weeks of sertraline followed by placebo (Walker et al., 2000).

Many social phobic patients respond powerfully to placebo; the rates of much-improved patients on it vary from 0% to 66%.

Psychological Treatments Combined/Compared with Psycho-pharmacology

As both psychological and pharmacological treatments have been shown to be beneficial, some studies sought to compare them singly or in combination. The design and outcome of these studies are summarized in Table 10.6.

Table 10.3. *Comparative outcome of pharmacological approaches – anxiety reduction*

Study	Treatment conditions	Outcome				Comments
		Social Avoidance	Subjective Distress	Social Functioning	Responders	
I. Inhibitors of monoamine oxidase – MAOIs/RIMAs						
Noyes et al. (1997)	12 weeks 1. Moclobemide (75 mg/d); n = 84 2. Moclobemide (150 mg/d); n = 86 3. Moclobemide (300 mg/d); n = 86 4. Moclobemide (600 mg/d); n = 82 5. Moclobemide (900 mg/d); n = 83 6. Placebo; n = 85	—	1 = 2 = 3 = 4 = (5 > 6) (all improved)	—	1 – 4: Information taken from Figure 5. 35% 6. 33% 1 = 2 = 3 = 4 = 5 = 6	Moclobemide was not shown to have therapeutic effects beyond those of placebo.
IMCTGM. (1997)	12 weeks 1. Moclobemide (300 mg/d); n = 191 2. Moclobemide (600 mg/d); n = 193 3. Placebo; n = 194	(1, 2) > 3	(1, 2) > 3	1 = 3; 2 > 3	1. 41% 2. 47% 3. 34% 1 = 3; 2 > 3	35-center study conducted in 13 countries.

Table 10.3. (cont.)

Study	Treatment conditions	Outcome				Comments
		Social Avoidance	Subjective Distress	Social Functioning	Responders	
Schneier et al. (1998)	8 weeks 1. Moclobemide (200–800 mg/d); n = 40 2. Placebo; n = 37	1 > 2	1 > 2	1 = 2 (no improvement)	1. 18% 2. 14% 1 = 2	Magnitude of its clinical effect is small. Significant effect shown only on one of ten measures.
Stein et al. (2002a) Phase I	12 weeks 1. Moclobemide (450–750 mg/d); n = 188 2. Placebo; n = 189	1 > 2	1 > 2	—	1. 43% 2. 30% 1 > 2	Effect maintained at 6 months with continuing medication 1. 86% 2. 58%.
van Vliet et al. (1992)	12 weeks 1. Brofaromine (150 mg/d); n = 15 2. Placebo; n = 15	1 > 2	1 > 2	—	1. 73% 2. 0% 1 > 2	Decrease in social sensitivity.
Falhén et al. (1995)	12 weeks 1. Brofaromine (150 mg/d); n = 37 2. Placebo; n = 40	1 > 2	1 > 2	—	1. 78% 2. 23% 1 > 2	Clinical effects were not significantly correlated with plasma concentration of brofaromine.

Study	Duration & treatment			
Lott et al. (1997)	10 weeks 1. Brofaromine (50–150 mg/d); n = 50 2. Placebo; n = 52	1 > 2	1 = 2 (no improvement)	1. 50% 2. 19% 1 > 2

II. Serotonin selective reuptake inhibitors – SSRIs

Study	Duration & treatment			
Stein et al. (1998b)	12 weeks 1. Paroxetine (20–50 mg/d); n = 91 2. Placebo; n = 92	1 > 2	1 > 2	1. 55% 2. 24% 1 > 2
Stein et al. (1999)	12 weeks 1. Paroxetine (20–50 mg/d); n = 45 2. Placebo; n = 48	—	1 > 2	1 = 2 (both improved)	1. 71% 2. 48% 1 > 2
Baldwin et al. (1999)	12 weeks 1. Paroxetine (20–50 mg/d); n = 139 2. Placebo; n = 151	—	1 > 2	1 > 2	1. 66% 2. 32% 1 > 2
Allgulander (1999)	12 weeks 1. Paroxetine (20–50 mg/d); n = 44 2. Placebo; n = 48	1 > 2	1 > 2	1. 71% 2. 8% 1 > 2

Table 10.3. (cont.)

Study	Treatment conditions	Outcome			Responders	Comments
		Social Avoidance	Subjective Distress	Social Functioning		
Stein et al. (2001b)	10 weeks ⇧ 4 weeks ⇧ 4 weeks 1. Paroxetine (46.4 mg/d*) ⇧ Paroxetine** + Pindolol (15 mg/d) ⇧ Placebo; n = 8 2. Paroxetine (46.4 mg/d*) ⇧ Paroxetine** + Placebo ⇧ Pindolol (15 mg/d); n = 6 * mean dose before randomization ** last dose maximally tolerated	—	1 = 2	—	1. 0% 2. 0%	Pindolol does not potentiate paroxetine.
Liebowitz et al. (2002)	12 weeks 1. Paroxetine (20 mg/d); n = 97 2. Paroxetine (40 mg/d); n = 95 3. Paroxetine (60 mg/d); n = 97 4. Placebo; n = 95	1 > 4; 2, 3 = 4	1 > 4; 2, 3 = 4	1, 3 > 4; 2 = 4	1. 45% 2. 47% 3. 43% 4. 28% 2 > 4; 1, 3 = 4	Although statistical differences were found, the difference between the 3 doses appears negligible.

Study	Treatment				Response	Comments
Stein et al. (2002)	12 weeks ⇨ 24 weeks maintenance phase 1. Paroxetine (20–50 mg/d) ⇨ Paroxetine (week 12 dosage level); n = 162 2. Paroxetine (20–50 mg/d) ⇨ Placebo; n = 161	—	1 > 2	1 > 2	12 weeks 1. 93% 2. 92%: 1 = 2 24 weeks 1. 78% 2. 51%: 1 > 2	Patients who discontinued paroxetine were 3 times as likely to relapse as those who took paroxetine for a further 24 weeks.
Lepola et al. (2004)	12 weeks 1. Paroxetine CR (12.5–37.5 mg/d); n = 186 2. Placebo; n = 184	1 > 2	1 > 2	1 > 2	1. 57% 2. 30% 1 > 2	Remitters 1. 24% 2. 8% 1 > 2
van Vliet et al. (1994)	12 weeks 1. Fluvoxamine (150 mg/d); n = 15 2. Placebo; n = 15	1 = 2 (both improved)	1 > 2	—	1. 46% 2. 7% 1 > 2	Most patients attended behavioral or cognitive therapy before but did not respond.

Table 10.3. (cont.)

Study	Treatment conditions	Outcome			Responders	Comments
		Social Avoidance	Subjective Distress	Social Functioning		
Stein et al. (1999)	12 weeks 1. Fluvoxamine (100–300 mg/d); n = 48 2. Placebo; n = 44	1 > 2	1 > 2	1 = 2 (no improvement)	1. 43% 2. 23% 1 > 2	
Davidson et al. (2004b)	12 weeks 1. Fluvoxamine CR (100–300 mg/d); n = 139 2. Placebo; n = 140	1 > 2	1 > 2	1 > 2	1. 34% 2. 17% 1 > 2	
Westenberg et al. (2004b)	12 weeks 1. Fluvoxamine CR (100–300 mg/d); n = 149 2. Placebo; n = 151	1 > 2	1 > 2	1 = 2 (both improved)	1. 48% 2. 44% 1 = 2 1. 40%	Effects maintained at 24 weeks even when medication is switched for placebo.
Stein et al. (2003) Kobak et al. (2002)	14 weeks 1. Fluoxetine (20–60 mg/d); n = 30 2. Placebo; n = 30	1 = 2 (both improved)	1 = 2 (both improved)	—	2. 30% 1 = 2	Rated normal post-therapy. 1. 27% 2. 24% 1 = 2

Study	Design				Results
Katzelnick et al. (1995)	10 weeks ⇨ 10 weeks (switch) 1. Sertraline (50–200 mg/d) ⇧ Placebo; n = 6 2. Placebo ⇧ Sertraline (50–200 mg/d); n = 6	—	Sertraline > Placebo	Sertraline > Placebo	Sertraline > Placebo Sertraline > Placebo	1. 50% 2. 9% — When switching to placebo, the risk of relapse increases tenfold.
Walker et al. (2000)	20 weeks 24 weeks maintenance phase 1. Sertraline (50–200 mg/d) ⇧ Sertraline (week 20 dosage level); n = 25 2. Sertraline (50–200 mg/d) ⇧ Placebo; n = 25 3. Placebo ⇧ Placebo; n = 15	1 > 2	—	1 = 2 (no improvement)	1. 20% 2. 24% 1 = 2
van Ameringen et al. (2001)	20 weeks 1. Sertraline (50–200 mg/d); n = 134 2. Placebo; n = 69	1 > 2	1 > 2	1 > 2	1. 53% 2. 29% 1 > 2

Table 10.3. (*cont.*)

Study	Treatment conditions	Outcome				Comments
		Social Avoidance	Subjective Distress	Social Functioning	Responders	
Liebowitz et al. (2003)	12 weeks 1. Sertraline (50–200 mg/d); n = 205 2. Placebo; n = 196	1 > 2	1 > 2	1 > 2	1. 47% 2. 26% 1 > 2	
Blomhoff et al. (2001)	24 weeks 1. Sertraline (50–150 mg/d); n = 96 2. Placebo + SE (I: 8 × 15–20 min during the first 12 weeks); n = 98	1, 3 > 4 2 = 4	1, 2, 3 = 4 (all improved)	1, 2, 3 > 4	1. 40% 2. 33% 3. 46% 4. 24% (1 = 3 > 4) = 2	At 12-months follow-up, exposure and placebo resulted in a significant drop in anxiety and avoidance while sertraline led to a significant increase in avoidance.
Haug et al. (2003)	3. Sertraline (50–150 mg/d) + SE (I: 8 × 15–20 min. during the first 12 weeks); n = 98 4. Placebo; n = 95					

Study	Treatment arms				Response	Remitters
Rickels et al. (2004)	12 weeks 1. Venlafaxine ER (75–225 mg/d); n = 126 2. Placebo; n = 135	1 > 2	1 > 2	1 > 2	1. 50% 2. 34% 1 > 2	Remitters 1. 20% 2. 7% 1 > 2
Liebowitz et al. (2005b)	12 weeks 1. Venlafaxine ER (75–225 mg/d); n = 133 2. Placebo; n = 138	1 > 2	1 > 2	1 > 2	1. 44% 2. 30% 1 > 2	
Stein et al. (2005)	6 months 1. Venlafaxine ER (75 mg/d); n = 119 2. Venlafaxine ER (150–225 mg/d); n = 119 3. Placebo; n = 126	1 = 2 > 3	1 = 2 > 3	1, 2 > 3	1 + 2: 58% 3. 33% 1 = 2 > 3	Remitters 1 + 2: 31% 3. 16% 1 = 2 > 3
Allgulander et al. (2004)	12 weeks 1. Venlafaxine ER (75–225 mg/d); n = 129 2. Paroxetine (20–50 mg/d); n = 128 3. Placebo; n = 132	1 = 2 > 3	1 = 2 > 3	1 = 2 > 3	1. 69% 2. 66% 3. 36%	Remitters 1. 38% 2. 29% 3. 13% 1 = 2 > 3

Table 10.3. (*cont.*)

Study	Treatment conditions	Outcome				Comments
		Social Avoidance	Subjective Distress	Social Functioning	Responders	
Liebowitz et al. (2005a)	12 weeks 1. Venlafaxine ER (75–225 mg/d); n = 133 2. Paroxetine (20–50 mg/d); n = 136 3. Placebo; n = 144	1, 2 > 3	1, 2 > 3	1, 2 > 3	1. 59% 2. 63% 3. 36% 1, 2 > 3	
Lader et al. (2004)	24 weeks 1. Paroxetine (20 mg/d); n = 169	1, 2, 4 > 5; 3 = 5	1, 2, 3, 4 > 5	1, 2, 3, 4 > 5	1. 80% 2. 79%	Strong placebo response.
Stein et al. (2004)	2. Escitalopram (5 mg/d); n = 167 3. Escitalopram (10 mg/d); n = 167 4. Escitalopram (20 mg/d); n = 170 5. Placebo; n = 166				3. 76% 4. 88% 5. 66% 1, 2, 4 > 5; 3 = 5	The treatment effects of escitalopram were independant of gender, phobic severity and chronicity, and comorbid depressive mood.

III. Other regulators of synaptic activity

Reference	Treatment				Comments
van Vliet et al. (1997a)	12 weeks; 1. Buspirone (30 mg/d); n = 15; 2. Placebo; n = 15	1 = 2 (both improved)	1 = 2 (both improved)	1 = 2	1. 7% 2. 7% 1 = 2 1 = 2
Barnett et al. (2002)	8 weeks; 1. Olanzapine (5–20 mg/d); n = 7; 2. Placebo; n = 5	—	1 = 2	1 = 2	

IV. Suppressants of neural excitability
a. Benzodiazepines

Reference	Treatment				Comments
Davidson et al. (1993b)	10 weeks; 1. Clonazepam (up to 3 mg/d); n = 39; 2. Placebo; n = 36	1 > 2	1 > 2	1 > 2	1. 78% 2. 20% 1 > 2
Sutherland et al. (1996)		—			

b. Miscellaneous

Reference	Treatment				Comments
Pande et al. (1999)	14 weeks; 1. Gabapentin (900–3600 mg/d); n = 34; 2. Placebo; n = 35	—	1 > 2	1 > 2	Treatment site 1 1. 38% 2. 29% — Treatment site 2 1. 41% 2. 11%

At 24 months follow-up, all patients sought further treatment (medication or psychotherapy) and reported significant distress and avoidance.

Table 10.3. (*cont.*)

Study	Treatment conditions	Outcome				Comments
		Social Avoidance	Subjective Distress	Social Functioning	Responders	
Pande et al. (2004)	10 weeks 1. Pregabalin (150 mg/d); n = 42 2. Pregabalin (600 mg/d); n = 47 3. Placebo; n = 46	2 > 3; 1 = 3	2 > 3; 1 = 3	1 = 2 = 3	1. 21% 2. 43% 3. 22% 2 > 3; 1 = 3	
Kobak et al. (2005)	12 weeks 1. St John's Wort (600–1800 mg/d); n = 20 2. Placebo; n = 20	—	1 = 2 (both improved)	—	—	The end point score for both groups was still in the clinical range.

Note: CR: Controlled release; ER: Extended release; SE: Instructions for self-exposure; +: combined with; ⇨: followed by.

Table 10.4. *Comparative outcome of various classes of medication*

Study	Treatment conditions	Outcome				Responders	Comments
		Social Avoidance	Subjective Distress	Social Functioning			
RIMA vs. MAOI							
Versiani et al. (1992) Phase I	8 weeks 1. Moclobemide (600 mg/d); n = 26 2. Phenelzine (90 mg/d); n = 26 3. Placebo; n = 26	2 > 1 > 3	1 = 2 > 3	1, 2 > 3		1. 81% 2. 96% 3. 27%	Responders defined as showing at least minimal change.
Versiani et al. (1992) Phase II	Patients who showed minimal response at 8 weeks continued treatment for 8 weeks 1. Moclobemide (600 mg/d); n = 17 2. Phenelzine (90 mg/d); n = 21 3. Placebo; n = 7	—	1 = 2 (both improved)	—		1. 82% 2. 91% 3. 43%	Patients who continued to respond to active drugs were randomized and treated for another 8 weeks. Improvement was greater for both active drugs after 16 weeks than after 8 weeks. Patients who switched to placebo reported considerable increase in anxiety at week 24 relative to week 16.

Table 10.4. (cont.)

Study	Treatment conditions	Outcome			Responders	Comments
		Social Avoidance	Subjective Distress	Social Functioning		
SSRI vs. RIMA						
Atmaca et al. (2002)	8 weeks 1. Citalopram (20−60 mg/d); n = 36 2. Moclobemide (300−900 mg/d); n = 35	1 = 2 (both improved)	1 = 2 (both improved)	—	1. 75% 2. 74% 1 = 2	
SSRI with and without benzodiazepines						
Seedat & Stein (2004)	10 weeks ⇨ 8 weeks 1. Paroxetine (20−40 mg/d) + Clonazepam (1−2 mg/d) ⇨ Paroxetine (20−50 mg/d); n = 14 2. Paroxetine (20−40 mg/d) + Placebo ⇨ Paroxetine (20−50 mg/d); n = 14	—	1 = 2 (both improved)	1 = 2 (both improved)	1. 86% 2. 57% 1 = 2	
β − adrenergic blocker vs. MAOI						
Liebowitz et al. (1992)	8 weeks 1. Atenolol (50−100 mg/d); n = 28 2. Phenelzine (45−90 mg/d); n = 29 3. Placebo; n = 28	2 > 1 = 3	2 > 1 = 3	1 = 2 = 3	1. 25% 2. 55% 3. 21% 2 > 1 = 3	Significant results were reported on ratings by independent evaluators but not on self-ratings by patients.

Note: +: combined with; ⇨: followed by.

Table 10.5. *Undesirable effects of medication*

Category of medication	Undesirable effects*																	
	Nausea	Asthenia	Abnormal ejaculation	Sweating	Anorgasmia	Somnolence	Insomnia	Decreased libido	Dizziness	Dry mouth	Constipation	Diarrhea	Headache	Drowsiness	Blurred vision	Forgetfulness	Impaired concentration	Vertigo
I[a]	×	×	×				×	×	×	×	×		×					×
II[b]	×	×	×	×		×	×	×	×	×	×		×					
III[c]				×						×	×			×				
IVa[d]					×										×	×	×	
IVb[e]	×	×				×			×	×		×			×	×		×

Note: I: inhibitors of monoamine oxidase; II: serotonin selective reuptake inhibitors; III: other regulators of synaptic activity; IVa: benzodiazepines; IVb: miscellaneous.

[a]Fahlén et al. (1995); Versiani et al. (1992)
[b]Allgulander et al. (2004); Liebowitz et al. (2005a)
[c]Barnett et al. (2002); Clark & Agras (1991); van Vliet et al. (1997a)
[d]Davidson et al. (1993b)
[e]Pande et al. (1999); Pande et al. (2004)
*Note: selected by the standard of having been endorsed by at least 10% of the patients on medication while simultaneously being at least twice the rates of endorsement of patients receiving placebo

Table 10.6. *Comparative outcome of psychological and pharmacological approaches*

Study	Treatment conditions	Outcome				Follow-up	Comments
		Social Avoidance	Subjective Distress	Social Functioning			
Psychological treatment vs. medication							
Clark & Agras (1991)	6 weeks **1. EXP + CR (G: 5 × ? h) + Placebo; n = 9** 2. EXP + CR (G: 5 × ? h) + Buspirone (15–50 mg/d); n = 8 **3. Buspirone (15–50 mg/d); n = 9** 4. Placebo; n = 8	——	(1, 2) > (3, 4); 3 = 4 ——			Improvement stable at 1 month	Although gains in the CBT conditions were statistically significant, it is not clear how clinically meaningful they were.
Gelernter et al. (1991)	12 weeks **1. EXP + CR (G: 2 h); n = 20** 2. Phenelzine (30–90 mg/d) + SE (I: 15–30 min); n = 15	1 = 2 = 3 = 4 (all improved)	1 = 2 = 3 = 4 (all improved)	2 > 3, 4 (1 was not rated)		Improvement stable at 2 months	Remitters 1. 24% 2. 63%

Study	Treatment	Outcome			Follow-up
	3. Alprazolam (2.1–6.3 mg/d) + SE (I: 15–30 min); n = 15			3. 38%	
	4. Placebo + SE (I: 15–30 min); n = 15			4. 20% $1 = 2 = 3 = 4$	
Turner et al. (1994)	12 weeks 1. EXP (I: 20 x 90 min); n = 27 2. Atenolol (25–100 mg/d); n = 24 3. Placebo; n = 21	$1 = 2 = 3$ (all improved)	$2 = (1 > 3)$	—	Improvement stable at 6 months
Heimberg et al. (1998) Liebowitz et al. (1999)	12 weeks 1. EXP + CR (G: 12 x 2.5 h); n = 36 2. Phenelzine (60–90 mg/d); n = 31 3. Placebo; n = 33 4. NSP (G); n = 33	$2 > (1 > 3,4)$	$2 > (1 > 3,4)$	—	Improvement stable Responders at 12 months 1. 58% (2 > 1). 2. 65% Phenelzine 3. 33% patients showed 4. 27% a trend toward $1 = 2 > 3, 4$ greater relapse

Table 10.6. (*cont.*)

Study	Treatment conditions	Outcome			Follow-up	Comments
		Social Avoidance	Subjective Distress	Social Functioning		
Otto et al. (2000)	12 weeks 1. **Clonazepam (1–4 mg/d);** **n = 25** 2. **EXP + CR** **(G: 12 x 2.5 h);** **n = 20**	1 = 2 (both improved)	1 = 2 (both improved)	—	—	Remitters 1. 20% 2. 25% **1 = 2**
Clark et al. (2003)	16 weeks 1. **CR (I: 75 min);** **n = 20** 2. **Fluoxetine (20–60 mg/d) +** **SE** **(30–40 min);** **n = 20** 3. Placebo + SE (30–40 min); n = 20	1 > 2 (both improved) = 3 (no change)	1 > 2 = 3 (all improved)	—	Treatment gains were maintained at 12 months (1 = 2)	

Study				Responders
Davidson et al. (2004a)	14 weeks	**1. EXP + CR + SST(G); n = 60**	$1 = 2 = 3 = 4 > 5$	**1.** 52%
		2. EXP + CR + SST (G) + Fluoxetine (10–60 mg/d); n = 59		2. 54%
		3. EXP + CR + SST(G) + Placebo; n = 59		3. 51%
		4. Fluoxetine (10–60 mg/d); n = 57		**4.** 51%
		5. Placebo; n = 60		5. 32%
				$1 = 2 = 3 = 4 > 5$

Psychological treatment with or without medication

Study				Improvement stable at 6 months
Falloon et al. (1981)	2 × 6 h + real life rehearsal with the assigned partner and therapist ⇨ medication	**1. SST; n = 8 ⇧ Placebo; n = 6**	$1 = 2$ (both improved)	$1 = 2$ (both improved)
		2. SST; n = 8 Propranolol (160–320 mg/d); n = 6		

Table 10.6. (cont.)

Study	Treatment conditions	Outcome				
		Social Avoidance	Subjective Distress	Social Functioning	Follow-up	Comments
Clark & Agras (1991)	6 weeks **1. EXP + CR** **(G: 5 × ? h)** **+ Placebo;** **n = 9** **2. EXP + CR** **(G: 5 × ? h) +** **Buspirone (15–50** **mg/d);** **n = 8** 3. Buspirone (15–50 mg/d); n = 9 4. Placebo; n = 8	——	(1, 2) > (3, 4); 3 = 4	——	Improvement stable at 1 month	Although gains in the CBT conditions were statistically significant, it is not clear how clinically meaningful they were.

| Davidson et al. (2004a) | 14 weeks | 1. EXP + CR + SST(G); n = 60
 2. **EXP + CR + SST (G) + Fluoxetine (10–60 mg/d); n = 59**
 3. **EXP + CR + SST(G) + Placebo; n = 59**
 4. Fluoxetine (10–60 mg/d); n = 57
 5. Placebo; n = 60 | — | $1 = 2 = 3 = 4 > 5$ | — | Responders
 1. 52%
 2. 54%
 3. 51%
 4. 51%
 5. 32%
 $1 = 2 = 3 = 4 > 5$
 Medication did not enhance combined psychological treatment. |

Note: CR: Cognitive restructuring; EXP: Exposure in vivo; NSP: Non-specific psychotherapy; SE: Instructions for self-exposure; SST: Social skills training; WL: Waiting list; G: Group modality; I: Individual modality; +: combined with; ⇨: followed by; **Highlighted areas** = treatments compared.

In summary, in comparisons of psychological therapies with medication, the behavioral and cognitive approaches were found to be equivalent in their short-term effects or better than pharmacotherapy in 5 out of 6 studies depending on the medication used. In one study (Heimberg et al., 1998) phenelzine resulted in better outcome than CBT both at the end of treatment and at 1-year follow-up.

The combination of psychological treatments and medication was on the whole disappointing: in the studies under review it did not exceed the effects of the psychological approaches alone. With the exception of phenelzine, the main medications that have been promising in the treatment of social phobia have yet to be compared to and/or combined with psychological approaches.

Discussion

Psychological Treatments

Principally anxiety-reduction methods, namely exposure and variants of cognitive restructuring, but also approaches aiming at improving social functioning (albeit with a smaller number of studies), were shown to be useful psychological treatments. Following such treatments social phobic patients typically reported a clinically meaningful lessening in their experience of anxiety and a reduction in their tendency to avoid threatening social situations.

While the treatments effected significant improvements relative to pretreatment levels, it remains unknown how meaningful these are in absolute terms (e.g. in reference to normal individuals). This point needs clarification.

Furthermore, results vary between good to modest, especially if criteria other than anxiety reduction are taken into account (e.g. meaningful reduction in passivity/avoidance, improved social functioning both in quantity and quality).

The most gratifying aspects of the outcomes resulting from psychological treatments are their relatively low rates of dropout allied to durable gains resulting from relatively brief treatments; these were shown to last over follow-ups of up to 2.5 and 5 years. Not least, these therapies have proven quite benign. With the exception of mounting anxious distress at the initial stages of treatment when avoidance is tackled, no systematic unwished-for ill effects were recorded.

Exposure has been clearly established as a robust and reliable treatment principle for social phobia. This makes it an indispensable ingredient in any therapeutic package seeking reduction of anxiety as its primary gain (Marks, 1987). It probably contributes to a certain extent to the effects reported under pharmacological treatment as well. Crucially, similar levels of anxiety reduction are systematically achieved by approaches seeking to promote better social functioning (e.g. Stravynski et al., 2000a). Whether this is due to the fact that inadvertently such approaches enforce a course of exposure, or rather that interpersonally patients feel less threatened and more powerful because they have become better able to stand up to the rigors of social life and to take advantage of opportunities, remains to be determined.

Cognitive restructuring enhanced the outcome of neither exposure nor social-skills training in most studies of psychological treatment. This may be due to the fact that the conceptually and nominally "non-cognitive" therapies unfold in sessions during which many words pass between therapist and patient. A psychological treatment without such talk is unimaginable. During the exchanges patients' statements are challenged and set straight – albeit not in the formal way taught by the proponents of cognitive treatments. Excuses for non-performance of homework or rationalizations for passivity, for instance, are typically addressed and disposed of. Rules of probability, cost–benefit analysis, taking perspectives, and the spellbinding power of words are routinely mooted. Unlike the chasm that separates behavioral and cognitive outlooks in theory, the practice of exposure and "cognitive" treatments may differ only in the systematic use of certain verbal tactics and jargon; the actual treatments might not be as different as their theoretical underpinnings would have it. CBT may therefore be a somewhat complex way of practicing exposure while relying on rather questionable assumptions (discussed in chapter 7). This is underscored by the equivalent cognitive changes (i.e. in beliefs) reported after both cognitive and non-cognitive treatments (Hope et al., 1995a; Heimberg, Dodge, Hope, Kennedy, Zollo, & Becker, 1990a; Stravynski et al., 1982b).

Anxiety-reduction methods, although effective in achieving their aims on their own terms, have disappointingly not been shown to generate automatically meaningful improvements in social functioning. Conceptually, this might reflect the fundamental ambiguity and ultimately the inadequacy of the term anxiety construed *intrapersonally* – as an enduring psychological characteristic of the individual (see chapter 3). The link between what one *feels* (anxious) and what one *does* is in all likelihood indeterminate.

Practically, an envisageable possibility is that the issue is one of measurement; the effect occurs but is poorly detected. Indeed the assessment of social functioning is rudimentary and needs refinement.

Alternatively, certain facts suggest that the problem may be substantive and go to the heart of what social phobia is. As may be seen in Stravynski et al. (1982b), only social behaviors that have been systematically singled out for therapeutic attention would meaningfully improve; otherwise behaviors not subjected to treatment hardly changed. Extrapolating from this finding, we might conclude that lesser experience of anxiety (whatever this might be) does not spontaneously "release" adequate social functioning. Where would it come from? After all, much of such conduct was never in evidence before. Hoping it will materialize spontaneously goes against the fact that social behavior is developed over time and is culturally constituted. Clinically, if improved social functioning is wished for (as it should be), deliberate treatment efforts to dismantle self-protective patterns of behavior and promote participatory ones need to be made.

Content aside, what means ought these efforts involve? Is SST the necessary choice? The record is actually mixed. In Wlazlo et al. (1990) and Mersch et al. (1989) the anxiety reported by social phobic patients who underwent a course of social-skill training lessened but their social functioning remained unchanged. By contrast Stravynski et al. (2000a, 1982b) reported both a reduction of anxiety and an improved social functioning at work, with friends, and in other areas.

What accounts for the difference in outcome? Perhaps the better social functioning obtained in the latter approach was due to the fact that its content of treatment was not driven by the strategy of building up generic hypothetical skills deemed necessary for social functioning, be they molecular (e.g. appropriate eye contact, timing) or molar (e.g. assertion). In other words, it did not seek to build up deficient social skills. Rather, individual patients were trained to develop *non-defensive* personal ways of dealing with their real-life social/interpersonal circumstances and to use them in situations very much a part of their daily lives. Admitting to being keen or red-faced, volunteering, and speaking in a more forthright manner are examples of behaviors targeted and encouraged in such a therapy.

As we have seen earlier (Stravynski et al., 2000a), SST is not necessary for improvement in the social functioning of social phobic patients to take place, for similar gains were obtained by a therapy promoting better social functioning without the benefit of SST. Moreover, 60% of patients in each condition no longer met DSM-IV criteria for social phobia at 1-year follow-up.

It may well be that this functional (and interpersonal) approach is better suited to the treatment of social phobic individuals whereas the use of SST guided by notions of skills deficits is more appropriate in improving the social functioning of other problems encountered in the clinic (e.g. schizophrenia; Kopelowicz & Liberman, 1995).

Can it be said with confidence that psychological treatments are far more than intricate ways of mobilizing a non-specific healing (psychological "placebo") effect? The studies under review do not allow this question to be answered with confidence. In that sense, the specific effects of psychological treatments are less securely established than those of the pharmacological treatments. On the one hand, studies featuring a no-treatment or waiting-list period in their designs (e.g. Mersch, 1995; Butler, Cullington, Munby, Amies, & Gelder, 1984; Stravynski et al., 1982b) did show little evidence of spontaneous remission or strong "placebo" effects. Additionally, given the chronic nature of social phobia, it would appear that the treatment gains observed in the studies under review were not instances of spontaneous remission; this is unlikely. On the other hand, a waiting list may not be the most suitable control for treatment, as it does not simulate it. It might therefore not be as evocative of the healing response as are culturally sanctioned treatments (Moerman, 2002). A limited number of comparisons of treatment with supportive (Heimberg et al., 1998; Cottraux, Note, Albuisson, Yao, Note, Mollard, Bonasse, Jalenques, Guérin, & Coudert, 2000) and associative (Taylor et al., 1997) therapies that might be construed as a psychological placebo have been reported so far. In 2 out of 3, treatment yielded significantly better results but in one study the results were nearly equivalent. For this reason, further comparisons of treatments with control conditions (e.g. counseling) that mimic them, are imperative. Interactive computer-assisted treatments (see Kirkby, 1996) and other methods that encourage self-care (see Marks, 1994), await properly controlled evaluation.

Psycho-Pharmacological Treatments

By now a fairly wide and growing range of compounds (e.g. moclobemide, phenelzine, clonazepam, fluvoxamine, and sertraline) drawn from four classes of medication have all been shown to effect a fairly rapid reduction in social anxiety over and above that observed under placebo. Speed of relief is the singular strength of the pharmacological treatments. Significant lessening of avoidance was observed with moclobemide, phenelzine, brofaromine, clonazepam and paroxetine, fluvoxamine, vanlafaxine, escitalopram, citalopram, sertraline, pregabalin, and gabapantin. Patients on medication usually reported lessening in the disruption in their social functioning (e.g. Sheehan, Harnett-Sheehan, & Raj, 1996), although it was by and large quite modest.

The above benefits conferred by the psycho-pharmacological treatments have to be set against various co-occurring undesirable effects of the same medication ranging from dry mouth – a mild inconvenience – to interference with sexual functioning or altogether loss of libido – serious drawbacks.

Furthermore, relapse rates following discontinuation of medication are likely to be high (e.g. 43% after atenolol; see also Pato, Zohar-Kadouch, Zohar, & Murphy, 1988). These need to be systematically studied. Neither follow-ups nor generalization of gains were reported.

In comparisons of psychological and pharmacological approaches, the short-term effects of therapy were either equivalent or superior to those of medication. In one study, phenelzine resulted in significantly greater improvement. The addition of medication to psychological treatments did not enhance their impact.

Considered imaginatively, the potential for the combination of medication with psychological treatments is dazzling, for the effects of both appear highly complementary. At its best, medication induces rapid (e.g. 6 weeks) lessening in the anxious distress reported by the patients. In principle, this ought to facilitate exposure to widen gains and allow therapeutic work on improving social functioning. In turn, the improvements resulting from psychological treatment are commonly stable and might protect against the relapses often seen when medication is stopped.

When put to the test, however, the available combinations proved disappointing on the whole, failing to exceed the effects of the psychological approach alone in the 3 studies that tested this. Combinations with the newest compounds, however, were not tested. Other kinds of combinations: psychotherapy either preceding or following an independent course of pharmacotherapy might be more promising, but are yet to be tried.

General Comments

The DSM proposes that social phobia comes in two types: the circumscribed ("specific") and the generalized. Is the distinction warranted so far as response to treatment is concerned? Hardly; both types seem to respond equally well to phenelzine (Liebowitz et al., 1992), to exposure with and without cognitive restructuring (see Turner et al., 1996b; Scholing and Emmelkamp, 1993a,b) and to a CBT regimen (Brown et al., 1995). Conversely, additional coexisting clinical problems (DSM: Axes I or II) did not affect response to treatment

(Turner et al., 1996b). For example, patients also meeting criteria for avoidant personality disorder responded as well as those who did not to either exposure alone or in combination with a cognitive treatment and SST (Mersch et al., 1995). However, in Turner (1987) social phobic patients with any personality disorder responded less well to a cognitive treatment. All in all, in their similar response to treatment, the putative social phobic subtypes fit better the hypothesis of a different degree of severity of a unitary problem than that of distinct categories.

Treatment of social phobia is in demand; a market in various services and products has sprung up to satisfy it. Naturally, providers attempt to draw attention to their wares and to drum up more demand (e.g. Gilbody, Wilson, & Watt, 2004; Moynihan et al., 2002, p. 888). In a recent Internet search for "treatment of social phobia," I identified 64,000 pages providing information cum advertisement to perplexed potential customers. A limited and informal perusal of some of the websites found a mixed bag of advice. Sound recommendations (based on demonstrated effects) and consistent with this review jostle with unwarranted claims on behalf of, among others, "humanistic therapy" or St John's Wort. The irrevocable severing of the normal neurological basis for blushing (Drott, Claes, Olsson-Rex, Dalman, Fahlen, & Gothberg, 1998) for example can hardly be considered treatment. My own advice is: *caveat emptor.*

Although concerned with the treatment of the same problem, namely social phobia, both psychological and pharmacological approaches tend to self-involvement. Tools developed or results obtained within one approach are typically ignored by the other. For instance, the measurement of the seemingly similar construct of social anxiety – the bedrock of outcome in both approaches – is conducted with separate assessment scales.

Such solipsism is inimical to progress for it systematically chooses to overlook the conceptual challenges generated by results arising from the other approach (accounting perhaps for the wish to ignore them). For the fact that the diverse psychological and pharmacological treatments under review resulted in fairly similar effects, at least in the immediate term, calls into question two kinds of theoretical claims put forward in justification of specific treatments: namely, the putative therapeutic processes provided by the treatments and their ability to undo the corresponding hypothetical causes of social phobia postulated by each approach.

First, as all treatments obtain similar outcomes across various facets of psychopathology it is doubtful that each triggers a specific therapeutic process unique to it. Concretely, it is unlikely that CBT achieves its effects by improving thinking, SST by correcting deficient social skills, and the various classes of medication by remedying each — a somewhat different defect in neuro-transmission.

Second and for the same reasons, there are grounds to doubt that each treatment deals with the causes of social phobia construed in terms of its own concepts and used as justification for that particular treatment. It is most unlikely therefore that irrational thinking, deficient social skills or a malfunctioning of various processes of neuro-transmission are each the cause of social phobia. This skeptical conclusion is strengthened by the fact that the direct evidence in support of the various causal claims (as reviewed in Part III) is flimsy at best.

Overall, results although useful are modest. Mostly, outcomes are reported in terms of reduction in subjective anxiety and to a lesser extent avoidance; although helpful (and statistically significant) the case for these being in themselves clinically meaningful is uncertain. This is highlighted by the fact that few of the studies have had such effects that would result in a radical change in clinical status (i.e. remission).

The results available suggest that improvements are rather domain-specific; gains seem to generalize poorly to spheres of social life not dealt with successfully in therapy (Scholing & Emmelkamp, 1996a,b; Stravynski et al., 1982b). This implies that a less anxious patient now entering (usually under the pressure of necessity) specific situations (e.g. team-meetings), may not be necessarily doing more or functioning meaningfully better within different situations in the same sphere (e.g. joining colleagues at the cafeteria) let alone in other spheres (e.g. seeking out and wooing potential mates).

Greater research efforts ought to be invested in finding even better ways of eroding the excessively fearful and self-protective pattern of conduct that is social phobia while simultaneously endeavoring to improve the social and interpersonal life of such individuals. The fact that fully 60% of patients seen in a program (Stravynski et al., 2000a) focusing on the difficulties of social functioning (e.g. social participation, assuming social roles) of the socially phobic no longer met DSM-IV criteria for social phobia at 1-year follow-up illustrates the promise of such an approach.

Part V

Concluding Remarks

"The cardinal sin is to confuse words with concepts and concepts with real things."   Johann Georg Hamann

11 Conclusions and Integration

Conclusions

The preceding chapters have overviewed a variety of conceptual schemes and a considerable amount of research work involving social phobia. Four questions have been used to structure this undertaking. Where available, multiple perspectives towards providing an answer have been considered. However, overall conclusions still need to be drawn.

What is Social Phobia?

The answer to this question must necessarily blend conception with observation. Without a theoretical statement delineating the construct, how could we observe (measure) the manifestation of what is properly socially phobic and distinguish it from what is not? Without further studying individuals who are socially phobic, how could we tell if the conception is apt?

Oddly, in view of the claim that social phobia can be identified by criteria specified in classificatory systems and its severity measured by various instruments, few formulations and descriptive statements of social phobia are found. The measurement schemes are likely the product of implicit and mostly unarticulated notions of what the construct of social phobia might be. In measurement certain features are singled out and made prominent but the overall structure and the relationship among its constituting elements remain ambiguous. Are the features salient for measurement also theoretically vital? Are they the quintessence of social phobia? In confronting these issues we were adrift in a theoretical void. I attempted to fill the gap in fleshing out the construct of social phobia in chapter 1. So as to avoid needless repetition I shall restate the main points later on, in the integrative section.

337

What is the Nature of Social Phobia?

What good is it to ponder what social phobia is an instance of? The answer to this question is of some moment, for it determines the proper terminology to be used as well as setting in train wider consequences for research and treatment (e.g. what ought to be investigated, what constitutes a proper treatment, what should be considered an improvement) implied by the membership in a particular category.

Three classes have been considered: social phobia as an anxiety disorder, as a disease and as an entity.

The formulation of social phobia *as a disorder of anxiety* is widely accepted; its popularity is on the whole unjustified. Conceptually, the scientific use of the term social anxiety so as to illuminate social phobia stumbles on the fact that anxiety itself is such a muddled notion (although the word is straightforward as the rough synonym of fear).

The ambiguity of its status is well illustrated by the availability of multiple competing definitions on the one hand and numerous measurement inventories devised without reference to a specific construct of anxiety on the other hand. Furthermore, most studies surveyed had actually relied on a *lay* construct of anxiety since the participants in those studies have defined it subjectively and idiosyncratically.

In absolute terms no specific sort of social phobic (or abnormal social) anxiety has been identified. As to the somatic aspect, palpitations, trembling, and sweating, for example, are self-reported not only by social phobic subjects but also by various other individuals (e.g. with other anxiety disorders) – notably the normal. In interpersonal terms, social phobic patterns of behavior (e.g. keeping quiet, smiling ingratiatingly, blushing) are rendered meaningful by the context in which they occur and their manifest interpersonal function; the term anxiety offers no added explanatory value.

Relatively speaking, no specific demarcation point cuts abnormal social anxiety off from the normal sort. Thus, although social phobic individuals typically rate themselves subjectively as more anxious than do normal individuals, the difference between the two is one of degree rather than in kind. If intermediate degrees of severity are admitted (e.g. of the shy or individuals with other clinical problems) these become consistent with a continuum of social fears, with social phobic individuals, as a group, at its high end. Furthermore, when physiological indices of fear are objectively measured in the laboratory, the differences – often significant on the continuum of subjective anxiety – blur or vanish altogether. Thus, the social phobic fear reaction is very much an exacerbation of normal fear. It is exaggerated in intensity, over-generalized in scope and prolonged in duration.

As children mature towards adolescence and then young adulthood, social fears become prominent while fears of harm and punishment wane. Social fears, unlike social phobia, remain commonplace. Naturally, so are the situations evoking these. Speaking in public, dealing with people in authority, competing in full view of others, evoke anxious discomfort in most people. In the final analysis, although at times extreme, so far as anxiety is concerned social phobic individuals display normal tendencies.

Why is then the construct of social anxiety so widely used despite its evident flaws and rather tenuous empirical support? Likely, the outlook in which the term anxiety serves as a cornerstone is not formed in response to solid theorizing and supporting evidence alone. Underpinning it is a widely held but unspoken assumption that (social) anxiety is the expression of a dysfunction of certain (as yet unknown) regulatory mechanisms within the individual; social phobia would be its ultimate consequence. In short, social phobia might be a *disease* of sorts.

If rhetoric were the deciding factor, there would be little doubt that social phobia is a disease. It is named as such in many publications (with the term disorder as a blander synonym). Social phobia is found in diagnostic manuals and studies of epidemiology. That much is also suggested by the vocabulary in use: individuals seeking help are "diagnosed with" or are "suffering from" social phobia. Apprehensions about and a strong preference toward avoidance of some social occasions are said to be its "symptoms" and so is the dread of humiliation. According to the DSM-IV, "individuals with social phobia almost always experience symptoms of anxiety e.g. palpitations, tremors, sweating, blushing." A closer inspection of both conception and the supporting evidence suggests that the medical vocabulary does not snugly fit reality.

Conceptually, disease is viewed in medicine materialistically; in terms of (observable) lesions to cells, tissues or organs, identifiable biochemical imbalances, etc. These manifest themselves through signs (e.g. fever, swelling, weight loss). Symptoms are experiential and subjective expressions of suffering. Both sets of indicators are used to arrive at tentative diagnoses. In medical practice, some diagnoses may never be validated independently. As a matter of principle, however, there is a concrete and verifiable (by means of tests, biopsies, autopsies) disease independent of its manifest indicators. In the absence of disease, as is the case with social phobia, the use of the related term of diagnosis hardly makes sense, for social phobia cannot be independently confirmed. Agreement among diagnosticians cannot count as validation; such reliability as occurs could be the result of shared preconceptions.

Empirically, the proposition that social phobia is a neurological disease – the consequence of defects in the brain – has little going for it, for no major structural, neurochemical or endocrine abnormalities were found to be in evidence. Conversely, the biological functions (e.g. sleep, appetite) of social phobic individuals are alike those of normal subjects rather than at variance with them.

Ultimately, if disease is defined as a physical problem, objectively measured and scientifically demonstrated, social phobia is not a disease and the medical terminology surrounding it, a figure of speech.

If considering social phobia as an instance of disordered anxiety fits it poorly and categorizing it as a disease is a bit rich and requiring a considerable leap of faith, could it nevertheless be considered an *entity*, reflecting an intrinsic order of nature? This would imply a highly defined pattern with a well-ordered inner structure consistently found in every instance of social phobia. Unlike earlier questions (i.e. is it an anxiety disorder or disease?) the latter is not bedeviled by conceptual and linguistic confusions and in principle can be answered in a straightforward manner. Empirically, however, not all the research one might wish for has been carried out and therefore large gaps in information still prevail. In that sense any assessment is bound to be provisional.

On current knowledge the evidence for and against the hypothesis that social phobia is a fixed entity might be considered a qualified draw. On the one hand, a self-reported social phobic pattern of responding could be fairly reliably agreed on from interviews. Social phobia was consistently associated with difficulties in more social situations evoking more severe anxiety reactions. Although social fears characterizing social phobia were in varying degrees widely shared with normal individuals and other anxiety disorders, these were highly distinguishable not only in degree but as a kind (i.e. patterned configuration). Social phobia was associated with poorer social functioning (e.g. lower employment and marriage rates, and fewer friends). Social phobia has a fairly distinctive age range of onset (15 to 18) and equal sex distribution; it usually precedes other anxiety, affective, and alcoholism disorders with which it has affinities.

On the other hand, social phobia cannot be separated from the obviously related hypothetical entity of avoidant personality disorder; the two doubtless represent degrees of severity of the same pattern. Of considerable importance by its absence is the fact that no specific factors on any level of analysis (social, psychological, biological) have been firmly established as characterizing the social phobic pattern despite considerable research effort.

Large discrepancies in the prevalence of social phobia reported by various studies cast a serious doubt on what is being measured by the defining criteria. Regarding social phobia as a natural entity would lead us to expect a certain (rather high, given the definition) prevalence rate that would fluctuate to a degree in view of the somewhat different life-demands that various cultures make on its members in terms of the social-roles they fulfill. International and same-country (e.g. USA) discrepancies, however, are of such magnitude as to throw into doubt what is being measured each time. Similar inconsistencies were encountered when co-occurring psychopathological constructs were delineated. The variability and incomparability of rates of prevalence across studies throw into doubt the very measurement and ultimately the meaningfulness of social phobia as an entity.

The fact that social phobia has both close links with other hypothetical entities with pronounced anxious features (e.g. panic, Anorexia/Bulimia Nervosa, alcoholism, and depression) as well as various personality disorders, raises the possibility of social phobia being an element in an even larger pattern also encompassing, for example, other anxieties, depression and wider interpersonal difficulties. It is also consistent with a possibility that social phobia is an idiosyncratic loosely defined multi-tiered protean pattern extended in time, sometimes fading out of existence and reincarnated as a myriad of manifestations in particularly trying evoking circumstances. Such a conception is incompatible with the assumption of stable independent entities favored by the DSM (III, III-R and IV).

Although we presume social phobia does obtain naturally – hence the hypothetical construct – and believe we detect it through interviews, the social phobic pattern has not yet been shown independently. The crucial test will lie in studies documenting actual social phobic behavior in real-life situations as well as delineating the social phobic pattern of behavior extended in time and ranging over various areas of social functioning.

What Causes Social Phobia?

Any attempt at understanding complex human phenomena has to start with a theoretical choice of level of analysis. In principle, this could range from the astronomic (e.g. planetary positions at birth) to sub-atomic physics; the plausible range is likely narrower. It could be represented as a continuum of ever-decreasing units of analysis or vice versa.

If what needs to be explained is social phobic behavior, the options in terms of where the explanation might lie are roughly: extra-personal, interpersonal and intra-personal factors. At the sizeable end (in terms of scope of potential units of analysis), there is the physical environment but especially the social world in which humans operate. This could mean group or society-wide structures (sociology) and processes (anthropology) or at a somewhat more individual focus – an interpersonal level of analysis – the manner one engages others and the resulting interplay. This would constitute the study of a person operating in its natural habitat (ethology). Lower down along the continuum are found intra-personal explanatory notions. From a psychological perspective these would deal with postulated mental systems (cognitive). From a biological perspective these would concern biological structures and processes (anatomy, physiology) within the person. These in turn could be approached on various levels (e.g. systems, organs or cells). Further reductions in the level of analysis are conceivable: the molecular as in the case of genes and their products. In principle, a purely atomic or even subatomic level of analysis is conceivable. At some stage in the process of adopting ever smaller constituent units, we confront a theoretical problem: at what level to stop?

What constitutes a cause? The Aristotelian analysis of explanation (Hocutt, 1974) distinguishes between efficient or proximate and final or ultimate causes. In principle, an analysis of efficient causes yields an answer to the question of "how" did something occur. The answer to the question is typically in terms of how one thing leads to another; it is therefore often "mechanical." In complexity, it could range from the simple (e.g. a car hits a pedestrian) to the very intricate (e.g. cause of death). Answering why the event (e.g. the accident) took place is beyond the scope of such an analysis.

An analysis of final causes, by contrast, allows one to answer "why" questions. The answers that it provides to such questions are in terms of ends that define a pattern of dynamic elements, intertwined and integrated by their common purpose. Thus, "in a system with a certain goal, a form of behavior will occur because it brings about that goal" (Looren de Jong, 1997, p. 160).

The behavior of soldiers belonging to various military units attempting a pincer movement against their opponents, and dancers each seemingly executing slightly different movements, over time integrating into small sections of dancers, coalescing in turn into a larger ballet movement, are both examples of complex patterns woven as it were into a larger pattern extended in time, identified by their function. These patterns are the final causes of the behavior of the individual participants. Whereas the ballet (usually) unfolds predictably, the pattern of the two-pronged attack might be transformed while meeting resistance or even become disorganized under the pressure of counter-attacks. These examples illustrate the fact that final causes are to their effect what a pattern is to its elements (Rachlin, 1992, p. 1372).

Whereas an efficient cause invariably precedes its effect, the effect of a final cause is folded into the cause (i.e. a pattern denoting an end). Such functions are relative to their surroundings and — as is the case with social anxiety — when obviously enhancing security in a particular environment, not problematic in ascription. However, the final cause of a particular pattern of behavior might be understood only a considerable time after it took place. This will occur when a pattern started in the past and extending into the future as well as the context molding it, has become sufficiently pronounced and its function in the environment clear. Ultimate causation is often a historically contingent process. The function of a larger pattern into which a smaller pattern fits might be considered a more ultimate cause than the final cause (i.e. the purpose characterizing the sub-pattern considered by itself). Enhancing survival might be considered the ultimate cause of all other final causes. Ultimately, the richest understanding results from clarifying both proximate and final causes.

With these considerations in mind, I shall summarize the various research programs which have attempted to elucidate what causes social phobia. The cognitive and biomedical approaches rely on a subpersonal level of analysis to test efficient causation of social phobia. Such programs might be characterized as reductionistic, (i.e. seeking to understand the behavior of the whole [person] in terms of the properties of certain of its constituting elements). Such research programs are typically framed by a dualistic conception of the human as expounded by Descartes: a disembodied mind housed within a machine-like body. Non-human animals in that scheme of things are mindless automatons of sorts.

It is difficult to classify the social skills deficit program in terms of level of analysis. Social skills are at times treated as plain social behavior and at times characterized as a mental ability, thus a sub-personal system conceived of as an efficient cause. The developmental research program, by contrast, is bound up with final causation. Within that framework different levels of analysis were chosen as each theory emphasized a particular element in the process of development as decisive. The "attachment" approach is situated at an interpersonal level, namely the historical pattern of interactions between a particular caregiver and a child whereas the "behavioral inhibition" approach is situated at a sub-personal one in terms of a certain feature of the young organism (i.e. temperament).

How have the various research program fared? The biomedical outlook, namely that: (1) The social phobic pattern of behavior is caused by (molecular or cellular) events in particular brain regions of the individual exhibiting it; (2) Something coded in the genes of the individual displaying the social phobic pattern predisposes him/her to social phobia; has been found to have little support. In absolute terms, no major structural, neurochemical or endocrine abnormalities were in evidence. Relatively speaking, the biological functions of social phobic individuals were altogether more alike those of normal subjects rather than different from them. When statistical differences were detected, these were exacerbations of normal fear responses. On current evidence, the proposition that social phobic conduct is caused by some (hereditary) brain defects is unsupported and seems unlikely in the highest degree.

Similarly to the biomedical outlook, the cognitive approach failed to identify the cause of social phobia on its own terms. Although social phobic individuals differed from normal participants to some extent on certain cognitive measures, these were differences in (often minuscule) degree. Altogether, there is no evidence to support the claim that these reflect "cognitive biases" that are inherently social phobic. In fact, no "cognitive" process inherently and exclusively typifies social phobia.

One of the implications of these results is that social phobia is not reducible to sub-personal (e.g. molecular–genetic) units of analysis (see Looren de Jong, 2000). Although reductionism is considered the hallmark of science in some quarters, it is plain that assuming that causation necessarily runs from lower to higher levels has offered no privileged understanding in our case. Examining patterns of activity in the brain, for example, will say nothing about why the socially anxious individual is dreading approaching his attractive neighbor and pretends not to notice her instead. Wealth or rank (and the self-assurance that goes with it) might be inherited – but not genetically. Arguably, the interpersonal and somatic facets of social phobia are best characterized functionally.

As with the cognitive and the biomedical outlooks, no evidence has emerged to link social phobia consistently with "deficits of social skills" of any sort. The simulated enactment of various social interactions by social phobic individuals did not differ markedly or systematically from that of normal subjects on any specific parameters. When statistically significant differences between the averages of social phobic and contrast groups emerged, the performance overlapped to a large degree.

Since many normal individuals were as skillful or even less so than those socially phobic without turning socially phobic, this makes it highly unlikely that "deficient" social skills play a causal role in social phobia.

Within the historical perspective on social phobia, two approaches (behavioral inhibition, attachment) stood out for the lucidity and refinement of their theoretical analysis as well as the quality of their longitudinal studies.

Both predicted a decisive role for what they took to be a key factor in the historic development of the pattern of social phobia: a constitutional inhibited temperament on the one hand and a relationship of insecure attachment between caregiver and child on the other. Although in both cases associations between the key theoretical factors (i.e. inhibited temperament, insecure pattern of attachment in early childhood, and social phobia in late adolescence/early adulthood) were established, these were not shown to be necessary conditions for the evolution of social phobia. Proportionately fewer children with the predicted requisite characteristics did develop social phobia later on than those who did not. Conversely, a sizeable proportion of children lacking these characteristics turned socially phobic.

Whatever the theoretical framework, both approaches might be interpreted as suggesting that some individuals will have a stronger propensity to behave defensively and react with greater alarm (i.e. anxiously). Some exhibit it early on, others somewhat later. It is likely a necessary but, emphatically, not a sufficient condition for social phobia to emerge. For the maladjusted pattern of social functioning to crystallize, the propensity to engage people defensively or for the same reason withdraw from social contacts altogether, requires a social environment (characterized by certain social practices and insistent age-appropriate cultural demands) in which such individuals repeatedly struggle and in some respects fail to participate fully in the life of the community to which they belong. The fact that no single factor (inhibited temperament, insecure attachment) was shown as decisive in the emergence of social phobia strengthens the argument that the ultimate cause of the myriad of fearful interpersonal acts coalescing as social phobia is wider in scope: it is the self-protective extended historic pattern of conduct, incorporating as it were all the necessary conditions (environmental and otherwise) for its emergence. I shall return to this point later.

What Helps Social Phobic Individuals?

The widespread categorization of social phobia as a disorder of anxiety is of greatest moment at the level of treatment. In consequence of such construal, most psychological and pharmacological treatments aim directly or indirectly at anxiety reduction. Improvement is similarly defined. Psychological treatments achieve this by variations on the principle of exposure, itself likely based on the naturally occurring phenomenon of habituation; pharmacological treatments by chemically dampening – through different pathways – neuronal excitability. Perhaps for this reason, the effects of psychological treatments are durable, whereas the therapeutic effects of medication cease with its withdrawal. They are on the whole benign, without any of the undesirable effects of medication.

No psychological therapy or medication is properly speaking a treatment specific to social phobia, for they are applied with equal degrees of success to various other problems. Nor is the reduction of anxiety achieved by repairing, as it were, the alleged cause(s) of anxiety.

Conceptually, the narrow construal of social phobia as a disorder of anxiety has the effect of ignoring extensive difficulties of social functioning characterizing it, for these are considered secondary consequences. Contrary to this view, although some alleviation of anxiety doubtlessly provides relief in various social settings, there is little evidence to support the assumption that the extensive self-protective interpersonal patterns typical of social phobia dissipate as a consequence and appropriately participatory ones emerge in their stead. Conversely, evidence shows that treatment aiming at improving social functioning, additionally and simultaneously produces a lessening of anxiety to levels comparable to those found in the anxiety-reduction approaches (Stravynski et al., 1987).

An Integration

The previous statement of conclusions listed summaries of extensive research programs that inadvertently clarified what social phobia was not.

Although possibly disappointing, this need not be dispiriting. After all, these were productive programs that have made important contributions, for considered from a Popperian perspective, knowledge advances best through the winnowing of ultimately untenable hypotheses. Thus, an inkling of what social phobia is not clears the ground for a positive statement of what social phobia is or is likely to be. I shall use this as a point of departure for the integration of current knowledge into a single theoretical framework.

What is Social Phobia?

Social phobia is both an inordinate fear of humiliation resulting from public degradations that one is powerless to prevent and that might end in subsequent loss of standing or membership in the social worlds to which one belongs, as well as a comprehensive defensive interpersonal pattern (constituted of various sub-patterns) protective against the threat of being treated hurtfully by others by means of strategies geared to minimize such risk. In addition to a general preference for avoiding or escaping threatening social situations whenever possible, the main self-protective sub-patterns are: concealing manifestations of fear; striving to be likeable and its flip-side, keeping out of trouble by guarding against provoking or giving offence; being scrupulously proper and participating passively in social life so as not to draw attention or put oneself in harm's way.

The above self-protective measures are evoked by certain classes of dangers embedded in social situations acting as the warp as it were, for the weft of the earlier described patterns of social phobic responses. The main types of social situations are: dealing with powerful and authoritative individuals within social hierarchies; actively seeking group membership and taking part in (at times competitive) group activities; dealing with strangers; and initiating and sustaining intimate relationships.

Fearful and self-protective responses are not monolithic; they are highly differentiated from situation to situation, the danger inherent in each dependent on the class it belongs to and other parameters. Among the most dangerous are performances as a social actor on public occasions (e.g. toasting the bride and groom); the formality, the quality and quantity of participants acting as exacerbating factors. The easiest would be embarking on an intimate relationship that is obviously requited, under conditions guaranteeing privacy – at least initially.

The interlacing of dangerous and therefore fear-evoking context and defensive response to it – to pursue the carpet-weaving metaphor – holds the fabric together; it is solid yet out of sight while some bright designs (e.g. blushing, being at a loss for words) catch the eye.

The comprehensive social phobic pattern (as well as the various sub-patterns comprising it) has simultaneously a somatic and an interpersonal locus. Whereas defensive interpersonal behavior in various guises aims at minimizing risk from others at the present, the body is constantly readied for self-protective maneuvers in the face of both immediate dangers as well as those likely to lie ahead. This results in an often-chronic somatic "state of alert." Among others, this involves: palpitations, fast breathing, tensed muscles, sweating, urges to relieve oneself, speech difficulties, and diminished responsiveness. Inadvertently, because of its potential for drawing attention, the state of over-preparedness for possible future emergencies constitutes a danger in itself and hence evokes persistent attempts to hide both blushing and physical manifestations of fear from scrutiny. Negatively put, fears of blushing, shaking, panicking or of eating, writing, speaking (in public) or their avoidance – on occasion invoked as descriptions of social phobia – only point to some of its facets. These are the bright patterned designs – the pile, figuratively speaking – knotted on top of the weave.

Most importantly, the integrated social phobic self-protective pattern compromises the ability of the individual to carry out desired personal goals and to participate fully in the life of the groups and communities to which she or he belongs. The abnormality of social phobia resides in this; it is the demarcation between the socially phobic and the socially anxious or shy who – although somewhat diminished in ability – carry on and muddle through.

If the conceptually pure definition of social phobia were widened so as to better mirror broader associations that obtain naturally, it might also include other (non-social) fears and reliance on additional self-protective measures – a second line of defense as it were – for instance, alcohol and medication. Lying low while the going gets rough might be considered a third such figurative line – a refuge of last resort. Thus, intermittent or chronic depressed mood and further withdrawal from social life accompany setbacks and the ensuing disappointment and self-blame. Which is the true social phobia? The equivocal answer is that it is a matter of definition. The choice – wide or narrow – reflects the theoretical outlook of the classifier rather than the state of nature; the latter is amorphous and lacks sharply drawn boundaries.

What is the Nature of Social Phobia?

Social phobia might be best considered a pragmatic category as on evidence gathered in chapter 5, it is unlikely to be a natural kind – an entity with highly regular features and internally consistent in all instances (see Zachar, 2001, p. 167). Although a practical kind is a fuzzier category than a natural kind, it is not necessarily arbitrary (2001, p. 167) and as such could still be useful. Such designation has two advantages. First, it is rich in theoretical potential for it admits the possibility of different ways of conceptualizing the category. In this sense, it is less constraining than narrowly seeking what social phobia is "really" like. The relative merits of the different perspectives could subsequently be judged by their explanatory power.

Second, it allows considering its membership as existing on a continuum, varying in degree of resemblance; with no members necessarily identical. Moreover, the category itself could be on a continuum with normality with distinctions at times blurred and made on pragmatic grounds.

What then are the characteristics of social phobia as a pragmatic construct?

The social phobic pattern is consistently associated with difficulties in more social situations evoking more severe anxiety reactions than other contrast groups. It occupies the high end of a continuum of social fears characterizing in varying degrees also normal individuals and those with anxiety and various other disorders (see Kollman, Brown, Liverant, & Hofmann, 2006). Nevertheless, social phobic fears are distinguishable not only in degree but also as a patterned configuration of fears. Moreover, they seem sufficiently well defined in terms of salient features to be fairly reliably agreed on from interviews.

Nevertheless, no characteristics on any level of analysis (social, e.g. skills deficits; mental, e.g. cognitive biases or biological, e.g. neurotransmission) are typical of and exclusive to social phobic individuals. Although at times (but not always) higher in degree, social phobic responding is within normal range. Similarly, no developmental characteristic, fraught as it might seem, in itself irrevocably leads to social phobia. In sum, regardless of the dimension examined at any particular moment, social phobic individuals are more alike those who are normal than different from them.

The overemphasis of social phobic individuals on self-protection by various interpersonal tactics has serious social consequences in the long run. Social phobia is associated with poorer social functioning, for instance in terms of lower employment and marriage rates, and fewer friends.

Social phobia has a fairly equal sex distribution and a distinctive age-range of onset (15 to 18). In light of the evidence reviewed in chapter 9, I consider it likely that the social phobic pattern is forged gradually but appears suddenly with the advent of adult demands made on the individual by the way of life of the community to which he or she belongs. As these crystallize in late adolescence or early adulthood, so does the onset of social phobia. While various social fears might (and indeed often do) precede it in childhood, social phobia – as a fully-fledged pattern – is a problem of young adulthood. Viewed in such light, social phobic children (e.g. Warren, Umylny, Aron, & Simmens, 2006) are incongruous. The very notion needs careful reconsideration.

Social phobia usually precedes other anxiety and affective disorders as well as alcoholism with which it has affinities; these are likely subsequent and inadequate attempts to shore up self-protection. The degree and kind of association in each instance of social phobia varies widely and is idiosyncratic.

In nosological terms, social phobia is simultaneously a disorder of anxiety and personality. Incongruously with the structure of current manuals of classification, it straddles two domains of psychopathology considered independent: functioning in situations and functioning with people, correspondingly Axis I and II in DSM-IV.

Considered pragmatically, social phobia might be regarded as an idiosyncratic loosely defined multi-tiered protean self-protective (and fearful) interpersonal pattern extended in time, resulting in a significant impairment in the ability to engage in deliberate social action and to participate in the social practices of the community. Once in train, the fully fledged social phobic pattern is typically confining and unvarying with predictable consequences in terms of a heightened state of fear and poorer social functioning, at least among individuals seeking treatment. Altogether, however, under auspicious circumstances (e.g. a particularly helpful spouse) the social phobic pattern might fall in disuse and fade out of existence and if − or when − social conditions become particularly trying, be reincarnated.

Pragmatic need not imply arbitrary for social phobia stands in direct link with a myriad of social fears and self-protective interpersonal tactics prevailing naturally and seemingly universally among humans (see chapter 3). A sensitivity to other people's wishes, a desire for approval and recognition from others, a preference for fitting in with the group, coupled with fears of being at variance with others, losing their esteem, provoking their anger and subsequent strife − especially with powerful individuals − are common to humans. Their survival value − seen in an evolutionary light − is obvious both for humans and other sociable animals. Social phobia is simultaneously an exacerbation of normal social fears commonly evoked by life in groups and corresponding interpersonal defensive tactics woven into an abnormal pattern that hinders adequate social functioning.

What Causes Social Phobia?

A comprehensive understanding of any pattern of human behavior, including social phobia, might be seen as the outcome of three levels of historic processes of selection by consequences (Skinner, 1981). The first is the process of natural selection that, building on ancestor populations, resulted in the organic evolution of the human species. Among others, being human and alive includes the capacity for sociability and, conversely, fearing others; both make social phobia possible. In comparison to the scope of the first process, the second is on a human scale. It refers to the development of a fearful individual pattern of self-protection through constant and insistent molding of certain relevant characteristics by the social environment. Such a pattern arises over childhood and adolescence and is consolidated in early adulthood. If unattended, it might last a lifetime. As in evolution by natural selection, the overall behavioral pattern and the sub-patterns that comprise it are shaped by its consequences – relief and safety from harm.

The third process characterizes the emergence of the social world set in a physical environment. This includes a community or a set of communities to which an individual belongs, characterized by a way of life. Such culture involves social institutions and patterns of practices. Like glaciers, although natural and seemingly immutable at any moment, cultures constantly evolve, a process molded by various impersonal historic processes and singular events (natural and man-made), the group's responses to them and their consequences. Humans are social beings; for them, life in groups is a necessity and otherwise unimaginable. All the same, it is not without its dangers (see chapter 3).

For all intents and purposes being human and being born into a cultural community and therefore a way of life are given. Social phobia must arise out of the two, but how? I shall attempt to sketch the process.

A key necessary ingredient is social fear or anxiety (used interchangeably) considered interpersonally or relationally. Some dealings with others obviously induce fear. What characterizes these? Social anxiety is closely associated with the parameters of *power* and *status* inherent in social transactions (see chapter 3). It is worth emphasizing that these are relational notions – not individual attributes – describing the dynamic transactions between two individuals or, a pattern of relationships between an individual and others that form a group. Power is a construct tightly bound up with the ability to deny and to inflict pain, ultimately death. To accord status, in contrast, is to elevate someone as possessing superior qualities (e.g. charm, decisiveness, integrity) and treat them accordingly. Correspondingly, to suffer diminished regard, losing it altogether or worse to be excluded from a group, is experienced painfully as loss (MacDonald & Leary, 2005).

Dominance (a synonymous notion to power) and corresponding submission constitute a relationship; this is played out in sequences of carefully "choreographed" exchanges. A fixed stare is met with lowered eyes and averted gaze, a fierce expression or one of indifference with an ingratiating smile; criticisms delivered cuttingly or orders barked in a loud and imperious voice are acknowledged (or obeyed) with bowed head, a submissive posture, and in soft-spoken and apologetic tones. Dominance is recognized by deference; the dominant party is not treated in a familiar manner, ignored, or dismissed.

Briefly put, insufficient power, an erosion or loss of it (and correspondingly the interlocutor's ascendancy) at the present, or previously established disparities of power, are typically associated with feelings of fear or anxiety (see chapter 3). The degradation of status as manifested in the manner one is treated is associated with shame (e.g. one is not up to standard) and humiliation (e.g. loss of respect).

The recognition of one's weakness for not having been able to prevent the harm or counter it in a specific confrontation opens the possibility of similar defeats in future confrontations. It counsels caution: avoidance of further conflict if possible; submission if not. When existence or the realization of cherished plans depend on someone who pays little heed to one's welfare, or if one is compelled to do things one does not wish to do while being ignored or worse (e.g. one's impotence mocked), one feels threatened, ashamed, and humiliated. Such exchanges could equally involve a fierce bully, a rigidly rule-bound official or a flirtatious stranger.

Social fears are normal and commonplace (see chapter 3). While exaggerated, over-generalized and over-extended in time, the social anxiety of social phobic individuals is undifferentiated from normal social anxiety although they seem to experience it more keenly. Qualitatively, it involves the same subjective experiences (e.g. focus on threat, suspiciousness, apprehension, worry); similar physical preparation towards the danger ahead (e.g. increased circulation of blood, tensing up of muscles); and self-protective social behaviors (e.g. avoidance, immobility, submission, aggression, see chapter 3). It is orchestrated by the same systems of emotional regulation in the brain. These very systems (as well as other activities of the brain) are stifled by medication, prescribed and otherwise (alcohol, placebo).

Normal social anxiety, then, and the interpersonal insufficiency of power associated with it are the necessary conditions for social phobia, making it possible. These, however, are elicited relationally by engaging literally or imaginatively in dangerous transactions with threatening individuals or groups.

Imaginative does not imply delusional; the terrorized citizens of dictatorships know well enough what boundaries are not to be crossed without ever putting the issue to a precise test.

It is the objects of fear, then, that constitute the proximate causes of normal social anxiety and by extension and in aggregate, social phobia; they determine whether normal socially anxious as well as social phobic episodes might take place and their extent.

Although responding not dissimilarly on specific occasions when threatened and in a fearful state, normal individuals are nevertheless not socially phobic; for over time they do not display the interpersonal pattern of powerlessness and self-protection inimical to satisfactory social functioning. This is the exclusive domain of social phobic individuals. The pattern, and its self-protective function are put in high relief by the manner of its coming into being.

The distress occasioned by separation from a caregiver (age range between 8 to 24 months, peaking at 9 to 12 months; see Chapter 3) is in all likelihood the earliest form of social anxiety experienced by a child. A fear of strangers – prominent at about the same time – might be added to this. This is but the first experience in the young individual's life as a supplicant, depending entirely on the goodwill of his or her caregivers and later in life on that of strangers. Such goodwill may at times falter or be altogether unavailable. A self-involved caregiver might not be very responsive to the insistent demands of the child and attend to it intermittently and inadequately – only when the child is very upset. Another parent might be quite anxious about, and more concerned with, diffusing various potential dangers (e.g. catching a cold) than responding to the requests of the child. Conversely a parent could be domineering and short-tempered, exasperated with the nagging child, and terrifying it into submission. To the parents the child may appear difficult for being slow to adapt, tending to withdraw from new situations, and reacting with excessive emotional intensity. Situations outside the home (e.g. family gatherings, playground, kindergarten) where the child might be teased, ignored, punished or bullied might evoke similar reactions.

Over extended periods of time, from the interplay of various environmental elements, the responses to long series of unresponsive, unrewarding social interactions or worse – intimidating or wounding – gradually coalesce into an overall defensive pattern. On the one hand it will be characterized by a high degree of vigilance to threat and physical activation in preparation against it, with some difficulties in modulating arousal. On the other hand and in behavioral terms, it might involve distancing strategies such as outright avoidance or a precarious and passive manner of participation in social life, with a tendency to stay away from other children and from competitive group activities. Additionally, children who might have been ill-used (being mocked or rebuffed) at school, for example, would respond by means of acts of appeasement and submissiveness (e.g. giving no cause for offence, not leaving oneself open to rejection or ridicule by reaching out or showing off).

Traumatic experiences (e.g. standing panting and speechless in front of the class) are triggering events of a previously existing pattern of difficulties and level of adjustment, rather than causes of social phobia.

As can be gathered from the above examples, no single all-important factor, no one particular experience, unsettling as it might have been, leads inexorably towards social phobia. Neither temperament nor parent−child relationships are determinant in the development of social phobia, although they might constitute a serious liability towards it. This is underscored by the fact (see chapter 9) that some of the children assumed to be the most at risk did not become social phobic whereas some of those considered least likely to develop social phobia, did. Furthermore, in longitudinal studies (Chapter 5) no developmental factor singly or in combination predicted the emergence of social phobia; only fully formed social phobia predicted social phobia later on.

The above considerations fit best with the proposition that social phobic interpersonal patterns are the product of widely extended but ceaseless demands placed by a certain social environment on an individual with a specific endowment and a certain history of (mal)adjustment, who systematically and repeatedly fails to engage various aspects of the social life of his or her community in a participatory and self-directed manner and, instead, responds anxiously and defensively.

Social environment in the abstract denotes a variety of ways of life characterizing various communities. It provides values (e.g. what is good, beautiful, true). It determines worthwhile things to do, who is admirable and who is important. It inculcates approved practices (e.g. showing respect, reaching an agreement). It assigns social roles and designates social units. It structures important human activities (e.g. relations between parents and children, women and men, neighbors). Communities, however, are often stratified, with quite different patterns of life (e.g. working from age 14 and struggling to make a living or studying till 26 to occupy choice positions subsequently) characterizing each stratum.

Concrete people enacting the various practices of their community woven into the fabric of social institutions and informal structures provide the context − the danger − evoking socially anxious or socially phobic (depending on the overall pattern) reactions. This is determined by the power embedded in their social role (defined by institutions), their place in the ruling hierarchy or the fact that they possess desirable characteristics, much admired in the community. Who is powerful, and why one needs to take them into account, is culturally constituted. Their powers to grant or deny what one wishes for (e.g. a position, a loan, but also love) or mock one's impudence make them important and dangerous.

If some of the social roles rooted in social structures or practices (e.g. public competitions) were to disappear, so would the corresponding danger. A female member of a religious community that limits women to the family sphere of life cannot by definition become socially phobic — temperament notwithstanding. Similarly, the young son of an aristocratic family surrounded with wealth and privilege, raised by nannies and educated by private tutors who treat him with great deference and whose every utterance is greeted respectfully, can hardly be imagined socially anxious, let alone socially phobic, never mind the relationship with the parents.

By contrast, a woman living in a society that encourages female participation in its economy and therefore in public life is expected to advertise her abilities and compete. The consequences provided by the social environment will be different for those able to rise to the challenge than those who cannot systematically muster the courage to do it.

In the final analysis, social phobia cannot be considered the result of defects in normal functioning on the sub-personal (i.e. brain, mind) level. Rather, it is a purposeful interpersonal pattern or strategy made up of a variety of normal fearful self-protective tactics used in threatening occasions. The strategy is a historically constituted and extended fearful pattern of powerlessness, interpersonally aiming at self-protection in a specific social and cultural environment. Unfortunately, it simultaneously results in a significant restriction on the ability to engage in deliberate social activities and thereby to participate meaningfully in the social practices of the community to which the individual belongs. In this sense the pattern, and the pattern alone, is abnormal. It is characteristic only of social phobic individuals. Naturally, it is in evidence in every case of social phobia.

The ultimate cause of social phobia, then, is the overall fearful pattern of interpersonal behavior whose function is minimizing risk and otherwise providing relief from and enhanced security against social dangers.

What Helps Social Phobic Individuals?

If the fearful and interpersonally defensive pattern is the ultimate cause of social phobia, its dissolution and replacement by a participatory pattern allowing the pursuit of personal goals through meaningful involvement in the life of the community ought to be the goal of treatment. This is the position adopted by treatment aiming at improving social functioning.

Treatments seeking to reduce anxiety generally aim at the enabling systems of social anxiety. Exposure-type treatments, however, (wittingly or not) attempt to undermine certain elements of the general pattern. They do this by encouraging the patient to seek out and confront fear-evoking situations, thereby undermining avoidance and simultaneously bringing about a reduction of anxious arousal, likely through a normal process of habituation (this is not precisely understood). In contrast, pharmacological treatments achieve anxiety reduction by interfering rather broadly (by various chemical ways with varying qualitative results) with the brain, among others, but not exclusively, dampening the activity of the systems involved in emotional regulation. Similar results are produced by non-prescribed medicines (e.g. alcohol, placebo) at least with some individuals. For this reason when medication is discontinued (everything else remaining the same), the physical sensations associated with an anxious state return and the unwished for effects of medication disappear.

The various compounds constituting pharmacological treatment of social phobia stifle some of the normal processes sustaining the fear response (but also depression, pain, and others) while inadvertently interfering with other processes in the brain, with various undesired consequences ("secondary effects"). Sometimes two compounds are better able to achieve a wider suppression of various somatic aspects of fear (i.e. anxiety reduction). Connor, Cook, & Davidson (2004) for example added botox to paroxetine for social phobic patients complaining of "excessive" sweating. The enhancement to paroxetine (a standard medication) consists of the botulinum toxin (produced by the bacterium clostridium botulinum) that has the effect of blocking – for a time – the chemical that stimulates underarm sweating. Surgically severing the sympathetic nerve supply that mediates underarm sweating or blushing is on offer to the desperate (Rex, Drott, Claes, Gothberg, & Dalman, 1998). Such drastic "treatments" have undesirable effects too (e.g. increased sweating in the lower part of the body; 1998).

An unspoken assumption of the anxiety-reduction therapeutic strategy is that in addition to providing welcome relief, it will "release" adaptive social functioning. This seems unwarranted both on empirical (i.e. the evidence is tenuous) and on conceptual grounds. Acting powerlessly and defensively (e.g. appeasing, escaping notice) is a long-standing habit, at this stage likely to be functionally independent and only loosely related to levels of anxiety. While the social anxiety element in social phobia might have weakened in intensity, the ultimate cause (i.e. self-protection as a ruling passion) would likely remain wholly intact. Moreover acting powerfully (i.e. critically, authoritatively or seductively) is something that a social phobic individual has little or no experience of doing and in all likelihood needs to be built up.

The benefits of a strategy of tackling both proximate and final causes of social phobia through changing environment wherever possible, but mostly by means of improving social functioning, are highly encouraging (see Stravynski et al., 2000a). During such therapy, social phobic individuals are taught to behave with greater autonomy (e.g. being outspoken or theatrical), assume social roles, and enact them in a participatory rather than self-protective manner. The emphasis on adaptive behaviors (e.g. that facilitate participation) in therapy and putting them into practice in real life seem the key ingredients toward improvement in social functioning. Similar results are achieved by various training methods ranging from brief individual supervision of performance of interpersonal tasks in vivo to a full-blown training (including modeling and role-rehearsal) in a group setting (Stravynski et al., 2006).

Such an approach, in addition to improving social functioning, achieves, simultaneously, meaningful reductions of anxiety reaching levels comparable to those found in the anxiety-reduction approaches. This provides an indirect support for the link between relative powerlessness (being cornered, scrambling to safety) and high levels of anxiety and conversely, between committed and involved social participation with normal (i.e. modest) and well-modulated levels of fearfulness.

The most beneficial consequence of a widespread change in interpersonal behavior, however, is that it drives the dissolution of the social phobic pattern – the ultimate goal of treatment. Fully 60% of the patients treated in Stravynski et al. (2000a) were no longer meeting criteria of social phobia at 1-year follow-up with similar rates prevailing at 2-years follow-up. This outcome is also brought in high relief by the fact that social phobia is typically a long-standing problem (e.g. average duration of 24 years; 2000). Luckily, treatment duration need not be proportional; 12 weekly sessions with 2 additional follow-up sessions were sufficient in many cases. A long-term (5–8 years) follow-up of this approach is now being carried out.

Whatever the therapeutic means in use, the antidote to social phobia is the development of a more autonomous (and therefore less fearful) interpersonal pattern of social functioning. This provides security through a judicious mixture of collaboration with others so as to create and sustain environments where coexistence can flourish, combined with defensive and offensive tactics of self-protection when need arises. Such fruitful collaborations include the creation of intimate emotional bonds (love, friendship) and participation – as an actor in various social capacities – in the life (economic, political, cultural) of the communities to which the individual attaches herself or himself. In the final analysis, greater autonomy is achieved when an interpersonal pattern of self-creation rather than one narrowly aimed at survival (i.e. self-protection) becomes predominant.

References

Abou-Saleh, M. T., Ghubash, R., & Daradkeh, T. K. (2001) Al Ain community psychiatric survey. I. Prevalence and sociodemographic correlates. *Social Psychiatry & Psychiatric Epidemiology*, *36*, 20–28.

Adams, H. B. (1964) "Mental illness" or interpersonal behavior? *American Psychologist*, *19*, 191–197.

Adams, J. A. (1987) Historical review and appraisal of research on the learning retention and transfer of human motor skills. *Psychological Bulletin*, *101*, 41–74.

Ainsworth, M. D. S., Blehar, M. C., Waters, E., & Wall, S. (1978) *Patterns of attachment: a psychological study of the Strange Situation*. Hillsdale, New Jersey: Lawrence Erlbaum.

Alden, L. E., & Wallace, S. T. (1995) Social phobia and social appraisal in successful and unsuccessful social interactions. *Behaviour Research & Therapy*, *33*, 497–505.

Alexander, D. A., & Klein, S. (2003) Biochemical terrorism: too awful to contemplate, too serious to ignore. *British Journal of Psychiatry*, *183*, 491–497.

Allan, S., & Gilbert, P. (1997) Submissive behaviour and psychopathology. *British Journal of Clinical Psychology*, *36*, 467–488.

Allgulander, C. (1999) Paroxetine in social anxiety disorder: a randomized placebo-controlled study. *Acta Psychiatrica Scandinavica*, *100*, 193–198.

Allgulander, C., Mangano, R., Zhang, J., Dahl, A. A., Lepola, U., Sjödin, I., & Emilien, G. (2004) Efficacy of Venlafaxine ER in patients with social anxiety disorder: a double-blind, placebo-controlled, parallel-group comparison with paroxetine. *Human Psychopharmacology*, *19*, 387–396.

Alpert, J. E., Uebelacker, L. A., McLean, N. E., Nierenberg, A. A., Pava, J. A., Worthington III, J. J., Tedlow, J. R., Rosenbaum, J. F., & Fava, M. (1997) Social phobia, avoidant personality and atypical depression: co-occurrence and clinical implications. *Psychological Medicine*, *27*, 627–633.

Amies, P. L., Gelder, M. G., & Shaw, P. M. (1983) Social phobia: a comparative clinical study. *British Journal of Psychiatry*, *142*, 174–179.

Amir, N., McNally, R. J., Riemann, B. C., Burns, J., Lorenz, M., & Mullen, J. T. (1996) Suppression of the emotional Stroop effect by increased anxiety in patients with social phobia. *Behaviour Research & Therapy*, *34*, 945–948.

Amir, N., Foa, E. B., & Coles, M. E. (1998a) Automatic activation and strategic avoidance of threat relevant information in social phobia. *Journal of Abnormal Psychology*, *197*, 285–290.

(1998b) Negative interpretation bias in social phobia. *Behaviour Research & Therapy*, *36*, 945–957.

Anderson, J. C., Williams, S., McGee, R., & Silva, P. A. (1987) DSM-III disorders in preadolescent children: prevalence in a large sample from the general population. *Archives of General Psychiatry*, *44*, 69–76.

Andreasen, N. C. (1984) *The broken brain: the biological revolution in psychiatry.* New York: Harper & Row.

Andrews, G. (1996) Comorbidity and the general neurotic syndrome. *British Journal of Psychiatry*, *168*, 76–84.

Andrews, G., Stewart, G., Morris-Yates, A., Holt, P., & Henderson, S. (1990) Evidence for a general neurotic syndrome. *British Journal of Psychiatry*, *157*, 6–12.

Andrews, G., Slade, T., & Peters, L. (1999) Classification in psychiatry: ICD-10 versus DSM-IV. *British Journal of Psychiatry*, *174*, 3–5.

Antony, M. M., Purdon, C. L., Huta, V., & Swinson, R. P. (1998a) Dimensions of perfectionism across the anxiety disorders. *Behaviour Research & Therapy*, *36*, 1143–1154.

Antony, M. M., Roth, D., Swinson, R. P., Huta, V., & Devins, G. M. (1998b) Illness intrusiveness in individuals with panic disorder, obsessive-compulsive disorder or social phobia. *The Journal of Nervous & Mental Disease*, *186*, 311–315.

APA (1994) *Diagnostic and statistical manual of mental disorders (DSM-IV).* Washington, District of Colombia: American Psychiatric Association.

Arbel, N., & Stravynski, A. (1991) A retrospective study of separation in the development of adult avoidant personality disorder. *Acta Psychiatrica Scandinavica*, *83*, 174–178.

Argyle, M., & Kendon, A. (1967). The experimental analysis of social performance. In L. Berkowitz (Ed.), *Advances in experimental social psychology.* Volume *3*. New York: Academic Press, pp. 55–98.

Arnarson, E. O., Gudmundsdotttir, A., & Boyle, G. J. (1998) Six-month prevalence of phobic symptoms in Iceland: an epidemiological postal survey. *Journal of Clinical Psychology*, *54*, 257–265.

Arrindell, W. A., & van der Ende, J. (1985) Cross-sample invariance of the structure of self-reported distress and difficulty in assertiveness. *Advances in Behaviour Research & Therapy*, *7*, 205–243.

Arrindell, W. A., Emmelkamp, P. A., Monsma, A., & Brilman, E. (1983) The role of perceived parental rearing practice in the aetiology of phobic disorders: a controlled study. *British Journal of Psychiatry*, *143*, 183–187.

Arrindell, W. A., Sanderman, R., van der Molen, H., van der Ende, J., & Mersch, P. P. (1988) The structure of assertiveness: a confirmatory approach. *Behaviour Research & Therapy*, *26*, 337–339.

Arrindell, W. A., Kwee, M. G. T., Methorst, G. J., van Der Ende, J., Pol, E., & Moritz, B. J. M. (1989) Perceived parental rearing styles of agoraphobic and socially phobic inpatients. *British Journal of Psychiatry*, *155*, 526–535.

Arrindell, W. A., Pickersgill, M. J., Merckelbach, H., Ardon, M. A., & Cornet, F. C. (1991a) Phobic dimensions III: factor analytic approaches to the study of common phobic fears. *Advances in Behaviour Research & Therapy*, *13*, 73–130.

Arrindell, W. A., Sanderman, R., Hageman, W. M., Pickersgill, M. J., Kwee, M. G. T., van der Molen, H. T., & Lingsma, M. M. (1991b) Correlates of assertiveness in normal and clinical samples: a multidimensional approach. *Advances in Behaviour Research & Therapy*, **12**, 153–282.

Asendorf, J. B. (1990) Development of inhibition during childhood: evidence for situational specificity and a two-factor model. *Developmental Psychology*, **26**, 721–731.

Asendorf, J. B., & Meier, G. H. (1993) Personality effects on children's speech in everyday life: sociability-mediated exposure and shyness-mediated reactivity to social situations. *Journal of Personality & Social Psychology*, **64**, 1072–1083.

Asmundson, G. J. G., & Stein, M. B. (1994) Vagal attenuation in panic disorder: an assessment of parasympathetic nervous system function and subjective reactivity to respiratory manipulations. *Psychosomatic Medicine*, **56**, 187–193.

Atmaca, M., Kuloglu, M., Tezzcan, E., & Unal, A. (2002) Efficacy of citalopram and moclobemide in patients with social phobia: some preliminary findings. *Human Psychopharmacology & Clinical Experience*, **17**, 401–405.

Baker, S. R., & Edelmann, R. J. (2002) Is social phobia related to lack of social skills? Duration of skill related behaviours and ratings of behavioural adequacy. *British Journal of Clinical Psychology*, **41**, 243–257.

Baldwin, D., Bobes, J., Stein, D. J., Scharwächter, I., & Faure, M. (1999) Paroxetine in social phobia/social anxiety disorder: randomised, double-blind, placebo-controlled study. *British Journal of Psychiatry*, **178**, 120–126.

Bandelow, B., Charima Torrento, A., Wedkin, D., Broocks, A., Hajak, G., & Ruther, E. (2004) Early traumatic life events, parental rearing styles, family history of mental disorders, and birth factors in patients with social anxiety disorder. *European Archives of Psychiatry & Clinical Neuroscience*, **254**, 397–405.

Barber, B. (1957) Social stratification: a comparative analysis of structure and process. New York: Harcourt, Brace, & World.

Barnett, S. D., Kramer, M. L., Casat, C. D., Connor, K. M., & Davidson, J. R. T. (2002) Efficacy of olanzapine in social anxiety disorder: a pilot study. *Journal of Psychopharmacology*, **16**, 365–368.

Baron, J. (1988) *Thinking & deciding*. Cambridge: Cambridge University Press.

Barrett, P. M., Rapee, R. M., Dadds, M. M., & Ryan, S. M. (1996) Family enhancement of cognitive style in anxious and aggressive children. *Journal of Abnormal Child Psychology*, **24**, 187–203.

Bartlett, S. J. (1990) The etiology of work-engendered depression. *New Ideas in Psychology* **8**, 389–396.

Beattie, M., & Stevenson, J. (1984) Measures of social functioning in psychiatric outcome research. *Evaluation Review*, **8**, 631–644.

Bebchuk, J., & Tancer, M. (1994–95) Growth hormone response to clonidine and L-dopa in normal volunteers. *Anxiety*, **1**, 278–281.

Beck, A. T. (1976). *Cognitive therapy & the emotional disorders*. New York: International Universities Press.

Beck, A. T., Emery, G., & Greenberg, R. L. (1985). *Anxiety disorders and phobias: a cognitive perspective*. New York: Basic Books.

Beck, J. G., & Barlow, D. H. (1984) Current conceptualizations of sexual dysfunction: a review and an alternative perspective. *Clinical Psychology Review*, **4**, 363–378.

Beidel, D. C. (1991) Social phobia and overanxious disorder in school-age children. *Journal of the American Academy of Child & Adolescent Psychiatry*, **30**, 545–552.

Beidel, D. C., & Turner, S. M. (1997) At risk for anxiety: I. Psychopathology in the offspring of anxious parents. *Journal of the American Academy of Child & Adolescent Psychiatry*, **36**, 918–924.

Beidel, D. C., Turner, S. M., & Morris, T. L. (1999) Psychopathology of childhood social phobia. *Journal of the American Academy of Child & Adolescent Psychiatry*, **38**, 643–650.

Bellack, A. S. (1979) A critical appraisal of strategies for assessing social skill. *Behavioral Assessment*, **1**, 157–176.

Bell-Dolan, D. J., Last, C. G., & Strauss, C. C. (1990) Symptoms of anxiety disorders in normal children. *Journal of the American Academy of Child & Adolescence Psychiatry*, **29**, 759–765.

Benjamin, R., Costello, E., & Warren, M. (1990) Anxiety disorders in a pediatric sample. *Journal of Anxiety Disorders*, **4**, 293–316.

Benkelfat, C., Bradwejn, J., Meyer, E., Ellenbogen, M., Milot, S., Gjedde, A., & Evans, A. (1995) Functional neuroanatomy of CCK4-induced anxiety in normal healthy volunteers. *American Journal of Psychiatry*, **152**, 1180–1184.

Bergner, R. M. (1997) What is psychopathology? And so what? *Clinical Psychology; Science & Practice*, **4**, 235–248.

Berrios, G. (1999) Anxiety disorders: a conceptual history. *Journal of Affective Disorders*. **56**, 83–94.

Biederman, J., Rosenbaum, J. F, Hirshfeld, D. R., Faraone, S. V., Bolduc, E. A., Gersten, M., Meminger, S. R., Kagan, J., Snidman, N., & Reznick, J. S. (1990) Psychiatric correlates of behavioral inhibition in young children of parents with and without psychiatric disorders. *Archives of General Psychiatry*, **47**, 21–26.

Biederman, J., Rosenbaum, J. F, Bolduc-Murphy, E. A., Faraone, S. V., Chaloff, J., Hirshfeld, D. R., & Kagan, J. (1993) A 3-year follow-up of children with and without behavioral inhibition. *Journal of the American Academy of Child & Adolescent Psychiatry*, **32**, 814–821.

Biederman, J., Hirshfeld-Becker, D. R., Rosenbaum, J. F., Hérot, C., Friedman, D., Snidman, N., Kagan, J., & Faraone, S. V. (2001) Further evidence of association between behavioral inhibition and social anxiety in children. *American Journal of Psychiatry*, **158**, 1673–1679.

Bienvenu, O. J., Nestadt, G., Samuels, J. F., Costa, P. T., Howard, W. T., & Eaton, W. W. (2001) Phobic, panic and major depressive disorders and the five-factor model of personality. *The Journal of Nervous & Mental Disease*, **189**, 154–161.

Bijl, R. V., Ravelli, A., & Van Zessen, G. (1998) Prevalence of psychiatric disorder in the general population: results of the Netherlands Mental Health Survey and Incidence Study (NEMESIS). *Social Psychiatry & Psychiatric Epidemiology*, **33**, 587–595.

Birbaumer, N., Grodd, W., Diedrich, O., Klose, U., Erb, M., Lotze, M., Schneider, F., Weiss, U., & Flor, H. (1998) fMRI reveals amygdala activation to human faces in social phobics. *Neuroreport*, **9**, 1223–1226.

Bland, R. C., Oran, H., & Newman, S. C. (1988) Lifetime prevalence of psychiatric disorders in Edmonton. *Acta Psychiatrica Scandinavica*, **338** (Suppl.), 24–32.

Blashfield, R. K., & Livesley, W. J. (1991) Metaphorical analysis of psychiatric classification as a psychological test. *Journal of Abnormal Psychology*, **100**, 262–270.

Blomhoff, S., Haug, T. T., Hellström, K., Holme, I., Humble, M., Madsbu, H. P., & Wold, J. E. (2001) Randomised controlled general practice trial of sertraline, exposure therapy and combined treatment in generalised social phobia. *British Journal of Psychiatry*, **179**, 23–30.

Bodinger, L., Hermesh, H., Aizenberg, D., Valevski, A., Marom, S., Shiloh, R., Gothelf, D., Zemishly, Z., & Weitzman, A. (2002) Sexual function and behavior in social phobia. *Journal of Clinical Psychiatry*, **63**, 874–879.

Bögels, S. M., van Oosten, A., Muris, P., & Smulders, D. (2001) Familial correlates of social anxiety in children and adolescents. *Behaviour Research & Therapy*, **39**, 273–287.

Bohlin, G., Hagekull, B., & Rydell, A. M. (2000) Attachment and social functioning: a longitudinal study from infancy to middle childhood. *Social Development*, **9**, 24–39.

Boissy, A. (1995) Fear and fearfulness in animals. *The Quarterly Review of Biology*, **70**, 165–191.

Bond, R., & Smith, P. R. (1996) Culture and conformity; a meta-analysis of studies using Asch's line judgement task. *Psychological Bulletin*, **119**, 111–137.

Boone, M. L., McNeil, D. W., Masia, C. L., Turk, C. L., Cartier, L. E., Ries, B. J., & Lewin, M. R. (1999) Multimodal comparisons of social phobia subtypes and avoidant personality disorder. *Journal of Anxiety Disorders*, **13**, 271–292.

Bowlby, J. (1981a) *Attachment and loss*. Harmondsworth: Penguin Books.

Bowlby, J. (1981b) *Separation: anxiety and anger*. Harmondsworth: Penguin Books.

Bradwejn, J., Koszycki, D., & Shriqui, C. (1991) Enhanced sensitivity to cholecystokinin tetrapeptide in panic disorder: clinical and behavioral findings. *Archives of General Psychiatry*, **48**, 603–610.

Bremner, J. (2004) Brain imaging in anxiety disorders. *Expert Review of Neurotherapeutics*, **4**, 275–284.

Bridges, K. R., Sanderman, R., Breukers, P., Ranchor, A., & Arrindell, W. A. (1991) Sex differences in assertiveness on the U.S. version of the Scale for Interpersonal Behavior (SIB). *Personality & Individual Differences*, **12**, 1239–1243.

Brown, A. M., & Crawford, H. J. (1988) Fear Survey Schedule-III: oblique and orthogonal factorial structures in an American college population. *Personality & Individual Differences*, **9**, 401–410.

Brown, E. J., Heimberg, R. G., & Juster, H. R. (1995) Social phobia subtype and avoidant personality disorder: effect on severity of social phobia impairment and outcome of cognitive-behavioral treatment. *Behavior Therapy*, **26**, 467–486.

Brown, G. W. (1996) Genetics of depression: a social science perspective. *International Review of Psychiatry*, **8**, 387–401.

Brown, T. A., Campbell, L. A., Lehman, C. L., Grisham, J. R., & Mancill, R. B. (2001a) Current and lifetime comorbidity of the DSM-IV anxiety and mood disorders in a large clinical sample. *Journal of Abnormal Psychology*, **110**, 585–599.

Brown, T. A., Di Nardo, P. A., Lehman, C. L., & Campbell, L. A. (2001b) Reliability of DSM-IV anxiety and mood disorders: implications for the classification of emotional disorders. *Journal of Abnormal Psychology*, **110**, 49–58.

Bruch, M. A., & Heimberg, R. G. (1994) Differences in perceptions of parental and personal characteristics between generalized and non-generalized social phobics. *Journal of Anxiety Disorders*, **8**, 155–168.

Bruch, M. A., Gorsky, J. M., Collins, T. M., & Berger, P. A. (1989) Shyness and sociability re-examined: a multicomponent analysis. *Journal of Personality & Social Psychology*, **57**, 904–915.

Bruch, M. A., Heimberg, R. G., & Hope, D. A. (1991) States of mind model and cognitive change in treated social phobics. *Cognitive Therapy & Research*, **15**, 429–441.

Bruch, M. A., Fallon, M., & Heimberg, R. G. (2003) Social phobia and difficulties in occupational adjustment. *Journal of Counseling Psychology*, **50**, 109–117.

Bryant, B., & Trower, P. E. (1974) Social difficulty in a student sample. *British Journal of Educational Psychology*, **44**, 13–21.

Bulik, C. M., Beidel, D. C., Duchmann, E., Weltzin, T. E., & Kaye, W. H. (1991) An analysis of social anxiety in anorexic, bulimic, social phobic and control women. *Journal of Psychopathology & Behavioral Assessment*, **13**, 199–211.

Burnam, A., Karno, M., Hough, R. L., Escobar, J. I., & Forsythe, A. B. (1983) The Spanish Diagnostic Interview Schedule: reliability and comparison with clinical diagnoses. *Archives of General Psychiatry*, **40**, 1189–1196.

Burton, R. (1621) *The anatomy of melancholia* (11th edn. 1813, Volume. *1*). London: Chatto & Windus.

Buss, D. (1990) The evolution of anxiety and social exclusion. *Journal of Social & Clinical Psychology*, **9**, 196–201.

Butler, G., Cullington, A., Munby, M., Amies, P., & Gelder, M. (1984) Exposure and anxiety management in the treatment of social phobia. *Journal of Consulting & Clinical Psychology*, **52**, 642–650.

Cacioppo, J. T., Bernston, G. G., Sheridan, J. F., & McClintock, M. K. (2000) Multilevel integrative analyses of human behavior: social neuroscience and the complementing nature of social and biological approaches. *Psychological Bulletin*, **126**, 829–843.

Caldirola, D., Perna, G., Arancio, C., Bertani, A., & Bellodi, L. (1997) The 35% CO_2 challenge test in patients with social phobia. *Psychiatry Research*, **71**, 41–48.

Canetti, E. (1981) *Crowds and power*. Harmondsworth: Penguin.

Canino, G. J., Bird, H. R., Shrout, P. E., Rubio-Stipec, M., Bravo, M., Martinez, R., et al. (1987) The prevalence of specific psychiatric disorders in Puerto Rico. *Archives of General Psychiatry*, **44**, 727–735.

Caraveo-Anduaga, J. J., & Colmenares, E. (2000) Prevalencia de lo trastornos de ansiedad fóbica en la población adulta de la ciudad de México. *Salud Mental*, **23**, 10–19.

Caspi, A., Moffitt, T. E., Newman, D. L., & Silva, P. A. (1996) Behavioral observations at age 3 years predict adult psychiatric disorders. *Archives of General Psychiatry*, **53**, 1033–1039.

Cassidy, J., & Berlin, L. J. (1994) The insecure/ambivalent pattern of attachment: theory and research. *Child Development*, **65**, 971–991.

Caster, J. B., Inderbitzen, H. M., & Hope, D. (1999) Relationship between youth and parent perceptions of family environment and social anxiety. *Journal of Anxiety Disorders*, **13**, 237–251.

Chalmers, A. F. (1976) *What is this thing called science?* Milton Keynes: Open University Press.

Chambless, D. L., Tran, G. Q., & Glass, C. R. (1997) Predictors of response to cognitive-behavioral group therapy for social phobia. *Journal of Anxiety Disorders*, **11**, 221–240.

Chartier, M. J., Walker, J. R., & Stein, M. B. (2001) Social phobia and potential childhood risk-factors in a community sample. *Psychological Medicine*, **31**, 307–315.

Chatterjee, S., Sunitha, T., Velayudhan, A., & Khanna, S. (1997) An investigation into the psychobiology of social phobia: personality domains and serotonin function. *Acta Psychiatrica Scandinavica*, **95**, 544–550.

Chavira, D. A., Stein, M. B., & Malcarne, V. L. (2002) Scrutinizing the relationship between shyness and social phobia. *Journal of Anxiety Disorders*, **16**, 585–598.

Cheek, J. M., & Buss, A. H. (1981) Shyness and sociability. *Journal of Personality & Social Psychology*, **41**, 330–339.

Chen, X., Hastings, P. D., Rubin, K. H., Chen, H., Cen, G., & Stewart, S. L. (1998) Child-rearing attitudes and behavioral inhibition in Chinese and Canadian toddlers: a cross-cultural study. *Developmental Psychology*, **34**, 677–686.

Chess, S., & Thomas, A. (1987) *Origins and evolution of behavior disorders.* Cambridge, Massachusetts: Harvard University Press.

Chisholm, J. S. (1999) *Death, hope and sex.* Cambridge: Cambridge University Press.

Chorpita, B., & Barlow, D. (1998) The development of anxiety: the role of control in the early environment. *Psychological Bulletin*, **124**, 3–21.

Chua, P., Krams, M., Toni, I., Passingham, R., & Dolan, R. (1999) A functional anatomy of anticipatory anxiety. *Neuroimage*, **9**, 563–571.

Claparede, E. (1902) L'obsession de la rougeur: a propos d'un cas d'éreuto-phobie. *Archives de Psychologie de la Suisse Romande*, *Avril*, 307–334.

Clark, D. B., & Agras, W. S. (1991) The assessment and treatment of performance anxiety in musicians. *American Journal of Psychiatry*, **148**, 598–605.

Clark, D. M. (1999) Anxiety disorders: why they persist and how to treat them. *Behaviour Research & Therapy*, **37**, S5–S27.

Clark, D. M., & Steer, R. A. (1996) Empirical status of the cognitive model of anxiety and depression. In Salkovskis, P. (Ed.), *Frontiers of cognitive therapy*. New York: Guilford Press, pp. 75–96.

Clark, D. M., & Wells, A. (1995) A cognitive model of social phobia. In R. G. Heimberg, M. R. Liebowitz, D. A. Hope, & F. R. Schneier (Eds.), *Social phobia: diagnosis, assessment, and treatment: theoretical and empirical approaches*. New York: Guilford Press, pp. 69–93.

Clark, D. M., Ehlers, A., McManus, F., Hackmann, A., Fennell, M., Campbell, H., Flower, T., Davenport, C., & Louis, B. (2003) Cognitive therapy versus fluoxetine in generalized social phobia: a randomized placebo-controlled trial. *Journal of Consulting & Clinical Psychology*, *71*, 1058–1067.

Cloitre, M., Heimberg, R. G., Holt, C. S., & Liebowitz, M. R. (1992) Reaction time to threat stimuli in panic disorder and social phobia. *Behaviour Research & Therapy*, *30*, 609–617.

Cohen, J. (1960) A coefficient of agreement for nominal scales. *Educational & Psychological Measurement*, *20*, 37–46.

Coles, M. E., Turk, C. L., Heimberg, R. G., & Fresco, D. M. (2001) Effects of varying levels of anxiety within social situations: relationship to memory perspective and attributions in social phobia. *Behaviour Research & Therapy*, *39*, 651–665.

Condren, R., Sharifi, N., & Thakore, J. (2002a) A preliminary study of dopamine-mediated prolactin inhibition in generalized social phobia. *Psychiatry Research*, *111*, 87–92.

Condren, R., O'Neill, A., Ryan, M., Barrett, P., & Thakore, J. (2002b) HPA axis response to a psychological stressor in generalised social phobia. *Psychoneuroendocrinology*, *27*, 693–703.

Connor, K. M., Cook, J. L., & Davidson, J. R. (2004) Botulinum toxin treatment of social anxiety disorder with hyperhidrosis: a double-blind, placebo-controlled trial. *Neuropsychopharmacology*, *29* (Suppl. 1), S96.

Conquest, R. (1990) *The great terror: a reassessment*. New York: Oxford University Press.

Contesse, V., Lefebvre, H., Lenglet, S., Kuhn, J., Delarue, C., & Vaudry, H. (2000) Role of 5-HT in the regulation of the brain-pituitary-adrenal axis: effects of 5-HT on adrenocortical cells. *Canadian Journal of Physiology & Pharmacology*, *78*, 967–983.

Corner, P. (2002) Italian fascism: whatever happened to dictatorship? *Journal of Modern History*, *74*, 325–351.

Costello, C. G. (1982) Fears and phobias in women: a community study. *Journal of Abnormal Psychology*, *91*, 280–286.

Cotran, R. S., Kumar, V., & Robbins, S. L. (1994) *Robbins' pathologic basis of disease*. Philadelphia: Saunders.

Cottraux, J., Note, I., Albuisson, E., Yao, S. N., Note, B., Mollard, E., Bonasse, F., Jalenques, I., Guérin, J., & Coudert, A. J. (2000) Cognitive behavior therapy versus supportive therapy in social phobia: a randomized controlled trial. *Psychotherapy & Psychosomatics*, *69*, 137–146.

Coupland, N., Wilson, S., Potokar, J., Bell, C., & Nutt, D. (2003) Increased sympathetic response to standing in panic disorder. *Psychiatry Research*, *118*, 69–79.

Cox, B. J., Rector, N. A., Bagby, R. M., Swinson, R. P., Levitt, A. J., & Joffe, R. T. (2000) Is self-criticism unique for depression?: a comparison with social phobia. *Journal of Affective Disorders*, **57**, 223–228.

Cox, B. J., MacPherson, P. S. R., & Enns, M. W. (2005) Psychiatric correlates of childhood shyness in a nationally representative sample. *Behaviour Research & Therapy*, **43**, 1019–1027.

Craddock, A. E. (1983) Family cohesion and adaptability as factors in the aetiology of social anxiety. *Australian Journal of Sex, Marriage & Family*, **4**, 181–190.

Craig, W. M. (1998) The relationship among bullying, victimization, depression, anxiety and aggression in elementary school children. *Personality & Individual Differences*, **24**, 123–130.

Craighead, E., Kazdin, A., & Mahoney, M. (1981) *Behavior modification: principles, issues and applications*. Boston: Houghton Mifflin.

Crick, N. R., & Grotpeter, J. K. (1996) Children's treatment by peers: victims of relational and overt aggression. *Development & Psychopathology*, **8**, 367–380.

Crits-Christoph, P. (1986) The factor structure of the CSAQ. *Journal of Psychosomatic Research*, **30**, 685–690.

Cronbach, L. J., & Meehl, P. E. (1955) Construct validity in psychological tests. *Psychological Bulletin*, **56**, 81–106.

Curran, J. P. (1979) Social skills: methodological issues and future directions. In A. S. Bellack & M. Hersen (Eds.), *Research and practice in social skills training*. New York: Plenum, pp. 319–354.

  (1982) A procedure for the assessment of social skills: the Simulated Social Interaction Test. In J. P. Curran & P. M. Monti (Eds.), *Social skills training: a practical handbook for assessment and treatment*. New York: Guilford, pp. 348–373.

Curran, J. P., Wessberg, H. W., Monti, P. M., Corriveau, D. P., & Coyne, N. A. (1980) *Patients versus controls on a social skill/anxiety role-play test*. Paper presented at the 88th annual convention of the American Psychological Association, Montreal, Canada, September 1980.

Curran, J. P., Wessberg, H. W., Farrell, A. D., Monti, P. M., Corriveau, D. P., & Coyne, N. A. (1982) Social skills and social anxiety: are different laboratories measuring the same construct? *Journal of Consulting & Clinical Psychology*, **50**, 396–406.

Dadds, M. R., Barrett, P. M., Rapee, R. M., & Ryan, S. (1996). Family process and child anxiety and aggression: An observational analysis. *Journal of Abnormal Child Psychology*, **24**, 715–734.

Daniels, D., & Plomin, R. (1985) Origins of individual differences in infant shyness. *Developmental Psychology*, **21**, 118–121.

David, D., Giron, A., & Mellman, T. A. (1995) Panic-phobic patients and developmental trauma. *Journal of Clinical Psychiatry*, **56**, 113–117.

Davidson, J. R. T., Hughes, D. L., George, L. K., & Blazer, D. G. (1993a) The epidemiology of social phobia: findings from the Duke Epidemiological Catchment Area Study. *Psychological Medicine*, **23**, 709–718.

Davidson, J. R. T., Potts, N., Richichi, E., Krishnan, R., Ford, S. M., Smith, R., & Wilson, W. H. (1993b) Treatment of social phobia with clonazepam and placebo. *Journal of Clinical Psychopharmacology*, **13**, 423–428.

Davidson, J. R. T., Foa, E. B., Huppert, J. D., Keefe, F. J., Franklin, M. E., Compton, J. S., Zhao, N., Connor, K. M., Lynch, T. R., & Gaddle, K. M. (2004a) Fluoxetine, comprehensive cognitive behavioral therapy and placebo in generalized social phobia. *Archives of General Psychiatry*, **61**, 1005–1013.

Davidson, J. R. T., Yaryura-Tobias, J., DuPont, R., Stallings, L., Barbato, L. M., van der Hoop, R. G., & Li, D. (2004b) Fluvoxamine-controlled release formulation for the treatment of generalized social anxiety disorder. *Journal of Clinical Psychopharmacology*, **24**, 118–125.

Davidson, R. J., Marshall, J., Tomarken, A., & Henriques, J. (2000) While a phobic waits: regional brain electrical and autonomic activity in social phobics during anticipation of public speaking. *Biological Psychiatry*, **47**, 85–95.

Davies, D. (2002) D-lactate and the false suffocation alarm. *Archives of General Psychiatry*, **59**, 287–288.

Davis, S. (1996) The cosmobiological balance of the emotional and spiritual worlds: phenomenological structuralism in traditional Chinese medical thought. *Culture, Medicine & Psychiatry*, **20**, 83–123.

Dawkins, R. (1976) *The selfish gene*. Oxford: Oxford University Press.

Deater-Deckard, K. (2001) Recent research examining the role of peer relationships in the development of psychopathology. *Journal of Child Psychology & Psychiatry*, **42**, 565–579.

Degonda, M., & Angst, J. (1993) The Zurich study: XX. social phobia and agoraphobia. *European Archives of Psychiatry and Clinical Neuroscience*, **243**, 95–102.

DeGood, D. E., & Tait, R. C. (1987) The CSAQ: psychometric and validity data. *Journal of Psychopathology & Behavioral Assessment*, **9**, 75–87.

Delmonte, M. M., & Ryan, G. M. (1983) The CSAQ: a factor analysis. *British Journal of Clinical Psychology*, **22**, 209–212.

Dewar, K., & Stravynski, A. (2001) The quest for biological correlates of social phobia: an interim assessment. *Acta Psychiatrica Scandinavica*, **103**, 244–251.

DeWit, D. J., Ogborne, A., Offord, D. R., & MacDonald, K. (1999) Antecedents of the risk of recovery from DSM-III-R social phobia. *Psychological Medicine*, **29**, 569–582.

Dick, C. L., Sowa, B., Bland, R. C., & Newman, S. C. (1994) Phobic disorders. *Acta Psychiatrica Scandinavica*, **338** (Suppl.), 36–44.

DiLalla, L. F., Kagan, J., & Reznick, J. S. (1994) Genetic etiology of behavioural inhibition among two-year-old children. *Infant Behavior & Development*, **17**, 405–412.

Dilsaver, S. C., Qamar, A. B., & Del Medico, V. J. (1992) Secondary social phobia in patients with major depression. *Psychiatry Research*, **44**, 33–40.

Dimsdale, J., & Moss, J. (1980) Short-term catecholamine response to psychological stress. *Psychosomatic Medicine*, **42**, 493–497.

DiNardo, P. A., Moras, K., Barlow, D. H., Rapee, R. P., & Brown, T. A. (1993) Reliability of DSM-III-R anxiety disorder categories using the Anxiety

Disorders Interview Schedule–Revised (ADIS-R). *Archives of General Psychiatry*, **50**, 251–256.

Dinwiddie, S., Heath, A. C., Dunne, M. P., Bucholz, K. K., Madden, P. A. F., Slutske, W. S., Bierut, L. J., Statham, D. B., & Martin, N. G. (2000) Early sexual abuse and lifetime psychopathology: a co-twin-control study. *Psychological Medicine*, **30**, 41–52.

Dixon, J. J., De Monchaux, C., & Sandler, J. (1957) Patterns of anxiety: an analysis of social anxieties. *British Journal of Medical Psychology*. **30**, 107–112.

Dodge, C. S., Hope, D. A., Heimberg, R. G., & Becker, R. E. (1988) Evaluation of the SISST with a social phobic population. *Cognitive Therapy & Research*, **12**, 211–222.

Donkin, R. (2000) *Blood, sweat and tears: the evolution of work*. London: Texere.

Douglas, A. R., Lindsay, W. R., & Brooks, D. N. (1988) The three systems model of fear and anxiety: implications for assessment of social anxiety. *Behavioural Psychotherapy*, **16**, 15–22.

Drott, C., Claes, G., Olsson-Rex, L., Dalman, P., Fahlen, T., & Gothberg, G. (1998) Successful treatment of facial blushing by endoscopic transthoracic sympathicotomy. *British Journal of Dermatology*, **138**, 639–643.

Dugas, L. (1898) *Timidité*. Paris: Alcan.

Dyck, I. R., Phillips, K. A., Warshaw, M. G., Dolan, R. T., Shea, T., Stout, R. L., et al. (2001) Patterns of personality pathology in patients with generalized anxiety disorder, panic disorder with and without agoraphobia and social phobia. *Journal of Personality Disorders*, **15**, 60–71.

Eastburg, M., & Johnson, B. (1990) Shyness and perception of parental behavior. *Psychological Reports*, **66**, 915–921.

Eckman, P. S., & Shean, G. D. (1997) Habituation of cognitive and physiological arousal and social anxiety. *Behaviour Research & Therapy*, **35**, 1113–1121.

Edelmann, R., & Baker, S. (2002) Self-reported and actual physiological responses in social phobia. *British Journal of Clinical Psychology*, **41**, 1–14.

Ehlert, U., & Straub, R. (1998) Physiological and emotional response to psychological stressors in psychiatric and psychosomatic disorders. *Annals of the New York Academy of Sciences*, **851**, 477–486.

Eifert, G. H., & Wilson, P. H. (1991) The triple response approach to assessment: a conceptual and methodological reappraisal. *Behaviour Research & Therapy*, **29**, 283–292.

El-Islam, M. F. (1994) Cultural aspects of morbid fears in Qatari women. *Social Psychiatry & Psychiatric Epidemiology*, **29**, 137–140.

Emmelkamp, P. M. G., Mersch, P. P., Vissia, E., & Van Der Helm, M. (1985) Social phobia: a comparative evaluation of cognitive and behavioral interventions. *Behaviour Research & Therapy*, **23**, 365–369.

Epstein, S. (1972) The nature of anxiety with emphasis upon its relationship to expectancy. In C. D. Spielberger (Ed.), *Anxiety: Current trends in theory and research*. New York: Academic Press, pp. 292–337.

Eren, I., Tukel, R., Polat, A., Karaman, R., & Unal, S. (2003) Evaluation of regional cerebral blood flow changes in panic disorder with Tc99m-HMPAO SPECT. *Psychiatry Research*, **123**, 135–143.

Ernst, C., Angst, J., & Földényi, M. (1993) The Zurich Study: XVII. Sexual abuse in childhood, frequency and relevance for adult morbidity data of a longitudinal epidemiological study. *European Archives of Clinical Neuroscience*, *242*, 293–300.

Errera, P. (1962) Some historical aspects of the concept of phobia. *Psychiatric Quarterly*, *36*, 325–336.

Essau, C. A., Conradt, J., & Petermann, F. (1999) Frequency and comorbidity of social phobia and social fears in adolescents. *Behaviour Research & Therapy*, *37*, 831–843.

Eysenck, H. J., & Eysenck, S. B. J. (1969) *Personality structure and measurement*. London: Routledge & Kegan Paul.

Fahlén, T., Nilsson, H. L., Borg, K., Humble, M., & Pauli, U. (1995) Social phobia: the clinical efficacy and tolerability of the monoamine oxidase-A and serotonin uptake inhibitor brofaromine. *Acta Psychiatrica Scandinavica*, *92*, 351–358.

Falloon, I., Lloyd, G. G., & Harpin, R. E. (1981) The treatment of social phobia: real life rehearsal with non-professional therapists. *Journal of Nervous & Mental Disease*, *169*, 180–184.

Faravelli, C., Guerrini Degl'Innocenti, B., & Giardinelli, L. (1989) Epidemiology of anxiety disorders in Florence. *Acta Psychiatrica Scandinavica*, *79*, 308–312.

Faravelli, C., Zucchi, T., Vivani, B., Salmoria, R., Perone, A., Paionni, A., Scarpato, A., Vigliaturo, D., Rosi, S., D'Adamo, D., Bartolozzi, D., Cecchi, C., & Abrardi, L. (2000) Epidemiology of social phobia: a clinical approach. *European Psychiatry*, *15*, 17–24.

Faravelli, C., Abrardi, L., Bartolozzi, D., Cecchi, C., Cosci, Fiammetta, C., D'Adamo, D., Lo Iacono, B., Ravaldi, C., Scarpato, M. A., Truglia, E., & Rosi, S. (2004) The Sesto Fiorentino study: background, methods and preliminary results. *Psychotherapy & Psychosomatics*, *73*, 216–225.

Fatis, M. (1983) Degree of shyness and self-reported physiological, behavioural and cognitive reactions. *Psychological Reports*, *52*, 351–354.

Feehan, M., McGee, R., Nada Raja, S., & Williams, S. M. (1994) DSM-III-R disorders in New Zealand 18-years-olds. *Australian & New Zealand Journal of Psychiatry*, *28*, 87–99.

Feske, U., Perry, K. J., Chambless, D. L., Renneberg, B., & Goldstein, A. J. (1996) Avoidant personality disorder as a predictor for treatment outcome among generalized social phobics. *Journal of Personality Disorders*, *10*, 174–184.

Figueira, I., Possidente, E., Marques, C., & Hayes, K. (2001) Sexual dysfunction: a neglected complication of panic disorder and social phobia. *Archives of Sexual Behavior*, *30*, 369–377.

Finnie, V., & Russell, A. (1988) Preschool children's social status and their mother's behavior and knowledge in the supervisory role. *Developmental Psychology*, *24*, 789–801.

Foa, E. B., Franklin, M. E., Perry, K. J., & Herbert, J. D. (1996) Cognitive biases in generalized social phobia. *Journal of Abnormal Psychology*, *105*, 433–439.

Foa, E. B., Gilboa-Schechtman, E., Amir, N., & Freshman, M. (2000) Memory bias in generalized social phobia: remembering negative emotional expressions. *Journal of Anxiety Disorders*, *14*, 501–519.

Fodor, J. (1983) *The modularity of mind*. Cambridge, Massachusetts: The MIT Press.

Frances, A., Mack, A. H., First, M. B., Widiger, T. A., Ross, R., Forman, L., & Davis, W. W. (1994) DSM-IV meets philosophy. *The Journal of Medicine & Philosophy*, *19*, 207–218.

Francis, G., Last, C. G., & Strauss, C. C. (1992) Avoidant disorder and social phobia in children and adolescents. *Journal of the American Academy of Child & Adolescent Psychiatry*, *31*, 1086–1089.

Freedland, K. E., & Carney, R. M. (1988) Factor analysis of the CSAQ. *Journal of Psychopathology & Behavioral Assessment*, *10*, 367–375.

Friend, R., & Gilbert, J. (1972) Threat and fear of negative evaluation as determinants of locus of social comparison. *Journal of Personality*, *41*, 328–340.

Friman, P. C., Hayes, S. C., & Wilson, K. G. (1998) Why behavior analysts should study emotion: the example of anxiety. *Journal of Applied Behavior Analysis*, *31*, 137–156.

Furlan, P., DeMartinis, N., Schweizer, E., Rickels, K., & Lucki, I. (2001) Abnormal salivary cortisol levels in social phobic patients in response to acute psychological but not physical stress. *Biological Psychiatry*, *50*, 254–259.

Furmark, T., Tillfors, M., Everz, P. O., Marteinsdottir, I., Gefvert, O., & Fredrikson, M. (1999) Social phobia in the general population: prevalence and sociodemographic profile. *Social Psychiatry & Psychiatric Epidemiology*, *34*, 416–424.

Furmark, T., Tillfors, M., Marteinsdottir, I., Fischer, H., Pissiota, A., Langstrom, B., & Fredrikson, M. (2002) Common changes in cerebral blood flow in patients with social phobia treated with citalopram or cognitive-behavioral therapy. *Archives of General Psychiatry*. *59*, 425–433.

Furmark, T., Tillfors, M., Garpenstrand, H., Marteinsdottir, I., Langstrom, B., Oreland, L., & Fredrikson, M. (2004) Serotonin transporter polymorphism related to amygdala excitability and symptom severity in patients with social phobia. *Neuroscience Letters*, *362*, 189–192.

Fydrich, T., Chambless, D. L., Perry, K. J., Buergener, F., & Beazley, M. B. (1998) Behavioral assessment of social performance: a rating system for social phobia. *Behaviour Research & Therapy*, *36*, 995–1010.

Fyer, A. J., Mannuzza, S., Chapman, T. F., Liebowitz, M. R., & Klein, D. F. (1993) A direct interview family study of social phobia. *Archives of General Psychiatry*, *50*, 286–293.

Fyer, A. J., Mannuzza, S., Chapman, T. F., Martin, L. Y., & Klein, D. F. (1995) Specificity in familial aggregation of phobic disorders. *Archives of General Psychiatry*, *52*, 564–573.

Garcia Coll, C., Kagan, J., & Reznick, J. S. (1984) Behavioral inhibition in young children. *Child Development*, *55*, 1005–1019.

Gardner, S. (1993) *Irrationality and the philosophy of psychoanalysis*. Cambridge: Cambridge University Press.

Gelder, M., Gath, D., Mayou, R., & Cowen, P. (1996) *Oxford textbook of psychiatry*. Oxford: Oxford University Press.

Gelernter, C. S., Uhde, T. W., Cimbolic, P., Arnkoff, D. B., Vittone, B. J., Tancer, M. E., & Bartko, J. J. (1991) Cognitive-behavioral and pharmacological treatments of social phobia: a controlled study. *Archives of General Psychiatry*, **48**, 938–945.

Gelernter, C. S., Stein, M. B., Tancer, M. E., & Uhde, T. W. (1992) An examination of syndromal validity and diagnostic subtype in social phobia and panic disorder. *Journal of Clinical Psychiatry*, **53**, 23–27.

Gelernter, J., Page, G., Stein, M., & Woods, S. (2004) Genome-wide linkage scan for loci predisposing to social phobia: evidence for a chromosome-16 risk locus. *American Journal of Psychiatry*, **161**, 59–66.

Geraci, M., Anderson, TS., Slate-Cothren, S., Post, R., & McCann, U. (2002) Pentagastrin-induced sleep panic attacks: panic in the absence of elevated baseline arousal. *Biological Psychiatry*, **52**, 1183–1189.

Gerlach, A. L., Wilhelm, F. H., Gruber, K., & Roth, W. T. (2001) Blushing and physiological arousability in social phobia. *Journal of Abnormal Psychology*, **110**, 247–258.

Gerlach, A. L., Wilhelm, F., & Roth, W. (2003) Embarrassment and social phobia: the role of parasympathetic activation. *Journal of Anxiety Disorders*, **17**, 197–210.

Gerlach, A. L., Mourlane, D., & Rist, F. (2004) Public and private heart rate feedback in social phobia: a manipulation of anxiety visibility. *Cognitive Behaviour Therapy*, **33**, 36–45.

Gerth, H., & Mills, C. W. (1953) *Character and social structure*. New York: Harcourt, Brace, & World.

Ghaziuddin, N., King, C., Welch, K., Zaccagnini, J., Weidmer-Mikhail, E., & Mellow, A. (2000) Serotonin dysregulation in adolescents with major depression: hormone response to meta-chlorophenylpiperazine (mCPP) infusion. *Psychiatry Research*, **95**, 183–194.

Gilbert, P. (2001) Evolution and social anxiety: the role of attraction, social competition, and social hierarchies. *The Psychiatric Clinics of North America*, **24**, 723–751.

Gilboa-Schechtman, E., Foa, E. B., & Amir, N. (1999) Attentional biases for facial expressions in social phobia: the face-in-the-crowd paradigm. *Cognition & Emotion*, **13**, 305–318.

Gilboa-Schechtman, E., Franklin, M. E., & Foa, E. B. (2000) Anticipated reactions to social events: differences among individuals with generalized social phobia, obsessive compulsive disorder and nonanxious controls. *Cognitive Therapy & Research*, **24**, 731–746.

Gilbody, S., Wilson, P., Watt, I. (2004) Direct-to-consumer advertising of psychotropics: an emerging and evolving form of pharmaceutical company influence. *British Journal of Psychiatry*, **185**, 1–2.

Gilmartin, B. G. (1987) Peer group antecedents of severe love-shyness in males. *Journal of Personality*, **55**, 467–489.

Glas, G. (1996) Concepts of anxiety: a historical reflection on anxiety and related disorders. In H. G. M. Westenberg, J. A. Den Boer, & D. L. Murphy

References 373

(Eds.), *Advances in the neurobiology of anxiety disorders*. New York: Wiley, pp. 3–19.

Glass, C. R., & Furlong, M. (1990) Cognitive assessment of social anxiety: affective and behavioural correlates. *Cognitive Therapy & Research*, **14**, 365–384.

Glass, C. R., Merluzzi, T. V., Biever, J. L., & Larsen, K. H. (1982) Cognitive assessment of social anxiety: development and validation of a self-statement questionnaire. *Cognitive Therapy & Research*, **6**, 37–55.

Glassman, M. (2000) Mutual-aid theory and human development: sociability as primary. *Journal for the Theory of Social Behaviour*, **30**, 391–412.

Godart, N. T., Flament, M. F., Lecrubier, Y., & Jeammet, P. (2000) Anxiety disorders in anorexia nervosa and bulimia nervosa: co-morbidity and chronology of appearance. *European Psychiatry*, **15**, 38–45.

Goering, E., & Breidenstein-Cutspec, P. (1989) The web of shyness: a network analysis of communicative correlates. *Communication Research Reports*, **6**, 111–118.

Goisman, R. M., Goldenberg, I., Vasile, R. G., & Keller, M. B. (1995) Comorbidity of anxiety disorders in a multicenter anxiety study. *Comprehensive Psychiatry*, **36**, 303–311.

Gold, P., & Chrousos, G. (2002) Organization of the stress system and its dysregulation in melancholic and atypical depression: high vs. low CRH/NE states. *Molecular Psychiatry*, **7**, 254–275.

Goldenberg, I. M., White, K., Yonkers, K., Reich, J., Warshaw, M. G., Goisman, R. M., & Keller, M. B. (1996) The infrequency of "pure culture" diagnoses among the anxiety disorders. *Journal of Clinical Psychiatry*, **57**, 528–533.

Goldsmith, J. B., & McFall, R. (1975) Development and evaluation of an interpersonal skill-training program for psychiatric patients. *Journal of Abnormal Psychology*, **84**, 51–58.

Goldsmith, H. H., Buss, A. H., Plomin, R., Rothbart, M. K., Thomas, A., Chess, S., Hinde, R. A., McCall, R. B. (1987) What is temperament? Four approaches. *Child Development*, **58**, 505–529.

Goodwin, D. W. (1986) *Anxiety*. New York: Oxford University Press.

Goodwin, R. D., Fergusson, D. M., & Horwood, L. J. (2004) Early anxious/withdrawn behaviours predict later internalising disorders. *Journal of Child Psychology & Psychiatry*, **45**, 874–883.

Gopnik, A. (1993) How we know our minds: the illusion of first-person knowledge of intentionality. *Behavioral & Brain Sciences*, **16**, 1–14.

Gorenstein, E. E. (1992) *The science of mental illness*. San Diego: Academic Press.

Gorman, J. M., Papp, L. A., Martinez, J., Goetz, R. R., Hollander, E., Liebowitz, M. R., & Jordan, F. (1990) High-dose carbon dioxide challenge test in anxiety disorder patients. *Biological Psychiatry*, **28**, 743–757.

Gorman, J., Kent, J., Sullivan, G., & Coplan, J. (2000) Neuroanatomical hypothesis of panic disorder, revised. *American Journal of Psychiatry*, **157**, 493–505.

Grant, B. F., Hasin, D. S., Stinson, F. S., Dawson, D. A., Chou, S. P., Ruan, W. J., & Huang, B. (2005) Co-occurrence of 12-month mood and anxiety disorders and personality disorders in the US: results from the national epidemiologic survey on alcohol and related conditions. *Journal of Psychiatric Research, 39,* 1–9.

Gray, J. A. (1979) Anxiety and the brain. *Psychological Medicine, 9,* 605–609.

(1970) The psychophysiological basis of introversion – extraversion. *Behaviour Research & Therapy, 8,* 249–266.

Green, L. (1994) Fear as a way of life. *Cultural Anthropology, 9,* 227–256.

Greenberg, D., Stravynski, A., & Bilu, Y. (2004) Social phobia in ultra-orthodox Jewish males: culture-bound syndrome or virtue? *Mental Health, Religion, & Culture, 7,* 289–305.

Griesinger, W. (1845) *Die pathologie und therapie der psychischen krankheiten für aerzte und studirende.* Amsterdam: Bonset.

Grüner, K., Muris, P., & Merckelbach, H. (1999) The relationship between anxious rearing behaviours and anxiety disorders symptomatology in normal children. *Journal of Behavior Therapy & Experimental Psychiatry, 30,* 27–35.

Gullone, E., & King, N. J. (1993) The fears of youth in the 1990s: contemporary normative data. *The Journal of Genetic Psychology. 154,* 137–153.

(1997) Three-year follow-up of normal fear in children and adolescents, aged 7 to 18 years. *British Journal of Developmental Psychology, 15,* 97–111.

Gündel, H., Wolf, A., Xidara, V., Busch, R., & Ceballos-Baumann, A. O. (2001) Social phobia in spasmodic torticollis. *Journal of Neurology, Neurosurgery, & Psychiatry, 71,* 499–504.

Gursky, D. M., & Reiss, S. (1987) Identifying danger and anxiety expectancies as components of common fears. *Journal of Behavior Therapy & Experimental Psychiatry, 18,* 317–324.

Hacking, I. (1996) Les aliénés voyageurs: how fugue became a medical entity. *History of Psychiatry, 7,* 425–449.

Hackmann, A., Surawy, C., & Clark, D. (1998) Seeing yourself through others' eyes: a study of spontaneously occurring images in social phobia. *Behavioural & Cognitive Psychotherapy, 26,* 3–12.

Hallam, R. (1985) *Anxiety: psychological perspectives on panic and agoraphobia.* New York: Academic Press.

Ham, L. S., Hope, D. A., White, C. S., & Rivers, P. C. (2002) Alcohol expectancies and drinking behavior in adults with social anxiety disorder and dysthymia. *Cognitive Therapy & Research, 26,* 275–288.

Harris, J. R. (1995) Where is the child's environment? A group socialization theory of development. *Psychological Review, 102,* 458–489.

Hart, T. A., Turk, C. L., Heimberg, R. G., & Liebowitz, M. R. (1999) Relation of marital status to social phobia severity. *Depression & Anxiety, 10,* 28–32.

Hartenberg, P. (1901/1921) *Les timides et la timidité.* Paris: Alcan.

Harvey, J. M., Richards, J. C., Dziadosz, T., & Swindell, A. (1993) Misinterpretation of ambiguous stimuli in panic disorder. *Cognitive Therapy & Research, 17,* 235–248.

Haug, T. T., Blomhoff, S., Hellstrom, K., Holme, I., Humble, M., Madsbu, H. P., & Wold, J. E. (2003) Exposure therapy and sertraline in social phobia: 1-year follow-up of a randomised controlled trial. *British Journal of Psychiatry, 182,* 312–318.

Hawker, D. S. J., & Boulton, M. J. (2000) Twenty years' research on peer victimization and psychosocial maladjustment: A meta-analytic review of cross-sectional studies. *Journal of Child Psychology & Psychiatry*, *41*, 441–455.

Hawley, P. H. (1999) The ontogenesis of social dominance: a strategy-based evolutionary perspective. *Developmental Review*, *19*, 97–132.

Hayward, C., Killen, J. D., Kraemer, H. C., & Taylor, B. (1998) Linking self-reported childhood behavioural inhibition to adolescent social phobia. *Journal of American Academy of Child & Adolescent Psychiatry*, *37*, 1308–1316.

Healy, D., & Thase, M. E. (2003) Is academic psychiatry for sale? *British Journal of Psychiatry*, *182*, 388–390.

Heils, A., Teufel, A., Petri, S., Stober, G., Riederer, P., Bengel, D., & Lesch, K. (1996) Allelic variation of human serotonin transporter gene expression. *Journal of Neurochemistry*, *66*, 2621–2624.

Heimberg, R. G. (1994) Cognitive assessment strategies and the measurement of outcome of treatment for social phobia. *Behaviour Research & Therapy*, *32*, 269–280.

Heimberg, R. G., & Holt, C. S. (1989) The issue of subtypes in the diagnosis of social phobia: a report to the social phobia subworkgroup for DSM-IV. Unpublished manuscript. American Psychiatric Association.

Heimberg, R. G., Becker, R. E., Goldfinger, K., & Vermilyer, J. A. (1985) Treatment of social phobia by exposure, cognitive restructuring and homework assignments. *Journal of Nervous & Mental Disease*, *173*, 236–245.

Heimberg, R. G., Gansler, D., Dodge, C. D., & Becker, R. E. (1987) Convergent and discriminant validity of the CSAQ in a social phobic population. *Behavioral Assessment*, *9*, 379–388.

Heimberg, R. G., Dodge, C. S., Hope, D. A., Kennedy, C. R., Zollo, L. J., & Becker, R. E. (1990a) Cognitive behavioral group treatment for social phobia: comparison with a credible placebo control. *Cognitive Therapy & Research*, *14*, 1–23.

Heimberg, R. G., Hope, D. A., Dodge, C. S., & Becker, R. E. (1990b) DSM-III-R subtypes of social phobia, comparison of generalized social phobics and public speaking phobics. *Journal of Nervous & Mental Disease*, *178*, 172–179.

Heimberg, R. G., Mueller, G. P., Holt, G. S., Hope, D. A., & Liebowitz, M. R. (1992) Assessment of anxiety in social interaction and being observed by others: the Social Interaction Anxiety Scale and the Social Phobia Scale. *Behavior Therapy*, *23*, 53–73.

Heimberg, R. G., Salzman, D. G., Holt, C. S., & Blendell, K. A. (1993) Cognitive-behavioral group treatment for social phobia: effectiveness at five-year follow-up. *Cognitive Therapy & Research*, *17*, 325–339.

Heimberg, R. G., Liebowitz, M. R., Hope, D. A., Schneier, F. R., Holt, C. S., Welkowitz, L. A., Juster, H. R., Campeas, R., Bruch, M. A., Cloitre, M., Fallon, B., & Klein, D. F. (1998) Cognitive behavioral group therapy vs. phenelzine therapy for social phobia: 12-week outcome. *Archives of General Psychiatry*, *55*, 1133–1141.

Heimberg, R. G., Horner, K. J., Juster, H. R., Safren, S. A., Brown, E. J., Schneier, F. R., & Liebowitz, M. R. (1999). Psychometric properties of the Liebowitz Social Anxiety Scale. *Psychological Medicine*, *29*, 199–212.

Herbert, J. D., Hope, D. A., & Bellack, A. S. (1992) Validity of the distinction between generalized social phobia and avoidant personality disorder. *Journal of Abnormal Psychology*, *101*, 332–339.

Herbert, J. D., Gaudiano, B. A., Rheingold, A. A., Myers, V. H., Dalrymple, K., & Nolan, E. M. (2005) Social skills training augments the effectiveness of cognitive behavioral group therapy for social anxiety disorder. *Behavior Therapy*, *36*, 125–138.

Hersen, M. (1979) Modification of skill deficits in psychiatric patients. In A. S. Bellack & M. Hersen (Eds.), *Research and practice in social skills training*. New York: Plenum Press, pp. 189–236.

Hietala, J., West, C., Syvalahti, E., Nagren, K., Lehikoinen, P., Sonninen, P., & Ruotsalainen, U. (1994) Striatal D2 dopamine receptor binding characteristics in vivo in patients with alcohol dependence. *Psychopharmacology*, *116*, 285–290.

Hirshfeld, D. R., Rosenbaum, J. F., Biederman, J., Bolduc, E. A., Faraone, S. V., Snidman, N., Reznick, J. S., & Kagan, J. (1992) Stable behavioral inhibition and its association with anxiety disorder. *Journal of the American Academy of Child & Adolescent Psychiatry*, *31*, 103–111.

Hocutt, M. (1974) Aristotle's four becauses. *Philosophy*, *49*, 385–399.

Hoes, M. J. (1986) Biological markers in psychiatry. *Acta Psychiatrica Belgica*, *86*, 220–241.

Hofmann, B. (2002) On the triad disease, illness and sickness. *Journal of Medicine & Philosophy*, *27*, 651–673.

Hofmann, S. G., & Roth, W. T. (1996) Issues related to social anxiety among controls in social phobia research. *Behavior Therapy*, *27*, 79–91.

Hofmann, S. G., Newman, M. G., Becker, E., Barr Taylor, C., & Roth, W. T. (1995a) Social phobia with and without avoidant personality disorder: preliminary behavior therapy outcome findings. *Journal of Anxiety Disorders*, *9*, 427–438.

Hofmann, S. G., Newman, M. G., Ehlers, A., & Roth, W. T. (1995b) Psychophysiological differences between subgroups of social phobia. *Journal of Abnormal Psychology*, *104*, 224–231.

Hofmann, S. G., Gerlach, A. L., Wender, A., & Roth, W. (1997) Speech disturbances and gaze behavior during speaking in subtypes of social phobia. *Journal of Anxiety Disorders*, *11*, 573–585.

Hollander, E., Kwon, J., Weiller, F., Cohen, L., Stein, D., DeCaria, C., Liebowitz, M., & Simeon, D. (1998) Serotonergic function in social phobia: comparison to normal control and obsessive-compulsive disorder subjects. *Psychiatry Research*, *79*, 213–217.

Holmes, R. (1985) *Acts of war: the behavior of men in battle*. New York: Free Press.

Holt, C. S., Heimberg, R. G., & Hope, D. A. (1992) Avoidant personality disorder and the generalized subtype of social phobia. *Journal of Abnormal Psychology*, *101*, 318–325.

Holt, P. E., & Andrews, G. (1989) Hyperventilation and anxiety in panic disorder, social phobia, GAD and normal controls. *Behaviour Research & Therapy*, **27**, 453–460.

Homel, R., Burns, A., & Goodnow, J. (1987) Parental social networks and child development. *Journal of Social & Personal Relationships*, **4**, 159–177.

Hope, D. A., Rapee, R. M., Heimberg, R. G., & Dombeck, M. J. (1990) Representations of the self in social phobia: vulnerability to social threat. *Cognitive Therapy & Research*, **14**, 177–189.

Hope, D. A., Heimberg, R. G., & Bruch, M. A. (1995a) Dismantling cognitive-behavioral group therapy for social phobia. *Behaviour Research & Therapy*, **33**, 637–650.

Hope, D. A., Herbert, J. D., & White, C. (1995b) Diagnostic subtype, avoidant personality disorder, and efficacy of cognitive-behavioral group therapy for social phobia. *Cognitive Therapy & Research*, **19**, 399–417.

Howarth, E. (1980) Major factors of personality. *Journal of Psychology*, **104**, 171–183.

Hoyer, J., Becker, E. S., & Roth, W. T. (2001) Characteristics of worry in GAD patients, social phobics, and controls. *Depression & Anxiety*, **13**, 89–96.

Hudson, J. L., & Rapee, R. M. (2001) Parent–child interactions and anxiety disorders: an observational study. *Behaviour Research & Therapy*, **39**, 1411–1427.

(2002) Parent–child interactions in clinically anxious children and their siblings. *Journal of Clinical Child & Adolescent Psychology*, **31**, 548–555.

Hume, D. (1739/1961) *A treatise of human nature* (Ed. Selby-Bigge). Oxford: Clarendon Press.

Humphrey, N. K. (1976) The social function of intellect. In P. P. G. Bateson & R. A. Hinde (Eds.), *Growing points in ethology*. Cambridge: Cambridge University Press, pp. 303–317.

Hunt, N., & McHale, S. (2005) The psychological impact of alopecia. *British Medical Journal*, **331**, 951–953.

Hwu, H. G., Yeh, E., & Chang, L. Y. (1989) Prevalence of psychiatric disorders in Taiwan defined by the Chinese Diagnostic Interview Schedule. *Acta Psychiatrica Scandinavica*, **79**, 136–147.

Hymel, S., Rubin, K. H., Rowden, L., & LeMare, L. (1990) Children's peer relationships: longitudinal prediction of internalizing and external-izing problems from middle to late childhood. *Child Development*, **61**, 2004–2021.

IMCTGM – The International Multicenter Clinical Trial Group on Moclobemide in social phobia (1997) Moclobemide in social phobia: a double-blind, placebo-controlled clinical study. *European Archives of Psychiatry & Clinical Neurosciences*, **247**, 71–80.

Irwin, W., Davidson, R., Lowe, M., Mock, B., Sorenson, J., & Turski, P. (1996) Human amygdala activation detected with echo-planar functional magnetic resonance imaging. *Neuroreport*, **7**, 1765–1769.

Ishiguro, H., Arinam, I. T., Yamada, K., Otsuka, Y., Toru, M., & Shibuya, H. (1997) An association study between a transcriptional polymorphism in the serotonin transporter gene and panic disorder in a Japanese population. *Psychiatry & Clinical Neurosciences*, **51**, 333–335.

Ishiyama, F. I. (1984) Shyness: anxious social sensitivity and self-isolating tendency. *Adolescence*, **19**, 903–911.

Izard, C. E., & Youngstrom, E. A. (1996) The activation and regulation of fear and anxiety. *Nebraska Symposium on Motivation*, **43**, 1–59.

James, B. (1997) Social phobia: a debilitating disease with a new treatment option – based on presentations at the XXth congress of the Collegium Internationale Neuro-Psychopharmacologicum. *International Clinical Psychopharmacology* **12** (Suppl. 6), S1.

Janet, P. (1903) *Les obsessions et la psychasthénie*. Paris: Alcan.

Janicak, P. G. (1999) *Handbook of psychopharmacotherapy*. Philadelphia: Lippincott, Williams, & Wilkins.

Jansen, M. A., Arntz, A., Merckelbach, H., & Mersch, P. P. A. (1994) Personality disorders and features in social phobia and panic disorder. *Journal of Abnormal Psychology*, **103**, 391–395.

Jason, L. A., Richman, J. A., Friedberg, F., Wagner, L., Raylor, R., & Jordan, K. M. (1997) Politics, science, and the emergence of a new disease. *American Psychologist*, **52**, 973–983.

Johnson, M., Marazziti, D., Brawman-Mintzer, O., Emmanuel, N. P., Ware, M. R., Rossi, A., Cassano, G. B., & Lydiard, R. B. (1998) Abnormal peripheral benzodiazepine receptor density associated with generalized social phobia. *Biological Psychiatry*, **43**, 306–309.

Jones, E. E., & Nisbett, R. E. (1971) *The actor and the observer: divergent perceptions of the causes of behavior*. Morristown, New Jersey: General Learning Press.

Juster, H. R., Heimberg, R. G., & Holt, C. S. (1996a) Social phobia: diagnostic issues and review of cognitive behavioral treatment strategies. *Progress in Behavior Modification*, **30**, 74–98.

Juster, H. R., Heimberg, R. G., Frost, R. O., Holt, C. S., Mattia, J. I., & Faccenda, K. (1996b) Social phobia and perfectionism. *Personality & Individual Differences*, **21**, 403–410.

Kachin, K. E., Newman, M. G., & Pincus, A. L. (2001) An interpersonal problem approach to the division of social phobia subtypes. *Behavior Therapy*, **32**, 479–501.

Kagan, J. (1989) Temperament contributions to social behavior. *American Psychologist*, **44**, 668–674.

Kagan, J., & Moss, H. A. (1962) *Birth to maturity: a study in psychological development*. New York: Wiley.

Kagan, J., & Snidman, N. (1991a) Infant predictors of inhibited and uninhibited profiles. *Psychological Science*, **2**, 40–44.

(1991b) Temperamental factors in human development. *American Psychologist*, **46**, 856–862.

Kagan, J., & Zentner, M. (1996) Early childhood predictors of adult psychopathology. *Harvard Review of Psychiatry*, **3**, 341–350.

Kagan, J., Reznick, J. S., Clarke, C., Snidman, N., & Garcia Coll, C. (1984) Behavioral inhibition to the unfamiliar. *Child Development*, **55**, 2212–2225.

Kagan, J., Reznick, J. S., & Snidman, N. (1987) The physiology and psychology of behavioral inhibition in children. *Child Development*, **58**, 1459–1473.

(1988) Biological bases of childhood shyness. *Science*, **240**, 167–171.

Kagan, J., Reznick, J. S., & Gibbons, J. (1989) Inhibited and uninhibited types of children. *Child Development*, **60**, 838–845.

Karen, R. (1998) *Becoming attached: first relationships and how they shape our capacity to love.* New York: Oxford University Press.

Kashani, J. H., & Orvaschel, H. (1988) Anxiety disorders in mid-adolescence: a community sample. *American Journal of Psychiatry*, **145**, 960–964.

Katzelnick, D. J., Kobak, K. A., Greist, J. H., Jefferson, J. W., Mantle, J. M., & Serlin, R. C. (1995) Sertraline for social phobia: a double-blind, placebo-controlled crossover study. *American Journal of Psychiatry*, **152**, 1368–1371.

Katzman, M., Koszycki, D., & Bradwejn, J. (2004) Effects of CCK-tetrapeptide in patients with social phobia and obsessive-compulsive disorder. *Depression & Anxiety*, **20**, 51–58.

Kaye, W. H., Bulik, C. M., Thornton, L., Barbarich, N., & Masters, K. (2004) Comorbidity of anxiety disorders with anorexia and bulimia nervosa. *American Journal of Psychiatry*, **161**, 2215–2221.

Keedwell, P., & Snaith, R. P. (1996) What do anxiety scales measure? *Acta Psychiatrica Scandinavica*, **93**, 177–180.

Keegan, J. (1988) *The mask of command.* Harmondsworth: Penguin.

Keller, M. B. (2003) The lifelong course of social anxiety disorder: a clinical perspective. *Acta Psychiatrica Scandinavica*, **108**, 85–94.

Kelman, H. C., & Hamilton, J. L. (1989) *Crimes of obedience: toward a social psychology of authority and responsibility.* New Haven: Yale University Press.

Keltner, D., & Buswell, B. N. (1997) Embarrassment: its distinct form and appeasement functions. *Psychological Bulletin*, **122**, 250–270.

Kemp Smith, N. (1941) *The philosophy of David Hume.* London, Macmillan

Kemper, T. D. (1978) *A social interactional theory of emotions.* New York: Wiley.

(2000) Social models in the explanation of emotions. In M. Lewis & J. M. Haviland-Jones (Eds.), *Handbook of emotions.* New York: Guilford Press, pp. 45–58.

Kemper, T. D., & Collins, R. (1990) Dimensions of microinteraction. *American Journal of Sociology*, **96**, 32–68.

Kendell, R. E. (1986) What are mental disorders? In A. M. Freedman, R. Brotman, I. Silverman & D. Hutson (Eds.), *Issues in psychiatric classification: science, practice and social policy.* New York: Human Sciences Press, pp. 23–45.

(1989) Clinical validity. *Psychological Medicine*, **19**, 45–55.

Kendler, K. A., Neale, M. C., Kessler, R. C., Heath, A. C., & Eaves, L. J. (1992) The genetic epidemiology of phobias in women: the interrelationship of agoraphobia, social phobia, situational phobia, and simple phobia. *Archives of General Psychiatry*, **49**, 273–281.

Kennedy, J., Neves-Pereira, M., King, N., Lizak, M., Basile, V., Chartier, M., & Stein, M. (2001) Dopamine system genes not linked to social phobia. *Psychiatric Genetics*, **11**, 213–217.

Kerr, M., Lambert, W. W., Stattin, H., & Klackenberg-Larssen, I. (1994) Stability of inhibition in a Swedish longitudinal sample. *Child Development*, **65**, 138–146.

Kessler, R. C., McGonagle, K. A., Zhao, S., Nelson, C. B., Hugues, M., Eshleman, S., Wittchen, H.-U., & Kendler, K. S. (1994) Lifetime and 12-month prevalence of DSM-III-R psychiatric disorders in the United States: results from the National Comorbidity Survey. *Archives of General Psychiatry*, *51*, 8–19.

Kessler, R. C., Davis, C. G., & Kendler, K. S. (1997) Childhood adversity and adult psychiatric disorder in the US national comorbidity survey. *Psychological Medicine*, *27*, 1101–1119.

Kessler, R. C., Stang, P., Wittchen, H.-U., Stein, M., & Walters, E. E. (1999) Lifetime comorbidities between social phobia and mood disorders in the US National Comorbidity Survey. *Psychological Medicine*, *29*, 555–567.

King, W. L. (1993) *Zen and the way of the sword.* Oxford: Oxford University Press.

Kirkby, K. C. (1996) Computer-assisted treatment of phobias. *Psychiatric Services*, *47*, 139–142.

Klein, D. (1993) False suffocation alarms, spontaneous panics, and related conditions: an integrative hypothesis. *Archives of General Psychiatry*, *50*, 306–317.

(2002) Response differences of spontaneous panic and fear. *Archives of General Psychiatry*, *59*, 567–569.

Klonsky, B. G., Dutton, D. L., & Liebel, C. N. (1990) Developmental antecedents of private self-consciousness, public self-consciousness and social anxiety. *Genetic, Social, & General Psychology Monographs*, *116*, 273–297.

Kobak, K. A., Greist, J. H., Jefferson, J. W., & Katzelnick, D. J. (2002) Fluoxetine in social phobia: a double-blind, placebo-controlled pilot study. *Journal of Psychopharmacology*, *22*, 257–262.

Kobak, K. A., Taylor, L. H., Warner, G., & Futterer, R. (2005) St John's Wort versus placebo in social phobia: results from a placebo-controlled pilot study. *Journal of Clinical Psychopharmacology*, *25*, 51–58.

Kochanska, G. (1991) Patterns of inhibition to the unfamiliar in children of normal and affectively ill mothers. *Child Development*, *62*, 250–263.

Kochanska, G., & Radke-Yarrow, M. (1992) Inhibition in toddlerhood and the dynamics of the child's interaction with an unfamiliar peer at age five. *Child Development*, *63*, 325–335.

Kollman, D. M., Brown, T. A., Liverant, G. I., & Hofmann, S. G. (2006) A taxometric investigation of the latent structure of social anxiety disorder in outpatients with anxiety and mood disorders. *Depression & Anxiety*, *23*, 190–199.

Kopelowicz, A., & Liberman, R. (1995) Biobehavioral treatment and rehabilitation of schizophrenia. *Harvard Review of Psychiatry*, *3*, 55–64.

Kringlen, E., Torgersen, S., & Cramer, V. (2001) A Norwegian psychiatric epidemiological study. *American Journal of Psychiatry*, *158*, 1091–1098.

La Greca, A. M., Dandes, S. K., Wick, P., Shaw, K., & Stone, W. L. (1988) Development of the Social Anxiety Scale for Children: reliability and concurrent validity. *Journal of Clinical Child Psychology*, *17*, 84–91.

Lacey, H. (1995) Teleological behaviorism and the intentional scheme. *Behavioral & Brain Sciences*, *18*, 134–135.

Lader, M., & Marks, I. M. (1971) *Clinical anxiety.* New York: Grune & Stratton.

Lader, M., Stender, K., Burger, V., & Nil, R. (2004) Efficacy and tolerability of escitalopram in 12- and 24-week treatment of social anxiety disorder: randomized, double-blind, placebo-controlled, fixed-dose study. *Depression & Anxiety*, **19**, 241–248.

Lamb, M. E., Thompson, R. A., Gardner, W. P., Charnov, E. L., & Estes, D. (1984) Security of infantile attachment as assessed in the "Strange Situation." *Behavioral & Brain Sciences*, **7**, 127–171.

Lampe, L., Slade, T., Issakidis, C., & Andrews, G. (2003) Social phobia in the Australian National Survey of Mental Health and Well-being. *Psychological Medecine*, **33**, 637–646.

Laufer, N., Zucker, M., Hermesh, H., Marom, S., Gilad, R., Nir, V., Weizman, A., & Rehavi, M. (2005) Platelet vesicular monoamine transporter density in untreated patients diagnosed with social phobia. *Psychiatry Research*, **136**, 247–250.

Lazarus, P. J. (1982) Incidence of shyness in elementary school age children. *Psychological Reports*, **51**, 904–906.

Leary, M. R. (1983) Social anxiousness: the construct and its measurement. *Journal of Personality Assessment*, **47**, 66–75.

Lecrubier, Y., & Weiller, E. (1997) Comorbidities in social phobia. *International Clinical Psychopharmacology*, **12**, S17–S21.

Lederman, R. J. (1989) Performing arts medicine. *New England Journal of Medicine*, **320**, 221–227.

LeDoux, J. (1996) *The emotional brain.* New York: Simon & Schuster.

Lee, C. K., Kwak, Y. S., Yamamoto, J., Rhee, H., Kim, Y. S., Han, J. H., Choi, J. O., & Lee, Y. H. (1990a) Psychiatric epidemiology in Korea: Part 1. Gender and age differences in Seoul. *Journal of Nervous & Mental Disorders*, **178**, 242–246.

(1990b) Psychiatric epidemiology in Korea. Part II. Urban and rural differences. *Journal of Nervous & Mental Disorders*, **178**, 247–252.

Lelliott, P., McNamee, G., & Marks, I. M. (1991) Features of agora, social, and related phobias and validation of the diagnoses. *Journal of Anxiety Disorders*, **5**, 313–322.

Lépine, J. P., & Lellouch, J. (1995) Classification and epidemiology of social phobia. *European Archives of Psychiatry & Clinical Neuroscience*, **244**, 290–296.

Lépine, J. P., Wittchen, H.-U., Essau, C. A., & participants of the WHO/ ADAMHA CIDI field trials (1993) Lifetime and current comorbidity of anxiety and affective disorders: results from the international WHO/ ADAMHA CIDI field trials. *International Journal of Methods in Psychiatric Research*, **3**, 67–77.

Lepola, U., Bergtholdt, B., St. Lambert, J., Davy, K. L., & Ruggiero, L. (2004) Controlled-release paroxetine in the treatment of patients with social anxiety disorder. *Journal of Clinical Psychiatry*, **65**, 222–229.

Lesch, K., Bengel, D., Heils, A., Sabol, S., Greenberg, B., Petri, S., Benjamin, J., Muller, C., Hamer, D., & Murphy, D. (1996) Association of anxiety-related traits with a polymorphism in the serotonin transporter gene regulatory region. *Science*, **274**, 1527–1531.

Leung, A. W., & Heimberg, R. G. (1996) Homework compliance, perceptions of control, and outcome of cognitive-behavioral treatment of social phobia. *Behavior Research & Therapy*, *34*, 423–432.

Leung, A. W., Heimberg, R. G., Holt, C. H., & Bruch, M. A. (1994) Social anxiety and perception of early parenting among American, Chinese American and social phobic samples. *Anxiety*, *1*, 80–89.

Levenson, R. W. (1999) The intrapersonal functions of emotion. *Cognition & Emotion*, *13*, 481–504.

Levin, A. P., Saoud, J. B., Strauman, T., Gorman, J. M., Fyer, A. J., Crawford, R., & Liebowitz, M. R. (1993) Responses of generalized and discrete social phobics during public speaking. *Journal of Anxiety Disorders*, *7*, 207–221.

Levitt, E. E. (1980) *The psychology of anxiety*. Hillsdale, New Jersey: Lawrence Erlbaum.

Lewinsohn, P. M. (1974) Clinical and theoretical aspects of depression. In K. S. Calhoun, H. E. Adams & K. M. Mitchell (Eds.), *Innovative treatment methods in psychopathology*. New York: Wiley, pp. 63–120.

Lewis, A. (1967) Problems presented by the ambiguous word "anxiety" as used in psychopathology. *The Israel Annals of Psychiatry & Related Disciplines*, *5*, 105–121.

Liberzon, I., & Phan, K. (2003) Brain-imaging studies of posttraumatic stress disorder. *CNS Spectrum.*, *8*, 641–650.

Libet, J. M., & Lewinsohn, P. M. (1973) Concept of social skills with special reference to the behavior of depressed persons. *Journal of Consulting & Clinical Psychology*, *40*, 304–312.

Lieb, R., Wittchen, H. U., Hofler, M., Fuetsch, M., Stein, M. B., Merikangas, K. R. (2000) Parental psychopathology, parenting styles, and the risk of social phobia in offspring: a prospective-longitudinal community study. *Archives of General Psychiatry*, *57*, 859–866.

Liebowitz, M. R. (1987) Social phobia. In D. F. Klein (Ed.), *Modern problems of pharmacopsychiatry: anxiety*. Volume 22, New York: Karger.

Liebowitz, M. R., Gorman, J., Fyer, A., & Klein, D. (1985) Social phobia: review of a neglected anxiety disorder. *Archives of General Psychiatry*, *42*, 729–736.

Liebowitz, M. R., Schneier, F., Campeas, R., Hollander, E., Hatterer, J., Fyer, A., Gorman, J., Papp, L., Davies, S., Gully, R., & Klein, D. F. (1992). Phenelzine vs. atenolol in social phobia. *Archives of General Psychiatry*, *49*, 290–300.

Liebowitz, M. R., Heimberg, R. G., Shneier, F. R., Hope, D. A., Davies, S., Holt, C. S., Goetz, D., Juster, H. R., Lin, S. H., Bruch, M. A., Marshall, R. D., & Klein, D. F. (1999) Cognitive-behavioral group therapy versus phenelzine in social phobia: long term outcome. *Depression & Anxiety*, *10*, 89–98.

Liebowitz, M. R., Heimberg, R. G., Fresco, D. M., Travers, J., & Stein, M. B. (2000) Social phobia or social anxiety disorder: what's in a name? *Archives of General Psychiatry*, *57*, 191–192.

Liebowitz, M. R., Stein, M. B., Tancer, M., Carpenter, D., Oakes, R., & Pitts, C. D. (2002) A randomized, double-blind, fixed-dose comparison of paroxetine and placebo in the treatment of generalized social anxiety disorder. *Journal of Clinical Psychiatry*, *63*, 66–74.

Liebowitz, M. R., DeMartinis, N. A., Weihs, K., Londborg, P. D., Smith, W. T., Chung, H., Fayyad, R., & Clary, C. M. (2003) Efficacy of sertraline in severe generalized social anxiety disorder: results of a double-blind, placebo-controlled study. *Journal of Clinical Psychiatry*, *64*, 785–792.

Liebowitz, M. R., Gelenberg, A. J., & Munjack, D. (2005a) Venlafaxine extended release vs. placebo and paroxetine in social anxiety disorder. *Archives of General Psychiatry*, *62*, 190–198.

Liebowitz, M. R., Mangano, R. M., Bradwejn, J., & Asnis, G. (2005b) A randomized controlled trial of venlafaxine extended release in generalized social anxiety disorder. *Journal of Clinical Psychiatry*, *66*, 238–247.

Lima, S. L., & Dill, L. M. (1989) Behavioural decisions made under the risk of predation: a review and prospectus. *Canadian Journal of Zoology*, *68*, 619–640.

Lindal, E., & Stefanson, J. G. (1993) The lifetime prevalence of anxiety disorders in Iceland as estimated by the US National Institute of Mental Health Diagnostic Interview Schedule. *Acta Psychiatrica Scandinavica*, *88*, 29–34.

Lipowski, Z. J. (1989). Psychiatry: mindless or brainless, both or neither? *Canadian Journal of Psychiatry*, *34*, 249–254.

Lobitz, W. C., & LoPiccolo, J. (1972) New methods in the behavioral treatment of sexual dysfunction. *Journal of Behavior Therapy & Experimental Psychiatry*, *3*, 275–281.

Looren de Jong, H. (1997) Some remarks on a relational concept of mind. *Theory and Psychology*, *7*, 147–172.

(2000) Genetic determinism: how not to interpret behavioral genetics. *Theory & Psychology*, *10*, 615–637.

Lorberbaum, J., Kose, S., Johnson, M., Arana, G., Sullivan, L., Hamner, M., Ballenger, J., Lydiard, R., Brodrick, P., Bohning, D., & George, M. (2004) Neural correlates of speech anticipatory anxiety in generalized social phobia. *Neuroreport*, *5*, 2701–2705.

Lott, M., Greist, J. H., Jefferson, J. W., Kobak, K. A., Katzelnick, D. J., Katz, R. J., & Schaettle, S. C. (1997) Brofaromine for social phobia: a multi-center, placebo-controlled, double-blind study. *Journal of Clinical Psychopharmacology*, *17*, 255–260.

Lourenço, O. (2001) The danger of words: a Wittgensteinian lesson for developmentalists. *New Ideas in Psychology*, *19*, 89–115.

Lucock, M. P., & Salkovskis, P. M. (1988) Cognitive factors in social anxiety and its treatment. *Behaviour Research & Therapy*, *26*, 297–302.

Lundh, L. G., & Öst, L. G. (1996a) Stroop interference, self-focus and perfectionism in social phobics. *Personality & Individual Differences*, *20*, 725–731.

(1996b) Memory bias for critical faces in social phobics. *Behaviour Research & Therapy*, *34*, 787–794.

(1997) Explicit and implicit memory bias in social phobia: the role of subdiagnostic type. *Behaviour Research & Therapy*, *35*, 305–317.

MacDonald, G., & Leary, M. R. (2005) Why does social exclusion hurt? The relationship between social and physical pain. *Psychological Bulletin*, *131*, 202–223.

MacLeod, C. (1991) Clinical anxiety and the selective encoding of threatening information. *International Review of Psychiatry*, *3*, 279–292.

Maes, M., Meltzer, H., D'Hondt, P., Cosyns, P., & Blockx, P. (1995) Effects of serotonin precursors on the negative feedback effects of glucocorticoids on hypothalamic-pituitary-adrenal axis function in depression. *Psychoneuroendocrinology*, *20*, 149–167.

Maes, M., van West, D., De Vos, N., Westenberg, H., Van Hunsel, F., Hendriks, D., Cosyns, P., & Scharpe, S. (2001) Lower baseline plasma cortisol and prolactin together with increased body temperature and higher mCPP-induced cortisol responses in men with pedophilia. *Neuropsychopharmacology*, *24*, 37–46.

Magee, W. J. (1999) Effects of negative life experiences on phobia onset. *Social Psychiatry & Psychiatric Epidemiology*, *34*, 343–351.

Magee, W. J., Eaton, W. W., Wittchen, H. U., Mcgonagle, K. A., & Kessler, R. C. (1996) Agoraphobia, simple phobia and social phobia in the National Comorbidity Survey. *Archives of General Psychiatry*, *53*, 159–168.

Malcolm, N. (1977) The myth of cognitive processes and structures. In T. Mischel (Ed.), *Cognitive development and epistemology*. New York: Academic Press, pp. 385–392.

Manassis, K., Bradley, S., Goldberg, S., Hood, J., & Swinson, R. P. (1995) Behavioural inhibition, attachment and anxiety in children of mothers with anxiety disorders. *Canadian Journal of Psychiatry*, *40*, 87–92.

Mancini, C., van Ameringen, M., & MacMillan, H. (1995) Relationship of childhood sexual and physical abuse to anxiety disorders. *Journal of Nervous and Mental Disease*, *183*, 309–314.

Mancini, C., van Ameringen, M., Szatmari, P., Fugere, C., & Boyle, M. (1996) A high-risk pilot study of the children of adults with social phobia. *Journal of the American Academy of Child & Adolescent Psychiatry*, *35*, 1511–1517.

Mandelstam, N. (1970) *Hope against hope*. New York: Atheneum.

Mangelsdorf, S., Gunnar, M., Kestenbaum, R., Lang, S., & Andreas, D. (1990) Infant proneness-to-distress temperament, maternal personality and mother–infant attachment: associations and goodness of fit. *Child Development*, *61*, 820–831.

Manicavasagar, V., Silove, D., & Hadzi-Pavlovic, D. (1998) Subpopulations of early separation anxiety: relevance to risk of adult anxiety disorders. *Journal of Affective Disorders*, *48*, 181–190.

Mannuzza, S., Fyer, A. J., Martin, L. Y., Gallops, M. S., Endicott, J., Gorman, J., Liebowitz, M. R., & Klein, D. F. (1989) Reliability of anxiety assessment (I): diagnostic agreement. *Archives of General Psychiatry*, *46*, 1093–1101.

Mannuzza, S., Chapman, T. F., Martin, L. Y., & Klein, F. (1995a) Specificity in familial aggregation of phobic disorders. *Archives of General Psychiatry*, *52*, 564–573.

Mannuzza, S., Schneier, F. R., Chapman, T. F., Liebowitz, M. R., Klein, D. F., & Fyer, A. J. (1995b) Generalized social phobia: reliability and validity. *Archives of General Psychiatry*, *52*, 230–237.

Marks, I. M. (1985) Behavioral treatment of social phobia. *Psychopharmacology*, **21**, 615–618.

(1987) *Fears, phobias and rituals*. New York: Oxford University Press.

(1994) Behavior therapy as an aid to self-care. *Current Directions in Psychological Science*, **3**, 19–22.

Marks, I. M., & Dar, R. (2002) Fear reduction by psychotherapies. *British Journal of Psychiatry*, **176**, 507–511.

Marks, I. M., & Gelder, M. G. (1966) Different ages of onset of varieties of phobia. *American Journal of Psychiatry*, **123**, 218–221.

Martel, F., Hayward, C., Lyons, D., Sanborn, K., Varady, S., & Schatzberg, A. (1999) Salivary cortisol levels in socially phobic adolescent girls. *Depression & Anxiety*, **10**, 25–27.

Masia, C. L., Morris, T. L. (1998) Parental factors associated with social anxiety; methodological limitations and suggestions for integrated behavioral research. *Clinical Psychology: Science & Practice*, **5**, 211–228.

Mason, W. A., Kosterman, R., Hawkins, J. D., Herrenkohl, T. I., Lengua, L. J., & McCauley, E. (2004) Predicting depression, social phobia, and violence in early adulthood from childhood behavior problems. *Journal of the American Academy of Child & Adolescent Psychiatry*, **43**, 307–315.

Matheny, A. P. (1989) Children's behavioral inhibition over age and across situations: genetic similarity for a trait during change. *Journal of Personality*, **57**, 215–235.

Mattia, J. I., Heimberg, R. G., & Hope, D. A. (1993) The revised Stroop color-naming task in social phobics. *Behavior Research & Therapy*, **31**, 305–313.

Mattick, R. P., & Clarke, J. C. (1998) Development and validation of measures of social phobia scrutiny fear and social interaction anxiety. *Behaviour Research & Therapy*, **36**, 455–470.

Mattick, R. P., & Peters, L. (1988) Treatment of severe social phobia: effects of guided exposure with and without cognitive restructuring. *Journal of Consulting & Clinical Psychology*, **56**, 251–260.

Mattick, R. P., Peters, L., & Clarke, J. C. (1989) Exposure and cognitive restructuring for social phobia: a controlled study. *Behavior Therapy*, **20**, 3–23.

Mauss, I. B., Wilhelm, F. H., & Gross, J. J. (2003) Autonomic recovery and habituation in social anxiety. *Psychophysiology*, **40**, 648–653.

May, R. (1979) *The meaning of anxiety*. New York: Washington Square Press.

Mayr, E. (1974) Behavior programs and evolutionary strategies, *American Scientist*, **62**, 650–659.

Mazower, M. (2002) Violence and the state in the twentieth century. *American Historical Review*, **107**, 1158–1178.

McCabe, R. E., Antony, M. M., Summerfeldt, L. J., Liss, A., & Swinson, R. P. (2003) Preliminary examination of the relationship between anxiety disorders in adults and self-reported history of teasing or bullying experiences. *Cognitive Behavior Therapy*, **32**, 187–193.

McCann, U., Slate, S., Geraci, M., Roscow-Terrill, D., & Uhde, T. (1997) A comparison of the effects of intravenous pentagastrin on patients with social phobia, panic disorder and healthy controls. *Neuropsychopharmacology*, **16**, 229–237.

McFall, R. M. (1982) A review and reformulation of the concept of social skills. *Behavioral Assessment, 4,* 1–33.

McFall, R. M., & Townsend, J. T. (1998) Foundations of psychological assessment: implications for cognitive assessment in clinical science. *Psychological Assessment, 10,* 316–330.

McFall, R. M., Treat, T. A., & Viken, R. J. (1998) Contemporary cognitive approaches to studying clinical problems. In D. K. Routh & R. J. De Rubeis (Eds.), *The science of clinical psychology.* Washington, District of Columbia: American Psychological Association, pp.163–197.

McGee, R., Feehan, M., Williams, S., Partridge, F., Silva, P. A., & Kelly, J. (1990) DSM-III disorders in a large sample of adolescents. *Journal of the American Academy of Child & Adolescent Psychiatry, 29,* 611–619.

McNally, R. J. (1995) Automaticity and the anxiety disorders. *Behaviour Research & Therapy, 33,* 747–754.

McNamara, J. R., & Blumer, C. A. (1982) Role playing to assess social competence. Ecological validity considerations. *Behavior Modification, 6,* 519–549.

McNeil, D. W., Turk, C. L., & Ries, B. J. (1994) Anxiety and fear. In V. S. Ramachandran (Ed.), *Encyclopedia of human behavior.* Volume *1,* La Jolla, California: Academic Press, pp. 151–167.

McNeil, D. W., Ries, D. J., & Turk, C. L. (1995) Behavioral assessment: self-report, physiology, and overt behavior. In R. G. Heimberg, M. R. Liebowitz, D. A. Hope, & F. R. Schneier (Eds.), *Social phobia: diagnosis, assessment and treatment,* New York: Guilford, 202–231.

Medawar, P. B. (1977) Unnatural science. *The New York Review of Books, February, 3,* 13–18.

Meichenbaum, D. (1977) *Cognitive-behavior modification: an integrative approach.* NewYork: Plenum Press.

Melke, J., Landen, M., Baghei, F., Rosmond, R., Holm, G., Bjorntorp, P., Westberg, L., Hellstrand, M., & Eriksson, E. (2001) Serotonin transporter gene polymorphisms are associated with anxiety-related personality traits in women. *American Journal of Medical Genetics, 105,* 458–463.

Mennin, D. S., Heimberg, R. G., & Jack, M. S. (2000) Comorbid generalized anxiety disorder in primary social phobia: symptom severity, functional impairment, and treatment response. *Journal of Anxiety Disorders, 14,* 325–343.

Merikangas, K. R., Avenevoli, S., Acharyya, S., Zhang, H., & Angst, J. (2002) The spectrum of social phobia in the Zurich Cohort Study of young adults. *Biological Psychiatry, 51,* 81–91.

Mersch, P. P. A. (1995) The treatment of social phobia: the differential effectiveness of exposure in vivo and an integration of exposure in vivo, rational emotive therapy and social skills training. *Behaviour Research & Therapy, 33,* 259–269.

Mersch, P. P. A., Emmelkamp, P. M. G., Bogels, S. M., & van der Sleen, J. (1989) Social phobia: individual response patterns and the effects of behavioral and cognitive interventions. *Behaviour Research & Therapy, 27,* 421–434.

Mersch, P. P. A., Emmelkamp, P. M. G., & Lips, C. (1991) Social phobia: individual response patterns and the long-term effects of behavioral and cognitive interventions. A follow-up study. *Behavior Research & Therapy*, **29**, 357–362.

Mersch, P. P. A., Hildebrand, M., Mavy, E. H., Wessel, L., & van Hout, W. J. P. J. (1992a) Somatic symptoms in social phobia: a treatment method based on rational emotive therapy and paradoxical interventions. *Journal of Behaviour Therapy & Experimental Psychiatry*, **23**, 199–211.

Mersch, P. P. A., Breukers, P., & Emmelkamp, P. M. G. (1992b) The Simulated Social Interaction Test: a psychometric evaluation with Dutch social phobic patients. *Behavioral Assessment*, **14**, 133–151.

Mersch, P. P. A., Jansen, M. A., & Arntz, A. (1995) Social phobia and personality disorder: severity of complaint and treatment effectiveness. *Journal of Personality Disorders*, **9**, 143–159.

Michels, R., Frances, A., & Shear, M. K. (1985) Psychodynamic models of anxiety. In A. H. Tuma & J. D. Maser (Eds.), *Anxiety and the anxiety disorders*. Hillside, New Jersey: Lawrence Erlbaum, pp. 595–609.

Mick, M. A., & Telch, M. J. (1998) Social anxiety and history of behavioral inhibition in young adults. *Journal of Anxiety Disorders*, **12**, 1–20.

Millan, M. (2003) The neurobiology and control of anxious states. *Progress in Neurobiology*, **70**, 83–244.

Millon, T., & Martinez, A. (1995) Avoidant personality disorder. In W. J. Livesley (Ed.), *The DSM-IV personality disorders*. New York: Guilford Press, pp. 218–233.

Mineka, S., & Kihlstrom, J. (1978) Unpredictable and uncontrolled aversive events and experimental neurosis. *Journal of Abnormal Psychology*, **85**, 256–271.

Misslin, R. (2003) The defense system of fear: behavior and neurocircuitry. *Neurophysiologie Clinique*, **33**, 55–66.

Moerman, D. (2002) *Meaning medicine and the placebo effect*. Cambridge: Cambridge University Press.

Mooij, A. (1995) Towards an anthropological psychiatry. *Theoretical Medicine*, **16**, 73–91.

Morey, L. C. (1991) Classification of mental disorder as a collection of hypothetical constructs. *Journal of Abnormal Psychology*, **100**, 289–293.

Mousnier, R. (1969) *Les hiérarchies sociales de 1450 à nos jours*. Paris: Presses Universitaires de France.

Moynihan, R. (2002) Drug firms hype disease: a sales ploy, industry chief claims. *British Medical Journal*, **324**, 867.

Moynihan, R., Heath, I., & Henry, D. (2002) Selling sickness: the parmaceutical industry and disease mongering. *British Medical Journal*, **324**, 886–891.

Muris, P., Merckelbach, H., Meesters, C., & van Lier, P. (1997) What do children fear most often? *Journal of Behavior Therapy & Experimental Psychiatry*, **28**, 263–267.

Muris, P., Merckelbach, H., Wessel, I., & van de Ven, M. (1999) Psychopathological correlates of self-reported behavioural inhibition in normal children. *Behaviour Research & Therapy*, **37**, 575–584.

Myerson, A. (1945) The social anxiety neurosis: its possible relationship to schizophrenia. *American Journal of Psychiatry*, **101**, 149–156.

Nahshoni, E., Gur, S., Marom, S., Levin, J., Weizman, A., & Hermesh, H. (2004) QT dispersion in patients with social phobia. *Journal of Affective Disorders*, **78**, 21–26.

Naimark, N. M. (2002) *Fires of hatred: ethnic cleansing in twentieth-century Europe.* Harvard: Harvard University Press.

Nardi, A. E., Valença, A. M., Nascimento, I., Mezzasalma, M. A., & Zin, W. A. (2001) Hyperventilation in panic disorder and social phobia. *Psychopathology*, **34**, 123–127.

Neftel, K., Adler, R., Kappeli, L., Rossi, M., Dolder, M., Kaser, H., & Brugesser, H. (1982) Stage fright in musicians: a model illustrating the effect of beta blockers. *Psychosomatic Medicine*, **44**, 461–469.

Nelson, E. C., Grant, J. D., Bucholz, K. K., Glowinski, A., Madden, P. A. F., Reich, W., & Heath, A. C. (2000) Social phobia in a population-based female adolescent twin sample: comorbidity and associated suicide-related symptoms. *Psychological Medicine*, **30**, 797–804.

Nelson-Gray, R. O. (1991) DSM-IV: empirical guidelines from psychometrics. *Journal of Abnormal Psychology*, **100**, 308–315.

Neufeld, K. J., Swartz, K. L., Bienvenu, O. J., Eaton, W. W., & Cai, E. G. (1999) Incidence of DIS/DSM-IV social phobia in adults. *Acta Psychiatrica Scandinavica*, **100**, 186–192.

Newell, R., & Marks, I. (2000) Phobic nature of social difficulty in facially disfigured people. *British Journal of Psychiatry*, **176**, 177–181.

Newman, M. G., Hofmann, S. G., Trabert, W., Roth, W. T., & Taylor, C. B. (1994) Does behavioral treatment of social phobia lead to cognitive changes? *Behavior Therapy*, **25**, 503–517.

Newman, M. G., Shapira, B., & Lerer, B. (1998) Evaluation of central serotonergic function in affective and related disorders by the fenfluramine challenge test: a critical review. *International Journal of Neuropsychopharmacology*, **1**, 49–69.

Nickell, P. V., & Uhde, T. W. (1995) Neurobiology of social phobia. In R. G. Heimberg, M. R. Liebowitz, D. A. Hope & F. R. Schneier (Eds.), *Social phobia: diagnosis, assessment, and treatment.* New York: Guilford Press, pp. 113–133.

Noyes, R., & Hoehn-Saric, R. (1998) *The anxiety disorders.* Cambridge: Cambridge University Press.

Noyes, R., Woodman, C. L., Holt, C. S., Reich, J. H., & Zimmerman, M. B. (1995) Avoidant personality traits distinguishing social phobic and panic disorder subjects. *Journal of Nervous & Mental Disease*, **183**, 145–153.

Noyes, R., Moroz, G., Davidson, J. R., Liebowitz, M. R., Davidson, A., Siegel, J., et al. (1997) Moclobemide in social phobia: a controlled dose-response trial. *Journal of Clinical Psychopharmacology*, **17**, 247–254.

Nutt, D., Bell, C., & Malizia, A. (1998) Brain mechanisms of social anxiety disorder. *Journal of Clinical Psychiatry*, **59** (Suppl. 17), 4–11.

Oatley, K. (1992) Human emotions: function and dysfunction. *Annual Review of Psychology*, **43**, 55–85.

Oei, T. P. S., Kenna, D., & Evans, L. (1991) The reliability, validity and utility of the SAD and FNE scales for anxiety disorder patients. *Personality & Individual Differences*, *12*, 111–116.

Offord, D. R., Boyle, M. H., Campbell, D. C., Goering, P., Lin, E., Wong, M., & Racine, Y. A. (1996) One-year prevalence of psychiatric disorders in Ontarians 15 to 64 years of age. *Canadian Journal of Psychiatry*, *41*, 559–563.

Ohman, A. (2000) Fear and anxiety: evolutionary, cognitive and clinical perspectives. In M. Lewis & J. M. Haviland-Jones (Eds.), *Handbook of emotions*. New York: Guilford Press, pp. 573–593.

Ollendick, T. H., Matson, J. L., & Helsel, W. J. (1985) Fears in children and adolescents: normative data. *Behaviour Research & Therapy*, *23*, 465–467.

Ollendick, T. H., Neville, J. K., & Frary, R. B. (1989) Fears in children and adolescents: reliability and generalizability across gender, age and nationality. *Behaviour Research & Therapy*, *27*, 19–26.

Olweus, D. (1993) Victimization by peers: antecedents and long-term outcomes. In K. H. F Rubin & J. B. Asendorf (Eds.), *Social withdrawal, inhibition and shyness in childhood*. Hillsdale, New Jersey: Lawrence Erlbaum.

Orvaschel, H. (1994) *Schedule for affective disorders and schizophrenia for school-age children-epidemiologic version (K-SADS-E)*. 5th edn. Fort Lauderdale, Florida: Nova Southeastern University, Center for Psychological Studies.

Otto, M. W., Pollack, M. H., Gould, R. A., Worthington, J. J., McArdle, E. T., & Rosenbaum, J. F. (2000) A comparison of the efficacy of clonazepam and cognitive-behavioral group therapy for the treatment of social phobia. *Journal of Anxiety Disorders*, *14*, 345–358.

Oxford English Dictionary (1972) Oxford: Oxford University Press.

Page, A. C. (1994) Distinguish panic disorder and agoraphobia from social phobia. *Journal of Nervous & Mental Disease*, *182*, 611–617.

Pakriev, S., Vasar, V., Aluoja, A., & Shlick, J. (2000) Prevalence of social phobia in the rural population of Udmurtia. *Nordic Journal of Psychiatry*, *54*, 109–112.

Pande, A. C., Davidson, J. R. T., Jefferson, J. W., Janney, C. A., Katzelnick, D. J., Weisler, R. H., Greist, J. H., & Sutherland, S. M. (1999) Treatment of social phobia with gabapentin: a placebo-controlled study. *Journal of Clinical Psychopharmacology*, *19*, 341–348.

Pande, A. C., Feltner, D. E., Jefferson, J. W., Davidson, J. R. T., Pollack, M., Stein, M. B. et al. (2004) Efficacy of novel anxiolytic pregabalin in social anxiety disorder: a placebo-controlled, multicenter study. *Journal of Clinical Psychopharmacology*, *24*, 141–149.

Papadimitriou, G. N., & Linkowski, P. (2005) Sleep disturbance in anxiety disorders. *International Review of Psychiatry*, *17*, 229–236.

Papp, L., Gorman, J., Liebowitz, M., Fyer, A., Cohen, B., & Klein, D. (1988) Epinephrine infusion in patients with social phobia. *American Journal of Psychiatry*, *145*, 733–736.

Papp, L., Klein, D., & Martinez, J. (1993) Diagnostic and substance specificity of carbon dioxide-induced panic. *American Journal of Psychiatry*, *150*, 250–257.

Parker, G. (1979) Reported parental characteristics of agoraphobics and social phobics. *British Journal of Psychiatry*, *135*, 555–560.

Parker, I. (1996) Against Wittgenstein: materialist reflections on language in psychology. *Theory & Psychology*, *6*, 363–384.

Parker, K., Schatzberg, A., & Lyons, D. (2003) Neuroendocrine aspects of hypercortisolism in major depression. *Hormones & Behaviour*, *43*, 60–66.

Patel, A., Knapp, M., Henderson, J., & Baldwin, D. (2002) The economic consequences of social phobia. *Journal of Affective Disorders*, *68*, 221–233.

Pato, M. T., Zohar-Kadouch, R., Zohar, J., & Murphy, D. L. (1988) Return of symptoms after discontinuation of clomipramine in patients with obsessive-compulsive disorder. *American Journal of Psychiatry*, *145*, 1521–1525.

Paxton, R. O. (2004) *The anatomy of fascism*. New York: Knopf.

Pedersen, D. (2002) Political violence, ethnic conflict, and contemporary wars: broad implications for health and social well-being. *Social Science & Medicine*, *55*, 175–190.

Pélissolo, A., & Lépine, J. P. (1995) Les phobies sociales: perspectives historiques et conceptuelles. *L'Encéphale*, *21*, 15–24.

Pélissolo, A., André, C., Moutard-Martin, F., Wittchen, H. U., & Lépine, J. P. (2000) Social phobia in the community: relationship between diagnostic threshold and prevalence. *European Psychiatry*, *15*, 25–28.

Perez-Lopez, J. R., & Woody, S. R. (2001) Memory for facial expressions in social phobia. *Behaviour Research & Therapy*, *39*, 967–975.

Perugi, G., Simonini, E., Savino, M., Mengali, F., Cassano, G. B., & Akiskal, H. S. (1990) Primary and secondary social phobia: psychopathologic and familial differentiations. *Comprehensive Psychiatry*, *31*, 245–252.

Perugi, G., Nassini, S., Socci, C., Lenzi, M., Toni, C., Simonini, E., & Akistal, H. S. (1999) Avoidant personality in social phobia and panic-agoraphobic disorder: a comparison. *Journal of Affective Disorders*, *54*, 277–282.

Perugi, G., Frare, F., Toni, C., Mata, B., & Akiskal, H. S. (2001) Bipolar II and unipolar comorbidity in 153 outpatients with social phobia. *Comprehensive Psychiatry*, *42*, 375–381.

Philippot, P., & Douilliez, C. (2005) Social phobics do not misinterpret facial expression of emotion. *Behaviour Research & Therapy*, *43*, 639–652.

Pine, D. S., Cohen, P., Gurley, D., Brook, J., & Ma, Y. (1998) The risk for early-adulthood anxiety and depressive disorders in adolescents with anxiety and depressive disorders. *Archives of General Psychiatry*, *55*, 56–64.

Pini, S., Cassano, G. B., Simonini, E., Savino, M., Russo, A., & Montgomery, S. A. (1997) Prevalence of anxiety disorders comorbidity in bipolar depression, unipolar depression and dysthymia. *Journal of Affective Disorders*, *42*, 145–153.

Plomin, R., & Rowe, D. C. (1979) Genetic and environment etiology of social behavior in infancy. *Developmental Psychology*, *15*, 62–72.

Plomin, R., DeFries, J. C., & McClearn, G. E. (1990) *Behavioral genetics*. New York: W.H. Freeman.

Pollard, C. A., & Henderson, J. G. (1988) Four types of social phobia in a community sample. *The Journal of Nervous & Mental Disease*, *176*, 440–445.

Potts, N. L., Davidson, J. R., Krishnan, K. R., Doraiswamy, P. M., & Ritchie, J. C. (1991) Levels of urinary free cortisol in social phobia. *Journal of Clinical Psychiatry*, **52**, 41–42.

Potts, N. L., Davidson, J., Krishnan, K., & Doraiswamy, P. (1994) Magnetic resonance imaging in social phobia. *Psychiatry Research*, **52**, 35–42.

Poulton, R., Trainor, P., Stanton, W., McGee, R., Davies, S., & Silva, P. (1997) The (in)stability of adolescent fears. *Behaviour Research & Therapy*, **35**, 159–163.

Pribor, E. F., & Dinwiddie, S. H. (1992) Psychiatric correlates of incest in childhood. *American Journal of Psychiatry*, **149**, 52–56.

Purdon, C., Antony, M., Monteiro, S., & Swinson, R. P. (2001) Social anxiety in college students. *Journal of Anxiety Disorders*, **15**, 203–215.

Putallaz, M. (1987) Maternal behavior and children's sociometric status. *Child Development*, **58**, 324–340.

Putman, D. (1997) Psychological courage. *Philosophy, Psychiatry, & Psychology*, **4**, 1–11.

Quine, W. (1960) *Word and object*. Cambridge, Massachusetts: MIT Press.

Rachlin, H. (1992) Teleological behaviorism. *American Psychologist*. **47**, 1371–1382.

——— (1995) Self-control: beyond commitment. *Behavioral & Brain Sciences*, **18**, 109–159.

Rapee, R. M., & Lim, L. (1992) Discrepancy between self- and observer ratings of performance in social phobics. *Journal of Abnormal Psychology*, **101**, 728–731.

Rapee, R. M., & Melville, L. F. (1997) Recall of family factors in social phobia and panic disorder: comparison of mother and offspring reports. *Depression & Anxiety*, **5**, 7–11.

Rapee, R. M., Mattick, R., & Murrell, E. (1986) Cognitive mediation in the affective component of spontaneous panic attacks. *Journal of Behavior Therapy & Experimental Psychiatry*, **17**, 245–253.

Rapee, R. M., Sanderson, W. C., & Barlow, D. H. (1988) Social phobia features across the DSM-III-R anxiety disorders. *Journal of Psychopathology & Behavioral Assessment*, **10**, 287–299.

Rapee, R. M., McCallum, S. L., Melville, L. F., Ravenscroft, H., & Rodney, J. M. (1994) Memory bias in social phobia. *Behaviour Research & Therapy*, **32**, 89–99.

Regier, D. A., Rae, D. S., Narrow, W. E., Kaelber, C. T., & Schatzberg, A. F. (1998) Prevalence of anxiety disorders and their comorbidity with mood and addictive disorders. *British Journal of Psychiatry*, **173**, 24–28.

Reich, J., & Yates, W. (1988) Family history of psychiatric disorders in social phobia. *Comprehensive Psychiatry*, **29**, 72–75.

Reinherz, H. Z., Giaconia, R. M., Lefkowitz, E. S., Pakiz, B., & Frost, A. K. (1993) Prevalence of psychiatric disorders in a community population of older adolescents. *Journal of the American Academy of Child & Adolescent Psychiatry*, **32**, 369–377.

Reiss, D., & Neiderhiser, J. M. (2000) The interplay of genetic influences and social processes in developmental theory: specific mechanisms are coming into view. *Development & Psychopathology*, **12**, 357–374.

Renken, B., Egeland, B., Marvinney, D., Mangelsdorf, S., & Sroufe, L. A. (1989) Early childhood antecedents of aggression and passive-withdrawal in early elementary school. *Journal of Personality*, *57*, 257–281.

Rettew, D. C., Zanarini, M. C., Yen, S., Grilo, C. M., Skodol, A. E., Shea, T., McGlashan, T. H., Morey, L. C., Culhane, M. A., & Gunderson, J. G. (2003) Childhood antecedents of avoidant personality disorder: a retrospective study. *Journal of American Academy of Child & Adolescent Psychiatry*, *42*(9), 1122–1130.

Rex, L. L., Drott, C., Claes, G., Gothberg, G., & Dalman, P. (1998) The Boras experience of endoscopic thoracic sympathicotomy for palmar, axillary, facial hyperkidrosis and facial blushing. *European Journal of Surgery*, *580*, 23–26.

Reznick, J. S., Hegeman, I. M., Kaufman, E. R., Woods, S. W., & Jacobs, M. (1992) Retrospective and concurrent self-report of behavioral inhibition and their relation to adult mental health. *Developmental Psychopathology*, *4*, 301–321.

Richardson, F. C., & Tasto, D. L. (1976) Development and factor analysis of a social anxiety inventory. *Behavior Therapy*, *7*, 453–462.

Rickels, K., Mangano, R., & Khan, A. (2004) A double-blind, placebo-controlled study of a flexible dose of venlafaxine ER in adult outpatients with generalized social anxiety disorder. *Journal of Clinical Psychopharmacology*, *24*, 488–496.

Robins, E., & Guze, S. B. (1970) Establishment of diagnostic validity in psychiatric illness: its application to schizophrenia. *American Journal of Psychiatry*, *126*, 983–987.

Robinson, J. L., Kagan, J., Reznick, J. S., & Corley, R. (1992) The heritability of inhibited and uninhibited behavior: a twin study. *Developmental Psychology*, *28*, 1030–1037.

Roca, M., Gili, M., Ferrer, V., Bernardo, M., Montano, J. J., Salva, J. J., Flores, I., & Leal, S. (1999) Mental disorders on the island of Formentera: prevalence in general population using the Schedules for Clinical Assessment in Neuropsychology (SCAN). *Social Psychiatry & Psychiatric Epidemiology*, *34*, 410–415.

Roelcke, V. (1997) Biologizing social facts: an early 20th century debate on Kraepelin's concepts of culture neurasthenia and degeneration. *Culture, Medicine, & Psychiatry*, *21*, 383–403.

Rose, R. J., & Ditto, W. B. (1983) A developmental-genetic analysis of common fears from early adolescence to early adulthood. *Child Development*, *54*, 361–368.

Rose, S. (1995) The rise of neurogenetic determinism. *Nature*, *373*, 380–382.

Rose, S., Kamin, L. J., & Lewontin, R. C. (1984) *Not in our genes: biology, ideology and human nature*. Harmondsworth, Middlesex: Penguin Books.

Rosen, J. B., & Schulkin, J. (1998) From normal fear to pathological anxiety. *Psychological Review*, *105*, 325–350.

Rosenbaum, J. F., Biederman, J., Hirshfeld, D. R., Bolduc, E. A., Faraone, S. V., Kagan, J., Snidman, N., & Reznick, J. S. (1991a) Further evidence of an association between behavioral inhibition and anxiety disorders: results from a family study of children from a non-clinical sample. *Journal of Psychiatry Research*, **25**, 49–65.

Rosenbaum, J. F., Biederman, J., Hirshfeld, D. R., Bolduc, E. A., & Chaloff, J. (1991b) Behavioral inhibition in children: a possible precursor to panic disorder or social phobia. *Journal of Clinical Psychiatry*, **52**, 5–9.

Rosenbaum, J. F., Biederman, J., Bolduc, E. A., Hirshfeld, D. R., Faraone, S. V., & Kagan, J. (1992) Comorbidity of parental anxiety as risk for childhood-onset anxiety on inhibited children. *American Journal of Psychiatry*, **149**, 475–481.

Rosser, S., Erskine, A., & Crino, R. (2004) Pre-existing antidepressants and the outcome of group cognitive behaviour therapy for social phobia. *Australian & New Zealand Journal of Psychiatry*, **38**, 233–239.

Roth, D., Antony, M. M., & Swinson, R. P. (2001) Interpretations for anxiety symptoms in social phobia. *Behaviour Research & Therapy*, **39**, 129–138.

Rothgerber, H. K. (1997) External intergroup threat as an antecedent to perceptions of in-group and out-group homogeneity. *Journal of Personality & Social Psychology*, **73**, 1206–1212.

Rubin, K. H., Hastings, P. D., Stewart, S. L., Henderson, H. A., & Chen, X. (1997) The consistency and concomitants of inhibition: some of the children, all of the time. *Child Development*, **68**, 467–483.

Russell, A., & Finnie, V. (1990) Preschool children's social status and maternal instructions to assist group entry. *Developmental Psychology*, **26**, 603–611.

Russell, B. (1958) *The will to doubt*. New York: Philosophical Library.

Rutter, M., & Plomin, R. (1997) Opportunities for psychiatry from genetic findings. *British Journal of Psychiatry*, **171**, 209–219.

Ryle, G. (1949) *The concept of mind*. London: Hutchinson House.

Saboonchi, F., Lundh, L. G., & Öst, L. G. (1999) Perfectionism and self-consciousness in social phobia and panic disorder with agoraphobia. *Behaviour Research & Therapy*, **37**, 799–808.

Sachs, G., Anderer, P., Margreiter, N., Semlitsch, H., Saletu, B., & Katschnig, H. (2004) P300 event-related potentials and cognitive function in social phobia. *Psychiatry Research*, **131**, 249–261.

Safren, S. A., Heimberg, R. G., & Juster, H. R. (1997) Clients' expectancies and their relationship to pretreatment symptomatology and outcome of cognitive-behavioral group treatment for social phobia. *Journal of Consulting & Clinical Psychology.* **65**, 694–698.

Safren, S. A., Heimberg, R. G., Horner, K. J., Juster, H. R., Schneier, F. R., & Liebowitz, M. R. (1999) Factor structure of social fears: the Liebowitz Social Anxiety Scale. *Journal of Anxiety Disorders*, **13**, 253–270.

Safren, S. A., Gershuny, B. S., Marzol, P., Otto, M. W., & Pollack, M. H. (2002) History of childhood abuse in panic disorder, social phobia and generalized anxiety disorder. *The Journal of Nervous & Mental Disease*, **190**, 453–456.

Salaberria, K., & Echeburua, E. (1998) Long-term outcome of cognitive therapy's contribution to self-exposure *in vivo* to the treatment of generalized social phobia. *Behavior Modification*, **22**, 262–284.

Samochowiec, J., Hajduk, A., Samochowiec, A., Horodnicki, J., Stepien, G., Grzywacz, A., & Kucharska-Mazur, J. (2004) Association studies of

MAO-A, COMT, and 5-HTT genes polymorphisms in patients with anxiety disorders of the phobic spectrum. *Psychiatry Research*, *128*, 21–26.

Sampson, E. E. (1981) Cognitive psychology as ideology. *American Psychologist*, *36*, 730–743.

Sanderson, W. C., Wetzler, S., Beck, A. T., & Betz, F. (1994) Prevalence of personality disorders among patients with anxiety disorders. *Psychiatry Research*, *51*, 167–174.

Sapolsky, R. M. (1992) Behavioral endocrinology. In J. B. Becker, M. Breedlove & D. Crews (Eds.), *Behavioral Endocrinology*. Cambridge, Massachusetts: The MIT Press, pp. 287–324.

(1997) A gene for nothing. *Discover the World of Science*, *18*, 40–46.

Sarbin, T. R. (1964) Anxiety: reification of a metaphor. *Archives of General Psychiatry*, *10*, 630–638.

Sareen, J., Chartier, M., Kjernisted, K. D., & Stein, M. B. (2001) Comorbidity of phobic disorders with alcoholism in a Canadian community sample. *Canadian Journal of Psychiatry*, *46*, 733–740.

Sartorius, N., Kaelber, C. T., Cooper, J. E., Roper, M. T., Rae, D. S., Gulbinat, W., Üstün, B., & Regier, D. A. (1993) Progress toward achieving a common language in psychiatry: I. results from the field trial of the clinical guidelines accompanying the WHO classification of mental and behavioral disorders in ICD-10. *Archives of General Psychiatry*, *50*, 115–124.

Sartorius, N., Üstün, B., Korten, A., Cooper, J. E., & van Drimmelen, J. (1995) Progress toward achieving a common language in psychiatry: II. results from the international field trials of the ICD-10 diagnostic criteria for research for mental and behavioral disorders. *American Journal of Psychiatry*, *152*, 1427–1437.

Scarpa, A., Raine, A., Venables, P. H., & Mednick, S. A. (1995) The stability of inhibited and uninhibited temperament from ages 3 to 11 in Mauritian children. *Journal of Abnormal Child Psychology*, *23*, 607–618.

Schatzberg, A. F., Samson, J. A., Rothschild, A. J., Bond, T. C., & Regier, D. A. (1998) McLean Hospital depression research facility: early onset phobic disorders and adult onset major depression. *British Journal of Psychiatry*, *173*, 29–34.

Schlenker, B. R., & Leary, M. R. (1982) Social anxiety and self-presentation: a conceptualization and model. *Psychological Bulletin*, *92*, 641–669.

Schmidt, L. A., & Fox, N. A. (1995) Individual differences in young adults' shyness and sociability: personality and health correlates. *Personality & Individual Differences*, *19*, 455–462.

Schneider, F., Grodd, W., Weiss, U., Klose, U., Mayer, K., Nagele, T., & Gur, R. (1997) Functional MRI reveals left amygdala activation during emotion. *Psychiatry Research*, *76*, 75–82.

Schneider, F., Weiss, U., Kessler, C., Miller-Gartner, H. W., Posse, S., Salloum, J. B., Grodd, W., Himmelmann, F., Gaebel, W., & Birbaumer, N. (1999). Subcortical correlates of differential classical conditioning of aversive reactions in social phobia. *Biological Psychiatry*, *45*(7), 863–871.

Schneier, F. R., Johnson, J., Hornig, C. D., Liebowitz, M. R., & Weissman, M. M. (1992) Social phobia: comorbidity and morbidity in an epidemiological sample. *Archives of General Psychiatry*, **49**, 282–288.

Schneier, F. R., Heckelman, L. R., Garfinkel, R., Campeas, R., Fallon, B. A., Gitow, A., Street, L., Del Bene, D., & Liebowitz, M. R. (1994) Functional impairment in social phobia. *Journal of Clinical Psychiatry*, **55**, 322–331.

Schneier, F. R., Goetz, D., Campeas, R., Fallon, B., Marshall, R., & Liebowitz, M. R. (1998) Placebo-controlled trial of moclobemide in social phobia. *British Journal of Psychiatry*, **172**, 70–77.

Schneier, F. R., Liebowitz, M., Abi-Dargham, A., Zea-Ponce, Y., Lin, S., & Laruelle, M. (2000) Low dopamine D(2) receptor binding potential in social phobia. *American Journal of Psychiatry*, **157**, 457–459.

Scholing, A., & Emmelkamp, P. M. G. (1993a) Cognitive and behavioural treatments of fear of blushing, sweating or trembling. *Behaviour Research & Therapy*, **31**, 155–170.

(1993b) Exposure with and without cognitive therapy for generalized social phobia: effects of individual and group treatment. *Behaviour Research & Therapy*, **31**, 667–681.

(1996a) Treatment of generalized social phobia: results at long-term follow-up. *Behaviour Research & Therapy*, **34**, 447–452.

(1996b) Treatment of fear of blushing, sweating and trembling – results at long-term follow up. *Behavior Modification*, **20**, 338–356.

Schuckit, M. A., Tipp, J. E., Bucholz, K. K., Nurnberger, J. I., Hesselbrock, V. M., Crowe, R. R., et al. (1997) The life-time rates of three major mood disorders and four major anxiety disorders in alcoholics and controls. *Addiction*, **92**, 1289–1304.

Schwalberg, M. D., Barlow, D. H., Alger, S. A., & Howard, L. J. (1992) Comparison of bulimics, obese binge eaters, social phobics and individuals with panic disorder on comorbidity across DSM-III-R anxiety disorders. *Journal of Abnormal Psychology*, **101**, 675–681.

Schwartz, C. E., Snidman, N., & Kagan, J. (1999) Adolescent social anxiety as an outcome of inhibited temperament in childhood. *Journal of the American Academy of Child & Adolescent Psychiatry*, **38**, 1008–1015.

Schwartz, G. E., Davidson, R. J., & Goleman, D. J. (1978) Patterning of cognitive and somatic processes in the self-regulation of anxiety: effects of meditation versus exercise. *Psychosomatic Medicine*, **40**, 321–328.

Sebag Montefiore, S. (2003) *Stalin: In the court of the red tsar.* London: Weidenfeld & Nicholson.

Seedat, S., & Stein, M. B. (2004) Double-blind, placebo-controlled assessment of combined clonazepam with paroxetine compared with paroxetine monotherapy for generalized social anxiety disorder. *Journal of Clinical Psychiatry*, **65**, 244–248.

Sheehan, D. V. (1986) *The anxiety disease.* New York: Scribner's.

Sheehan, D. V., Harnett-Sheehan, K., & Raj, B. A. (1996) The measurement of disability. *International Clinical Psychopharmacology*, **11**, 89–95.

Shepherd, M. (1993) The placebo: from specificity to the non-specific and back. *Psychological Medicine*, **23**, 569–578.

Shin, L., Wright, C., Cannistraro, P., Wedig, M., McMullin, K., Martis, B., Macklin, M., Lasko, N., Cavanagh, S., Krangel, T., Orr, S., Pitman, R., Whalen, P., & Rauch, S. (2005) A functional magnetic resonance imaging study of amygdala and medial prefrontal cortex responses to overtly presented fearful faces in posttraumatic stress disorder. *Archives of General Psychiatry*, *62*, 273–281.

Shlik, J., Maron, E., Tru, I., Aluoja, A., & Vasar, V. (2004) Citalopram challenge in social anxiety disorder. *International Journal of Neuropsychopharmacology*, *7*, 177–182.

Shumyatsky, G. B., Malleret, G., Shin, R-Y., Tokizawa, S., Tully, K., Tsvetkov, E., Zakharenko, S. S., Joseph, J., Vronskaya, S., Yin, D., Schubart, U. K., Kendel, E. R., & Bolshakov, V. Y. (2005). Stathmin, a gene enriched in the amygdala controls both learned and innate fear. *Cell*, *123*, 697–709.

Sidanius, J., & Pratto, F. (1999) *Social dominance: an intergroup theory of social hierarchy and oppression*. New York: Cambridge University Press.

Simon, N., Blacker, D., Korbly, N., Sharma, S., Worthington, J., Otto, M., & Pollack, M. (2002) Hypothyroidism and hyperthyroidism in anxiety disorders revisited: new data and literature review. *Journal of Affective Disorders*, *69*, 209–217.

Skinner, B. F. (1981) Selection by consequences. *Science*, *213*, 501–504.

Skre, I., Onstad, S., Torgersen, S., & Klingen, E. (1991) High interrater reliability for the Structured Clinical Interview for DSM-III-R Axis-I (SCID-I). *Acta Psychiatrica Scandinavica*, *84*, 167–173.

Skre, I., Onstad, S., Torgersen, S., Lygren, S., & Kringlen, E. (1993) A twin study of DSM-III-R anxiety disorders. *Acta Psychiatrica Scandinavica*, *88*, 85–92.

Slee, P. T. (1994) Situational and interpersonal correlates of anxiety associated with peer victimization. *Child Psychiatry & Human Development*, *25*, 97–107.

Sofsky, W. (1997) *The order of terror: the concentration camp*. Princeton: Princeton University Press.

Spence, S. H., Rapee, R., McDonald, C., & Ingram, M. (2001) The structure of anxiety symptoms among preschoolers. *Behaviour Research & Therapy*, *39*, 1293–1316.

Spitzer, R., & Endicott, J. (1978) Medical and mental disorder: proposed definition and criteria. In R. L. Spitzer & D. F. Klein (Eds.), *Critical issues in psychiatry*. New York: Raven Press, pp. 15–39.

Spitznagel, E. L., & Helzer, J. E. (1985) A proposed solution to the base rate problem in the kappa statistic. *Archives of General Psychiatry*, *42*, 725–728.

Sprigge, T. L. S. (1984) *Theories of existence*. Harmondsworth, Middlesex: Penguin.

Spurr, J., & Stopa, L. (2002) Self-focused attention in social phobia and social anxiety. *Clinical Psychology Review*, *22*, 947–975.

Sroufe, L. A. (1983) Infant caregiver attachment and patterns of adaptation in preschool: the roots of maladaptation and competence. In M. Perlmutter (Ed.), *Development and policy concerning children with special needs*.

Minnesota Symposia on Child Psychology, Volume. *16*, Hillsdale, New Jersey: Lawrence Erlbaum.

(1996) *Emotional development: the organization of emotional life in the early years*. Cambridge: Cambridge University Press.

(1997) Psychopathology as an outcome of development. *Development & Psychopathology*, *9*, 251–268.

Sroufe, L. A., & Waters, E. (1977) Attachment as an organizational construct. *Child Development*, *48*, 1184–1199.

Sroufe, A., Carlson, E. & Shulman, S. (1993) Individuals in relationships: development from infancy through adolescence. In D. C. Funder, R. Parke, C. Tomlinson-Keesey, & K. Widaman (Eds.), *Studying lives through time: approaches to personality and development*. Washington DC, USA: American Psychological Association, pp. 315–342.

Stangier, U., Heidenreich, T., Peitz, M., Lauterbach, W., & Clark, D. M. (2003) Cognitive therapy for social phobia: individual versus group treatment. *Behaviour Research & Therapy*, *41*, 991–1007.

Statman, D. (2000) Humiliation, dignity and self-respect. *Philosophical Psychology*, *13*, 523–540.

Stein, D. J., & Bouwer, C. (1997) Blushing and social phobia: a neuroethological speculation. *Medical Hypotheses*, *49*, 101–108.

Stein, D. J., Berk, M., Els, C., Emsley, R. A., Gittelson, L., Wilson, D., Oakes, R., & Hunter, B. (1999) A double-blind placebo-controlled trial of paroxetine in the management of social phobia (social anxiety disorder) in South Africa. *South African Medical Journal*, *89*, 402–406.

Stein, D. J., Cameron, A., Amrein, R., & Montgomery, S. A. (2002a) Moclobemide is effective and well tolerated in the long-term pharmacotherapy of social anxiety disorder with and without comorbid anxiety disorder. *International Clinical Psychopharmacology*, *17*, 161–170.

Stein, D. J., Stein, M. B., Pitts, C. D., Kumar, R., & Hunter, B. (2002b) Predictors of response to pharmacotherapy in social anxiety disorder: an analysis of 3 placebo-controlled paroxetine trials. *Journal of Clinical Psychiatry*, *63*, 152–155.

Stein, D. J., Versiani, M., Hair, T., & Kumar, R. (2002c) Efficacy of paroxetine for relapse prevention in social anxiety disorder. *Archives of General Psychiatry*, *59*, 1111–1118.

Stein, D. J., Westenberg, H. G. M., Yang, H., Li, D., & Barbato, L. M. (2003) Fluvoxamine CR in the long-term treatment of social anxiety disorder: the 12- to 24- week extension phase of a multicentre, randomized, placebo-controlled trial. *International Journal of Neuropsychopharmacology*, *6*, 317–323.

Stein, D. J., Kasper, S., Wreford Andersen, E., Nil, R., & Lader, M. (2004) Escitalopram in the treatment of social anxiety disorder: analysis of efficacy for different clinical subgroups and symptom dimensions. *Depression & Anxiety*, *20*, 175–181.

Stein, M. B., & Kean, Y. M. (2000) Disability and quality of life in social phobia: epidemiologic findings. *American Journal of Psychiatry*, *157*, 1606–1613.

Stein, M. B., & Leslie, W. (1996) A brain single photon-emission computed tomography (SPECT) study of generalized social phobia. *Biological Psychiatry*, *39*, 825–828.

Stein, M. B., Tancer, M. E., & Uhde, T. W. (1992) Heart rate and plasma norepinephrine responsitivity to orthostatic challenge in anxiety disorders: comparison of patients with panic disorder and social phobia and normal control subjects. *Archives of General Psychiatry*, *49*, 311–317.

Stein, M. B., Huzel, L., & Delaney, S. (1993) Lymphocyte beta-adrenoceptors in social phobia. *Biological Psychiatry*, *34*, 45–50.

Stein, M. B., Asmundson, G. J. G., & Chartier, M. (1994a) Autonomic responsivity in generalized social phobia. *Journal of Affective Disorders*, *31*, 211–221.

Stein, M. B., Walker, J. R., & Forde, D. R. (1994b) Setting diagnostic thresholds for social phobia: considerations from a community survey of social anxiety. *American Journal of Psychiatry*, *151*, 408–412.

Stein, M. B., Delaney, S., Chartier, M., Kroft, C., & Hazen, A. (1995) ³H Paroxetine binding to platelets of patients with social phobia: comparison to patients with panic disorder and healthy volunteers. *Biological Psychiatry*, *37*, 224–228.

Stein, M. B., Walker, J. R., & Forde, D. R. (1996) Public-speaking fears in a community sample: prevalence, impact on functioning and diagnostic classification. *Archives of General Psychiatry*, *53*, 169–174.

Stein, M. B., Chartier, M. J., Hazen, A. L., Kozak, M. V., Tancer, M. E., Lander, S., Furer, P., Chubaty, D., & Walker, J. (1998a) A direct-interview family study of generalized social phobia. *American Journal of Psychiatry*, *155*, 90–97.

Stein, M. B., Liebowitz, M., Lydiard, R. B., Pitts, C. D., Bushnell, W., & Gergel, I. (1998b) Paroxetine treatment of generalized social phobia (social anxiety disorder). *Journal of the American Medical Association*, *280*, 708–713.

Stein, M., Chartier, M., Kozak, M., King, N., & Kennedy, J. (1998c) Genetic linkage to the serotonin transporter protein and 5HT2A receptor genes excluded in generalized social phobia. *Psychiatry Research*, *81*, 283–291.

Stein, M. B., Fyer, A. J., Davidson, J. R. T., Pollack, M. H., & Wiita, B. (1999) Fluvoxamine treatment of social phobia (social anxiety disorder): a double-blind, placebo-controlled study. *Americal Journal of Psychiatry*. *156*, 756–760.

Stein, M. B., Torgrud, L. J., & Walker, J. R. (2000) Social phobia symptoms, subtypes and severity: findings from a community survey. *Archives of General Psychiatry*, *57*, 1046–1052.

Stein, M. B., Fuetsch, M., Müler, N., Höfler, M., Lieb, R., & Wittchen, H. U. (2001a) Social anxiety disorder and the risk of depression: a prospective community study of adolescents and young adults. *Archives of General Psychiatry*, *58*, 251–256.

Stein, M. B., Sareen, J., Hami, S., & Chao, J. (2001b) Pindolol potentiation of paroxetine for generalized social phobia: a double-blind, placebo-controlled, crossover study. *American Journal of Psychiatry*, *58*, 1725–1727.

Stein, M. B., Goldin, P., Sareen, J., Zorrilla, L., & Brown, G. (2002) Increased amygdala activation to angry and contemptuous faces in generalized social phobia. *Archive of General Psychiatry*, *59*, 1027–1034.

Stein, M. B., Pollack, M. H., Bystritsky, A., Kelsey, J. E., & Mangano, R. M. (2005) Efficacy of low and higher dose extended-release venlafaxine in generalized social anxiety disorder: a 6-month randomized controlled trial. *Psychopharmacology*, *177*, 280–288.

Stevenson-Hinde, J. (1991) Temperament and attachment. In P. Bateson (Ed.), *The development and integration of behaviour*. Cambridge: Cambridge University Press.

Stevenson-Hinde, J., & Glover, A. (1996) Shy girls and boys: a new look. *Journal of Child Psychology & Psychiatry*, *37*, 181–187.

Stich, S. (1983) *From folk psychology to cognitive science*. Cambridge, Massachusetts: MIT Press.

Stopa, L., & Clark, D. M. (1993) Cognitive processes in social phobia. *Behaviour Research & Therapy*, *31*, 255–267.

(2000). Social phobia and interpretation of social events. *Behaviour Research & Therapy*, *38*, 273–283.

Storch, E. A., Brassard, M. R., & Masia-Warner, C. L. (2003) The relationship of peer victimization to social anxiety and loneliness in adolescence. *Child Study Journal*, *33*, 1–18.

Straube, T., Kolassa, I., Glauer, M., Mentzel, H., & Miltner, W. (2004) Effect of task conditions on brain responses to threatening faces in social phobics: an event-related functional magnetic resonance imaging study. *Biological Psychiatry*, *56*, 921–930.

Stravynski, A., & Greenberg, D. (1989) Behavioural psychotherapy for social phobia and dysfunction. *International Review of Psychiatry*, *1*, 207–218.

Stravynski, A., Marks, I., & Yule, W. (1982a) Social skills training with and without cognitive modification. *Archives of General Psychiatry*, *39*, 1378–1385.

Stravynski, A., Marks, I., & Yule, W. (1982b) Social skills problems in neurotic outpatients. *Archives of General Psychiatry*, *39*, 1378–1385.

Stravynski, A., Lamontagne, Y., & Lavallée, Y. (1986) Clinical phobias and avoidant personality disorder among alcoholics admitted to an alcoholism rehabilitation setting. *Canadian Journal of Psychiatry*, *31*, 714–719.

Stravynski, A., Grey, S., & Elie, R. (1987) Outline of the therapeutic process in social skills training with socially dysfunctional patients. *Journal of Consulting & Clinical Psychology*, *55*, 224–228.

Stravynski, A., Lesage, A., Marcouiller, M., & Elie, R. (1989) A test of the therapeutic mechanism in social skills training with avoidant personality disorder. *The Journal of Nervous & Mental Disease*, *177*, 739–744.

Stravynski, A., Basoglu, M., Marks, M., Sengun, S., & Marks, I. M. (1995a) The distinctiveness of phobias: a discriminant analysis of fears. *Journal of Anxiety Disorders*, *9*, 89–101.

(1995b) Social sensitivity: a shared feature of all phobias. *British Journal of Clinical Psychology*, *34*, 343–351.

Stravynski, A., Arbel, N., Bounader, J., Gaudette, G., Lachance, L., Borgeat, F., Fabian, J., Lamontagne, Y., Sidoun, P., & Todorov, C. (2000a) Social phobia treated as a problem in social functioning: a controlled comparison of two behavioural group approaches. *Acta Psychiatrica Scandinavica*, *102*, 188–198.

Stravynski, A., Arbel, N., Lachance, L., & Todorov, C. (2000b) Social phobia viewed as a problem in social functioning: a pilot study of group behavioral treatment. *Journal of Behavior Therapy & Experimental Psychiatry*, *31*, 163–175.

Stravynski, A., Arbel, N., Chenier, N., Lachance, L., Lamontagne, Y., Sidoun, P., & Todorov, C. (2006) Treating social phobia interpersonally: dismantling the ingredients of a behavioural approach (submitted for publication).

Sutherland, S. M., Tupler, L. A., Colket, J. T., & Davidson, J. R. T. (1996) A 2-year follow-up of social phobia: status after a brief medication trial. *Journal of Nervous and Mental Disease*, *184*, 731–738.

Szasz, T. (1987) *Insanity: the idea and its consequences*. New York: Wiley.

Taggart, P., Carruthers, M., & Summerville, W. (1973) Electrocardiograms, plasma catecholamines and lipids, and their modification by oxprenolol when speaking before an audience. *Lancet*, *2*, 341–346.

Takahashi, T. (1989) Social phobia syndrome in Japan. *Comprehensive Psychiatry*, *30*, 45–52.

Tamaren, A. J., Carney, R. M., & Allen, T. W. (1985a) Assessment of cognitive and somatic anxiety: a preliminary validation study. *Behavioral Assessment*, *7*, 197–202.

(1985b) Predictive validity of the cognitive vs. somatic anxiety distinction. *Pavlovian Journal of Biology & Science*, *20*, 177–180.

Tancer, M. E., Stein, M. B., & Uhde, T. W. (1990a) Effects of thyrotropin-releasing hormone on blood pressure and heart rate in phobic and panic patients: a pilot study. *Biological Psychiatry*, *27*, 781–783.

Tancer, M., Stein, M., Gelernter, C., & Uhde, T. (1990b) The hypothalamic-pituitary-thyroid axis in social phobia. *American Journal of Psychiatry*, *147*, 929–933.

Tancer, M. E., Stein, M., & Uhde, T. (1993) Growth hormone response to intravenous clonidine in social phobia: comparison to patients with panic disorder and healthy volunteers. *Biological Psychiatry*, *34*, 591–595.

Tancer, M. E., Mailman, R., Stein, M., Mason, G., Carson, S., & Goldeen, R. (1994) Neuroendocrine responsivity in monoaminergic system probes in generalized social phobia. *Anxiety*, *1*, 216–223.

Tancer, M. E., Lewis, M., & Stein, M. (1995) Biological aspects. In M. Stein (Ed.), *Social phobia: clinical and research perspectives*, Washington DC, American Psychiatric Press, pp. 229–257.

Taylor, S., Woody, S., Koch, W. J., Mc Lean, P., Paterson, R. J., & Anderson, K. W. (1997) Cognitive restructuring in the treatment of social phobia: efficacy and mode of action. *Behavior Modification*, *21*, 487–511.

Thomas, K., Drevets, W., Dahl, R., Ryan, N., Birmaher, B., Eccard, C., Axelson, D., Whalen, P., & Casey, B. (2001) Amygdala response to fearful faces in anxious and depressed children. *Archives of General Psychiatry, 58,* 1057–1063.

Thomas, S. E., Thevos, A. K., & Randall, C. L. (1999). Alcoholics with and without social phobia: a comparison of substance use and psychiatric variables. *Journal of Studies on Alcohol, 60,* 472–479.

Tiihonen, J., Kuikka, J., Bergstrom, K., Hakola, P., Karhu, J., Ryynanen, O., & Fohr, J. (1995) Altered striatal dopamine re-uptake site densities in habitually violent and non-violent alcoholics. *Nature Medicine, 1,* 654–657.

Tiihonen, J., Kuikka, J., Bergstrom, K., Lepola, U., Koponen, H., & Leinonen, E. (1997) Dopamine reuptake site densities in patients with social phobia. *American Journal of Psychiatry, 154,* 239–242.

Tillfors, M. (2004) Why do some individuals develop social phobia? A review with emphasis on the neurobiological influences. *Nordic Journal of Psychiatry, 58,* 267–276.

Tillfors, M., Furmark, T., Marteinsdottir, I., Fischer, H., Pissiota, A., Langstrom, B., & Fredrikson, M. (2001a) Cerebral blood flow in subjects with social phobia during stressful speaking tasks: a PET study. *American Journal of Psychiatry, 158,* 1220–1226.

Tillfors, M., Furmak, T., Ekselius, L., & Fredrikson, M. (2001b) Social phobia and avoidant personality disorder as related to parental history of social anxiety: a general population study. *Behaviour Research & Therapy, 39,* 289–298.

Tillfors, M., Furmak, T., Marteinsdottir, I., & Fredrikson, M. (2002) Cerebral blood flow during anticipation of public speaking in social phobia: a PET study. *Biological Psychiatry, 52,* 1113–1119.

Torgersen, S. (1983) Genetic factors in anxiety disorders. *Archives of General Psychiatry, 40,* 1085–1089.

Tran, G. Q., & Chambless, D. L. (1995) Psychopathology of social phobia: effects of subtype and of avoidant personality disorder. *Journal of Anxiety Disorders, 9,* 489–501.

Trower, P. (1995) Adult social skills: state of the art and future directions. In W. O'Donohue & L. Krasner (Eds.), *Handbook of psychological skills training: Clinical techniques and applications.* Boston: Allyn & Bacon, pp. 54–80.

Trower, P., & Gilbert, P. (1989) New theoretical conceptions of social anxiety and social phobia. *Clinical Psychology Review, 9,* 19–35.

Trower, P., Bryant, B., & Argyle, M. (1978) *Social skills and mental health.* London: Methuen.

Tükel, R., Kiziltan, E., Demir, T., & Demir, D. (2000) A comparison of clinical characteristics in social phobia and panic disorder. *Behavior Therapist, 23,* 55–57.

Tupler, L., Davidson, J., Smith, R., Lazeyras, F., Charles, H., & Krishnan, K. (1997) A repeated proton magnetic resonance spectroscopy study in social phobia. *Biological Psychiatry, 42,* 419–424.

Turk, C. L., Heimberg, R. G., Orsillo, S. M., Holt, G. S., Gitow, A., Street, L. L., Schneier, F. R., & Liebowitz, M. R. (1998) An investigation of gender differences in social phobia. *Journal of Anxiety Disorders, 12,* 209–223.

Turner, R. M. (1987) The effects of personality disorder diagnosis on the outcome of social anxiety symptom reduction. *Journal of Personality Disorders*, *1*, 136–143.

Turner, S. M., Beidel, D. C., & Larkin, K. T. (1986) Situational determinants of social anxiety in clinic and nonclinic samples: physiological and cognitive correlates. *Journal of Consulting & Clinical Psychology*, *54*, 523–527.

Turner, S. M., McCanna, M., & Beidel, D. C. (1987) Validity of the Social Avoidance and Distress and Fear of Negative Evaluation scales. *Behavioral Research & Therapy*, *25*, 113–115.

Turner, S. M., Beidel, D. C., & Townsley, R. M. (1992) Social phobia: a comparison of specific and generalized subtypes and avoidant personality disorder. *Journal of Abnormal Psychology*, *101*, 326–331.

Turner, S. M., Beidel, D. C., & Jacob, R. G. (1994) Social phobia: a comparison of behavior therapy and atenolol. *Journal of Consulting & Clinical Psychology*, *62*, 350–358.

Turner, S. M., Beidel, D. C., & Wolff, P. L. (1996a) Is behavioral inhibition related to the anxiety disorders? *Clinical Psychology Review*, *16*, 157–172.

Turner, S. M., Beidel, D. C., Wolff, P. L., Spaulding, S., & Jacob, R. G. (1996b) Clinical features affecting treatment outcome in social phobia. *Behaviour Research & Therapy*, *34*, 795–804.

Tweed, J. L., Schoenbach, V. J., George, L. K., & Blazer, D. G. (1989) The effects of childhood parental death and divorce on six-month history of anxiety disorders. *British Journal of Psychiatry*, *154*, 823–828.

Tyrer, P. (1985) Neurosis divisible? *Lancet*, *23*, 685–688.

Tyrer, P. (1996) Diagnostic anomalies in social phobia. *International Journal of Clinical Psychopharmacology*, *11*(3), 29–33.

Uhde, T. W. (1994) Anxiety and growth disturbance: is there a connection? A review of biological studies in social phobia. *Journal of Clinical Psychiatry*, *55* (Suppl.), 17–27.

Uhde, T. W., Tancer, M., Black, B., & Brown, T. (1991) Phenomenology and neurobiology of social phobia: comparison with panic disorder. *Journal of Clinical Psychiatry*, *52* (Suppl.), 31–40. Review.

Uhde, T. W., Tancer, M., Gelernter, C., & Vittone, B. (1994) Normal urinary free cortisol and postdexamethasone cortisol in social phobia: comparison to normal volunteers. *Journal of Affective Disorders*, *30*, 155–161.

van Ameringen, M., Mancini, C., & Oakman, J. M. (1998) The relationship of behavioral inhibition and shyness to anxiety disorder. *Journal of Nervous & Mental Disease*, *186*, 425–431.

van Ameringen, M., Lane, R. M., Walker, J. R., Bowen, R. C., Chokka, P. R., Goldner, E. M., Johnston, D. G., Lavallee, Y. J., Nandy, S., Pecknold, J. C., Hadrava, V., & Swinson, R. P. (2001) Sertraline treatment of generalized social phobia: a 20-week, double-blind, placebo-controlled study. *American Journal of Psychiatry*, *158*, 275–281.

van Ameringen, M., Mancini, I. C., Szechtman, H., Nahmias, C., Oakman, J., Hall, G., Pipe, B., & Farvolden, P. (2004a) A PET provocation study of generalized social phobia. *Psychiatry Research*, *132*, 13–18.

van Ameringen, M., Oakman, J., Mancini, C., Pipe, B., & Chung, H. (2004b) Predictors of response in generalized social phobia: effect of age of onset. *Journal of Clinical Psychopharmacology, 24*, 42–48.

van Dam-Baggen, R., & Kraimaat, F. (2000) Group social skills training or cognitive group therapy as the clinical treatment of choice for generalized social phobia? *Journal of Anxiety Disorders, 14*, 437–451.

van Den Hout, M., & Griez, E. (1984) Panic symptoms after inhalation of carbon dioxide. *British Journal of Psychiatry, 144*, 503–507.

van Praag, H., Lemus, C., & Kahn, R. (1987) Hormonal probes of central serotoninergic activity: do they really exist. *Biological Psychiatry, 22*, 86–98.

van Velzen, C. J. M., Emmelkamp, P. M. G., & Scholing, A. (1997) The impact of personality disorders on behavioral treatment outcome for social phobia. *Behaviour Research & Therapy, 35*, 889–900.

(2000) Generalized social phobia versus avoidant personality disorder: differences in psychopathology, personality traits and social and occupational functioning. *Journal of Anxiety Disorders, 14*, 395–411.

van Vliet, I. M., Den Boer, J. A., & Westenberg, H. G. M. (1992) Psychopharmacological treatment of social phobia: clinical and biochemical effects of brofaromine, a selective MAO-A inhibitor. *European Neuropsychopharmacology, 2*, 21–29.

(1994) Psychopharmacological treatment of social phobia; a double blind placebo controlled study with fluvoxamine. *Psychopharmacology, 115*, 128–134.

van Vliet, I. M., den Boer, J. A., Westenberg, H. G. M., & Kamini, L. H. P. (1997a) Clinical effects of buspirone in social phobia: a double-blind placebo-controlled study. *Journal of Clinical Psychiatry, 58*, 164–168.

van Vliet, I., Westenberg, H., Slaap, B., den Boer, J., & Ho Pian, K. (1997b) Anxiogenic effects of pentagastrin in patients with social phobia and healthy controls. *Biological Psychiatry, 42*, 76–78.

Vega, W. A., Kolody, B., Aguilar-Gaxiola, S., Alderete, E., Catalano, R., & Caraveo-Anduaga, J. (1998) Lifetime prevalence of DSM-III-R psychiatric disorders among urban and rural Mexican Americans in California. *Archives of General Psychiatry, 55*, 771–778.

Veit, R., Flor, H., Erb, M., Hermann, C., Lotze, M., Grodd, W., & Birbaumer, N. (2002) Brain circuits involved in emotional learning in antisocial behavior and social phobia in humans. *Neuroscience Letters, 328*, 233–236.

Vernberg, E. M., Abwender, D. A., Ewell, K. K., & Beery, S. H. (1992) Social anxiety and peer relationships in early adolescence: a prospective analysis. *Journal of Clinical Child Psychology, 21*, 189–196.

Versiani, M., Nardi, A. E., Mundim, F. D., Alves, A. B., Liebowitz, M. R., & Amrein, R. (1992) Pharmacotherapy of social phobia: a controlled study with moclobemide and phenelzine. *British Journal of Psychiatry, 161*, 353–360.

Versiani, M., Amrein, R., & Montgomery, S. A. (1997) Social phobia: long-term treatment outcome and prediction of response – a moclobemide study. *International Clinical Psychopharmacology, 12*, 239–254.

Vieira, A., Ramos, R., & Gentil, V. (1997) Hormonal response during a fenfluramine-associated panic attack. *Brazilian Journal of Medical Biological Research*, **30**, 887–90. Erratum in: *Brazilian Journal of Medical Biological Research*, **30**, 1145.

Vorcaro, C. M., Rocha, F. L., Uchoa, E., & Lima-Costa, M. F. (2004) The burden of social phobia in a Brazilian community and its relationship with socioeconomic circumstances, health status and use of health services: the Bambui study. *International Journal of Social Psychiatry*, **50**, 216–226.

Wacker, H. R., Müllejans, R., Klein, K. H., & Battegay, R. (1992) Identification of cases of anxiety disorders and affective disorders in the community according to ICD-10 and DSM-III-R by using the Composite International Diagnostic Interview (CIDI). *International Journal of Methodology in Psychiatric Research*, **2**, 91–100.

Wakefield, J. C., Pottick, J. J., & Kirk, S. A. (2002) Should the DSM-IV diagnostic criteria for conduct disorder consider social context? *American Journal of Psychiatry*, **159**, 380–386.

Walker, J. R., van Ameringen, M. A., Swinson, R., & Bowen, R. C. (2000) Group social skills training of cognitive group therapy as the clinical treatment of choice for generalized social phobia? *Journal of Anxiety Disorders*, **14**, 437–451.

Wallace, C. J., & Liberman, R. P. (1985) Social skills training for patients with schizophrenia: a controlled clinical trial. *Psychiatric Research*, **15**, 239–247.

Wallace, S. T., & Alden, L. E. (1997) Social phobia and positive social events: the price of success. *Journal of Abnormal Psychology*, **106**, 416–424.

Walters, K. S., & Hope, D. A. (1998) Analysis of social behavior in individuals with social phobia and nonanxious participants using a psychobiological model. *Behavior Therapy*, **29**, 387–407.

Walters, K. S., & Inderbitzen, H. M. (1998) Social anxiety and peer relations among adolescents: Testing a psychobiological model. *Journal of Anxiety Disorders*, **12**, 183–198.

Warren, S. L., Huston, L., Egeland, B., & Sroufe, L. A. (1997) Child and adolescent anxiety disorders and early attachment. *Journal of the American Academy of Child & Adolescent Psychiatry*, **36**, 637–644.

Warren, S. L., Umylny, P., Aron, A., & Simmens, S. J. (2006) Toddler anxiety disorders: a pilot study. *Journal of the Academy of Child & Adolescent Psychiatry*, **45**, 859–866.

Watson, D., & Friend, R. (1969) Measurement of social evaluative anxiety. *Journal of Consulting & Clinical Psychology*, **33**, 448–457.

Webster's New Collegiate Dictionary (1962) Springfield, Massachusetts: G. & C. Merriam.

Weiller, E., Bisserbe, J.-C., Boyer, P., Lépine, J.-P., & Lecrubier, Y. (1996) Social phobia in general health care an unrecognised undertreated disabling disorder. *British Journal of Psychiatry*, **168**, 169–174.

Wells, A., & Papageorgiou, C. (1999) The observer perspective: biased imagery in social phobia, agoraphobia and blood/injury phobia. *Behaviour Research and Therapy*, **37**, 653–658.

Wells, J. E., Bushnell, J. A., Hornblow, A. R., Joyce, P. R., & Oakley-Browne, M. A. (1989) Christchurch psychiatric epidemiology study: Part I. Methodology and lifetime prevalence for specific psychiatric disorders. *Australian & New Zealand Journal of Psychiatry*, **23**, 315–326.

Westenberg, P. M., Drewes, M. J., Goedhart, A. W., Siebelink, B. M., & Treffers, P. D. A. (2004a) A developmental analysis of self-reported fears in late childhood through mid-adolescence: social evaluative fears on the rise? *Journal of Child Psychology & Psychiatry*, **45**, 481–495.

Westenberg, H. G. M., Stein, D. J., Yang, H., Li, D., & Barbato, L. M. (2004b) A double-blind placebo-controlled study of controlled release fluvoxamine for the treatment of generalized social anxiety disorder. *Journal of Clinical Psychopharmacology*, **24**, 49–55.

Wetzler, S., Asnis, G., DeLecuona, J., & Kalus, O. (1996) Serotonin function in panic disorder: intravenous administration of meta-chlorophenylpiperazine. *Psychiatry Research*, **64**, 77–82.

Whaley, S. H., Pinto, A., & Sigman, M. (1999) Characterizing interactions between anxious mothers and their children. *Journal of Consulting & Clinical Psychology*, **67**, 826–836.

Wiggins, O. P., & Schwartz, M. A. (1994) Psychiatric knowledge and classification. In J. Z. Sadler, O. P. Wiggins, & M. A. Schwartz (Eds.), *Philosophical perspectives on psychiatric diagnostic classification*. London: The Johns Hopkins University Press, pp. 89–103.

Wilhelm, S., Otto, M. W., Zucker, B. G., & Pollack, M. H. (1997) Prevalence of body dysmorphic disorder in patients with anxiety disorders. *Journal of Anxiety Disorders*, **11**, 499–502.

Williams, J. H. G. (1998) Using behavioural ecology to understand depression. *British Journal of Psychiatry*, **173**, 453–454.

Williams, M. (1985) Wittgenstein's rejection of scientific psychology. *Journal for the Theory of Social Behaviour*, **15**, 203–223.

Wittchen, H. U., Robins, L. N., Cottler, L. B., Sartorius, N., Burke, J. D., & Regier, D. (1991) Cross-cultural feasibility, reliability and sources of variance of the Composite International Diagnostic Interview (CIDI). *British Journal of Psychiatry*, **159**, 645–653.

Wittchen, H. U., Ahmoi Essau, C., Von Zerssen, D., Krieg, J. C., & Zaudig, M. (1992) Lifetime and six-month prevalence of mental disorders in the Munich follow-up study. *European Archives of Psychiatry Clinical Neuroscience*, **241**, 247–258.

Wittchen, H. U., Fuetsch, M., Sonntag, H., Müller, N., & Liebowitz, M. (1999a) Disability and quality of life in pure and comorbid social phobia: findings from a controlled study. *European Psychiatry*, **14**, 118–131.

Wittchen, H. U., Stein, M. B., & Kessler, R. C. (1999b) Social fears and social phobia in a community sample of adolescents and young adults: prevalence, risk factors and co-morbidity. *Psychological Medicine*, **29**, 309–323.

Wittgenstein, L. (1958) *Philosophical investigations.* Oxford: Blackwell.

Wlazlo, Z., Schroeder-Hartig, K., Hand, I., Kaiser, G., & Münchau, N. (1990) Exposure in vivo vs. social skills training for social phobia: long-term outcome and differential effects. *Behaviour Research & Therapy*, **28**, 181–193.

Wolpe, J. (1983) *The practice of behavior therapy.* New York: Pergamon Press.

Woodruff-Borden, J., Morrow, C., Bourland, S., & Cambron, S. (2002) The behavior of anxious parents: examining mechanisms of transmission of anxiety from parent to child. *Journal of Clinical Child & Adolescent Psychology*, **31**, 364–374.

Woody, S. R., & Rodriguez, B. F. (2000) Self-focused attention and social anxiety in social phobics and normal controls. *Cognitive Therapy & Research*, **24**, 473–488.

World Health Organization (1992) *The ICD-10 Classification of Mental and Behavioural Disorders.* Geneva: WHO.

Yehuda, R. (1998) Psychoneuroendocrinology of post-traumatic stress disorder. *Psychiatric Clinics of North America*, **21**, 359–379.

Yonkers, K. A., Dyck, I. R., & Keller, M. B. (2001) An eight-year longitudinal comparison of clinical course and characteristics of social phobia among men and women. *Psychiatric Services*, **52**, 637–643.

Young, A. (1995) *The Harmony of Illusions.* Princeton: Princeton University Press.

Zachar, P. (2001) Psychiatric disorders are not natural kinds. *Philosophy, Psychiatry & Psychology*, **7**, 167–182.

Zimbardo, P., Pilkonis, P., & Norwood, R. (1975) The social disease called shyness. *Psychology Today*, **8**, 68–72.

Zimmerman, M., & Mattia, J. I. (2000) Principal and additional DSM-IV disorders for which outpatients seek treatment. *Psychiatric Services*, **51**, 1299–1304.

Zweig, D. R., & Brown, S. D. (1985) Psychometric evaluation of a written stimulus presentation format for the SISST. *Cognitive Therapy & Research*, **9**, 285–295.

Author Index

Abi-Dargham, A. 146, 150
Abou-Saleh, M. T. 129
Abrardi, L. 129, 131
Abwender, D. A. 272
Acharyya, S. 115
Adams, H. B. 45, 227
Adams, J. A.
Adler, R. 152
Agras, W. S. 216, 217, 322, 326
Aguilar-Gaxiola, S. 126
Ahmoi Essau, C. 128
Ainsworth, M. D. S. 276
Aizenberg, D. 90
Akiskal, H. S. 100, 101, 107, 117, 124, 169
Albuisson, E. 295, 331
Alden, L. E. 195, 196, 235
Alderete, E. 126
Alexander, D. A. 32
Alger, A. A. 109, 121
Allen, S. 79
Allen, T. W. 192
Allgulander, C. 218, 309, 315
Alpert, J. E. 108, 120
Aluoja, A. 128, 132, 146, 150
Alves, A. B. 218, 319
Amies, P. L. 119
Amir, N. 198–201, 207–10, 219, 221
Amrein, R. 95, 97, 161, 218, 308, 311, 319
Anderer, P. 165
Anderson, J. C. 172
Anderson, K. W. 213, 294, 331
Anderson, T. S. 154–6
André, C. 55, 128
Andreas, D. 278
Andreasen, N. C. 71
Andrews, G. 77, 85, 92, 106, 115, 130
Andrews, S. 176
Angst, J. 115, 129, 275
Antony, M. M. 42, 117, 203, 273
APA (American Psychiatric Association)
xv, 28, 31, 67
Arana, G. 159–65

Arancio, C. 154, 156, 167
Arbel, N. 45, 133, 240, 242, 244, 245,
265, 266, 274, 300, 301, 303, 304,
329, 330, 358
Ardon, M. A. 29, 37
Argyle, M. 226, 227
Arinam, I. T. 180
Arnarson, E. O. 127
Arnkoff, D. B. 216, 217, 322
Arntz, A. 98, 118, 333
Arrindell, W. A. 29, 37, 229, 230, 264
Asendorf, J. B. 59–60, 254
Asmundson, G. J. G. 91, 93, 126, 148, 153
Asnis, G. 151
Atmaca, M. 320
Avenevoli, S. 115
Axelson, D. 165

Bagby, R. M. 120
Baghei, F. 180–1
Baker, S. R. 43, 61, 66, 112, 153, 235
Baldwin, D. 114–15, 309
Ballenger, J. 159–65
Bandelow, B. 99, 171, 274, 275
Barbarich, N. 109
Barbato, L. M. 312
Barber, B. 38
Barlow, D. H. 31, 79, 86, 109, 119, 121
Barnett, S. D. 317
Baron, J. 220
Barr Taylor, C. 98, 122, 206
Barrett, P. M. 157, 158, 270
Bartko, J. J. 216, 217, 322
Bartlett, S. J. 77
Bartolozzi, D. 129, 131
Basile, V. 178, 179
Basoglu, M. 37, 66, 105, 118
Battegay, R. 129, 132
Beattie, M. 290
Beazley, M. B. 235
Bebchuk, J. 147, 151
Beck, A. T. 111, 185, 186

407

Index